T0385566

SMALL WARS, BIG DATA

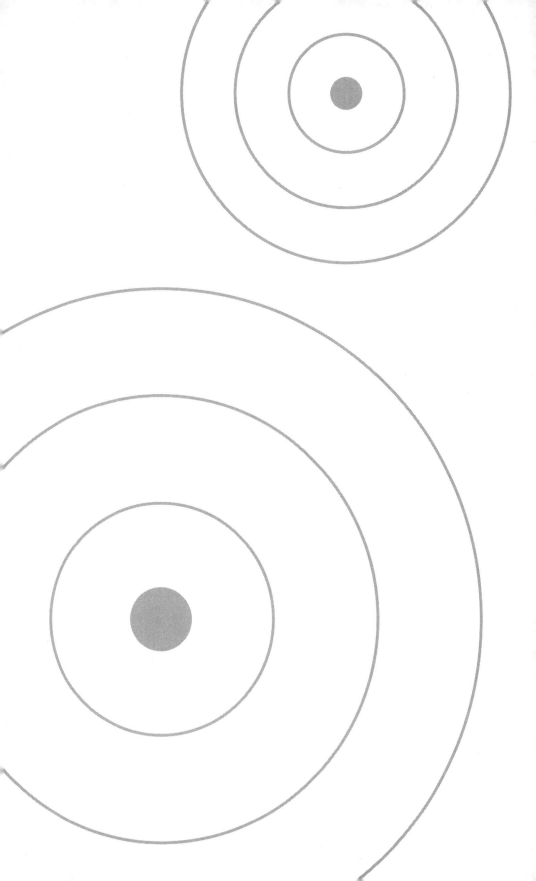

SMALL WARS, BIG DATA

THE INFORMATION REVOLUTION IN MODERN CONFLICT

ELI BERMAN, JOSEPH H. FELTER, AND JACOB N. SHAPIRO

WITH VESTAL McINTYRE

PRINCETON UNIVERSITY PRESS   PRINCETON AND OXFORD

Copyright © 2018 by Princeton University Press

Published by Princeton University Press
41 William Street, Princeton, New Jersey 08540

In the United Kingdom: Princeton University Press
6 Oxford Street, Woodstock, Oxfordshire OX20 1TR

press.princeton.edu

Jacket design by Amanda Weiss

All Rights Reserved

Library of Congress Control Number 2017959003
ISBN 978-0-691-17707-6

British Library Cataloging-in-Publication Data is available

This book has been composed in Adobe Text Pro, FRAC, and Motor

Printed on acid-free paper. ∞

Printed in the United States of America

10 9 8 7 6 5 4 3 2 1

To our friends and comrades in the field, running the projects, and standing the watch. This is for you.

CONTENTS

PREFACE

WHY IT IS IMPORTANT TO READ THIS BOOK NOW

A drowned boy pulled from the Mediterranean, kidnapped schoolgirls sitting helpless at gunpoint in a field in Nigeria, shoppers lying dead in a market in Iraq, more than 350 killed on a Saturday afternoon in Mogadishu, the Twin Towers spewing smoke as they collapse: these images, now seared in our common experience, reflect the direct and indirect effects of modern wars.

The death toll in these "small" or intrastate wars is staggering. As we go to press, the war in Syria has claimed 400,000 lives in seven years, the much longer war in Somalia 500,000, the younger conflict in Yemen 10,000. Civil wars grind on in Afghanistan and Iraq while insurgencies continue to claim lives in India, Mali, Nigeria, Pakistan, the Philippines, South Sudan, and many other countries around the world.

Fatalities tell only part of the story. These conflicts slow economic growth, impoverishing entire generations.[1] The effects on human health are persistent, lasting long after the fighting has ended.[2] When you consider the brutal tactics employed by the self-proclaimed "Islamic State" (IS, aka Daesh, ISIS, ISIL) and other combatants in today's conflicts, add the years of misery experienced by refugees and internally displaced people, and include the global terrorism that extends from these local conflicts making almost all of humanity feel at risk, the burden becomes overwhelming.

How do these small wars occur, and what can be done to reduce the damage?

A first step is to better understand the inner workings of intrastate warfare. That is our purpose in this book. The logic of these wars is quite different from the mechanisms that drive interstate wars—that is, wars between nations. That matters because the intuitive response to interstate wars often fails when applied to intrastate wars. We will look closely at the differences presently, but first let's examine how the prevailing form of warfare has changed over the past several decades.

THE RISE OF INTRASTATE WARFARE

Figure 0.1 charts the incidence and effects of conflicts worldwide since the Vietnam War. The graph on the left plots battle deaths, and the one on the right, the number of conflicts. This period has seen far more civil wars—and they have been far more costly—than wars between nations. The number of interstate wars in any year (right panel) has not exceeded five and has hovered close to zero for the past decade. Meanwhile, the number of intrastate wars peaked at fifty in the early 1990s, subsided to a level roughly equivalent to that in the 1960s, and has risen again since 2005.

The character of these intrastate wars has also changed over time. During the Cold War most were proxy wars between governments and insurgents, each backed by the opposing superpower. Those were extremely violent conflicts, as reflected in the high number of battle deaths. The 1990s saw a peak in the number, but not the lethality, of civil wars, characterized by two sides with equivalent (and usually low) military sophistication. This rise was driven by the civil wars that broke out across Africa over the decade, many of which became long-running conflicts, like the horrible on-and-off civil war in Liberia (1989–2003), which resulted in the death of 6 percent of the population and the displacement of 25 percent.[3] The increase in fatalities since 2005 is fueled almost entirely by the conflicts in Iraq and Syria, with Yemen and Afghanistan each contributing to the toll. Those conflicts are unbalanced, pitting militarily weak insurgents against a government supplied by technologically sophisticated allies.

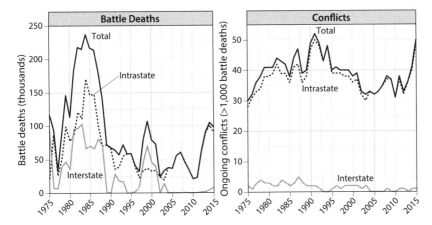

FIGURE 0.1. Trends in conflict since 1975. The figure on the left describes in thousands the number of individuals killed in battle for intrastate and interstate conflicts in each year. The figure on the right shows the count of conflicts with at least 25 battle-related deaths occurring in the given year. Data from the UCDP/PRIO Armed Conflict Dataset (Marie Allansson, Erik Melander, and Lotta Themnér, "Organized Violence, 1989–2016," *Journal of Peace Research* 54, no. 4 [2017]: 574–87).

Interstate conflicts are those in which belligerents on both sides include nation-states defined in Gleditsch and Ward as well as a subset of microstates (e.g., Tonga). Kristian S. Gleditsch and Michael D. Ward, "A Revised List of Independent States since the Congress of Vienna," *International Interactions* 25, no. 4 (1999): 393–413. Intrastate conflicts coded as those where one or both sides of the conflict are not a state government or coalition of sovereign states.

The United States, NATO, and other Western powers routinely intervene in such conflicts, as illustrated in figure 0.2. While the number of new interventions has varied (around two to three per year), the right graph indicates that they endure and accumulate as conflicts go unresolved. And many other countries have faced conflicts on their own soil, including India, with the Naxalite conflict in the heart of the country, as well as ethnic separatist movements in its northeastern regions, and Pakistan, which has been fighting militant groups in the Federally Administered Tribal Areas since the mid-2000s.

Since the 1990s the United Nations has responded to the increase in civil wars with new peacekeeping missions. Between 1989 and 1994 alone, for example, the UN Security Council authorized 20 new operations, raising the number of peacekeeping troops from 11,000 to 75,000.[4] And those numbers have continued to grow, with more than 112,000 UN personnel deployed around the world as of June 2017.[5]

The experience of American troops intervening in places such as Somalia and Yugoslavia in the late 1990s prompted General Charles

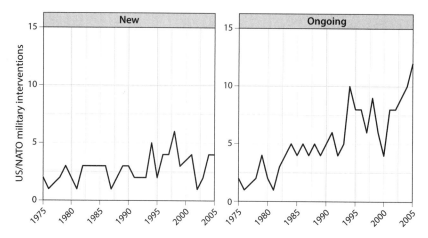

FIGURE 0.2. Trends in foreign military intervention by the United States and NATO since 1975. The figure on the left denotes the number of new overseas interventions starting in a given year involving the United States alone, the United States as part of a coalition force, or NATO. The figure on the right depicts the number of ongoing interventions in each year (i.e., the total number for which some portion of the conflict took place in that year), starting with conflicts beginning in 1975. All data are from the IMI data set (Jeffrey Pickering and Emizet F. Kisangani, "The International Military Intervention Dataset: An Updated Resource for Conflict Scholars," *Journal of Peace Research* 46, no. 4 [2009]: 589–99).

C. Krulak, then Commandant of the Marine Corps, to theorize about the dramatic change in the *type* of warfare America was conducting.

> In one moment in time, our service members will be feeding and clothing displaced refugees, providing humanitarian assistance. In the next moment, they will be holding two warring tribes apart— conducting peacekeeping operations—and, finally, they will be fighting a highly lethal mid-intensity battle—all on the same day . . . all within three city blocks. It will be what we call "the Three Block War."[6]

Krulak predicted that demographic shifts and globalization would continue to push different ethnic, class, and nationalist groups crowded together in growing cities to spark conflicts, which would eventually require U.S. intervention.[7]

Krulak was prescient about the rise of the Three Block War and the need for outsiders to intervene in civil conflicts with what the U.S. military has called "full spectrum operations." And these are the types of military engagements the West can expect to fight for the foreseeable future because no non-state threat will be able to challenge Western nations in head-to-head combat for control over territory anytime soon. The gap in weapons and surveillance technology has widened since Krulak wrote. As we write, IS has high-powered assault rifles, commercial drones jury-rigged to drop grenades, guided anti-tank missiles, and no shortage of ammunition.[8] But these systems do not compare to the weapons of the coalition opposing it: air power, GPS-guided munitions, long-range drones carrying precision-guided missiles, and spy satellites.[9]

While conventional combat is off the table, guerrilla warfare, as we will see in the coming chapters, remains a viable and sustainable strategy for heavily disadvantaged forces whenever they can depend on the local population for support and protection.

Information and how it is leveraged, we will argue, play a key role in governments' efforts to defeat or contain insurgencies. During the Algerian civil war, for example, it was the government's ability to use information to infiltrate the Islamist rebellion, as much as its brutal tactics, that led to victory. India and Nepal have both used tips from civilians to contain rural Maoist insurgencies. In the NATO operation in Libya in 2011 and the French-led intervention in Mali in 2013, local information allowed the intervening parties to effectively use their military advantages to target combatants.

THE GLOBAL EFFECTS OF SMALL WARS

While it is tempting to think of these wars as a horror that plagues distant places, the effects of today's civil wars are felt far beyond the borders of the countries where they simmer. First of all, they tend to spill over borders to create violence and instability in neighboring nations, the way Boko Haram has in Chad and Cameroon.

Second, they can lead to terrorist attacks in faraway nations. The examples of this are clear and numerous, but we can start by thinking of what Paris suffered: hundreds killed in the Métro bombings of the 1990s at the hands of the Groupe Islamique Armé (GRE), which was waging an insurgency in Algeria, and 130 on the night of 15 November 2015 at the hands of IS. The subnational conflicts so common in recent years are particularly potent incubators of terrorism, as they create pockets of poorly governed space where terrorists can organize and train. When space is governed by non-state actors aligned with terrorists, there is no stable entity responsible, so there is no address for punishment or deterrence.

Third, insurgencies create opportunities for network building among terrorists—the kind al Qaeda fostered and that enabled the planning of the 9/11 attacks.

Fourth, ungoverned spaces within sovereign states can breed a range of pernicious threats beyond terrorism: drug trafficking and human trafficking, as in Afghanistan and Mexico, and infectious diseases such as Ebola, which was enabled by the collapse of health services in post–civil war Liberia.

Finally, small wars have the potential to catalyze big wars; as powerful nations intervene on one side or another, an intrastate conflict can develop into a multinational conflagration. The current civil war in Yemen, for example, has dramatically escalated the potential for conflict between Saudi Arabia and Iran.

For all these reasons we need a far greater understanding of how insurgencies are sustained, who joins them and why, who funds them, how they interact with the communities in which they hide, and what can be done to defeat them.

On the more hopeful side, weakening today's insurgencies would be largely good for democracy worldwide. In 2014, Afghanistan had its first ever peaceful democratic election and transfer of power. In 2015, Nigeria did the same. An increasingly powerful Taliban or Boko Haram would threaten these nascent democracies. The fledgling governments of Iraq and Afghanistan are making real efforts at economic development, improving health care, and empowering women.[10] The West can help these governments navigate their minefields, both literal and metaphorical.

Persistent intrastate conflict is one of the great scourges of our era. It stymies economic development, directly and indirectly kills hundreds of thousands every year, breeds terrorism, and saps policy attention from other threats (such as climate change). The way to deal with these conflicts is becoming less and less mysterious, though. As we will show in the pages ahead, a broad body of research contains lessons on how to do so. If applying those insights can help open up political space to get deals done, then winning small fights can lead to big gains. We hope this book provides an important step in that direction.

ACKNOWLEDGMENTS

This book is the fruit of over a decade of work by a revolving team of coauthors, mentors, and research associates. We've been uniquely fortunate to have such a community, so we're going to do our best to thank them here.

Above all others, we acknowledge Vestal McIntyre, our stalwart science writer turned colleague, taskmaster, coach, and friend. Vestal worked with us—and at times carried us—throughout this journey: outlining the book, crafting clear prose to illuminate key points, and translating our ideas from jargon to accessible English. We would have surely lost our way without him. Thank you, Vestal—and also Asim, Rohini, and Mike for recommending Vestal to us. You were right!

None of this would have happened without the dedication and talent of our program managers, Katherine Levy at the University of California-San Diego (UCSD) and Kristen Seith at Princeton. They embraced our vision and adopted it as their own, working creatively and tirelessly to keep the Empirical Studies of Conflict Project (ESOC) running. The safety and success of our research teams have relied on their diligence and thoughtfulness. The book would never have been written without the wisdom and encouragement of Steve Biddle, David Laitin, David Lake, and Tjip Walker, who began compelling us to synthesize the emerging data-driven literature on asymmetric conflict in 2012. After three years of them beating up on us, we finally got the message and began working with Vestal to craft the text.

We owe an immense debt to those whose ideas formed the foundation of what you are about to read, including Jon Bendor, Steve Biddle, Ethan Bueno de Mesquita, Jim Fearon, Martin Feldstein, Ashraf Ghani, Clark Gibson, Roger Gordon, Paul Huth, Laurence Iannaccone, Ethan Kapstein, Alan Krueger, David Laitin, David Lake, Adam

Meirowitz, Gerard Padró i Miquel, Chick Perrow, Kris Ramsay, Scott Sagan, Susan Shirk, Tjip Walker, Barry Weingast, Jeremy Weinstein, and Richard Zeckhauser.

Much of this book and of the broader ESOC agenda draws on data collected by various government and nongovernmental organizations. Many individuals have helped us access and understand data over the years, including the Freedom of Information Act (FOIA) officers across the U.S. government whose impressive devotion to their mission, of making as much information publicly accessible as legal limits allow, has made much of this work possible.

Beyond the FOIA officers, our work on Iraq would have been impossible without the assistance of Jim Glackin and Fran Woodward (then at the Gulf Region Division of the Army Corps of Engineers), who helped us locate and understand the data on aid spending, Jeffrey Cadman and the MNC-I C2 Foreign Disclosure Office, who helped to secure release of the "significant activity" (SIGACT) data on combat incidents, Pat Buckley and Lee Ewing, who helped us understand the biases and problems with many different data sources, and David Petraeus, who was instrumental in gaining the support needed to authorize the first declassification of SIGACT data.

Our work on Afghanistan benefited from efforts by Stanley McChrystal and Michael Flynn to declassify civilian casualty data. It is immeasurably richer thanks to Kyle Pizzey, who helped us and our colleagues understand many different data sources and whose long service at the International Security Assistance Force (ISAF) Joint Command's Assessment Cell make him the world expert on data from that conflict.

Our research on the Philippines was enabled by senior officers and members of the Armed Forces of the Philippines (AFP), including AFP Chiefs of Staff Generals Narcisso Abaya, Victor Ibrado, Dionisio Santiago, and Alexander Yano. Other senior military and civilian officials supporting our efforts include Delfin Lorenzana, Victor Corpus, Eduardo Davalan, Teodoro Llamas, Corazon "Dinky" Soliman, Gilbert Teodoro, and countless others. Technical Sergeant Erwin Augustine and the many dedicated coding team members he helped motivate and lead for nearly a decade did an amazing job pulling information from paper records into spreadsheets. And Erwin Olario was tireless in his efforts as a one-stop shop for analytical, coding, and geospatial support in building the ESOC Philippines data from the very beginning in 2004. But most especially, we thank our colleague Colonel Dennis Eclarin, who made our extensive research efforts in the Philippines possible for over a decade and shared our commitment to making these efforts matter. Joe will forever consider him a brother.

Our understanding of the internal workings of terrorist and insurgent groups benefited tremendously from hard work by Liam Collins and Bryan Price to continue the precedent of releasing data from the Harmony database that Joe started when he led the Combating Terrorism Center at the United States Military Academy. Seth Jones and Chris White had the foresight to persuade their organizations to support that research before it was clear we would learn as much as we did.

Many other folks outside of government organizations helped us with different data sources. We could not have done any of our earlier work on the impact of civilian casualties without John Sloboda, Hamit Dardagan, and Josh Doughtery at Iraq Body Count (now everycasualty.org). Their steadfast belief that every human being deserves to have his or her death recorded, and their commitment to doing so in conflicts around the globe, is an inspiration. Lewis Shadle opened many doors for us in understanding the cell-phone networks of Afghanistan and Iraq and how their construction was shaped by violent events. Munqith Daghir generously shared his deep knowledge of the Iraqi public opinion as well as survey data that his firm, IIACSS, collected during the worst parts of the war in Iraq. And Ben Connable's well-informed skepticism about administrative data collection in war zones vastly improved how we approached the data you will read about.

In all of our research we strive to be sensitive to the details of how policies were implemented and data collected on a day-to-day basis. When we succeed it is usually thanks to hours and hours of conversation with the people who put their lives on the line in various conflict zones. On the military side Victor Corpus, Brian Cunningham, Dennis Eclarin, Brendan Gallagher, Mike Kelvington, Kevin McKiernan, Andrew Montalvo, Pete Newell, Douglas Ollivant, Brynt Parmeter, Jeff

Peterson, Ryan Shann, and Colin Supko were all extremely generous with their time, in addition to some of the folks mentioned above who also helped with data. On the civilian side Alexandra Courtney, Bob Crowley, Jason Foley, Stacia George, Nick Lawson, Stephen Lennon, Carter Malkasian, Tjip Walker, and Kael Weston all shared stories and reflections on the constraints aid professionals face in conflict zones.

Beyond those who helped us with their shared experiences, we owe a debt to our coauthors and collaborators on other projects, whose ideas permeate this book as much as do our own. Mike Callen, Luke Condra, Tarek Ghani, and Radha Iyengar have been good friends and even better coauthors on many different projects over the years, and valiantly spent time in the field in Afghanistan. Ben Crost and Patrick Johnston worked with Joe on the Philippines and have been great partners in understanding that conflict. Patrick and a large crew worked with Jake to understand the finances of al Qaeda in Iraq (AQI) and successor groups and how they paid their fighters, including Howard Shatz, Benjamin Bahney, Danielle Jung, Pat K. Ryan, Jonathan Wallace, and Barbara Sude. Andrew Shaver and Austin Wright are setting new standards for getting data released and have been a joy to write with as graduate students and colleagues. Tiffany Chou, Mitch Downey, Mohammad Isaqzadeh, Jen Keister, Lindsay Heger, Aila Matanock, and Erin Troland have helped us understand the big picture and results from Afghanistan, Iraq, and the Philippines. Working with Steve Biddle and Jeff Friedman helped Jake understand much more about the interaction of politics and military force. Running surveys with Graeme Blair, Christine Fair, Kosuke Imai, Neil Malhotra, Rebecca Littman, and Bryn Rosenfeld contributed to our knowledge on the political impact of violence. Oliver Kaplan, Abbey Steele, and Juan Vargas taught us a great deal about conflicts in Colombia, as Oliver Vanden Eynde did for conflicts in India. Projects with Jesse Driscoll, Daniel Egel, Patrick Kuhn, Nicolai Lidow, and James Long informed our understanding of how a range of policies affect political behavior, as did projects on mobile communications with Josh Blumenstock and Nils Weidmann. And Jake's work on the economy of the Islamic State with Mohamed Abdel-Jalil, Daniel Anh, Chris Elvidge, Jamie

Hansen-Lewis, and Quy Toan-Do opened our eyes to the potential of remote sensing for understanding conflict.

All of these projects have benefited from many excellent research assistants over the years (most of whom have now gone on to far bigger things—which does not make us feel old at all), including Emefa Agawu, Raizel Berman, Philip Clark, Benjamin Crisman, Jeff Decker, Mathilde Emeriau, Alexandra Hennessy, Carrie Lee, Crystal Lee, Alexa Liautaud, Jian Yang "Lumpy" Lum, Josh Martin, Ryan Mayfield, Torey McMurdo, Zach Romanow, Peter Schram, Manu Singh, Landin Smith, Adrienne von Schulthess, Elsa Voytas, and Neel Yerneni.

A number of other scholars provided thoughtful, detailed feedback on this project at various stages, including Richard English, who pointed us to a host of useful historical examples, Rick Morgan, who helped us understand India's lesser-known insurgencies, Dani Reiter, who showed us how to connect results to the broader security studies literature, and our anonymous reviewers, who identified a host of problems in earlier drafts and guided us in correcting them. Eric Crahan provided excellent editorial guidance and indulged our desire to tell our story alongside the research.

This research is expensive. A number of institutions and individuals have supported ESOC over the years. With persistence and vision Erin Fitzgerald built the U.S. Department of Defense's Minerva Research Initiative into a major force for social science and encouraged us to build the team. We owe a great debt to the late Terry Lyons, our first program manager at the Air Force Office of Scientific Research, who believed deeply in our mission, and to Nora Zelizer, who helped write the grant that got our first big chunk of funding. Terry's successor, Joe Lyons, and Stephanie Bruce were extremely supportive and helped us navigate several tricky research compliance issues. The USC Center for Risk and Economic Analysis of Terrorism Events (CREATE) provided important funding over the years, as did Ivy Estabrooke and Harold Hawkins's programs at the Office of Naval Research.

The leadership of the U.S. Military Academy's Combating Terrorism Center provided guidance and institutional support for many years, particularly Vinnie Viola, Wayne Downing, John Abizaid,

Mike Meese, and Cindy Jebb. Adnan Khan and the team at the International Growth Centre supported a range of research on links between governance, service delivery, and political behavior. And long discussions with Ali Cheema, Asim Khwaja, and Farooq Naseer helped us understand how terrorism does, and often does not, block economic development in peaceful regions of conflict-affected countries. The leadership of Princeton's Woodrow Wilson School—Anne-Marie Slaughter, Christina Paxson, and Cecilia Rouse—have provided core support to ESOC for years, enabling us to take risks and push the research frontier in new directions. Colleagues at Stanford's Center for International Security and Cooperation (CISAC) provided an intellectual home for Joe and the environment where we conceived the idea of ESOC, most especially Scott Sagan, Liz Gardner, Martha Crenshaw, Sigfried Hecker, Tino Cuellar, Amy Zegart, and David Relman. Colleagues at the Hoover Institution and especially its Library and Archives helped us bring many of the Philippines records to the United States and aided our efforts to archive valuable records from that conflict. David Brady, John Raisian, Richard Sousa, and Eric Wakin have been particularly helpful, as have Lew Davies, Bob Oster, and the Hoover Institution Board of Overseers. Colleagues at UCSD have responded with enthusiasm and insight to the unconventional idea of economists working on security, particularly Peter Cowhey, Peter Gourevitch, and the superb faculty in the Department of Economics, the School of Global Policy and Strategy, and the Department of Political Science. Tai Ming Cheung, Lynne Bush, and Helen Olow of the UC Institute on Global Conflict and Cooperation (IGCC) provided a logistical backbone.

Finally, our greatest debt is to family. For Eli, it is to his parents, Shaindel and Shier Berman, who teach "tikkun olam" with clarity and through example. For their patience Eli thanks his children, Ami and Raizel, and his wife, Linda, who once memorably declared "next book, next wife" but allowed an exception, this time. For Joe, it is to Colonel Joseph H. Felter Sr. and Colonel Joseph H. Felter Jr., who fought for the same causes at different times and in different wars, and were his role models for selfless service and sacrifice for a higher calling. Joe thanks Darby, Ben, and Max, whom he hopes will not be obliged to carry on this family tradition, and Lynn for helping him realize you can still contribute to the fight without being in the middle of it. For Jake, the debt is to his parents, Jim and Joan, who taught him that the measure of your life is how hard you worked to make the world a better place. Jake's motivation comes from Catherine, Felix, and Gus, who inspire him to get up every day and try to leave them a better world in some small measure.

1

KNOW THE WAR YOU'RE IN

The first, the supreme, the most far-reaching act of judgment that the statesman and commander have to make is to establish the kind of war on which they are embarking.

—Carl von Clausewitz

It seems unfathomable now, but by directive, at that time we weren't even allowed to use the term "insurgency" or "insurgents," even though everyone knew that's what we were facing every day. . . . It was very frustrating for soldiers operating in these conditions because they rarely saw the enemy but were constantly reacting to the variety of methods they employed to attack them. This was the reality we were settling into after a month or so on the ground.

—Colonel Brynt Parmeter, usa, Retired, on soldiers trained for a big conventional war finding themselves facing an asymmetric one, in Iraq in 2004

0630 hrs 6 June 2004, Tikrit, Iraq
1st Infantry Division Headquarters
Forward Operating Base "Danger"
- -

Major General Batiste, commanding general of the U.S. Army 1st Infantry Division, looked with some anticipation into the faces of the thirty-odd staff officers and NCOs filing in for the daily division operations update. Fatigue and stress had etched lines onto nearly all, though most were still young. Those nearing the end of a night shift supporting the division's maneuver elements conducting neighborhood sweeps, manning checkpoints, and other operations could be readily distinguished from those just beginning their day by their weary expressions or by the day's growth of beard on their chins.

The room was incongruously grand. Marble floors reflected the light from a crystal chandelier at the center, while Moorish arches opened onto darkened hallways at the periphery. The 1st Division staff occupied the palace where Saddam Hussein and his entourage used to stay when visiting his hometown of Tikrit—one of many such compounds across Iraq. One adaptation the soldiers had made was to erect crude, stadium-style seating in front of a podium and three large screens. The smell of fresh-cut plywood still permeated the room. The 1st Division members took their seats, many clutching the ubiquitous plastic water bottles with dust-coated hands. Before them hung blank white screens, and next to them maps of the town—a grid of streets with the dark braid of the Tigris River running from north to south. Operational graphics representing the disposition and location of friendly forces, unit boundaries, and other icons were neatly transcribed in fine-tipped Sharpie onto acetate sheets overlaying the maps.

The troops expected the operations update to refer to *this* geography, but when a map was projected on the screen, it showed the gentle curve where the English Channel meets the *coast of France*. This operations update was special: today was 6 June 2004, and the division staff had used computer-aided graphics and satellite imagery to develop an operations update reflecting the 1st Infantry Division's participation in the Allied landings in Normandy exactly sixty years earlier.

0630 hrs 6 June 1944
H-Hour D-Day
1st Infantry Division
Omaha Beach
Normandy, France
- -

Machine-gun fire ripped across the deck the moment the ramp dropped from the Higgins amphibious assault vehicle. Bullets wounded or killed many of the lead elements of the U.S. Army 1st Infantry Division's invasion force before their boots touched the sand.

Soon Omaha Beach was soaked in blood. German artillery fire rained down on the advancing forces. The soldiers who made it past submerged obstacles and through this gauntlet of fire to reach the crescent-shaped beach had to traverse an additional three hundred meters of fire-swept open ground laced with barbed wire and studded with land mines. Only then did they reach the first available cover at the base of the bluffs.

A number of the soldiers storming the beach on that historic morning were seasoned veterans of multiple campaigns. The 1st Infantry Division had initially seen combat in North Africa in 1942, then fought in the invasion of Italy in 1943. Given the extraordinary operations tempo the division had maintained and the major battles and campaigns it participated in early in the war, many believed it would be spared assignment to the first wave of Operation Overlord's invasion force. But the senior leaders developing the invasion plans decided to send this seasoned division in with the initial assault on Normandy. The soldiers were not expecting to land unopposed, but still they were shocked to meet with seemingly impenetrable resistance from German defenders securely dug in and well prepared, including the only full-strength enemy infantry division in France.

The first day, Allied forces suffered approximately ten thousand killed, wounded, or missing in action, and German forces approximately nine thousand, despite their well-prepared and fortified positions. In total, nearly half a million combatants would eventually be killed or wounded in the Normandy campaign. The Allied forces who survived the bloody amphibious assault, secured the beachhead, and made their way inland faced the extraordinary challenge of advancing across occupied France and into the German homeland. Missions of the storied 1st Infantry Division would include employing fire, maneuver, and shock effect to destroy German forces in the field, seize cities and key terrain from German control, and destroy industrial bases and other means of resistance.

The ultimate goal of the 1st Division was to secure the unconditional surrender of Hitler's regime—clearly defined, though by no means easy to achieve. Success on the battlefield was a necessary and nearly sufficient condition to achieve ultimate victory over the Axis Powers.

In this war, state capacity was readily translated into success on the battlefield. Allied forces would eventually prevail because the

industrial base of the United States, once mobilized by the fully supportive political leadership and committed American public, enabled
them to produce the massive amount of war matériel required to turn
the tide. Bombing raids over Germany increased and Allied infantry
forces progressed rapidly across France and into Germany itself. In
April 1945, less than ten months after the assault on the Normandy
coast, U.S. and British forces linked up with the Soviet Red Army and
secured Germany's unconditional surrender.

Major General Batiste turned off the projections and raised the
lights. He brought the formal ceremony to its culmination: "Commanders, present your soldiers the shoulder sleeve insignia of the 1st
Infantry Division on this day, sixty years after our forefathers landed
on the beaches of Normandy."

All of the 1st Infantry Division members now carried the striking
image of the division's "Big Red 1" insignia on both shoulders, the
left and now the right. In the U.S. Army, soldiers wear the patch of
the current unit on their left shoulder. By tradition, they wear the
insignia of units they have served with in combat on their right and
are authorized to wear them there for the rest of their time in service.
Save for a handful of senior noncommissioned officers and officers
who had served in Desert Storm or in the Panama invasion over a
decade earlier, this was the first time the division's soldiers earned
this privilege and distinction.

Major General Batiste recited the 1st Infantry Division's World War
I motto: *No mission too difficult, no sacrifice too great, duty first.*

- -

This story was told to us by Colonel Brynt Parmeter, USA, Retired. At
the time, he was Chief of Operations ("CHOPS") in charge of a critical
section of the 1st Infantry Division operation staff responsible for the
current and near-term operations of the division. Among his many
duties were morning updates and evening radio net calls, to ensure a
common understanding of current and future activities among commanders and staff.

Prior to deployment, the 1st Division had trained in much the same
way that U.S. Army units based in Germany had done throughout the

Cold War, maneuvering combat units to engage and destroy a conventional enemy. A number of the division's members were veterans of the first Gulf War. Ground fighting there had lasted just ninety-six hours and resulted in an overwhelming victory for the U.S. and Coalition forces over the Iraqi military. This had seemed a validation of the U.S. military's approach to defeating its foes through technological dominance of the battlefield from air, sea, and land. Aside from the recent peacekeeping missions in Bosnia and Kosovo, the unit had little experience with insurgency.

Unfortunately, neither the train-up nor the experience in the first Gulf War did much to prepare the 1st Division's leaders and soldiers for what they found in Iraq: roadside bombs, assassinations of village leaders friendly to the Coalition, and the destruction of bridges and other infrastructure. "Vehicle-borne explosives starting to pop up," Parmeter explained, "and you had small arms fire attacks just randomly through urban areas and land mines placed to hit our forces."

Though the 1st was suffering nowhere near the casualties seen on D-Day or throughout World War II, it was not uncommon to experience more than fifty enemy attacks a day across the division's area of operations, and there were casualties every day. These were not clustered around any front—attacks could happen at any moment, anywhere U.S. forces were deployed across the increasingly restive country.

Major General Batiste's purpose in reminding his soldiers of the 1st Division's powerful history at Normandy was to give them an additional source of support and stability to draw on during those challenging times. But his reminder also highlighted what a different tactical challenge the division faced and how, in essence, they were better prepared for battles like Normandy than for Tikrit. In Iraq, the 1st Division soldiers had a steep advantage over the enemy—unprecedented firepower, vehicles, and technology—but they rarely had the opportunity to use these against the elusive and seemingly invisible insurgents. Even the most advanced surveillance systems had a difficult time confirming whether an individual was the enemy and whether the people surrounding him were combatants or civilians.

Fortunately, Major General Batiste and most of the senior leaders quickly recognized that this fight was unlike the first Gulf War and more like the "small" subnational wars in Bosnia and Kosovo, where the U.S. military had played a peacekeeping role. Both the 2nd and 3rd Brigades had spent time in Kosovo, where they had encountered a similar, though much less violent, insurgency. Batiste knew that the 1st Division needed to conduct *precision* actions: raids and other operations to find and capture or kill the insurgent groups and individuals responsible for the violence. To do this, they first had to learn to engage with the local population, gain their trust, glean fragments of information from them, and piece these together into a coherent intelligence estimate. Each step in this process represented a major challenge.

About a month after the D-Day commemoration, an insurgent dressed in police uniform detonated a car bomb at a building occupied by 1st Division soldiers and Iraqi policemen, killing many of both in Samarra, a city forty miles from Tikrit. This marked the beginning of a period of intense insurgent activity: every patrol entering Samarra met some combination of small arms fire, rocket-propelled grenades, improvised explosive devices, and indirect fire. Later in the summer, the 1st Division and other units pushed into the city and drove out most of the insurgents. Afterward, 1st Battalion, 26th Infantry stayed to conduct "hold-and-build operations" while the other units withdrew. Parmeter described the variety of activities this entailed:

> On one day, patrolmen would go out and meet with a group of primary school teachers to figure out how we could set up an education program in a town. On the next patrol two hours later, we would try to set up a terrain-denial patrol around a known mortar-firing location. Two hours after that we would go and meet with the mayor and his city infrastructure team (which may or may not even have existed) to try to figure out how we could fix an electrical problem or water problem in the town. And then our last patrol would be to go to secure a police recruiting drive to protect the individuals that might want to sign up to attend a training academy— which we had to set up—to be future policemen. All of this was part of Major General Batiste's directive to conduct intelligence-driven operations and protect the population from the insurgents. This

made the population more likely to provide information on bad actors when they had it, which helped us interdict planned attacks and successfully target insurgents.

The months that followed the initiation of combat operations in Samarra were trying, with numerous attacks suffered, and a strong effort by the insurgents to push Coalition forces out. Parmeter described their strategy:

> It was during this stage that every one of the U.S. soldiers in Samarra realized that we gained very little through violence in the form of kinetic responses. They were often the worst response especially in urban and other areas with a high risk of collateral damage. In fact, we suspected that for every Iraqi killed or injured by U.S. forces, we were essentially creating more new insurgents. On the contrary, for every non-kinetic action where we were assisting the population, like helping with the hospitals, schools, critical infrastructure, and other similar activities, we were taking the power away from the insurgents and encouraging greater support and collaboration from among the population.

According to Parmeter, the 1st Infantry Division realized that they were in a war fought for the support and cooperation of the local population—a population who could provide information—completely different from the war their forefathers waged in 1944 and 1945 or that they themselves had fought in Kuwait and Iraq in 1991. It would be two years before Lieutenant General David Petraeus and Major General James Mattis would compile the lessons Parmeter and his fellow soldiers were learning into FM 3-24—the U.S. Army-Marine Corps counterinsurgency manual—the first resource of its kind since the Vietnam War era.

TWO TYPES OF WAR

One legendary division, two very different wars. There are innumerable technological and political differences from one conflict to another sixty years later. However, when it comes to theories of war and paths to victory, many of the starkest differences between those wars come down to one important dichotomy: symmetric versus asymmetric.

Symmetric wars include international contests such as the two world wars. The victor is generally the side with superior weapons and larger armies. They also include civil (or "subnational") wars where protagonists of roughly equal capacity fight primarily over territorial control. In the later stages of the Vietnam War, for instance, combatants from North and South Vietnam fought along well-defined fronts as in international wars, with victory secured by a combination of superior weaponry, numbers, and strategy. Civilians matter in these conflicts, of course, but mostly because they provide soldiers and resources to the battlefield.

Asymmetric wars, by contrast, are contests where one side enjoys a heavy matériel and capabilities advantage. These include the post-9/11 U.S. engagements in Iraq and Afghanistan, as well as numerous historical examples. In Napoleon's struggle to control the Iberian Peninsula, he didn't face one central opponent but instead fought many "little wars," the origin of the term "guerrilla." Nearly a century later, after Spain ceded the Philippines to American control, the United States waged a three-year war within this newly acquired territory against multiple semi-independent insurgent groups. It ended officially in victory in 1902 but saw sporadic violence for years afterward. On the Eastern Front in World War II, Hitler's army struggled to root out insurgencies, notably the Yugoslav Partisans and Polish Underground State, but also the Ukrainian Insurgent Army, who would go on to fight the Soviet Union until 1949, long after that war had slipped from public view.

In symmetric wars, the struggle is primarily over territory. Information plays an important role, to be sure, but it is not decisive in the same way. Both the D-Day landing in Normandy and the 1991 U.S. invasion of Kuwait involved deception campaigns designed to make the enemy think the main attack would be in a different location than it was. But the value of a given piece of information in symmetric conflicts can vary greatly. Knowing who the opposing commander is or where he is, for example, is of little value if he is in a well-protected bunker too far behind enemy lines to be targeted with available means.

In asymmetric wars, the struggle is fundamentally not over territory but over *people*—because the people hold critical information (which is true to a greater extent than in symmetric conflicts[1]), because the ability of the stronger side to take advantage of any given piece of information is always very high, and because holding territory is not enough to secure victory. The stronger party in asymmetric conflicts can physically seize territory for a short time whenever it chooses to do so. But holding and administering that territory is another thing altogether—as so many would-be conquerors have learned. If the stronger side knows the location of a commander, hideout, or arsenal it can remove that threat, but if it does not, then there is no well-defined front on which to push and the weaker side will continue to be able to operate. Put more simply, asymmetric conflicts are *information-centric*. We will use that term in the chapters to come to refer to asymmetric conflicts and specifically to discuss the role played by tips passed from civilians to the government or dominant combatant.

Consider the 1st Division in Iraq: they and their Iraqi allies had massively superior conventional military capacity. Insurgent strategy depended on being able to blend into the civilian population. If insurgents could enlist the support of the population, they could move forces, acquire weapons, and conduct attacks using roadside bombs and other improvised devices, thereby preventing the Iraqi government from consolidating control. On the other hand, if insurgents were identified and their movements reported, it was relatively easy for the Coalition and Iraqi government to suppress them, using advanced weaponry and skilled regular or special operations forces. The battle was not over territory. Victory required a flow of accurate information, mostly provided by civilians.

Globally, asymmetric civil wars have become the prevalent form of conflict since World War II. By one calculation, asymmetric subnational conflicts made up a majority (54 percent) of all subnational conflicts between 1944 and 2004, and were especially prevalent during the Cold War (66 percent).[2]

Understanding asymmetric warfare is especially important today from a Western strategic standpoint. For example, every major war the United States has fought since Korea, except for the first Gulf War and the first few weeks of the second, has been an asymmetric subnational conflict. As figure 1.1 illustrates, the United States and NATO launched new interventions in asymmetric conflicts almost year every between 1975 and 2005.

This trend will likely continue for the foreseeable future. Partly this is because geopolitics have generated a large number of fragile countries. Also, as drones, missiles, surveillance, and other weapons technologies applicable to subnational conflicts have improved, becoming more lethal, specialized, and expensive, the gap between the haves and have-nots is widening in terms of conventional war aimed at capturing territory. The weaker side is increasingly unlikely to survive when it tries to fight a conventional war, as ISIS's fate in Iraq and Syria so clearly demonstrates. With the United States as the last remaining military superpower, when it or NATO enters with their weapons technology, the conflict increasingly becomes asymmetric, even if only the local ally deploys forces on the ground. And when the weak side strategically switches to insurgency tactics (e.g., ambushes and improvised explosive devices [IEDs]), rather than fielding troops along some front in an attempt to control territory, the resources and technology advantage of the strong side are no longer enough to win the war, for reasons we will explain in a few chapters.[3]

In this book, we will examine the crucial role information plays in today's wars, particularly those the United States has fought since 9/11—and is still fighting and can expect to fight. We argue that taking a conventional approach, based on a symmetric warfare doctrine, will waste lives and resources, and risk defeat. However, taking a smarter approach can improve strategy and make dramatic gains in efficiency. Two major new tools enable this smart approach: research methods that were unavailable just fifteen years ago and data science, including the analysis of "big data." Our use of these tools has already yielded an important central finding: in information-centric warfare, small-scale efforts can have large-scale effects. Larger efforts may be neutral at best and counterproductive at worst. If this more nuanced view can guide policy, lives and money could be saved.

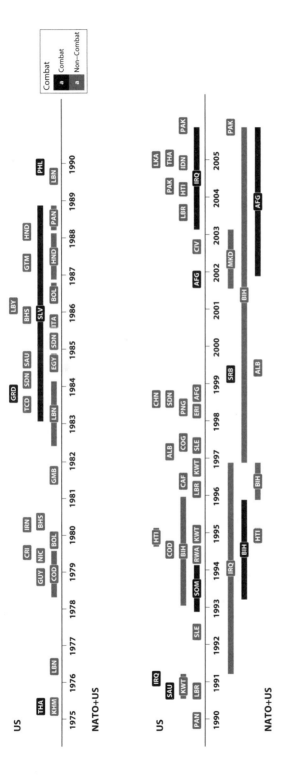

FIGURE 1.1. U.S. and NATO Interventions, 1975–2005.

Data are from the IMI data set. Jeffrey Pickering and Emizet F. Kisangani, "The International Military Intervention Dataset: An Updated Resource for Conflict Scholars," *Journal of Peace Research* 46, no. 4 (2009): 589–99.

Colonel Parmeter's story of the 1st Division being caught unprepared for an asymmetric conflict has analogues throughout the U.S. military and NATO and, more importantly, among aid and development agencies as well, both inside and outside government. In the next chapter, we describe our first contacts with development professionals in Kabul, who echoed the same theme: being caught unprepared, without a doctrine. More generally, the World Bank estimates that 1.5 billion people live in countries affected by fragility, conflict, or violence.[4] Because many of those are asymmetric conflict zones that lack front lines or forces in uniform, fragility means that people and property are unsafe. Those conditions, now familiar to conflict researchers, imply that many of the conventional approaches to addressing poverty through development programs may be ineffective and could even worsen violence.

BIG DATA

The first trend motivating our book is that small wars and their tragic costs are here to stay; the second is that society is increasingly using data to understand our world. Talk of "big data" is ubiquitous, but what professionals mean by the term is not so much that there's more data available—which of course there is—but that we have a growing set of computational and analytical tools to learn from it. The currently proliferating Internet of Things, for example, is already sending data from previously unconnected objects, like watches, toys, thermostats, pacemakers, and pet collars, back for analysis, informing decisions by doctors, government, manufacturers, and service providers. That should target products to suit our tastes and habits, save energy, and make us safer. Real-time analysis of high-precision weather data may save billions of dollars by allowing governments to ease traffic congestion, monitor pollution, and coordinate emergency services, for example.[5] And of course your every mouse movement and keyboard click online can be analyzed to figure out how companies like Google and Amazon can improve search results or induce you to click on ads.

Applications of big data from mobile phones are particularly promising for development and poverty reduction, as a large percentage of the population in poor countries are digitally connected, despite the lack of other infrastructure. After the 2010 earthquake in Haiti, for instance, researchers showed that call detail records predicted population movements, information that could be used to coordinate relief efforts in future disasters.[6] Analyzing mobile data in Côte d'Ivoire has given researchers insights into determinants of HIV transmission[7] and how cholera spreads.[8] A model combining Twitter and Google searches with environmental sensor data predicted the number of asthma emergency room visits with about 70 percent precision.[9] Additionally, an effort to use big data to identify biomarkers of Alzheimer's disease may be a step toward a cure.[10]

But what, specifically, do big data methods have to offer conflict studies? A lot, in two main areas.

First, big data allows us to measure things we never could before.

In Iraq and Afghanistan, the U.S. military recorded every "significant activity" involving U.S. forces with a precise time and location stamp (accurate to about one minute of time and ten meters in terms of location), including details such as the time and place of insurgent attacks, the type of attacks, and select outcomes. We managed to secure the declassification of certain fields from the resulting SIGACT-III database, which we could then match to economic and program data, making it possible to analyze the effects of economics and military interventions in asymmetric conflicts at an unprecedented granularity of detail. For example, some of our colleagues combined these data with records of cell-phone calls to show how violence displaced business activity.[11] Those kinds of analyses serve as a foundation for this book's empirics.

Innovation in data collection in theater has reshaped military practice as well as scholarship. In Afghanistan, the Joint Command of the NATO International Security Assistance Force (ISAF), which was responsible for the tactical side of the war, created an assessments cell to crunch through the massive amounts of information being collected. The cell conducted a wide range of analyses, from predicting IED attack patterns to measuring the effect of deploying persistent surveillance over major roads. Also in Afghanistan, the Defense Advanced Research Projects Agency (DARPA) funded the Nexus 7 project, which used data from a wide range of systems to support decision making at ISAF. One of the authors of this book worked on a Nexus 7 effort to use commercial satellite imagery to measure activity in rural markets in order to assess whether ISAF deployments were improving security from the population's point of view, reasoning that more people would go to market if they thought roads were secure.

Another project analyzed the movement patterns of ISAF units using the Blue Force Tracking (BFT) system that records the GPS locations of all U.S. combat vehicles.[12] The study found that while units in one regional command had an effective system for randomizing their departure times from base, which made it hard for insurgents to plan attacks, their return times were clearly scheduled, and thus they were being attacked routinely as they returned. After the study, new procedures were implemented to make sure that patrols were not returning to base at such predictable intervals. Further analysis with BFT data showed that the introduction of heavily armored vehicles that had trouble traveling off road led to shifts in patrol patterns away from remote areas, motivating investments in programs to develop lighter armor.

Years later, in another conflict, one of us worked with the researchers from the World Bank and Chris Elvidge's team at the National Oceanographic and Atmospheric Association to use nighttime satellite imagery to estimate IS oil revenue in Iraq and Syria.[13] The question had great relevance to world policy, since determining the groups' financial viability was essential to driving them out of the territory they had captured.

At its height in 2015, IS had seized 42 oil production sites in both Syria and Iraq. A reliable estimate of output at these sites before they fell under IS control put output at 70,000 barrels per day (BPD).[14] Based on those calculations, the media reported the group's oil revenues at up to $3 million per day,[15] while the U.S. Treasury put that number at $1 million.[16] After U.S. air strikes began targeting IS oil facilities, reports estimated income at anywhere between $260,000 and $1.5 million per day.[17]

One reason for the wide disparity in estimates was that they were each based on information about a small number of production sites obtained at a few points in time. The team took a new approach: conduct a real-time census of all of the oil production facilities under IS control. They used satellite multispectral imaging to estimate the radiant heat produced by flares at the oil fields. (Methane and other gases released when oil is pumped out of the ground are typically burned off in a constant flame atop a flare stack.) They compared these estimates with prewar data on the output of the oil wells and to output at production sites just outside IS territory. The radiant heat estimates clearly indicated that some fields were in modest productions and others seemed dormant: not only were they not producing heat, satellites didn't even pick up ambient electrical light.

Using these techniques, the team estimated that production levels increased from approximately 29,000 BPD from July to December 2014 to an average of 40,000 BPD throughout 2015 before dropping to approximately 14,000 BPD in 2016. These numbers were much lower than most estimates reported in the press but closely tracked internal numbers maintained by the Islamic State administrators.

These few examples illustrate how satellite imaging and GPS data previously unavailable, and collected at little or no risk, can help us understand economic and military activity in conflict zones.

Second, big data allows us to identify cause-and-effect relationships in ways we never could before.

When a scientist conducts an experiment, she is intervening in the world's normal functioning and measuring the effects. She might give test subjects a drug to see if it lowers their white blood cell count, or she might give poor children free school uniforms to see if that increases enrollment. These aspects of the world as it is—white blood cell count and school enrollment—are the measured outcomes. The interventions—the drug and the offer of school uniforms—are the treatments, sometimes referred to as *independent* variables. The outcome *depends* on how the intervention changes things, so it is sometimes called a *dependent* variable. Randomization of research subjects into different treatment conditions (different dosages of medication, for example) effectively holds everything but the treatment constant so you can reliably distinguish the effects of treatment from those of other factors.

Trying to determine how conflict works is tricky, first because violence depends on so many things that are out of the researcher's control and second because it's unthinkable to conduct actual experiments that vary real-world conditions in ways that could increase violence. Instead, you need rich data on where and when violent incidents happen so you can find ways to hold everything but one factor constant and see how violence *depends* upon it. As we will see, this is the kind of data Joe developed in the Philippines by convincing military officials to code huge numbers of paper records, and this is also the type of SIGACT data we relied on for analysis in Iraq.

THE WAY AHEAD

Our main contribution is to build a new theory of asymmetric conflict and test it with new sources of data. We will do this by telling a story—one that revolves around information. The simplest version goes like this:

> Information—and more specifically the knowledge citizens possess about insurgent activities—is the key factor determining which side has the upper hand in an asymmetric conflict. If governments have information, they can use their greater power to target insurgents and remove them from the battlefield. If governments lack that information then insurgents can get away with a range of attacks that continue to impose costs on the government, from IEDs and ambushes of government forces to violence against civilians supporting the government.
>
> Civilians will choose to share this information or choose to withhold it, depending on a rational calculation about what will happen to them if one side or the other controls the territory.[18] They will compare costs they will be subjected to if the government is not in control—the violence insurgents wreak in their area—to the ben-

efits the government will provide if it *is* in control—services such as schools, water systems, roads, and so on—all the while weighing these against their political preferences and the risks of retaliation by insurgents if they do inform. The government and rebels will make resource allocation decisions—the government choosing how much to invest in military force and services, the rebels deciding how much violence to attempt—taking into account what civilians will do as a result.

That basic three-way interaction between citizens, rebels, and government has several implications that we can look for in the historical record and in data from specific conflicts. Two of the most important are these.

First, changes in the communications infrastructure in a society that make it safer for citizens to inform—for example, the expansion of cell-phone coverage—should lead to reductions in insurgent violence. It should also be easy to find evidence that information-sharing by civilians poses serious challenges to the operations of rebels in asymmetric conflicts.

Second, governments can make citizens more willing to share information by doing a better job of delivering services, because doing so demonstrates the value of having government control the space, which will in turn lead to less insurgent violence. This mechanism works best for services whose value depends critically on government remaining in control (i.e., probably more for a clinic, which will close if staff flee when rebels take control, than for roads, which are functional regardless of who controls them) and is enhanced when those services are delivered effectively.

This book proceeds through several more implications of that three-way model, explaining, testing, describing the related literature (by ourselves and others), taking stock, and drawing out practical implications when possible.

Why should we tell this story, and why should leaders—or you for that matter—take interest? Because a detailed understanding of the interactions among citizens, governments, and insurgents provides a new set of tools to reduce violence and increase stability. As we will see, these tools may provide very cost-effective ways of saving lives and encouraging development. The story we will tell differs from previous analyses of asymmetric war in many ways. We will refute some widely accepted notions: that insurgencies can never be defeated or, alternatively, that counterinsurgency is best conducted with massive use of military force alone. We will show empirically, instead, that service delivery in conjunction with security provision provides a more cost-effective approach. Further, we will provide direct evidence linking the number of civilian casualties to changes in civilian attitudes, a flow of tips from civilians to government, and reduced insurgent violence.

Perhaps most important, you will learn why stronger powers so often seem to "win" locally, in the short term, but then fail to achieve their strategic outcomes nationally, in the longer run. While we will argue that there is an approach that works to win local battles, many of the cases we study also demonstrate that doing so is not enough to end many asymmetric conflicts. Our story is about how to reduce violence and increase stability once conflict has started. How to link those reductions to broader political settlements is a very different question.[19] In some places, those settlements may be out of reach for many years, and so knowing how to reduce violence in the meantime is valuable. In other places, stringing together local victories can lead to broader peace, as we will discuss in the conclusion.

Our central argument—that information flowing from noncombatants is the key resource in asymmetric conflicts—may be simple, but wars fought on city corners and along dusty rural roads, against enemies who are sometimes indistinguishable from allies, are anything *but* simple. To discover the forces causing the behavior of civilians and insurgents, you must examine many facets of economic activity and cultural norms.

Adding further complexity is the fact that conflicts can shift along the symmetric-asymmetric spectrum and that certain wars, like the Syrian civil war, have both symmetric and asymmetric fronts. Many of the traditional assumptions about conflict dynamics fall apart when exposed to the new tools of advanced empirical methods and data analysis. So we will proceed with care, addressing possible challenges, reviewing the literature, weighing the evidence, and allowing the discussion to take on more complexity. Note also that much of our discussion depends on some knowledge of statistical and economics concepts, and even a little game theory. As we go along, we will try gently to explain those, usually in the context of examples. Experts, of course, can skip these passages.

Although most of our quantitative data come from conflicts involving the United States, we will draw examples from a range of settings to build intuition. Sadly, we can draw evidence from (and crunch the data on) far too many current and historical conflicts—including those in Afghanistan, Algeria, Colombia, India, Nigeria, Pakistan, the Philippines, and Vietnam. That breadth should provide some confidence in the generalizability of the theory. This book is not about wars the United States has fought since 2001; it is about what sets asymmetric conflicts apart in a much broader way and the ways this informs how best to prosecute them.

The structure of this book reflects the three-way interaction of rebels, government, and civilians that we've just summarized. In chapter 2 we will explain who we are, what the Empirical Studies of Conflict research collective is, our approach to understanding conflict, and where we get our data. Because the story is one of scientific discovery by a community extending well beyond our team, we include a brief explanation of the broader empirical revolution that has disrupted the social sciences over the past few decades, and how we judge different types of evidence.[20] Readers not interested in our backgrounds, or in how knowing our biases and expertise will help you weigh evidence we present, can safely skip that part. Similarly, if you are familiar with modern research methods in economics and political science, as well as with how the move to microdata can help us better measure causal relationships, then large parts of chapter 2 will be redundant for you.

In chapter 3 we present the theoretical core of the book: an information-centric way of thinking about insurgency and other forms of asymmetric intrastate conflict. We explain the theory using an extended hypothetical narrative about a civilian who hears insurgents moving outside his home at night, and faces a series of difficult choices about whether to inform on them or not. This narrative introduces the three-way contest between violent rebels, a government seeking to minimize violence by mixing service provision and coercion, and civilians deciding whether to share information about insurgents.[21] Readers preferring full mathematical details of the models can find them in the original research papers and can skip to the six predictions of the model that we outline at the end of chapter 3.[22] For everyone else the story should provide rich intuition for the strategic logic behind asymmetric conflict and, we hope, provide a feel for the wrenching choices faced by those caught in the middle.

The chapters that follow work from this model and build off each other to examine different aspects of conflict—we don't suggest skipping any of chapters 4–9. Chapter 4 summarizes the most direct evidence we have for what we call the *information mechanism*. Our recent research suggests that manipulating this flow—for instance, by making it safer for civilians to share information—can reduce violence. Chapter 5 focuses on the role of development assistance—aid from the central government or other countries in various forms, from food deliveries to infrastructure projects to welfare payments. We review a large body of evidence suggesting that aid can actually stoke violence rather than ease it, and then we explore that question in greater detail, and discuss how aid can reduce violence. This gives a more detailed picture than previously available of the type of aid that reduces violence (and most likely also achieves its economic or social purpose) and demonstrates why. Chapter 6 examines the role of suppression—efforts on the part of security forces to suppress rebel activity. We will show how the returns to such efforts depend on the information provided by civilians. We will build on chapter 5 by exploring various synergies that our model predicts, particularly between certain kinds of aid and military force. Chapter 7 returns to the relationship between civilians and rebels, examining how the harm insurgents cause correlates with their political standing. One of our most interesting and strategically important discoveries is that providing information to civilians can affect their support for insurgencies.

A good deal of strategy and spending has worked off the assumption that insurgencies pull their recruits from a pool of disaffected, angry young men. In chapter 8 we examine the hypothesis that violence is caused by poverty, examine theoretical and empirical studies that support it, and consider other research that challenges it. We test the theory at the individual level (by using surveys to gauge the preferences of the poor) and then move to the national level (by comparing the rate of civil wars in rich versus poor countries). What we uncover will challenge traditional views and perhaps shed light on reasons behind the disappointing results of reconstruction campaigns that aim to reduce violence by simply raising incomes, without reference to local political conditions. In contrast, we will see that many of the elements at play in our theory of insurgency are common to asymmetric conflicts fought in many developing countries, including Colombia, India, and the Philippines, all of which have highly capable militaries that have fought lengthy campaigns against multiple insurgencies since the end of the Cold War.

In chapter 9 we focus on policies that enable government forces to gain information or generate goodwill. We draw on a wide variety of research from conflict zones and more peaceful regions to show the range of relatively inexpensive things governments can do. Evidence from a wide variety of studies suggests that subtle approaches can help. We then apply that research to our information-centric theory of conflict, showing why some small, targeted action might have large effects.

Chapter 10 concludes by considering what all this means in an era of increasing instability, large refugee flows out of conflict zones, growing militant organizations (including IS and others who practice both insurgency and terrorism), a reluctance among NATO countries to commit ground forces, a need for austerity, and the imperative of working through local allies. From Iraq to Syria to the Sahel and beyond, conditions around the world mean that dealing with insurgency and other asymmetric conflicts will remain a grave policy challenge for the foreseeable future. We will provide evidence for an approach that systematically enables stronger parties to control individual pieces of territory in even the hardest places. But winning the village is different from winning the war—as the U.S. experiences in Iraq and Afghanistan clearly demonstrate. The latter is a much harder political task. We therefore conclude by outlining how over a decade of research by ESOC and others can guide efforts to meet that challenge as well.

A NOTE ON STYLE

Throughout the book we will mix fairly informal narrative with precise technical language. Our objective is to make the book accessible to a broad set of readers without sacrificing precision when explaining the logic and evidence underlying our claims. In presentations and briefings over the years, that seems to have worked for us. We have also found that stories can help anchor our intuition. Most chapters therefore begin with short vignettes about particular people or moments in history that illustrate key ideas. Chapter 3 relies heavily on narrative, using a detailed *fictional* vignette to explain the logic of the theory. All these choices are designed to make it easy for readers to link the abstract concepts and evidence in the book to very concrete real-world events.

We will also tell the story of how some of these results were discovered. We hope this helps convey to prospective conflict researchers how rewarding this work is. We have enjoyed successful collaboration with superb academic teams, as well as deep engagement with practitioners and the broader policy community. The problems are vast and complex. Making progress requires understanding so many details of how policy is implemented on the ground in conflict zones that a cooperative "lab science" approach is efficient, perhaps even necessary.

Finally, Jake, Joe, and Eli will appear in the narrative. When we do, we'll introduce ourselves and provide a little background and context so that the intellectual journey will make a bit more sense. Knowing our backgrounds, experience, and perspectives will help you assess the biases we might carry and, we hope, better judge how much credence you should give to our arguments.

2

ESOC'S MOTIVATION AND APPROACH

Know your enemy and know yourself.

—Sun Tzu

1830 hrs 6 June 2010, Kabul, Afghanistan
Situation Awareness Room
International Security Assistance Force (ISAF) Headquarters

- -

A young woman stepped up to the microphone in the Situation Aware-ness Room in International Security Assistance Force (ISAF) Head-quarters, Kabul, Afghanistan. It was near the end of the evening com-mander's update briefing on 6 June 2010, and her audience included dozens of staff officers in various combat uniforms. Hundreds more joined via videoconference from the regional commands in Afghan-istan and NATO bases around the world. ISAF commander General Stanley McChrystal sat solemn-faced at the hub of a U-shaped array of plywood tabletops arranged to give him eye contact with his closest advisors. The woman called up the first slide of her presentation: the impact of civilian casualties on insurgent violence across Afghanistan.

Many in the audience were skeptical. What could a young academic with no operational or field experience tell them about civilian casualties —a challenging and sensitive topic—that they didn't already know? In a crisp, professional tone she presented the key finding: on average, *civilian deaths caused by ISAF units led to increased attacks directed against ISAF for a period that persisted fourteen weeks after each incident.*

The woman was Radha Iyengar, a Princeton-trained economist and then assistant professor at the London School of Economics, who had come to Afghanistan as part of the Counterinsurgency Advisory Assistance Team (CAAT), a new unit General McChrystal had created to help ISAF leaders at every level identify and implement best practices in counterinsurgency. The CAAT was led by Joe Felter, a U.S. Army Special Forces colonel—one of the authors of this book. On taking the position, Felter, himself a Stanford PhD who had earlier analyzed the sources of military effectiveness in counterinsurgency, had quickly realized that his team at the CAAT could benefit from some assistance with data analysis, modeling, and research, so he invited Iyengar and other volunteer academic researchers to spend time supporting the CAAT mission, including the other two authors of this book, Jake Shapiro and Eli Berman.

McChrystal tapped his microphone and directed the audience dialed in from multiple ISAF regional commands across Afghanistan as well as NATO countries in Europe and North America to take notice. Iyengar was presenting a graph indicating the expected increase in violence of different kinds after an ISAF-caused civilian-casualty event. Reducing civilian casualties was not only a moral imperative, it was also, he believed, a key to strategic victory.

General McChrystal was convinced that civilian casualties incurred in operations led to more damage and ultimately to more ISAF casualties. He and his advisors had encouraged commanders to assume increased tactical-level risks in the short term in some situations—such as minimizing use of air strikes and artillery for force protection when civilian lives could be at risk—in an effort to foster the relationships needed to secure critical long-term strategic gains. He had called this "courageous restraint"—accepting increased risk at tactical levels so as not to undermine strategic goals—and the idea became a hallmark of McChrystal's tenure as commander.[1]

- -

OUR STORY

Social scientists briefing commanders on fresh results in theater. That's unusual and a story worth telling for two reasons: first, in a controversial field, the reader should know what expertise and possible biases we bring to our findings; and second, cooperation with practitioners on the ground was critical, so we'd like to explain how that was achieved. How did the three of us, Joe, Eli, and Jake, and our ESOC project get to that point?

It started a few years before when we got excited about a core idea: there is a scientific agenda spanning security and development economics that coincides with policy challenges facing the international community. If we can traverse the gap between those two worlds, and maybe bring them a bit closer to each other, we can make better progress in both. Researchers on the science side lack access to high-resolution information on policies and outcomes, such as administrative data on aid programs and details of reported conflict episodes—data produced on a daily basis on the policy and practitioner side—as well as the context needed to interpret those data properly; substantive knowledge about how programs are implemented; and specific details of individual cases. Policymakers and practitioners in the field lack rigorous analysis from a wide range of scholars that would enable better bets about what will work in different contexts. Once we started to develop trust and build relationships across the gap, the bridge-building became a self-reinforcing process, and the Empirical Studies of Conflict (ESOC) project was the result.

The roots of our approach are in the field. Joe spent time advising and assisting the Armed Forces of the Philippines (AFP) from 1999 to 2002 while assigned to the U.S. Embassy in Manila as a military attaché. Prior to that he led U.S. Special Forces teams for several years, conducting security assistance missions throughout Southeast Asia. During his tour in the Philippines, Joe helped build the Philippine military's counterterrorist capabilities, in response to multiple international hostage crises involving U.S. citizens. In doing so he gained the trust and support of many senior leaders in the Philippine military and Department of National Defense. When Joe returned to the Philippines in 2004 to conduct research for his dissertation, his close friends in senior positions in the AFP helped him access a trove of written reports on the details of individual conflict incidents (e.g., firefights, ambushes, etc.) involving Philippine military units. Microdata coded from these incident reports for the years 2001–4 served as the key data source for Joe's doctoral work, which studied the optimal way to mix the ability of highly trained special forces with the operational intelligence of local forces.[2]

While Joe was working on his dissertation, Jake arrived at Stanford for graduate school. Fresh off of active duty in the navy and still a drilling reservist, Jake began working on applying insights from organizational economics (the literature on how the challenges of managing their people and relationships lead firms to adopt different organizational structures) to understanding terrorist groups. Jake's research, inspired by his involvement in counterterrorism planning shortly after the 9/11 attacks, focused on understanding what it would take to manage a group that was producing a hard-to-measure good like terrorism under the constraint that it had to remain undetected by the police and intelligence services to survive.

Joe's experience with the Philippine data informed his thinking when he took over as director of West Point's newly established Combating Terrorism Center (CTC) in the fall of 2005. The CTC had recently partnered with U.S. Special Operations Command (SOCOM) to analyze internal records from al Qaeda that were captured during raids in Afghanistan and elsewhere. The records were stored digitally in the Department of Defense's Harmony database and unavailable to scholars and researchers without active security clearances and access to the database.[3] Joe was familiar with Jake's ongoing dissertation research and recognized that many of the documents SOCOM declassified and released to the CTC for analysis might provide evidence to test a theory Jake had developed on how terrorist groups deal with managerial challenges. In the fall of 2005 Joe invited Jake to work on the CTC's first publication exploiting the Harmony documents. Joe's hunch was correct: Jake's theory formed the core theoretical frame for this analysis. In early March 2006, the CTC released "Harmony and Disharmony: Exploiting Al Qaeda's Organizational Vulnerabilities."[4]

The Harmony documents were hardly big data, but they got the ball rolling. This was the first time they had been declassified and made available to the public, which led to further collaboration with U.S. Special Operations Command and served as an example and precedent for demonstrating the value of declassification when we tried to gain access to the next batch of information.[5]

Following the publication of "Harmony and Disharmony," Joe, Jake, and the team at CTC succeeded in declassifying additional documents, which formed the core of the CTC's Project Harmony. One report looked al Qaeda's failed efforts in 1992–94 to establish a presence in the Horn of Africa. Al Qaeda had meant to use the Horn as a base for attacks against Western targets but was stymied by the challenges of operating in an ungoverned space. A key finding was that terrorism would be more likely to flourish in weak states rather than in failed ones.[6] A second publication used records of nearly seven hundred foreign nationals entering Iraq in 2006–7 to reveal insurgents' countries of origin (Saudi Arabia and Libya accounted for more than half), the background of recruits (largely self-described students), and how they were getting to Iraq (mostly along smuggling routes).[7] A third report used more declassified documents to elaborate on those findings, showing that in 2006–8 al Qaeda recruitment in Iraq was slowing, as militants were choosing other organizations.[8]

When Joe deployed to Iraq in 2008 to support a joint special operations task force, he had direct access to a wealth of conflict data and information maintained by Multi-National Force Iraq (MNF-I) and other U.S. military organizations.[9] Much of it was either overclassified or could meet the threshold requirements for declassification and release if certain sensitive fields in the data were deleted or sanitized. The SIGACT-III database, for example, recorded every "significant activity" reported by U.S. forces in Iraq and included details such as the time and place of insurgent attacks, the type of attacks, and select outcomes of these attacks. Four years of this detailed microconflict data had been compiled by 2008, but it was classified "Secret" and thus—sadly—out of reach for scholars and nongovernment analysts who could use it to test a range of hypotheses and theories of conflict and political violence.

Joe identified the fields in the database that weren't sensitive. Then, through a long process made possible by key allies and many trips from Balad to Baghdad, he secured their declassification to West Point's CTC and ESOC and thus for broader academic use.[10] He was able to get the memo releasing key fields in the SIGACT data signed by the MNF-I Foreign Disclosure Office (FDO) just a week before redeploying from Iraq. That single page led to all the others in this book. That's how important data is to our research.

In addition, Jake and Joe worked with the Army Corps of Engineers to release data on reconstruction spending in Iraq, which, while unclassified, were not publicly accessible or easily interpretable.[11] And to make these data usable, Jake and Joe assembled geospatial data to match them (an arduous task at the time that is now almost trivial thanks to Google Earth) as well as other pieces of the puzzle—for example, crucial data on unemployment, health, and population size from the World Food Programme in Iraq. For each piece, we worked with our sources to understand methods of data collection, possible biases, and other potential sources of inconsistencies.

Eli joined the team that same year. A veteran himself (counterinsurgency and counterterrorism in Israel), Eli had coauthored an article with David Laitin (one of Joe's advisors at Stanford) that took a new approach to understanding why organizations like Hamas and the Taliban are so effective. They employed "club" theory, which proposes that groups as diverse as the Sicilian Mafia and nineteenth-century utopian communities use costly sacrifices to select in only the most devoted new entrants, which in turn allows them to punch well above their weight by efficiently making greater demands of members.[12] Eli began to work with Jake and Joe to build a theoretical framework to explain why the trends in the SIGACT data varied so much from district to district and to test it with the rich data from Iraq. The results serve as the foundation for the central argument of this book.

After returning from Iraq, Joe began a yearlong Army War College fellowship at Stanford's Hoover Institution and soon returned to the Philippines. Some of his military friends had been promoted, most prominently Lieutenant General Victor Ibrado, then commanding general of the Philippine army. Ibrado tasked Captain Dennis Eclarin, a respected Scout Ranger commander and West Point graduate, with helping Joe with counterinsurgency research. Eclarin was showing Joe around the offices of the Assistant Chief of Staff at Fort Bonifacio, in Metro Manila, when they struck gold. In a dilapidated annex behind the main offices they came across a shelf of old incident journals gathering dust. These logbooks contained typed reports with details of every single incident reported by operational units conducting counterinsurgency and other internal security operations in the field, the material Joe had based his doctoral research on, but now dating back to 1975! It came complete with typos, corrected with white-out. The breadth and depth of these conflict data were extraordinary; Joe immediately saw the potential for new knowledge that these logbooks represented, as well as the risk to this unique archive to conflict research if a fire tore through the dilapidated structure.

General Ibrado agreed to support Joe's proposal to code the details of these incident reports and allowed him to enlist the support of Philippine army noncommissioned officers to work on-site to read the reports and manually code the information. Captain Eclarin supervised the team, who began an intensive, laborious multiyear effort, often working late into the night. The result is the longest-running microdata on insurgency and counterinsurgency to date.[13]

While Joe was tracking down data, Eli was seeking theories. In the summer of 2009, encouraged by policymakers at the U.S. Agency for International Development (USAID), Eli led a research team to Kabul with the objective of evaluating the effects of development assistance projects on violence at a local level, which, we hoped, would replicate encouraging results we had found in Iraq. They had a pretty standard research plan: take an existing finding and see if they could replicate and generalize the results, or explore hypotheses about mechanisms. Eli and his team were particularly interested in mechanisms: military and civilian practitioners had myriad theories about what affected civilian attitudes toward combatants and what civilian actions were consequential, ranging from angry citizens providing donations to insurgent groups to unemployed men becoming recruits. The goal for the trip was for the team to slowly chip away at a large set of conjectures—one of which might be the correct theory—as a sculptor would chip at a large block of marble, removing unnecessary pieces until the essential pattern emerges. It's a mistake-prone process and full of surprises. Sometimes pieces fall away unexpectedly, and sometimes an essential piece is falsely rejected. Fortunately, theory is more forgiving than marble, and removed chunks can be reattached later, on reconsideration.

A series of meetings with development practitioners at U.S. and international aid agencies about possible projects revealed anxiety and frustration. Local program administrators and implementing teams were reluctant to share data that would inform research.

In a rare and brave move, one of the American development contractors isolated Eli and his fellow researchers and offered a side meeting with his senior country staff one evening on a U.S. base outside Kabul. The base commander who hosted the meeting evicted a few noncommissioned officers playing video games in the lounge, and the researchers and staff officers gathered, about two dozen of them, to sit in a circle on ratty couches and mismatched old chairs.

Eli took no notes (to keep things informal), but from memory, the conversation went something like this. It started with a question from the researchers, designed to be neutral: "Let's say you decide to work with a village that Afghan and ISAF forces control by day and the Taliban control by night. You implement best practice: consult with the local community on their choice of project, and build it, maybe you dig a well, or maybe you build a schoolroom. How should the project help reduce Taliban presence?"

The experienced professionals in the room had worked in some very violent environments—Colombia, Iraq, and Pakistan, for example. And all of them were taking on tremendous personal risks to try to help make those places safer. The country director encouraged them to speak freely and speculate, noting that the funders of programs were not present and emphasizing that the research team could be trusted.

"We think that it's good to dig a well, because the children benefit from clean water, and the mothers save time fetching it. That can't hurt."

"It's difficult to know, as we seldom can actually visit the villages, so we rely on local staff."

"Sometimes the project can hurt, as the Taliban will come destroy it, frightening local families."

"The projects might come with increased troop presence, which increases confrontations and violence."

Ultimately, the hesitant answer was: "We're not sure. We don't know that the programs reduce Taliban presence."

The staff in charge of implementing programs had examined the block of marble, chipped at it in their own way, and now questioned whether there was a sculpture lurking inside at all. Their experience and accumulation of best practices from other countries—some just as poor, some even more violent—were not generating useful principles of program design. Echoing the theme of chapter 1, they were grappling with the development-assistance version of "know the war you're in."

The country director listened carefully to his staff, turned to us, and made the request that would summarize the evening: "We were hoping you would tell us."

In short, the contractor lacked a working theory that could serve as a doctrine for development in conflict environments. Anticipating further increases in development assistance—more roads and wells and schoolrooms—they hesitated to say it out loud, but they didn't know if their programs were dampening or igniting violence in Afghanistan. They needed to design programs that would work and they were looking for guidance. The stakes were high: programs sent staff to dangerous places with a lot of resources and put them at risk of attack or kidnapping. The impression that programs were failing was a powerful motivator for research and discovery.

Eli did not have a good answer for the contractor that evening, and certainly not one that would hold up to our standards of academic scrutiny. Clearly the team's research was not going to make incremental progress on a theory proposed by practitioners, as they had planned, because the practitioners did not have a consensus theory. The underlying theory would have to come from us.

This was the background we carried with us when Joe was selected to command the ISAF CAAT in Afghanistan in 2009. We had campaigned to make data available, had done it carefully to avoid any security repercussions, and in return had delivered policy-relevant analysis. At the same time, we were chipping away at various theories of insurgency—in an ongoing conversation with development practitioners and counterinsurgents—and had informed basic theoretical debates in security studies (at least in our opinion). When we started working on the briefing on civilian casualties, we already had positive feedback loops in place: the benefits of our analysis made more government officials willing to share their information and expertise with us, and that led to funding opportunities, more studies, and new results. It put us, along with Radha and the rest of the team, in the position to bring research to bear on the question of how ISAF should approach the painful subject of civilian casualties.

Our track record also put us in a position to help out on other issues. Shortly after that 2010 briefing, General Petraeus assumed command of ISAF from General McChrystal. Early one morning that autumn, Joe was heading out of the CAAT headquarters for a jog around the compound. When Petraeus approached, Joe anticipated an invitation to join him on his run, but instead the general tasked him with a real challenge: "Joe, I want you to fix CERP."

There were problems with the efficiency and effectiveness of the Commander's Emergency Response Program—development project funding administered by the U.S. military. Petraeus felt that improvements could be made in its implementation—the way funds were disbursed. He committed his personal support to the CAAT and promised to make the tasking a priority, ensuring access to the many subordinate commanders and organizations needed to accomplish this mission. Joe mobilized the organic resources he had in the CAAT, some of whom had extensive experience with aid distribution efforts from their careers in the U.S. Army Civil Affairs community.[14] To augment the effort with additional analytic expertise Joe assembled a group of academics, again including Eli and Jake, and invited them over to Afghanistan. We had already modeled and tested a theory of development in conflict zones using Iraqi data (which we will lay out in chapter 3 and elaborate upon in chapter 7), but the application to Afghanistan required specific knowledge of local conditions and institutions. The team partnered with development professionals, interviewed military staff, and conducted surveys. The effort culminated in a decision briefing for General Petraeus and senior leaders across U.S. Forces Afghanistan, where we laid out the main challenges to distribution in CERP and offered specific recommendations. Several of those were adopted.

OUR RESEARCH

In 2009, grant support from the U.S. Department of Defense's Minerva Research Initiative allowed ESOC to scale up considerably, supporting other researchers, hiring postdocs, and fostering our style of research in different conflict environments around the world. To date, ESOC has supported in one way or another more than sixty peer-reviewed articles on conflict and what can be done to prevent it in Afghanistan, Colombia, India, Iraq, Israel, Kenya, Liberia, Mexico, Northern Ireland, Pakistan, the Palestinian territories, Philippines, Sierra Leone, Somalia, Vietnam, and Yemen. We now turn to that research. In particular, we will look at the four defining aspects of our approach: using microdata to learn from local variance; employing diverse methods to identify causal relationships; iterating between theory and data (and back again); and steadily accumulating facts across multiple studies.

Our Epistemology: Exploiting Local Variance

Within any given conflict there is tremendous variance in violence, both across localities and within a locality over time. This is not just our intuition from spending time on the ground in conflicts (as soldiers and researchers), it's in the data.

Figure 2.1 shows monthly trends in combat incidents per capita in Afghanistan and Iraq for the twenty-four most violent districts in each country, for the years 2005–14, as recorded in the incident data (SIGACTs) we discussed earlier. Though they are reported here by district, these data are already "big"—every location in the country is potentially covered.

Since the source is the U.S. military, these incidents might undercount violence that happened where American forces and the units

A. Afghanistan

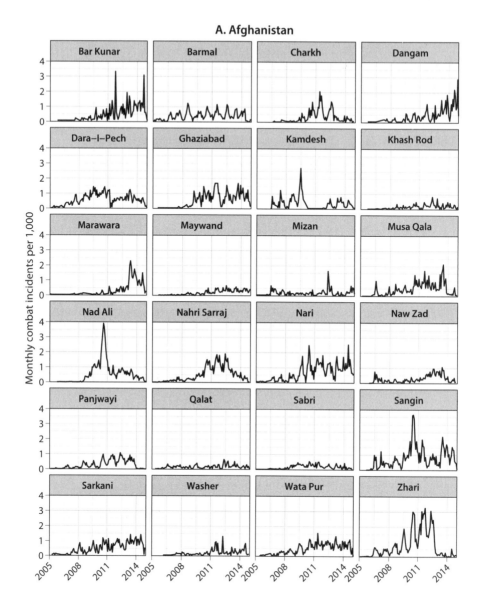

FIGURE 2.1. Monthly trends in combat incidents, 2005–14, per 1,000 people in the 24 most violent districts of Afghanistan and Iraq. Panel A shows the monthly number of combat incidents per 1,000 people for the 24 most violent districts of Afghanistan on a per capita basis from January 2005 to December 2014. Values for Nad Ali for August and September 2010 and for Sangin for July and August 2010 (all between 4 and 4.6) are not displayed due to scale. Data from the ISAF Combined Information Data Network Exchange (CIDNE) database, released through FOIA. Panel B shows the monthly number of combat incidents per 1,000 people for the 24 most violent districts on a per capita basis in Iraq from January 2005 to December 2011. The value for Al-Daur for January 2005 (4.2) is not displayed due to scale. Data from the MNF-I SIGACT-III database, released through FOIA.

B. Iraq

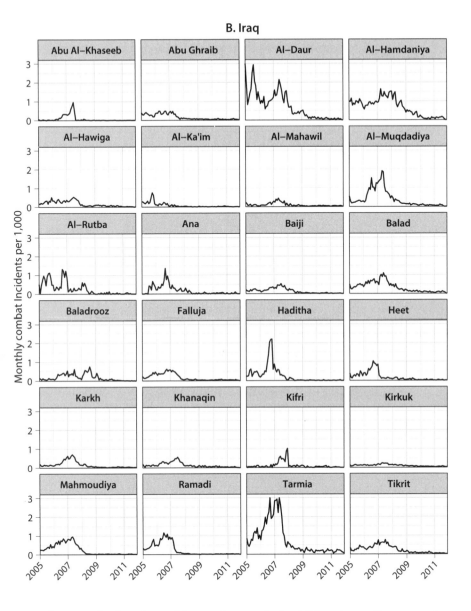

they worked with could not observe it. In Afghanistan, for example, they surely omit fighting involving the police (who could not easily report to ISAF due to low literacy among their officers), and in Iraq they omit a great deal of fighting between various militias.

Comparing plots across districts, you'll notice that *every district is a bit different*. Sure, there are some broad similarities, such as a clear seasonality to the fighting in Afghanistan and a downturn in general violence around 2007–8 in Iraq. Yet there are also a lot of local differences: peaks occur at different times in different places and per-capitized violence varies massively from place to place at any given time.

Look first at the set of graphs for Afghanistan. Barmal is a district in Paktika province near the border of North Waziristan, the Pakistani province that was a long-time haven for insurgent groups. This district had been violent since 2007, with the greatest spike during the 2008 summer fighting season and fairly regular annual spikes thereafter. Nad Ali is farther south in Helmand province. ISAF made no effort to take control of Nad Ali until the spring of 2008, then early in 2010 launched an offensive to take the town of Marja, a center of the poppy trade and a Taliban stronghold. The district was made relatively secure by 2012.[15] Hence, that large spike at the center of the graph reflects a struggle for control, preceded by relative calm under the Taliban and followed by relative calm under government control.

Now look at Kamdesh. It might appear that after a rough patch, ISAF started doing something right: 2010–12 seems remarkably peaceful. In fact, ISAF fully pulled out of the district during those years so there was no one for the Taliban to fight against and, moreover, no one to measure violence. If you went by the data alone, you'd be mistaking a lack of measurement for a successful effort to establish control. Accurate interpretation often requires doing significant qualitative research, particularly talking to the people who produced the data—another reason to engage tightly with the policy community.[16]

Now turn to Iraq. Ramadi, the capital and largest city in Anbar province, was the site of the first successful, large-scale realignment of Sunni tribes with Coalition forces during the Anbar Awakening. Violence peaked in mid-2006 and then began dropping sharply before falling off a cliff in 2007, reflecting the dramatic change in political tides. Balad, by contrast, is a mostly rural Sunni district north of Baghdad with a large Shi'ite-majority town and a major U.S. airbase nearby. Balad was one of the last locations the Awakening reached, and you can see that violence there peaked a full year after it did in Ramadi. Al-Hamdaniya is a mixed district south of Mosul in northern Iraq that saw fairly intense ethnic conflict from the start of the war. Here we see higher per capita violence and a later decline even than that of Balad.

Furthermore, we know from our policy contacts that in Iraq, unlike Afghanistan, very few places went uncontested by Coalition forces for long. Hence the absence of reported violence in these data indicates that the insurgency was lying low or defeated in an area.

Sorting out the forces causing local variance is necessary in order to discover ways to reduce violence. Of course, moving from finding the correlates of these patterns, like the winter in Afghanistan, to figuring out what caused some of the changes is a difficult task, one that requires delving deeply into the details of each local conflict. As we will see throughout the book, however, the nature of policy implementation in conflict zones affords us many opportunities to cut into the causal chain and learn lessons that can be applied to future conflicts.

Distinct local patterns of violence are also evident in other conflicts, as we see in the data from Pakistan and the Philippines illustrated in figure 2.2.[17] The data have again been per-capitized, but because these conflicts are roughly an order of magnitude less intense, we measure violence per 10,000 people. Once again note the massive differences in the trends across locations, which illustrate exactly why understanding local context and then exploiting local variance is so important.

In Pakistan there are clearly multiple conflicts going on. Areas in the tribal agencies bordering Afghanistan (e.g., Bajour, Khyber, and Orakzai) do not see significant levels of political violence until the mid-2000s. But from 2008 onward these sparsely populated regions begin seeing total counts of conflict incidents per month on par with those of the massive city of Lahore. Lahore itself sees a steady drumbeat of political violence over the decades, but on a per capita basis the intensity is quite low. Indeed, the only major city in Pakistan that saw significant violence on a per capita basis was Karachi in the mid-1990s during an intense period of ethnic conflict between the Sindhi majority and the Mohajir minority (descendants of those who had fled India at partition).

In the Philippines we see similar variability. Basilan is an island province in Southern Mindanao that saw some of the most intense violence in the recent Muslim separatist struggle as well as large amounts of fighting in the late 1970s. Negros Occidental is an agricultural province in the central Philippines that was long a stronghold of the communist New People's Army guerrilla group and experienced two major periods

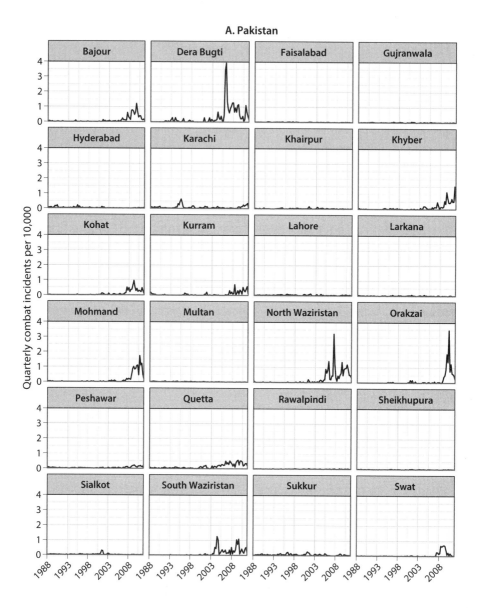

FIGURE 2.2. Quarterly trends in total violent incidents in the 24 most violent districts of Pakistan (1988–2010) and the Philippines (1975–2008). Panel A shows the quarterly number of combat incidents per 10,000 people for the 24 most violent districts of Pakistan on a per capita basis from January 1988 to December 2010. Data from the BFRS Dataset of Political Violence in Pakistan. Panel B shows the quarterly number of combat incidents per 10,000 people for the 24 most violent districts on a per capita basis in the Philippines from January 1975 through December 2008. Data from ESOC Philippines Database.

B. Philippines

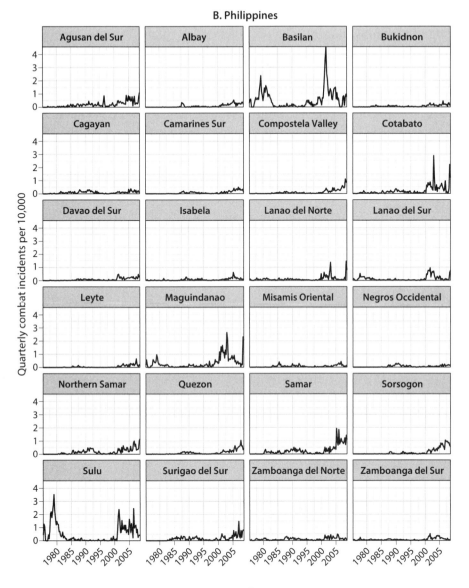

of violence, one from 1985 to 1995 and then a steady increase in the past decade. On an absolute basis the violence there approached that in Basilan, but as the region is much larger the intensity was not nearly as great. Jolo is the next big island south of Basilan in the Sulu Archipelago, and while it saw similar waves of violence to those of its northern neighbor it remained significantly violent much later than Basilan during the most recent wave of separatist insurgency.

What could be driving local patterns of insurgent violence? Support for rebel groups among civilian populations, perhaps? You might think that whether an Iraqi civilian supports the Islamic State today (or al Qaeda a decade ago) is as ingrained and slow to change as whether an American is a Democrat or a Republican. After all, Idaho has been largely Republican for generations, Massachusetts largely Democrat. But political attitudes in countries in conflict do not have the stability and continuity we see in more peaceful places. Like violence, support for rebel groups is largely heterogeneous district by district, and over time.

Have a look at figure 2.3. The data come from surveys conducted monthly over a five-year period by an Iraqi firm under contract with the U.S. military.[18] As a whole, the surveys elicited responses from 175,000 citizens across the city's ten *mahalas*, or neighborhoods, asking a variety of questions, including this one: "Do you support attacks against Multi-National Forces?" The graphs indicate that attitudes are also highly localized and have their own local dynamic. That's cause for hope, if we think that civilian attitudes might drive localized patterns of violence.

For many of the scientific and policy questions we're trying to answer, such as the effect of development programs on rebel violence, other local factors will in fact turn out to be very important. But if you only look at one or two places, it's very hard to distinguish between the effect of the program and the effects of those factors. In academic language, those other factors can *confound inference* (academics sometimes refer to them as "confounders"): some neighborhoods are predestined to have high levels of violence because of geography—a major intersection or proximity to a border, for example—while the same factors might also predispose them to getting development programs, perhaps because of the violence itself.[19] Collecting highly detailed subnational data on a wide variety of conflicts can substantially ameliorate this problem. For example, we will see enough places with development programs but no intersections, or intersections with no development programs, to be able to estimate separate effects of each.

A more familiar analogy can be useful for seeing how this works. Imagine that a secretary of labor for an American state receives a report that joblessness among young adults is high and rising.

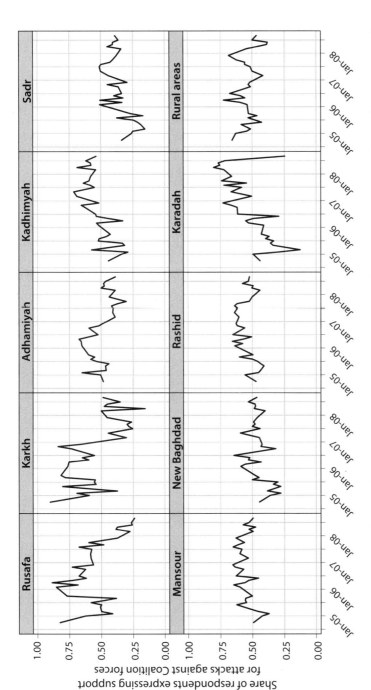

FIGURE 2.3. Support for insurgents from October 2004 to September 2008 in Baghdad. The figure shows average support for attacks on international forces by region (first stage sampling unit) of Baghdad over 33 waves of a large-scale public opinion survey. Regions used to draw the sample align roughly with the nine official districts of Baghdad plus the rural regions surrounding the city. Surveys were run approximately every two months from October 2004 through September 2008. The question was "Do you support attacks against Multi-National Forces?" "No" = 0, "Yes" = 1. Data provided by Independent Institute for Administration and Civil Society Studies (IIACSS).

He decides to conduct a survey to find out why; job counselors at state unemployment offices have claimants fill out the surveys. When he tallies up the answers, he sees that the most frequently cited reason for young job seekers being turned down is their lack of language skills. The secretary knows that there is a large immigrant population in the state, so he has English language programs offered at every unemployment center. After two years of this expensive program, joblessness among youth has declined only slightly. The program is canceled.

The neighboring state has the same problem. There, the secretary of labor conducts a similar survey, but instead of having responses tallied together, she separates them by district. This disaggregation exposes facts that the neighbor secretary missed: language skills are the most cited reasons in small enclaves—ones with very high unemployment rates and large immigrant populations. But in a majority of districts, where youth unemployment is lower, other reasons predominate: lack of low-skill positions available, a higher expected starting wage, poorly qualified candidates, and so on. This secretary targets the language-skills program at the districts that need it. The program lowers total (or *aggregate*) youth unemployment outside the enclaves by the same amount as in the first state—but success in immigrant neighborhoods is substantial. And because the program costs only a fraction of what it did in the first state, it is deemed a success and therefore keeps its funding.

Macrodata can mask small differences that can be extremely important for understanding how to help. In our example, language skills were not always a critical barrier to employment; only in places with a small population lacking employers who speak people's native language was language training critical to enabling youth employment. The local mismatch between employers and employees was critical, in other words, not the raw skill level of prospective employees in all regions. Microdata, analyzed using the right tools, capture such differences. Doing so is sometimes critical to understanding what is really going on in complex settings and how to target programs.

Academics know the value of microdata and have created advanced methods to analyze it (we cite some classic examples in note 25). In developed and some developing countries, policymakers are often willing to tailor programs based on data analysis. A major problem, however, is that demand and processing power have outpaced the actual data supply, particularly in poor and conflict-ridden countries. How do you put policies in place to stoke the economy when a large portion of it is informal and off-the-books? How do you tailor educational materials when there are no standardized tests measuring learning? How do you determine the effect of expenditures on clinics when you don't know who's attending them and what their health outcomes are?

In the study of conflict, too, we have the inferential machine but have lacked high-quality data to feed it. Traditionally, data sets available to researchers were highly aggregated or just absent. As the data revolution proceeds, collection tools have developed, especially over the past decade. As you read on you will see how this shift plays out in the literature.[20] Studies that used macrodata to give broad insights serve as a foundation in the field, while microlevel data sets, like the ones ESOC makes available, can test those insights, give detailed results, and reveal important exceptions to the rules.

In short, all conflict is local. This is especially true of asymmetric wars, which are against insurgents: these groups tend to organize locally, rather than nationally, so district-level data often capture their actions better. Our approach to testing theories exploits the localized nature of conflict. For a long time studies in the conflict literature were limited by the difficulty of saying anything credible about what *caused* what, based on country-level observations. There are lots of potential causes and not that many countries. By treating different regions, or even villages, within a country as different realizations of the process described in a theory we can do far more to make useful comparisons that let us net out the role of confounding factors.

Our Methods: Establishing Causal Relationships through Iterated Research

A core goal of both natural and social science is to identify cause-and-effect relationships. This not only answers academic questions but also provides the understanding required to make real-world decisions.

To see why, think of smoke and fire. If you want to find fires, you can do really well by looking for smoke, meaning you can *predict* the location of fires by looking for smoke. That's because fire causes smoke, a causal relationship. Conversely, there is not a causal relationship from smoke to fire: if I want to cause more fires, I shouldn't rent a smoke machine.

Correlations are great for prediction—for example, predicting the flow of populations after a disaster or the level of hospitalization at different times—and this accounts for much of the excitement about big data that we cited in chapter 1. Big data and data science can do well predicting what will happen in the world absent policy changes, but when predicting the effects of those policy changes, correlations are not enough. If you want to know what to do in the world to produce a certain outcome, then you need to establish causality. And when the goal is discovering causality, correlations can mislead: "smoke causes fire" is obviously an erroneous statement, but we see equivalent logic in policy all the time.

To take an example more germane to this book, imagine that a military tries a new technique, positioning dozens of vehicle checkpoints across a city in order to suppress rebel activity. The following month, instead of declining, violence increases. If commanders depend purely on correlation, they will conclude that the checkpoints *caused* more violence, dismantle them, and perhaps try something else. But maybe the program actually *was effective*: violence increased the following month because, quite separately, cheap weapons became available. In that case, violence might have been far worse without the checkpoints. We have no way of knowing because we can't compare the outcome to a *counterfactual*—the same city that following month without checkpoints in place.

Even if you question your dependence on correlation and start looking more closely, a number of factors can still trick you. A dip in the economy could spark more violence—or dampen it—and if you weren't watching out for that, you might attribute the effect to the checkpoints. A shift in the city's ethnic makeup due to an influx of refugees could do the same, and again you could misattribute that effect. Further, if there is more than one rebel group operating in the city, the determinants of the violence the two groups—and the government—produce could be different. Microdata allow you to shut down other channels because you can make more comparisons—ideally ones that let you rule out extraneous factors and find the ones that matter.

Broadly speaking, there are two ways you can identify causal relationships: with *theory* and with *research design*. Let's start with an example where we use *theory* to seek out causal relationships. In 2007, the Coalition changed strategy in Iraq. They deployed more troops in the communities, had them patrol more on foot, and charged them with providing more security for threatened Iraqi civilians, among other tasks. Now famous, "the surge" coincided with a large reduction in violence. Monthly U.S. military fatalities from June 2008 to June 2011 averaged less than 15 percent the rate from 2004 through mid-2007 and ten times less than the maximum. As news of this success sank in, three theories emerged attempting to explain why the surge had worked: surge tactics themselves; the Sunni uprising termed the "Anbar Awakening"; and "sectarian cleansing" that occurred in Iraq at the time (meaning, Sunnis had been run out of mixed areas, or killed, so fighting between sects decreased). Of course, there was no decisive test to tell us conclusively what caused the reduction in violence, but in a 2012 article, Jake and coauthors Jeff Friedman of Dartmouth College and Stephen Biddle of George Washington University examined these three theories one by one, applied data, and searched for patterns consistent with each.[21]

Combining 70 structured interviews with Coalition officers with extensive data on combat and sectarian attacks—193,264 "significant activities" (SIGACTs) recorded by Coalition forces and 19,961 incidents in which civilians were killed as recorded by Iraq Body Count—gave Jake and his coauthors a very strong idea of what caused the reduction in violence. The patterns of violence across Iraq and within Baghdad suggested that the "cleansing" theory was highly unlikely. Across Iraq sectarian violence began declining long after combat incidents did. Moreover, the onward advance of the combat frontier was far from exhausted when violence began to lessen in Baghdad in mid-2007. Instead, it seemed that a synergy of surge and Awakening mechanisms caused the reduction in violence. Previous movements among the

Sunni to realign loyalties had failed without the protection the surge now offered, and reciprocally, Coalition troops now encountered a political climate ripe for the new surge doctrine. Data that we will describe in detail in chapter 6 suggested that the Awakening could not have spread sufficiently without the surge and that the surge could not have succeeded without the Awakening.

Next, let's consider ways to use *research design* for causal identification. At ESOC we take a range of approaches to doing so, from looking for quirks of policy implementation that let us cut into the causal chain, to running surveys where we randomize the information provided to different respondents, to policy experiments where we work with officials to randomize some aspect of ongoing policy. It is easiest to understand how these approaches help us get at causality by starting with randomized experiments—the gold standard for identifying causal effects in one place and time—and then covering methods that we turn to when randomized experiments are impossible.

During the twentieth century the natural sciences worked out an efficient way to draw a line from cause to effect, the randomized controlled trial (RCT). The best way to test a new drug is to draw a large group of test subjects, randomly assign them to a treatment group, who receive it, and a control group, who do not, and measure the difference in results between the two groups. Randomization provides, on average, the real-world counterfactual we mentioned earlier. It allows researchers to say with confidence that all other observable factors have been averaged out and the effect of the drug is therefore simply the difference between the average measured outcome in treated subjects and that in control subjects. Strict standards for how randomization is conducted prevent researchers or subjects themselves from "selecting in" to treatment. (If another criterion is used to choose treated subjects—those needing it most, for example—then the results of the trial will be biased because that criterion, not the drug, can account for some of the measured ex post difference between treatment and control groups.) In many cases, study plans restrict what subjects know about their own treatment-versus-control status, or even what the researchers who interact with them know, because even the subject's knowledge, or the way researchers interact with them, might subtly affect results.

RCTs have generated a huge, robust, and constantly evolving body of knowledge. Over recent decades, the RCT has moved out of the natural sciences to revolutionize the social sciences and public policy research.[22]

In 2012 Jake and his colleagues Christine Fair and Neil Malhotra ran an experiment in Pakistan.[23] They wanted to understand, among other things, how the perception of living in a violent country affected citizens' support for the extremist groups that caused a lot of that violence. They surveyed approximately 16,000 Pakistanis, asking everyone a set of questions designed to evoke their like or dislike of extremist groups. Before subjects answered questions, though, enumerators primed them to feel that they lived in a relatively violent country or a relatively peaceful one by randomly telling them one of two true statements: "On average, Pakistan suffers from more extremist violence than Bangladesh" or "On average, Pakistan suffers from less extremist violence than Afghanistan." A randomly assigned control group wasn't primed on national violence, to provide a counterfactual. Randomization ensured that on average the only difference between the three groups was the prime they got, or the lack of any prime. In other words, adding the information prime and testing its effect against a control group allowed us to identify the causal effect of priming in the study. The difference in how they answered questions could then tell us how perceptions of violence caused support for extremists. We describe our results in detail in chapter 8.

While it would be enormously beneficial to deploy RCTs to analyze the determinants of violence and support for violent groups, unfortunately it's often impossible. We mentioned this in our discussion of dependent variables in chapter 1, but now let's look more closely at the three main barriers to running RCTs in conflict studies. The first is administrative: running experiments presents bureaucratic difficulties even in the best of environments, but those challenges loom even larger in conflict. Implementers and funders are often working incredibly long hours in conflict zones and simply lack the time to coordinate with researchers or add additional steps to their programs. Sharing data with academic researchers can create security concerns as well. Research could endanger human subjects and staff, as government agencies and university human subject research boards point out. And funders understandably resist launching studies in places where insecurity might shut them down.

The second reason is statistical. Say you wanted to test whether drone strikes reduced terrorist activity. The drone program is designed to affect a very rare outcome: attacks by al Qaeda and other groups. It might take decades of treatment to accumulate enough attacks to establish a precise statistical relationship. In medical terms the number of doses is large, but it all goes to very few patients actually at risk. Given the small number of places being targeted by the drone program we would simply have an insufficient sample to establish the treatment-control contrast. Moreover, imagine that a particular region, because of some institutional quirk, was allowed a sufficiently high number of randomized drone strikes (treatments) and potential targets that weren't struck (controls) to generate a precise estimated effect of drone strikes. Could we extrapolate from that region with the quirky institution to infer what we should expect the effect of treatment to be in other places, with different institutions? Probably not. Doing so would be like using the relationship between movie ticket sales and house prices in Beverly Hills to understand the broader U.S. real estate market.

The third reason is ethical. In medical trials, it is considered unethical to withhold a drug from the control group (i.e., those not receiving it) once one believes the treatment works. The U.S. government is not capacity constrained in drone strikes, at least not once the target is under sufficient surveillance to decide that a strike is worthwhile, and officials do not order strikes unless they strongly believe the target is of high value. Withholding a drone strike for research purposes (or, perish the thought, applying one for research purposes) necessarily fails a basic ethical test.[24]

So, RCTs are valuable but very often out of the question. If you are unable to conduct experiments, what is your next option? You gather all available knowledge on the situation and seek *natural experiments* you can use.

Like RCTs, natural experiments are not new to the social sciences, but it is only in the past decade that they have been used to assess the causal impact of different factors in the conflict space.[25] Here, researchers establish causality by exploiting quirks of the world that assign the treatment (or policy) in ways that are independent of the eventual outcomes. For example, Joe and coauthors wanted to examine whether the Philippines' flagship development program increased or decreased violence in treated villages.[26] The government had not randomly allocated the program to villages, so an RCT was not possible. However, the government did use an income threshold to determine whether communities were eligible for the program. The threshold was rather arbitrarily calculated (to reflect the government's idea of poverty), so aside from being just above or just below it, a large group of villages were arguably identical in expected outcomes. Thus Joe and his team were able to consider them as if they had been randomized into treatment and control groups. In chapter 5 we will describe our findings concerning the effect the program had on violence. This design of using only variation just above and just below some arbitrary threshold is called "regression discontinuity." It and other quasi-experimental methods represent an exciting direction in conflict research. Throughout the course of this book we will explain these methods and review how we and other scholars have used them.

Finally, we have qualitative studies, the traditional approach of security scholars: using archival materials on how a particular decision was made, for example. ESOC is still very much interested in gathering this type of *qualitative* (as opposed to *quantitative*) evidence: the store of al Qaeda records that we and others convinced the Department of Defense to release to CTC is an example. It included personal letters, expense reports, pocket litter, and a variety of primary-source material captured in the course of U.S. military operations in Afghanistan, Iraq, and elsewhere. These documents provided in-depth organizational knowledge of the groups that would later metamorphose into the so-called Islamic State, which we will also cover later in this book.

An encouraging result of this "empirical revolution" in social science is a healthy discussion of what we can learn from different types of evidence. The ESOC approach is to deploy all methods, depending on the circumstances: identification through theory when data alone cannot be decisive; RCTs where they are possible; design-based approaches to evaluate the effects of real-world programs when they are not; and qualitative evidence to understand important processes that cannot be studied quantitatively. Observational evidence interacts with experimental evidence and with theory, and the three check and corroborate one another. Numbers must back up the stories, and the quantitative evidence must be sensitive to the qualitative. A single method is seldom convincing in isolation, but the combination of theory and evidence is often compelling.

Our Process: Iterating between Theory and Data (and Back Again)

Scientific knowledge grows through the creation, testing, and modification of theories. This is true on the largest scale. In economics, theories about how markets strive toward equilibrium, with prices adjusting until supply meets demand, served well until the Great Depression showed that economies can enter prolonged periods with unemployed labor, and theory had to expand to encompass that possibility.

It is also true at the small scale. Every experiment must start with a theoretical framework, a hypothesis that the evidence will prove or disprove. You can think of data, such as the rich conflict data we described above, as a liquid—only really useful if you have a theoretical container to put them in.

Up to now, for example, most theories of conflict have not recognized important differences between asymmetric and symmetric warfare and as a result have largely assumed that they follow the same rules.[27] In part, this was because much work in the study of conflict has looked for one big answer—the kind of unifying theory physicists have been after.

We don't believe there is one big answer to why people engage in violence or to why civil wars start in the first place—the motivations that drive different militaries, rebel groups, and individuals are diverse, and the social forces present in different countries too different—but we do believe that asymmetric warfare has a common unifying logic at the tactical level, within the subnational units where violence is organized. A common approach—a theoretical lens if you will—can reveal which factors are likely to matter most in each microcontext and can help separate what is common across multiple conflicts from what is unique to a particular place and time. Getting the theoretical lens right, so to speak, can also make it easier to analyze new conflicts that spring up and allow researchers and governments to more efficiently implement a trial-and-error process that results in sustained insights. In other words, we're looking for the best first approximation of an answer, then iterating toward better answers.

By collecting data across conflicts and analyzing them through similar theoretical lenses—ones that acknowledge the very different motivations among actors in an asymmetric war—we gain two important inferential advantages. First, we can distinguish results that are common to counterterrorism and counterinsurgency across countries from those that are specific to a particular country or historical period. Consider the geopolitical factors that have changed the dynamics of counterterrorism and counterinsurgency in the past twenty-five years: the end of the Cold War, the rise of transnational Islamist activism, and so on. Also consider the technological factors: cell phones, the Internet. These factors only enter the theoretical approaches underpinning our research as intervening variables, so it is critical to test whether the dynamics we identify are fundamental to insurgency or are particular to a setting or point in time. If we can find what is common across many asymmetric conflicts, we are in a much better place to make predictions and strategize.

Second, by examining how our results vary across conflicts, we can identify which aspects of the environment—technology, availability of foreign support, ideologies, and the like—explain important variation in the efficacy of governance and development interventions. When you see something that works in one place but not another, that guides your search for the differences. And if you replicate across many places you start to rule out various factors that could account for those differences.

Say a government decides to start making welfare payments to citizens in the hope that it will win their loyalty and decrease rebel activity in a region. The program has varying levels of success in different districts. You gather data and see that places with successes and failures all have copper mines, but all places with successes have agricultural districts and all places with failures do not. Once you recognize that some aspect of an agricultural economy interacts well with the new welfare program, you can design it and deploy it more effectively.

As we mentioned, sometimes the iterative process yields big surprises. Eli's evening with development contractors in Kabul was one of those, revealing that they were themselves lacking a doctrine.

Since then, we have been chipping away at the question of how development assistance should be designed in an insurgency setting, iterating between a large set of theories and a growing set of empirical findings, as we will discuss at greater length in subsequent chapters. The practical question of how to use development assistance builds on deeper questions: What's the underlying model of insurgency and counterinsurgency in which development assistance might play a salutary role? As the set of empirical findings grows, the set of feasible answers to that question tends to shrink.

In terms of a metaphorical block of marble, we are chipping away, using as tools evidence that comes from different sources. Sometimes experimental evidence is the most revealing because it sharply refutes some hypothesis, cleaving off large chunks of false conjecture. Sometimes an accumulation of observational (nonexperimental) evidence is equally valuable. Where to strike the chisel is often guided by theory, the aspects of the sculpture we think will be revealed, but often we're guided by intuition and experience. Sometimes we just have to take the evidence offered by chance and generally by the research of others. The result is a refined and highly polished theoretical figure in places and a rough piece of speculation in others.

Critically, the resulting structure is now well enough defined that it serves two useful purposes. First, it can guide policy. Second, when refuting evidence arrives—from our research or that of others—the inferential effects are readily apparent: sections either emerge polished or they get removed completely.

Our Book: The Incremental Accumulation of Small Facts

While the setting is more exotic, the micro-empirical approach we've sketched implements the scientific method that most people learn in high school. In our setting rather than drawing on a large body of prior scientific research, you build a theory based on subject-matter knowledge and repeated interaction with experts and practitioners. Sometimes you lay this theory out through careful verbal elaboration, and at other times you use a game theoretic model to make sure you're being precise enough to avoid mistakes and misunderstandings.

But however you get there, you need to test the theory. In one particular context, say Afghanistan, you use the quirks of that place and time to establish causal relationships with confidence (using the kinds of methods we described). Then someone else repeats the test in another place, say Colombia, using its particular quirks to establish similar causal claims. Collaboratively, you look for where the theory works and where it doesn't, and you use that information to go back and modify the theory. Then you go through the whole cycle again. Theorize, test, repeat.

This approach is *not* like that of the physicist searching for a Theory of Everything that will explain the cosmos and the atom. It is more like a biologist attempting to explain how individual organisms interact with each other and with a complex environment. Exposure to data tends to dissuade empiricists from looking for one definitive statement about the world that will guide policy in all nations.

Compared to grand theories, the insight from an incremental iteration of the cycle may seem modest or particular to one little corner of the world. However, those modest localized findings contribute to big answers via the steady accumulation of small facts. In this book we will pull together results from nearly two hundred papers, articles, and books and present many diverse and contradictory findings. We are happy to report that doing so exposes major commonalities.

In the next chapter we will present a theoretical framework for asymmetric conflict. That framework is the answer we wish we would have had for the development contractor in Kabul the summer of 2009 and for Colonel Parmeter and the 1st Division in Tikrit in the summer of 2004. It is now validated by empirical testing. It also provides the intellectual framing for Radha's ISAF briefing on the effects of civilian casualties in June 2010. In the chapters that follow we will present the surprising and often counterintuitive findings that the micro-approach has yielded, shedding light on that framework and on related theories of conflict.

INFORMATION-CENTRIC INSURGENCY AND COUNTERINSURGENCY

- -

Imagine a civilian, maybe a father living in a small village (*barangay*) in the Philippines, awakened at night by a rustling outside, some muffled voices.

Careful not to awaken his wife, he swings his bare feet out of the bamboo frame of his family bed, ducks under the mosquito netting, and steps into a pair of clammy white plastic slippers. Quietly he slips into the courtyard that separates his house from the street. He peers cautiously over the bamboo partition that provides a modicum of privacy for his family's thatched-roof *nipa* hut from the daily whirl of tricycle cabs, mopeds, and foot traffic that ply the now deserted road. His brother, an overseas contract worker with a multinational construction firm in Dubai, had offered to send him funds to rebuild their home with cinder blocks and a solid corrugated tin roof, but for now it remains bamboo and palm thatch.

Two hunched figures are visible in the shadows several meters away, partially illuminated by the moon's reflection off the white concrete pavement. They whisper to each other as they pile up trash against the trunk of a palm tree, where the road turns sharply on its meandering path to the neighboring village of Magallanes, off to the father's left. A dog barks in the house to his right. He ducks his head as the two figures look across in his direction. He crouches behind the damp cinder blocks that support the thin bamboo partition and listens as rapid footsteps approach. The dog barks louder, making any footsteps inaudible. Then the barks lower to a growl. The footsteps are a few feet away, on the other side of the wall. The father holds his breath, listening. Then the footsteps move away, across the street and down to his left, toward the edge of town. He risks another glance over the partition and catches sight of the backs of two young men hurrying away, briefly touching shoulders as they turn up a path between two huts. The figures might have been familiar in daylight, but in the dark they could be anyone. He crouches again and leans his back against the cinder blocks, which scratch the sweat-soaked skin through his thin T-shirt. He exhales.

The father fumbles in his pocket for a small black cellular phone, checks for a signal and sees the time: 2:42 a.m. His brain is awakening, the pulse pounding in his temples, scenarios spinning in his mind. He starts with denial: Maybe it's not an explosive? Get real. Two men, in the middle of the night, just arranging garbage in a pile? He peeks over the partition again. The garbage surely conceals a bomb. He can picture the scene at the market outside an army camp in Sorsogon City, the municipal center not far from here, just last month: a military pickup truck was returning to base after a patrol, and a hidden explosive lifted it and rolled it over, screeching and skidding to the far side of the road. It ran over two market stalls, killing the driver and a young girl passing on her way to school.

When will this bomb explode? He instinctively shifts his weight back toward the protection of the house but hesitates to move for fear of waking his four children, wife, and mother-in-law. Traffic is unlikely until dawn, but in about three hours, just after sunrise, an army patrol will roll down the road from the center of town as it does every morning, probably in a noisy, lightly armored Korean-made one-ton truck. Where are the two men? If they station themselves on the upward slope of the hill behind the *nipa* huts across the road, they will be in position to spot the patrol. One of those huts is empty: the owner drives a taxi in Manila and just relocated the family to join him there. Since then, the teenagers of the village have been using the empty house as their hangout. His brain fully awake now, the pieces click into place. The ambush will begin with an explosion; any survivors will be exposed to gunfire from the thickly vegetated high ground opposite his courtyard, just north of the east-west running road. The communist rebels from the New People's Army (NPA) used that method, bomb followed by ambush, last month in the neighborhood north of here. Even the boys in the street could explain the tactical logic—they have made it part of their games.

The father's attention returns to the pile of garbage.

He pictures an overturned truck and a barrage of bullets from the ambush bounding against the pavement. The explosion would surely be powerful enough to knock down his flimsy bamboo screen. Would debris fly across the road and into his hut? Would the blast blow out the kitchen window and spray his family with nails, rocks, or other deadly objects? Would the kids be off at school by then? No, they would be dressing and eating. Would he offer water to the injured? Would his family be in range of some sniper if he did? Should the children see the injured or the dead? How dare the two young men endanger his family! The grip fear already had on his stomach tightens with anger.

What if he woke his wife, children, and mother-in-law now and moved everyone to his sister's place a couple of streets over, escaping out the back through his cassava fields? Would the two young men hear from their lookout? Would they interfere?

It would be safer if the two men thought he was asleep. Say a neighbor tipped off the patrol about the bomb—the two youths might suspect he had been the informer.

He studies the scratched NOKIA lettering on the phone, as if it would spell out the answer. The display reads 2:44. He breathes deeply. *Don't be in a hurry to make a mistake.* That's what his father would say to him. He breathes deeply and stares at the phone.

Ka Eming

Victor Corpus is a unique figure in the history of insurgency. As a young first lieutenant assigned to the Philippine Constabulary he was asked to conduct a political assassination. He refused. Eventually, disgusted by how ruling elites used the military to suppress opposition, he defected to the NPA in 1970. He fought government forces and trained cadres of the rebels under the nom de guerre Ka Eming, rising to become a member of the NPA Central Committee.

Yet his conscience started giving him trouble again. He became convinced that the NPA leadership was responsible for a grenade attack on civilian opposition politicians and, disillusioned, he surrendered to the military six years after defecting from it. He was sentenced to death, but not executed. A decade later, the dictator Ferdinand Marcos was replaced by President Corazon Aquino, who pardoned Victor at age forty-four. Rejoining the armed forces, his knowledge of the NPA proved invaluable. Shortly after being reinstated, he developed Lambat Bitag—a comprehensive population-centric counterinsurgency campaign plan that stemmed the rising tide of communist influence around the country and led to significant attrition of the NPA communist guerrilla fighters and their supporters in the field. He worked his way up the ranks, eventually to chief of the armed forces intelligence service in 2001 as a brigadier general. His book *Silent War* remains the definitive guide to understanding insurgency and counterinsurgency in the Philippines.

Joe developed a relationship with General Corpus when he was first assigned to the Philippines as a military attaché in 1999. He interviewed Victor in 2014. At age seventy, his quick, optimistic smile lit up a weathered face.

> Victor Corpus, on his time as NPA rebel Ka Eming: "Without people's support you're dead, because it's the support of the people that give[s] you all the intelligence that you need. They will be your eyes and ears, and that's a big difference between a guerrilla fighter and government forces."

Back in the courtyard the father sits on a wooden bench between rows of hanging laundry. The black phone lies in the palm of his hand. He listens vigilantly for sounds from the high ground across the road, beyond the tree which he is now certain has a bomb at its base. But he hears only the wind in the palms. One of the young men wore a windbreaker with a striped sleeve, like his sister's son does, a name-brand knockoff she bought him in Sorsogon City. Maybe he should go shout at them? Tell them to get lost, and take their explosives with them. Too late for that; they would have to know how to defuse it. And there could be retribution.

Should he move his family to his sister's house? Would his nephew be asleep in bed there? But wait. Why did they plant the explosive across the road directly opposite his house? They could have placed it facing another house or somewhere that the blast would engage the enemy patrol but not endanger any of the villagers. Has he done something to anger the rebels? Is someone getting even with him? He stares at the phone. The bastards want to get away, he concludes, so they planted the explosive at the base of the hill by the road, allowing them to escape using the reverse slope of the hill, masked from the road and unnoticed.

But is it fair to call them bastards? They promise justice and security. The government, on the other hand, is also promising justice and security and, if they can drive out the insurgents, a nurse in the clinic, a repaving of the pothole-strewn road, and an end to extortion on the highway—that one critical link to Sorsogon City and its market.

What if one of those men *was* his sister's son? He shakes the thought from his head. For years his entire extended family had been neutral, not volunteering for the security forces and avoiding recruitment into the insurgency. A bribe to the police or military when necessary, and some food to the rebels when they arrive at the back door, but never taking sides. Yet, now their damned explosive is across the street. He glances at the bamboo partition, slips back into the house, eyes the windows, and checks that the door to the children's room is firmly closed. He returns to the courtyard. It would be cowardly to hide in the house with his family, even though he is now sure that the blast will not come until dawn.

What if a neighbor had texted in a tip to the military already, to save the patrol? Then it would not matter if he did as well. He could pretend to sleep in bed.

What if he were the only one on the street, sitting in a courtyard staring at a phone? Then the decision would be his alone. He must act as if it is.

Colonel Kakilala

Brigadier General Joselito Kakilala of the 903rd Brigade, Armed Forces of the Philippines (AFP), is a solidly built man with a weathered face, intense gaze, and unmistakably military posture. He retired in April 2016 after a distinguished career in the AFP. He developed a reputation as a strategic thinker and effective "counterinsurgent" in the field. Both the 45th Infantry Battalion and 903rd Infantry Brigade that he commanded were officially recognized as the "Best Battalion" and "Best Brigade," respectively, in the Philippine army during his tenure in charge. Many in his Philippine Military Academy (PMA) class of 1984 expected him to compete for chief of staff—the lone four-star position in the AFP—but the all-important timing and upper-echelon politics did not quite work out for him before his retirement date, which is officially mandated to be no later than an officer's fifty-sixth birthday.

As a colonel conducting internal security operations in Sorsogon, in Bicol Province on the far southern end of Luzon Island, he faced an intelligence-collection problem. In towns near military installations he could dispatch messengers to community leaders to exchange (or even buy) necessary intelligence. However, closer to the rebel strongholds, villagers shied away from government patrols. Locals feared that rebel informants were everywhere, so even if they wanted to pass information to the military, it was not worth the risk. In late 2013, the brigade intelligence officer proposed an alternative: set up a text-and-talk tip hotline for anyone to pass on information. Initially, the line was quiet, but when messages arrived and the military followed through, it came alive.

Joe interviewed Brigadier General Kakilala on 11 December 2014.

Felter: How did you gain information from the population?

Kakilala: Because of your sincere interest in improving their quality of life. When you are a reliable unit that can decisively defeat the enemy, you can gain support. . . . Right now because of text messaging the people can support you without exposing themselves. . . . They share information by text but do not expose themselves.

The father imagines scenarios. If he texts in a tip, an AFP squad would avoid the street, approaching on foot though the fields, from the rear of the opposite hill. The firefight, if there was one, would be on the opposite hillside, so his family home would be at low risk of cross fire. But what if the military chose the wrong hut and the fight spilled down the hill onto his street?

The father checks the time again on the phone. 2:58 a.m. He has perhaps an hour to decide.

CAST OF CHARACTERS

The father in this vignette is a fictional composite of characters familiar to us from our research. Ka Eming, Brigadier General Kakilala, and the other officers we refer to in this chapter are quite real. The setting is typical of asymmetric conflicts not only in the Philippines but also in Afghanistan, Colombia, India, Iraq, Nigeria, Northern Ireland, and Pakistan. They share two key common elements. First, the father's choice is consequential. He has sufficient information to deliver control of his street to the patrol—or to the insurgents—should he choose to do so. Second, if he chooses to call in the tip, he can do so anonymously, with minimal danger of revealing himself as the informant.

Let's return to the father in the courtyard with the phone, deciding whether to text in a tip. To understand his predicament, we need to outline the strategic environment he is involuntarily embedded in: an asymmetric, information-centric war.

Information-Centric Insurgency and Counterinsurgency

The father faces a dilemma. Well-armed forces—government and insurgents—are vying for control of his street and are willing to use violence to win it. It's an asymmetric conflict, meaning that one side is better armed (in this case the government), allowing them to capture or kill the insurgents if they can only locate them. The rebels, though, have their own advantage: they can slip back into the population and circulate without detection, but only as long as civilians allow them to do so, by not sharing information about the identity and location of rebels. And so, it's an information-centric conflict.

How will it turn out? This type of problem lends itself to analysis using a mathematical tool called "game theory," in which actors pursue their objectives strategically by making certain choices, mindful that their choices can be anticipated by the other actors, who also behave as though their own choices can be anticipated. A key idea here is the difference between a "best response" and an equilibrium. A "best response" is simply the best action an actor can possibly choose, given what the other actors have chosen. An equilibrium, which we will explore below, is a possible result of those choices, an interaction between multiple actors where everyone chooses their best response given that everyone else is doing so as well. Put differently: a situation in which no one person can do better by changing his or her choice.

Though the term "game theory" may sound cavalier, it is in fact a valuable tool for thinking about a wide range of strategic interactions. Game theory has proven useful, for example, in predicting outcomes in economic interactions—for instance, how to maximize revenue from selling public resources like the radio spectrum, which has made the U.S. government billions of dollars. Game theory has also been a key tool for understanding security challenges: during the Cold War, the United States and USSR used it to think through how to deploy nuclear weapons to best deter each other from attacking.

Datu George Mandahay

George Mandahay was the tribal leader, or *datu*, of the Manobo tribe, indigenous peoples from the Paquibato District of Davao, located in the south-central region of Mindanao Island. Paquibato is a restive area with a long history of conflict between the AFP and the Communist New People's Army. The Manobo is one of several indigenous tribes—or Lumads—that had been controlled by the NPA but became disillusioned and opted to rise up against them in

2000. Since then, these Lumads have received weapons and other logistical support from local AFP units.

"It's like a chess game: there are things you want to pursue but then you will encounter enemies. You will fight with tactics and strategies, same with the military in the government forces and the enemies."

It's common in this type of analysis to make simplifying assumptions: the actors are well informed, understand their own objectives, are fully rational, and are quite disciplined in pursuing those objectives. Why make those assumptions? Science fiction is populated by characters like Mr. Spock, the Vulcan from *Star Trek* who acts on logic and never gets distracted by pretty aliens (as Captain Kirk might). He is resolute in the face of danger, never panicking. Yet earthly conflicts are not fought by Vulcans but by human beings. So why assume rationality? Because stripping down a strategic interaction to its simplest elements sometimes allows us to generate clear predictions about how Mr. Spock would behave. That often provides insight into how real people behave; better yet, we can often check our logic by testing those predictions against real-world data, rejecting some arguments and validating others (including those pesky rationality assumptions).[1] Besides, we can always add cowards, pretty aliens, and psychopaths later, if drama is lacking.

Actors and Actions

In this case, who are our actors and what choices do they make?

The father (representing civilians) we met already. He desperately needs security and would appreciate some other services from either government or insurgents, such as dispute adjudication and justice, education, health care, and perhaps some representation. He has one choice: whether or not to give the government information, in this case the location of the bomb and the possibility of an ambush. (What we're calling a bomb is often referred to as an IED, or improvised explosive device.) His neighbors, if they are awake, might be strongly committed to the government or insurgent side, which would make their choice easy. We've chosen the father who faces a dilemma, because it is civilians like him, on the margin of calling in a consequential tip, who will often decide the night's events.

The colonel (representing the government) is interested in controlling territory but has limited resources to do so, and suffers from insurgent attacks. He chooses how much of his limited resources to spend on counterinsurgency (COIN), which includes coercive use of force (i.e., pursuing insurgents) and providing public services to civilians. The services in question include all the things listed above that civilians want, so we will just call them "services" for short. The colonel does not know exactly what an individual civilian's political attitudes are, but he has some ideas about the range of attitudes in the population as a whole.

The rebel leader (representing the insurgency) might be interested in controlling territory, an objective he pursues by attacking government forces, or he may be attacking the government in order to extract some other concession. In an asymmetric war, common tactics are ambushes and roadside bombs. Like the colonel, the rebel would choose to spend his limited resources on attacks but could also spend them on providing public services. Like the colonel, the rebel leader does not know exactly what the civilians' attitudes are, though he has a rough idea of the range of attitudes in the population.

This setup is laid out schematically in figure 3.1, where rectangles are actors and arrows are actions. At the top are government and rebels, who attack each other. A conventional approach to war would

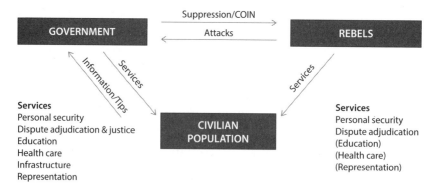

FIGURE 3.1. Asymmetric conflict modeled as a three-player game.

end there. The additional complication of information-centric insurgency is that it *necessarily includes* the bottom rectangle: civilians who can choose to provide information to government and might be influenced in doing so by the services provided to them by government, rebels, or both. For readers interested in linking the diagram to the mathematical model behind the discussion in this chapter, the diagram labels the choice variables in that model.[2]

Outcomes

So how will it turn out? It seems that there are lots of possibilities, but we can reduce the possible combinations of actions by actors by removing those that don't make sense, given choices by other actors. This is best explained by working through the father's decision on whether to text a tip and exploring how, under different conditions, the interaction might turn out in different ways. As a start, keep in mind that once the IED has been planted and once the government has deployed some level of troops to his town, there are only two choices for the father: he can text in a tip, or he can keep quiet.

The Tip

The father chooses. Concealing himself in a shed inside the courtyard, he taps out a long text message. He waits for confirmation. It comes within minutes. Emerging from the shed, he looks up at the stars and listens again for sounds in the street. Did someone hear him? Was he the only one texting to a tip line? He hopes not, as he quietly upends a workbench and leans it against the gate as a barricade. He goes inside and checks on the children, quietly asleep, three girls in one bed, a boy in the other. The sound of his mother-in-law's raspy sleeping breath comes from her curtained-off room. If his wife is awake, she hides it well.

Lieutenant Colonel Francis Alaurin
Lieutenant Colonel Alaurin commanded the Philippine army's 37th Infantry Battalion in the early 2000s. His unit's area of responsi-

bility included the towns of Sultan Kudarat, Sultan Mastura, Parang, Buldon, Baria, and Matanog, all of which had been hotbeds of conflict between government forces and the Moro Islamic Liberation Front (MILF). Prior to the "all-out war" declared by then president Joseph Estrada in 2000, the area also included one of its most sprawling MILF camps, which operated more like a community, as the separatist rebels' families lived on-site. The heightened possibility of civilian casualties vastly complicated the AFP's strategy. Shortly after the peak of fighting in 2000, Lieutenant Colonel Alaurin implemented a successful people-empowerment initiative to help rebuild this area.

"Now another thing is, the challenges there, one thing [that is] important is that for almost all the households in the area that know the hotline number, we have developed the sense of psychological security that means that with just one text there is a response. It fostered a working and trusting relationship between the police and the military and the population at large that were very much willing to respond to whatever concern."

Brigadier General Kakilala: "When I get information I immediately make a plan."

An hour later, the father sits in the courtyard, listening for sounds of soldiers and mentally rehearsing how a surprised family would respond to a firefight across the street and a sapper (i.e., bomb disposal expert) clearing an IED.

At 4:07 a.m. the phone lights up with a text:

(Undisclosed): WE ARE CLOSE. ARE YOU THERE?
Father: YES.
(Undisclosed): KEEP YOUR FAMILY INSIDE.
Father: OK.
(Undisclosed): THE HOUSE WITH SUSPECTS HAS A SINGLE THIN TREE IN THE REAR? CONFIRM.
Father: YES.
(Undisclosed): DOES THE HOUSE HAVE A REAR DOOR?

Father: NO. DOOR IN FRONT. ANOTHER DOOR ON WEST SIDE.

(Undisclosed): CONFIRM DOOR ON WEST SIDE?

Father: YES.

Father: SHOULD I MOVE MY FAMILY?

(Undisclosed): NO. STAY INSIDE. MOVE TO BACK OF HOUSE. FAR AWAY FROM THE STREET. IED MAY EXPLODE.

Father: WHAT DO I TELL THEM?

(Undisclosed): SAY YOU HEARD NOISES. PHONE ON SILENT. HIDE PHONE. CONFIRM.

Father: OK.

The father wakes his wife. Minutes later, three adults huddle in the rear bedroom of the house, watching four children sleep. The adults brace for an explosion.

No Tip

What if the father chose differently?

The father, sitting in the courtyard, slips the phone into his pocket and quietly barricades the entrance to the courtyard. The children are asleep when he checks, as is his mother-in-law. If his wife is awake, she hides it well.

> Datu George L. Mandahay, on tribal collaboration with government: "Our disadvantage is that we are in the open, they know where we are situated. They know our daily activities. While the NPAs, they are guerrillas in essence, they are moving, mobile, they could act as plain or ordinary citizen. In indigenous places, we do not know if they are already the enemies. . . . Of course we need a good intelligence."

He sits in the courtyard, imagining again a jeep blown onto its side, a shower of glass and rubble. He waits for the right moment to silently wake his family and move them to the back room. What questions would his wife ask, and how could he quickly answer? She would ask about the neighbors across the street, of course. How had he not thought of them? Her father's niece and her family. The bomb is even more of a threat to them. He curses his thoughtlessness.

He could sneak across the street in the dark to warn them, but that would put him directly in the line of fire of the men on the opposite slope. He stares at the phone. If he sends a text, will the neighbor know what he chose? He thinks it through.

Father: SORRY TO WAKE YOU. HEARD SOUNDS IN THE STREET.
   No answer.
Father: WAKE UP. SOUNDS IN STREET. SOMETHING OUTSIDE YOUR
   WALL ON STREET. DO NOT GO CHECK. SOMEONE MIGHT BE WATCH-
   ING.
   No answer.
Father: DANGER IN STREET. MOVE CHILDREN AWAY FROM FRONT OF
   HOUSE. TRUST ME, COUSIN.
   No answer.

Would he have to walk across the street to wake them? His son walks to school with their children; they play together in the afternoons. He could slip out the side entrance, cross a hundred meters up the street, double back behind the row of walls, and tap on his neighbor's window. What if the damned dog barks again?

That's what he'll do. He stands up to find a jacket, but then the phone lights up: SOMETHING ON MY SIDE OF STREET?
Father: YES. MOVE THE CHILDREN. QUIETLY.
Neighbor: WHAT IS IT? WHY?
Father: SUSPICIOUS OBJECT. MIGHT BE BOMB. WILL EXPLAIN IN
   MORNING. STAY IN HOUSE. MOVE TO BACK. QUIETLY.
Neighbor: OK. THANK YOU. BE SAFE.

The wind has died down. Minutes pass to the sound of insects buzzing in the fields behind his house. Is his cousin in bed or sitting alone staring at a phone like him? Perhaps he would call in a tip now. If that was his intention, he didn't mention it. Best that way.

The father goes inside and wakes his wife. Minutes later, three adults huddle in the rear bedroom of the house, watching four children sleep. His wife asks about the cousins. He reassures with a nod and gestures a caution not to speak of it. The adults brace for an explosion.

EQUILIBRIUM

The father's choices are consequential, as the tip provides a very different outcome for rebels and government than "no tip." Game theory provides us with a powerful tool for analyzing human interactions and predicting outcomes, using the concept of an *equilibrium*, which we noted above. An equilibrium is a combination of choices by people with a special property: they are the best possible responses to the choices made by the others. The idea of an equilibrium is familiar in markets, where prices adjust to an equilibrium level where supply meets demand (i.e., sellers and buyers choose quantities until there are no sellers left who would like to sell at a price lower than the last buyer wants to buy at—yielding what we call an *equilibrium price*). Markets provide a nice example, as they suggest a balance of actions, which is how the word originated.[3]

Much has been written on why we tend toward equilibria in many areas of life—whether we learn to do so through our experiences or if it's actually built into our brains. Striving for equilibrium is clearly something that we do, even without conscious consideration. For instance, if you've ever driven into a traffic circle or merged onto a freeway you've witnessed a situation where everyone acts in their own best interest, while carefully (if only semiconsciously) weighing everyone else's options, predicting what actions others will take, and adjusting by changing speed and direction. A reckless driver pushing in might induce you to adjust your choices drastically, as you yield to avoid a collision. Experienced drivers negotiate these interactions many times in a single trip, generally achieving equilibria without incident. Animals, too, interact in complicated equilibria successfully: locusts determine at what population density to socialize yet avoid cannibalism,[4] fish coordinate collective motion to dupe predators,[5] and ants coordinate to determine traffic flow (much like humans on a freeway).[6] Behavior in the natural world shows many instances of equilibrium of choices by actors.

Equilibrium is a powerful concept, but our case is a little more complex. Could the scenario with a tip be the result of actors making their best possible choices given what everyone else is doing? Well, not if the rebels and the colonel know what civilians will do. If the rebel leader knows that a civilian will tip off the military, he would realize that his ambush will surely fail, and the two young men on the hillside will be lucky to escape unharmed. So rebels will rationally not plant the IED or set the ambush if they know a tip will be called in. In our case, the rebels did indeed plant the IED and set the ambush, so they must not have predicted the father's tip or the squad on the way to trap them on the hillside. The scenario only happens if the insurgents were misinformed or miscalculated.

What about the scenario with an IED planted but no tip? If the colonel knows that the civilians on the street (including the father) are so strongly supportive of the rebels that they will never call in a tip, he must also know that his patrol will be ambushed. So he won't dispatch it. In that scenario, the rebels will also be confident that there will be no tip, so they can anticipate no patrol and will not have to bother with ambushes and IEDs. But in our scenario there was a patrol, an IED, and an ambush. Those are not the best possible choices by actors, so it cannot be an equilibrium, at least not according to the definition we provided.

We will resolve this puzzle shortly, but for the moment it's useful to review the cases that the two equilibria describe well. In the one favoring the government, the colonel knows that a civilian will tip off his forces about IEDs and he can confidently dispatch patrols, which will safely drive through the neighborhood in the morning. So a patrol with no IED (or ambush) is an equilibrium (in which the father has no information to tip about). That's a good description of many low-grade conflict zones, in which rebels are present but lack sufficient support among civilians to present a territorial threat to government, at least not locally.

There's also an equilibrium favoring the rebels in which everyone knows the civilians will not tip and so there is no patrol and no ambush. That is a useful representation of the peripheral areas of many countries today, including, at this writing, Afghanistan, the Philippines, Syria, and India. Rebel control is strong. Civilians do not share information with government (because of attitudes or because they are too frightened), thus government lacks the information it needs about possible ambushes to contest the space without incurring heavy casualties, and so the government stays away and rebels retain control.

Returning to our puzzle, in our vignette the two young men set the ambush, and the father lives in a neighborhood that is contested by both sides. We just argued that if the father's choice were known, then either the rebels would retreat or the government would. But then the neighborhood would not be contested. To explain a neighborhood with conflict, which is what we observe in the real world, we need another tool.

Sequence, and Chance

We can explain the father's setting, a contested neighborhood, if we introduce some chance and uncertainty. Tip or no tip, it's impossible to predict *with certainty* how the night will end in our vignette. If the father calls in the tip, a squad or possibly artillery rounds will probably arrive on time, and in the ensuing action the government will most likely win the street. But squads sometimes get lost, and rebels sometimes hear them coming, and indirect fire sometimes misses the intended targets. The patrol might even come through by accident—uninformed and early—and detonate the IED despite the tip. Or, even if no civilian calls in the tip, the IED might still malfunction or be detected by an alert sapper, or the two rebels on the slope might have misgivings and back off, or simply fall asleep. (In our experience all of these things and more are possible.) So even after the father decides, the outcome is uncertain.

Can people successfully negotiate simultaneous choices involving uncertainty? Reflecting back on the rotary, or the freeway, the answer is surely positive. In merging into traffic we can seldom predict exactly how the other cars will move, but that doesn't prevent an equilibrium from emerging composed of best guesses by all the drivers involved.

In our example, it will also matter who knows what and when. In the discussion so far, we've implicitly assumed that the father makes his choice after observing what the rebels and the colonel would do. Of course the father can't call in a tip until he sees the ambush being set, so the rebels must act before they can observe the father's decision. Let's assume that they also know that the colonel has deployed forces and is planning a morning patrol. The same is true of the colonel. He will typically deploy patrols before he knows if a tip might come and certainly must invest ahead of time in making sure people in the area know his tip number. More broadly speaking, because troops and services take a while to move around, both the rebels and the colonel must make decisions about deploying forces locally and providing services to that neighborhood in advance. The father, on the other hand, is flexible and can decide last. So let's now be explicit: first the rebels and the colonel make decisions simultaneously about services, patrols, and ambushes, then the father, having observed what they do, decides whether to text the tip.

Now let's think about the father and work backward. The unavoidable element of chance must gnaw at the stomach of the father in the courtyard. If he texts in the tip there is still some chance of an IED exploding fifteen meters away, endangering his family. If he does not, he cannot be absolutely sure that the rebels will win the ambush and secure the street. Either way, there may be firefights, artillery fire, and explosions while the government and the rebels fight it out, perhaps for weeks. Yet, despite the uncertainty, sitting there staring at the cell phone, he must make a decision.

Moreover, the father's decision is informed by his attitude toward rebels as opposed to government, which neither the rebel leader nor the colonel can possibly know with certainty.[7] For those two combatants, a civilian's decision to call in a tip, or not, must introduce even more uncertainty. We will discuss factors that affect civilian attitudes at length in this book, but for now the key points are that they influence the father's actions, and that they are at least somewhat unpredictable for the colonel and the rebel leader and thus increase the unpredictable element of chance for combatants.

Shifting back a step, both the rebels and the colonel now face two layers of uncertainty. Not only do they not know whether a tip will be shared, but there is also an unavoidable element of chance about how any battle might turn out. The father will decide, and the battle will be won by someone, but here's the thing: both the rebel leader and the colonel must decide before either layer of uncertainty is resolved.

Equilibrium with Uncertainty

Working out an equilibrium when there's uncertainty about outcomes and choices seems quite complicated. Fortunately, it is familiar territory for game theorists, and the idea of equilibrium still applies. The basic approach is what you might expect from personal experience: actors make decisions without being able to fully predict the consequences, then they watch reality play itself out. The choices they make are still best responses, as defined earlier—that is, the best choice given what they can predict, with the caveat that "best" now means the best outcomes given the choice, weighted by the probabilities associated with possible outcomes.[8] In that sense it's still an equilibrium because actors make the best choices they can, given that others are doing the same. In our example, the father makes the best decision he can, after observing what the rebels and the colonel do, considering the odds of all the terrible things that might happen and figuring in his ideological, religious, or patriotic allegiance. The rebel leader and the colonel guess as best they can what the civilians (including the father and possibly others) might decide, calculate some odds of their own—factoring in what they think civilians' attitudes on the street are—and decide if it's worth risking an ambush or a patrol, respectively, to contest the father's neighborhood.

An example might make this more concrete. Imagine that both the rebel leader and the colonel estimate the chance of a tip at about 60 percent if the IED is planted, which implies a chance of the colonel winning of perhaps 55 percent (lowered slightly by the inherent uncertainty in how any battle might turn out). Considering those odds, they decide how to spend their resources. For the rebel leader, a 45 percent chance of victory might be worth taking the risk of setting the IED and exposing his cadres to the possibility of capture, rather than holding back and ceding the neighborhood to the colonel. The colonel might make the same calculation at 55 percent and risk the patrol, rather than ceding the territory, leading to a confrontation.

We seldom know these probabilities exactly, but the main point of the example is that, even with uncertainty about the outcome, the equilibrium provides a plausible analytical tool to describe the situation in the vignette: a contested neighborhood in which the ambush is set and the patrol is dispatched. This is indeed what we see in real life: combatants actively contest neighborhoods even when both sides know that they might well lose.

Having decided to contest the neighborhood (with ambushes and patrols), both the rebel leader and the colonel can improve their chances of winning by providing services to the father and his neighbors, which will sway those civilians toward their side. A clinic or a new school provided by the government might shift civilians in the direction of more tips, in order to keep the clinic staffed and the school open. Conversely, rebel services, perhaps adjudicating disputes or protecting property from theft, will shift people away from providing tips to the government.[9]

Is it realistic to assume that actors so thoughtfully pursue their self-interest in such a complex environment with so much uncertainty? Well, yes. That's how we would think about a manager in baseball, for instance, choosing a relief pitcher with the best chance of reducing the probability of the next few hitters scoring. It's also how we think of opposing sides in an election—deploying speakers, advertisements, and arguments; anticipating responses and preparing counterresponses—all in an attempt to shift the odds in their favor as best they can, in a complex strategic interaction whose outcome will be influenced by chance—a hurricane or a scandal breaking just before election day.

The ultimate test of what's realistic, for any theory, is to confront its predictions with real-world data and see whether they are refuted. We will set out those predictions shortly and see how they do against data in subsequent chapters.

One implication we can already see is that combatants have a strong interest in winning over civilians, such as the father, who hold valuable information potentially shared as tips. So both the rebel leader and the colonel might find themselves in a bidding war for the support of those civilians, even if they have no ideological or political interest in providing services. Ironically, civilians in these settings are often terribly disenfranchised and would be provided very poor services by government, were it not for combatants' strategic generosity.

What Else Could Tip the Balance?

With an analytical approach in place, we can consider a more complete set of government and rebel actions that might either encourage civilians to provide tips or dissuade them from doing so. Referring to figure 3.1, so far we've discussed tips and service provision. We can now add civilian casualties, taxes, and extortion.

Return now to the father in the courtyard in the night, perhaps deciding the fate of the rebels or the patrol. He might well be furious at the rebels for endangering his family and the neighbors by placing the IED charge between their houses. As he mulls it over, though, he remembers cases in which the patrol *also* endangered civilians by being trigger-happy in dispersing crowds. How could either side claim to be fighting on behalf of civilians when they took so little effort to avoid civilian casualties?

Victor Corpus (on his time with the AFP): "Having been with the other side, I know that if you harmed one innocent civilian in an

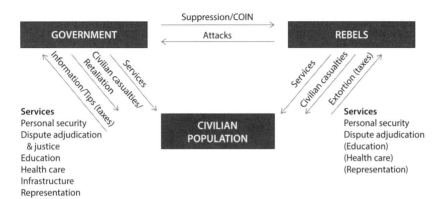

FIGURE 3.2. Asymmetric conflict as a three-player game, with added interactions: civilian casualties, retaliation, taxes, and extortion.

area, that whole area will become your enemy. For instance, in one village, you accidentally bomb and kill a child, the whole village will become your enemy. First they will get even and ambush you, so instead of neutralizing one guerrilla you create one whole village of enemies. And the more civilian casualties that get killed, the stronger and more powerful will be the resistance. Secondly, based on my experience also, the life of the guerrilla is with the civilian population. He who wins the popular support will win the insurgency war." (Interview in Makati City, Philippines, with Joe, 27 August 2015)

Even worse than accidental violence, thinks the father, is retribution. What will the two youths do to him if he texts a tip and they somehow find out? He grimaces at the thought and glances nervously at the phone. Even if they do not identify him as the informant, they might retaliate against the entire street. The "night letters" slipped under the doors in the town where the patrol had been attacked had promised exactly that. But if they do retaliate against the entire street they will be targeting innocents, and how can they subsequently claim to represent the people? And if he and his neighbors are going to suffer retaliation anyway, maybe he should just call in the tip and take his chances?

An ache in his stomach, he realizes, is not fear but hunger. The conflict along the road to Sorsogon City has made it too dangerous to bring his produce to market. He and his wife are now surviving on dinners of rice alone and saving the occasional chicken or *inihaw* (pork belly) for the children. There's been talk of the highway being made secure the following week, when the rebel offensive subsides, but then he will either be taxed by the military or extorted by the rebels. These days it is unclear which side is worse.

Victor Corpus (on his time as Ka Eming): "That's why the discipline of the guerrilla is very strict, because any violation of discipline that will cause the loss of popular support will diminish your team or be the end of you, because if the people are against you, we would get ambushed left and right. But if the people love you, they will tell you [when] the government forces are still far away and tell you to move to safety when they come closer."

PROPOSITIONS

The framework we've developed by thinking through the father in the courtyard has six major predictions, or testable propositions, some obvious and some a little more subtle. These propositions map directly onto the story we will tell throughout the book, which we summarized in a less formal style starting on page 16, in chapter 1. We hope that we've made the theoretical mechanisms very explicit—both here and in the original research papers—so that our assumptions are transparent and it's easy to see what kinds of patterns in the data would constitute evidence for or against the theory.[10]

A first, readily apparent proposition of our approach is that *innovations* that facilitate anonymous tips by civilians to government should reduce rebel violence. Such innovations are often technical in nature, and in recent years the introduction of cell-phone coverage in conflict-affected communities has been the most prominent. We will test this logic in the next chapter.

Second, *service provision* by government will reduce rebel violence, as it reduces the level of violence that will trigger civilian tips to government, which in turn increases the risk of failure for rebels, should they attack. When we discuss evidence on service provision, which was our original entry point into these research questions, we will expand the discussion to include three more specific implications about development projects in particular. Projects that are (a) created to *address* the *needs* of the civilians in the local community and (b) simply *better designed* will yield more violence reduction per dollar spent. In addition, projects that are (c) *conditioned* on information-sharing by the community (i.e., revoked when information is not shared) will be more violence reducing at a given level of spending. We take these propositions to evidence in chapters 5 and 6.

Third, security provided by the government and service provision are *complementary* activities, that is, providing more of one increases the effectiveness of the other. The greater the security that the government can give to service providers, the more effective will service provision be in suppressing violence. The converse is also true: the greater the capacity of government forces to suppress rebels, the more value they obtain from tips that flow as a result of service provision, making government forces more effective in suppressing violence when service provision is high. We test that proposition in chapter 6.

A fourth proposition, which we've alluded to already, is that *civilian casualties* reduce civilian support for whichever side caused the casualties. This has one general implication: combatants in asymmetric conflicts should be mindful that hurting civilians undermines their prospects for victory. It also has three more specific implications: (a) the average noncombatant in conflict-affected places should dislike groups causing harm, and those who suffer civilian casualties should be less supportive of the groups causing them; (b) an increase in support for rebels due to government-caused casualties should allow them to increase attacks because they correctly anticipate that civilians will tolerate more rebel violence before deciding to inform, while a decrease in support for rebels due to rebel-caused civilian casualties should have the opposite effect on rebel attacks; and (c) civilian casualties caused by government will lead to a short-term decrease in tips to government forces, while those perpetrated by rebels will do the opposite. We will test these propositions using evidence from Afghanistan and Iraq in chapter 7.[11]

Fifth, *economic conditions* should not have a consistent relationship to levels of violence. Our intuition from thinking about symmetric conflicts might lead us to expect that when the economy improves violence would decline, because it becomes harder for rebels to recruit fighters. But in asymmetric conflicts the most important obstacle for rebels is rarely their ability to recruit enough fighters. Their challenge in successfully contesting the father's street is averting the father's text message to government forces, not finding a few fighters to plant an explosive. We examine the role of economic conditions in chapter 8.

Finally, a sixth proposition is that both government and rebels have an incentive to provide services in order to encourage (or reduce) tips, an incentive that increases with the value of the information shared in the tip. So *both sides will provide services* even to disenfranchised civilians, and civilians with the most valuable information to share will get a disproportionate share of those services.

We do not dedicate a separate chapter to evidence for the last proposition, so we sketch it quickly here. A clear example is service provision by U.S. forces in Iraq and Afghanistan under the Commander's Emergency Response Program (CERP). These development funds, which were spent on projects chosen by battalions and brigades, were disproportionately allocated to communities with the highest predicted levels of violence rather than those with the largest population or the greatest economic need.[12] Land reform in Colombia provides another example, as documented by Mike Albertus and Oliver Kaplan: the government implemented it disproportionately in areas where violence posed the greatest risk to elites.[13]

Rebels also provide services. William Hinton, in 1966, documented land redistribution and other service provision by Maoist rebels in China in his book *Fanshen*.[14] More recent research has repeatedly replicated that finding, showing multiple instances of service provision by various rebel groups. For example, using retrospective surveys, Lindsay Heger documents community services provided by the Irish Republican Army, including security and dispute adjudication; Jennifer Keister describes similar services provided by the Moro Islamic Liberation Front and the Moro National Liberation Front in the southern Philippines; and Alberto Diaz-Cayeros and coauthors report on services provided by drug-trafficking organizations in Mexico.[15] Mary Flanagan uses personal interviews to document provision of similar sets of basic municipal services by the Liberation Tigers of Tamil Elam (LTTE) in Sri Lanka and Hezbollah in Lebanon.[16] Eli's book *Radical, Religious, and Violent: The New Economics of Terrorism* describes (using secondary sources) the provision of security, education, and health services by Hamas and Hezbollah, and basic municipal services by the Mahdi Army and the Taliban.[17] These sources and anecdotal evidence suggest that when rebels control territory, they *typically* divert effort from the fight to provide at least some form of security and dispute adjudication services to noncombatants. The phenomenon of rebel provision of services is now recognized as common.[18]

To summarize, we have six clearly testable propositions that we will look at in the following chapters (and refer to as *Proposition 1*, *Proposition 2*, and so on):

1. Making tipping safer reduces violence (chapter 4).
2. Service provision (modest, secure, and informed) does too (chapter 5).
3. Security provision and services are complements (chapter 6).
4. Civilian casualties affect expressed support for combatants, shift subsequent levels of violence, and affect information flow to the government side (chapter 7).
5. Economic conditions do not have a consistent relationship to levels of violence in asymmetric conflicts (chapter 8).
6. Both government and rebels will provide services, when tips are valuable (chapter 5).

IMPLICATIONS

We began this chapter with a civilian and an attempt to understand the strategic decision that he faces when suddenly forced to take sides by either sharing a tip or not. The result is a fully fleshed-out model: a three-sided game in which the civilian's decision is pivotal and in which small, noncoercive acts by combatants—such as staffing a clinic or circulating a tip line number—could have large consequences.

Along the way we also explained the analytical approach that has typically resulted in the discoveries we describe in this book, equilibrium analysis with rational actors, which yields clear propositions that lend themselves to testing.

Before we move on to the evidence, it is worth pointing out a broad implication of the information-centric approach. Because the choices of civilians are so central to how the night's battle will play out, the outcome will be determined not only by the count of cadres and weapons, or even by their training and motivation, but also by the attitudes of civilians toward government and rebels. Those attitudes might be driven by deep issues of representation, corruption, the rule of law, and fairness, or by day-to-day assessments of performance, like whether roads are fixed. These topics come more naturally to a social scientist than they do to an infantry company commander or to a military planner trained in operations research. So it should not be surprising that sociologists, anthropologists, political scientists, and even economists have increasingly made contributions to the study of asymmetric conflicts.

Once validated, the information-centric approach will have useful insights for practitioners who seek to provide security at lower cost and with less risk, and to govern and develop neighborhoods now cursed by asymmetric conflict. That menu will include methods such as development assistance and connectivity. We will discuss practical implications as we progress through the chapters, and then dedicate chapter 9 to specific implications for enabling a flow of tips.

And what about the father in the courtyard weighing his options? The best answer, as we move through the next chapters, is to leave that dramatic tension in place: *he has not decided yet*. Both government and rebel forces must make their choices without knowing if a civilian tip will be called in. As we look at data that come from contested neighborhoods and examine the results of decisions made by combatants, it will help to keep in mind the father staring at the cell phone. He is a civilian whose decision could go either way and who holds information that may well decide the outcome of the next battle. That's the environment that the colonel and the rebel leader face in making their choices, a three-sided game where a civilian will observe their actions before sharing a tip, or not.

4

THE INFORMATION MECHANISM

2011-13, Northern Nigeria

Boko Haram was founded in 2002 and began attacking the Nigerian state in 2009, but not until 2011 did it take center stage as a player in the global jihadist movement. That year the group bombed the United Nations headquarters in Abuja, the capital, in August, praising Osama bin Laden in the video that claimed responsibility.[1] On Christmas Day they attacked churches during services in four northern cities. In January 2012 they attacked again, with coordinated bombings and shootings in Kano, Nigeria's second-largest city.[2] Nigerian security forces managed to arrest the suspected mastermind of the Christmas attacks, Kabiru Sokoto, but he escaped in an attack on the convoy transporting him.[3]

Then, on 10 February, security agents re-arrested Sokoto in Taraba state, hundreds of miles east of Abuja. Soon after, a Boko Haram spokesman stated to the media: "We have realized that the mobile phone operators and the NCC [Nigerian Communications Commission] have been assisting security agencies in tracking and arresting our members by bugging their lines and enabling the security agents to locate the position of our members."[4] He went on to announce that Boko Haram would attack mobile telephone firms for their complicity with the government.

Boko Haram made good on that threat in September 2012, conducting a two-day coordinated campaign against cell-phone towers in five cities in northern Nigeria.[5] In case there was any doubt as to why, they declared that they launched "the attacks on masts of mobile telecom operators as a result of the assistance they offer security agents." By the end of that year, Boko Haram had damaged or destroyed 150 cell-phone base stations in northern Nigeria.[6] The group continued to disrupt telecommunications so completely over subsequent years that reports of their violence in the rural north would take days to reach the outside world.[7]

From the government's perspective, the dramatic increase in violence over 2011 and 2012 was *facilitated in part by the insurgents' ability to communicate using mobile phones.* In March 2011 the government mandated that all SIM cards be registered with the NCC, and in January 2012 it deactivated all unregistered accounts.

On 14 May 2013, President Goodluck Jonathan declared a state of emergency in three northeastern states and ordered the military to "take all necessary action, within the ambit of their rules of engagement, to put an end to the impunity of insurgents and terrorists."[8] One of those actions was a temporary *shutdown* of mobile phone networks, which the Nigerian government implemented between 23 May and 12 July for twelve million citizens, in an area of northern Nigeria the size of England. These were the same states in which Boko Haram had begun attacking cell-phone towers the previous year. During the blackout, the police and military communicated using alternative networking systems.

- -

So, each for their own reason, both the rebels and the government acted to shut down cell-phone networks, the main form of information and communications technology (ICT) available in the conflict zone. In a zero-sum conflict (i.e., one in which an act that advantages one side must equally disadvantage the other), one side must have made a mistake. But which one?

The information-centric model we laid out in the previous chapter implies that Boko Haram was right, since ICT facilitates tips, which advantage the government. But we've yet to report on empirical tests of that model or discuss whether it applies to the conflict in Nigeria. In this chapter we will do both. We'll start with testable implications of the model outlined in the previous chapter, focusing on how making information-sharing safer for noncombatants should affect rebel operations (*Proposition 1*). We will then turn to evidence from subnational data in Iraq on how connectivity affects violence. That evidence supports the information-centric model but is also consistent with another explanation—signals intelligence—so we will look at direct evidence on tips, which has recently become available, to adjudicate between those competing rationales.

With the information-centric model buttressed by evidence, we will ask how broadly it applies, returning to Nigeria but also examining the role of connectivity and information transfer in political mobilization and insurgencies ranging from the Arab Spring to rural Indonesia to the conflict against IS in Iraq.

TESTING THE INFORMATION-CENTRIC MODEL

The Father in the Courtyard: Testable Implications of the Model

Recall the logic of chapter 3. In an asymmetric conflict setting, if our fictional father decides to text in a tip, that information allows the government to limit rebel violence. Rebels should be highly sensitive to information-sharing such that anything which makes it safer for citizens to share information will make it harder for rebels to operate.

Now let's return to the father in the courtyard and consider how information-sharing looks to him, in terms of risk. Putting aside for a moment his sympathy or antipathy for the rebels or the quality of services the government or rebels provide, there is also the risk that the rebels might discover that the tip came from him and retaliate against him and his family. The greater that risk of discovery, the less likely the father is to text the tip, all else being equal.

Rebels know that risk levers can be influenced, so they sometimes act not only to improve civilian attitudes toward them but also to raise civilians' perception of the risk associated with informing. The Islamic State in Syria,[9] Hamas in Gaza,[10] al-Shabaab in Somalia,[11] and other militant groups have publicly executed suspected informers as a warning to the civilian population to keep their mouths shut.[12] In 2010 when the Wikileaks site released 92,000 U.S. military files, Taliban spokesman Zabihullah Mujahid promised to punish informants: "We knew about the spies and people who collaborate with US forces. We will investigate through our own secret service whether the people mentioned are really spies working for the United States. If they are US spies, then we know how to punish them."[13]

Informing must have been all the more risky in the days before tip lines, when face-to-face meetings had to be scheduled. In *Pacification in Algeria, 1956–1958*, David Galula describes the successful tactics he and other members of the French military used to acquire information on Algerian rebels.[14] Assuming that most citizens could finger at least the local rebels (*fellaghas*) who extorted monthly payments, soldiers would arrest men on petty criminal charges in groups of no fewer than four—giving each potential informer some degree of protection from being identified by rebels as the source. They would then interrogate the men individually, offering them cash for tips. One detainee said to Galula, "*Mon Capitaine*, you must understand our situation. We are not afraid of you. The most you will do to us is put us in jail. The *fellaghas*, they cut our throats. Even if we want to help you, we cannot; too dangerous."[15] Galula eventually convinced the man to reveal the name of the rebel leader in his village. He followed with a theatrical show, throwing the old man out of the interrogation room in a fury in order to prevent other detainees from becoming suspicious.

In those contexts the risk of exposure was high. Today, however, when cellular coverage arrives in a region, *cell phones allow anonymous tips*. Functioning cellular networks dramatically reduce the risk for informants.

Critically, in equilibrium rebels know approximately (but not precisely) where the average citizen's activation threshold lies (i.e., the level of cost and risk they can impose before the father decides to call in a tip).[16] A rebel leader, knowing that violence upsets citizens, will be reluctant to choose so much violence that he risks crossing the threshold at which citizens start sharing information. When ICT arrives, reducing the risk of informing for citizens and therefore the level of violence they will tolerate, rebels will adjust by reducing their violence.

That logic has two implications. First, restating *Proposition 1* of chapter 3, making coverage available to civilians will reduce rebel violence, as rebels will be forced to reduce violence (and other behavior objectionable to civilians) in order to keep potential informants (like the father in the previous chapter) below their activation threshold.[17] Second, an immediate corollary is that rebels will block cellular coverage whenever they can, while government will generally support it. As the Nigerian example makes clear, though, rebels can also exploit the cellular network to organize or to detonate explosives remotely, potentially reversing *Proposition 1* and its corollary. To decide which effect prevails in specific settings, we need to turn to data.

Evidence on Coverage and Violence

Let's look first at evidence on the corollary, to check whether rebels welcome cellular coverage or try to limit it to control the damage information flow can wreak on their activities.

India's Maoists treated cellular coverage as a threat when it began expanding into their core territories. They attempted to coercively ban cell-phone use in regions they controlled as early as 2008.[18] By 2016 they had destroyed over two hundred cell towers, and the government was replacing them with towers at police stations and military bases.[19] This led some to argue that weak cell-phone coverage was an important component of a poor infrastructure that allowed Maoists to continue to thrive in India's hinterlands.[20]

Likewise, the Taliban took control of ICT in their areas of influence in southern Afghanistan (with greater success than the Maoists or any other insurgency we know of). Telephone connectivity was slow to penetrate rural areas of Afghanistan but was widespread enough by 2006 that ISAF could establish a tip line and publicize the number. In 2008, the Taliban began sporadically demanding that mobile companies shut down their towers at night. Why only at night? Apparently the Taliban were motivated by a concern with tips, since citizens could phone in tips at night with less risk of being spotted than during the daytime.[21] But the Taliban seemed to also have a second concern: ISAF could triangulate mobile signals to track the nighttime activities of their operatives. The Afghan government rallied the three main mobile providers to keep the towers running. The Taliban responded by blowing up towers and killing mobile company employees. By 2010 the mobile companies caved to Taliban pressure. In several provinces, they began turning off their towers at night, typically from 5:00 p.m. to 6:30 a.m. Roshan, the country's largest provider (with 3.5 million customers), turned off at least 60 of its 800 towers every night. In an interview, Roshan's chief operating officer, Altaf Ladak, said of the Taliban, "We play by their rules—we don't like to play around when people's lives are at stake. . . . From a political perspective, it's quite a coup for them."[22]

While the evidence on rebels blocking ICT seems to support the information-centric model, it does admit a second interpretation: perhaps cellular coverage advantages government over rebels not because it facilitates tips but because it allows rebel activity to be tracked, or even listened to. In the language of intelligence collection that would be signals intelligence (SIGINT), as opposed to human intelligence (HUMINT).

The distinction is consequential. If all the government needs is SIGINT, neither government nor rebels need be concerned with the actions of civilians or with their attitudes; the three-sided game of the previous chapter collapses to a more standard two-sided model of conflict. We will return to that point when we look at direct evidence that tips matter. But first we turn to *Proposition 1* of the information-centric model, that cellular coverage reduced violence, recognizing now that it is a shared implication of a HUMINT mechanism (in the infocentric model) and a SIGINT mechanism (in a more standard two-sided model of conflict).

IS THE PHONE MIGHTIER THAN THE SWORD?

Does ICT reduce rebel violence? In a 2015 article, Jake and coauthor Nils B. Weidmann, now of the University of Konstanz in Germany, addressed that question in the context of Iraq, 2004–9.[23] This was the first systematic empirical research to examine whether cellular communications networks were security enhancing. Of course, any such study must confront the possibility of reverse causality, that is, that the rollout of cellular coverage was affected by the conflict (as opposed to the other way around). In particular, one might worry that insurgents would allow towers to be built only in places where they were so securely in control that civilian tips and SIGINT were not a concern for them. If so, an expansion of cell-phone coverage would be associated with no change in violence because the Taliban already controlled those uncontested areas without a need for violence.

Insurgent groups active in Iraq at the time must have recognized that ICT exposed them to risk. On the SIGINT side, tapping cell phones of al Qaeda in Iraq operatives had helped U.S. forces kill several of the organization's leaders, including Abu Musab al-Zarqawi in 2006.[24] On the HUMINT side, the Coalition's efforts to solicit tips were highly visible: a $10 million campaign advertised the National Tips Hotline as a way for civilians to "fight the war in secret."[25]

And yet, while Iraqi insurgent groups frequently attacked water and electricity networks, they carefully spared the cell-phone network.[26] This was perhaps because AQI was also *using* cell phones in two ways: to detonate their explosive devices and to coordinate operations. In 2005 the chairman of the Iraqi National Communications and Media Commission reported companies were being "threatened by terrorists for delays in setting up masts" because "terrorists like mobile companies."[27] Those insurgents must have believed that on balance ICT *helped* their cause more than hurt it. As in Nigeria, the effects of cellular coverage on violence in Iraq could have gone either way.

Now, returning to the concern about reverse causality, it would have been very hard for AQI and the other insurgents to anticipate the exact timing of the rollout of coverage. To see why, we need to first provide some background. In late autumn 2009, one of Jake's research assistants, Josh Martin, wanted to practice his Arabic skills, so we decided to have him reach out in Arabic to various cell-phone providers in Iraq to ask for data on how they built out their networks. After several months of discussion, Zain Iraq, the largest mobile provider in the country and the *monopoly* provider through 2007 in the areas where the vast majority of the civil war violence took place, agreed to share data on their towers.[28] The team was thus able to include 2,416 towers in the analysis. As a measure of attacks, they used the SIGACT data described in chapter 2.

ICT was relatively new to the country, and the period of study was a time of huge network expansion. By Jake and Nils's calculations, less than 10 percent of Iraq's population of approximately 25 million people had cell-phone coverage at the beginning of 2004, but by February 2009 (when our SIGACT data end) Zain alone reported over 10 million subscribers.

We wanted to estimate the effect of this cell-phone network expansion on insurgent violence, so out of concern with reverse causality, it was important first to check that construction of cell-phone towers did not depend on violence in the area. Jake's contacts at Zain had not been with the company or its predecessors in 2005–8 when most of the towers were built, so they couldn't address whether rollout was affected by insurgent threats. As a result, Jake and Nils could not be sure about the direction of causality.

Despite this concern, Nils and Jake knew that the question of whether cell-phone coverage was violence reducing was important to policy decisions in Afghanistan. So they conducted an initial analysis of the Iraqi data in the summer of 2010. Later that year, Jake was briefly in Kabul to do research with Joe at ISAF. Commanders in the next building were, coincidentally, debating whether NATO should subsidize extending cell-phone coverage to rural areas. To contribute some evidence, Jake briefed them on preliminary results from Iraq.

Immediately after the briefing a dapper American gentleman in a suit and tie, a very unusual sight at ISAF headquarters, approached Jake and introduced himself: "I'm Lew and I just spent the last four years in Iraq helping to build out the cell-phone network. How can I help?" Lew unzipped a notebook holder, revealing the business cards of senior executives at every Iraq cell-phone provider. "Say Lew sent you," he told Jake.

True to Lew's word, the CEOs and CTOs of all the major Iraqi providers (as well as one of Zain's key consultants) spent hours on the phone with Jake describing how the network was rolled out. The professionals told Jake that ICT companies' site acquisition teams employed various strategies to push expansion—even in difficult security situations such as Fallujah in 2004 and Ramadi in 2006. Given the myriad delays a project could encounter, the major firms often used what they described as a "scatter-shot" approach: as soon as site selection was complete they would try to secure titles to all of the property in their expansion plan at the same time, as opposed to securing them in the order that their marketing departments suggested. A quick test with the data backed this up: violence did not predict tower construction.[29]

With the system designers' description of a process free of intimidation validated by data, Jake and Nils proceeded to test *Proposition 1* about ICT and rebel violence, specifically, the effect of tower construction on violence. They did this at two geographic levels. First, because the insurgency was organized regionally, they conducted a district-level analysis and found that better coverage led to a clear and robust *decrease* in insurgent attacks during most of the war. In the average district in Zain's coverage area, the introduction of one new tower predicted approximately 2.8 fewer attacks in that month (on an average of 327,000 residents).[30] This effect was not large, as the average district in those data saw 36 attacks per month, but it was strongly statistically significant, robust to the inclusion of a battery of control variables, and consistent across the years of war and their varying levels of violence.

And second, when Jake and Nils separated districts by their ethnic mix, they saw that in Sunni and mixed-ethnicity districts, where the vast majority of violence took place, a one-standard-deviation[31] increase in towers (which is typically a shift from the median of a distribution to the 85th percentile) led to 3.9 fewer attacks in the next month—a 12.3 percent reduction relative to the average number of attacks per month. The violence-reducing effect of ICT was strongest in highly contested districts, as we might expect. It was also very strong in mixed and Sunni areas, the regions where we might expect that Coalition forces' ability to maintain face-to-face contact with their informants would be weakest and where in-group policing by insurgents would be most effective, such that the anonymity that cell-based tips allow would be particularly valuable.

Jake and Nils were also able to more precisely isolate the effects of adding towers that introduced new coverage, as opposed to adding towers that only improved signal quality in already covered areas. Because each tower covered a well-defined geographic area, this analysis could be conducted at much higher resolution, for 1,859 tower catchment areas (of 4- to 12-kilometer radius) over four years.

Consistent with the logic of *Proposition 1*, new coverage did indeed reduce violence more than did improvements in signal.[32] Adding towers to catchment areas that previously had only 10 percent coverage had about twice the violence-reducing effect of adding towers to areas that previously had 90 percent coverage.[33] This effect was statistically strongest for IED attacks. Introducing new coverage also led to a small local *increase* in indirect fire attacks, which indicates tactical substitution wherein insurgents seeking to attack newly covered areas did so with methods that did not require that they physically go there. The finding on IED attacks is particularly striking as delivering new coverage over an area gave insurgents more options for triggering IEDs, which would have increased violence—the information-channel effect alone might have been even larger than the study found, given the countervailing effect.

Taken together, these findings from Jake and Nils are consistent with the prediction of the information-centric model, that coverage favors government over rebels, forcing rebels to use less violence. More than that, the larger effect from introducing new coverage, what economists would call the *extensive margin*, is what the model would predict. Intensifying coverage, the *intensive margin* in economists' terms, just resolves uncertainty among rebels and government about whether the father can get a signal in the courtyard but does not reflect the same shift in risk for informing.

While the data are consistent with the theory in subtle ways, they don't go far to adjudicate between HUMINT and SIGINT in terms of which acts as the dominant mechanism. We will do that later in the chapter, but first it may be helpful to develop a little more intuition on tip lines by looking at domestic applications of the same idea.

ANTI-GANG INTERVENTIONS

An extension of the logic that insurgents will try to make tips by phone harder is that governments will try to make them easier. While there are relatively few asymmetric civil wars (thankfully), some form of organized crime is prevalent in all countries. There is a deep strategic analogy between governments opposing insurgency and police attempting to win over citizens who live in neighborhoods with a heavy gang presence. In particular, tips from civilians allow police to arrest gang members and reduce the gang's ability to control territory.

Indeed, when we first laid out the idea of asymmetric conflict as a three-player game, we used as a starting point a model of criminal gangs proposed in a 1994 article by Nobel Prize winner George Akerlof and former chair of the Federal Reserve Janet Yellen.[34] The article described the incentives faced by gangs and the citizens in areas where they operated. The authors argued that citizens must observe some share of gang activities, since operations such as extortion, prostitution, and selling drugs require visibility to customers. Gangs, meanwhile, may do favors for citizens, provide them protection, and often include their children and neighbors among their ranks. The intuition in the Akerlof and Yellen model was that when deciding whether to cooperate with gangs or law enforcement, citizens took into account how the government would treat gang members it arrested. If the government was expected to be overly punitive, imposing harsh mandatory minimum sentences for selling small amounts of drugs, for example, then citizens would choose not to share information, making it hard for the government to arrest and prosecute gang members. If, however, gang members were violating community norms but the prospective punishments they faced were acceptable, then citizens would tend to share information with police. At the heart of Akerlof and Yellen's model was a simple point: increased expenditure on punishment (lengthy incarceration for minor crimes) might actually *undermine* crime prevention because police depend on voluntarily shared information, that is, tips. The deterrent effect of punishment could be overwhelmed by the reluctance of civilians to see it imposed.

Not surprisingly, given the strategic similarities between the crime prevention problem and counterinsurgency, it turns out that police forces worldwide have attempted a range of policies to encourage citizens to share tips on criminal gangs. The Chicago Police Department (CPD) has been a leader in deploying new technology to allow citizens to share tips safely and anonymously.[35] In 2011, the CPD introduced a program called TXT2TIP.[36] People calling 911 are asked if they have any photographic or video evidence of an event. If they do, the dispatcher offers to send a text to the caller's cell phone (after explaining the privacy protocols of the program—police are completely walled off from the caller's identifying information). The caller responds to the text with the photo or video attached as an MMS. The dispatcher gives the caller an anonymous code uniquely associated with the tip provided, which can be used to claim any rewards through Crime Stoppers (a long-standing anticrime nonprofit organization). In the suburb of Skokie, the police launched a tip line, developed a "Skokie Tips" app,[37] and in 2016 posted tongue-in-cheek advertisements encouraging drug dealers to inform on each other, inviting them to "take your competition off the street for free."[38]

Thus if we expand our scope to other asymmetric conflicts in which civilians hold consequential information, we find that here as well the strong side is looking for ways to enable anonymous tips that will deprive the weak side of the ability to go undetected among the civilian population.

ALTERNATIVE INTERPRETATION: SIGNALS INTELLIGENCE

We've mentioned the possibility that ICT coverage reduces violence by enabling not tips but signals intelligence. It's worth, then, understanding better the role SIGINT can play in modern conflicts.

When rebels use their cellular phones to coordinate activities, they give government surveillance opportunities to gather information by listening in and/or to use technical analysis of call records to pinpoint the caller's location. This is the ICT version of technology-based spying, in the tradition of code breaking during World War II, for example. It has parallels in both symmetric and asymmetric conflict. On the surface, SIGINT concerns led Boko Haram to shut down ICT, as we saw in the vignette that opens this chapter.

The most famous recent example of successful SIGINT use comes from the search for Osama bin Laden. The U.S. National Security Agency tracked cell-phone calls and established calling patterns of al Qaeda personnel in many countries, allowing them to locate a phone owned by one of bin Laden's couriers and link it to the compound in western Pakistan where the group's leader was holed up.[39] SIGINT can also play a major role in a broad counterinsurgency effort; a senior Pakistani security official claimed in 2014 that signals intelligence drove 90 percent of army operations against Tehreek-e-Taliban Pakistan (TTP) and its affiliate terror outfits in tribal areas.[40]

Rebels around the world take dramatic steps to counteract ICT-based spying, providing strong qualitative evidence of the importance of the SIGINT channel. Bin Laden himself was famously vigilant about never having a phone. Uncovered correspondence from the Islamic State of Iraq (a precursor to IS) cites the need to maintain better communications security.[41] Maoist rebels in the Indian state of Bihar banned mobile phone use among their operatives after police captured ten leaders by tracking their signals in 2007.[42]

THE LINK FROM THE TIP TO THE RESPONSE

Sorting out the roles played by SIGINT and tips (HUMINT—the prosaic military acronym for human intelligence) in reducing violence requires directly observing tips themselves—and not just cell-phone coverage—and then demonstrating that they predict reduced violence. In 2015 ESOC scholar Andrew Shaver secured the declassification of documents that allowed him to directly observe data on tips. In a working paper he circulated in 2016, he used documents from the United Kingdom's Ministry of Defence to measure for the first time the effect of receiving a quality tip (as defined by the troops manning the lines) on subsequent levels of insurgent violence in Iraq.[43]

The data covered two time periods that together provided just under a year's worth of daily reports on the number and nature of calls received in Basra district, in southeastern Iraq. The first period was in 2006 when the insurgency raged and the number of calls was high; the second was in 2009 when both insurgents and callers were far less active.

Iraqi insurgent groups had responded to the establishment of tips hotlines by flooding them with illegitimate calls (more indirect evidence that they viewed tips as a threat). A 2006 *New York Times* article reported that in an apparent "effort by the insurgency to tie up the lines," prank callers attempted to overwhelm call center operators by "berat[ing] and threaten[ing them]. Women called to offer the operators sex or, they said, just to chat."[44] Internal U.S. government documents from the time confirm that while calls to hotlines exceeded 5,000 per day, three-quarters were death threats or made simply to harass.[45] The situation was as bad or worse in Basra specifically. On one day, 10 October 2006, the hotline received nine calls containing actual tips and 2,122 calls that were fake. Over the 2006 period in Andrew's data, only 1 percent of calls received were tips.[46]

To accurately capture the temporal progression from a genuine tip to its result, Andrew looked at how past tips relate to subsequent insurgent violence. In his analysis he controlled for variables that might confound our understanding of the effect of tips on subsequent violence, including the number of illegitimate calls received and changes in the number of civilian casualties inflicted by either side.

The data provide clear evidence that tips lead to a statistically significant increase in discoveries of IEDs and arms caches in the fourteenday window after a tip is shared. That's direct evidence for the information mechanism we invoked in the previous chapter's vignette. The increase ranges from .1 to .2 extra IEDs discovered each day in the first nine days after the tip but declines to zero by day fourteen. Each tip, in other words, leads to approximately one IED being found on average over the following two weeks. And discovery of IEDs meant fewer IED attacks, as one would expect.

All in all, Andrew found that for each additional tip there were approximately 0.4 fewer IED attacks and 0.5 fewer indirect-fire attacks one week later. In real terms, this meant a reduction of almost 50 percent from the average number of indirect-fire attacks per week in Basra (which was 1.1) and of 15 percent from the average number of

IED attacks (2.6). For the simple act of calling in a tip, those are large effects. The temporal profiles of the events following an increase in tips match the logic of the information-centric mechanism, which is to say, the father with the cell phone in the previous chapter.

This evidence is critically important for two reasons. First, it provides the first direct evidence on a link in our chain of logical argument that was previously only hypothesized. In the chapters that follow we will use that same chain to diagnose the effects of development programs and civilian casualties on rebel violence, appealing to the logic of the model to argue that the missing link must be tips, but without direct evidence. Though it comes later in the book, those results actually came earlier for us, so Andrew's direct evidence on tips provided us the previously missing golden ring in the evidentiary chain.

The second important implication of Andrew's evidence is that, in the context of interventions that improve the availability of cellular coverage, either HUMINT or SIGINT mechanisms could be in play. As we've pointed out, that's a consequential difference for policy. The SIGINT mechanism requires only passive information collection from rebels, allowing combatants to ignore the well-being of civilians altogether. Should the HUMINT mechanism, that is, the tips, be in play, then civilians, at least those with plastic attitudes toward one side relative to the other, must be protected and provided with services.

We will see more evidence in the chapters that follow that implicates the HUMINT rather than the SIGINT mechanism as being of primary importance in asymmetric conflicts. For now, let's return to Nigeria and the narrower question of whether the government should expand or suppress cellular communication in what is (at this writing) an ongoing conflict with the Boko Haram insurgency.

BACK TO NIGERIA: COULD ICT INCREASE VIOLENCE BY ADVANTAGING REBELS?

Both Boko Haram and the Nigerian government thought it strategically advantageous to shut down ICT. As we argued, they cannot both have been correct, since a win for one was a loss for the other. Who was right?

Jacob Udo-Udo Jacob and Idorenyin Akpan, both of the American University of Nigeria, wrote in 2015, "It is curious . . . that the Nigerian security forces saw the mobile phone blackout, a usual Boko Haram tactic, as a means of containing the insurgency."[47] Tellingly, a month into the blackout, the army tightened restrictions, declaring that they would arrest anyone using a satellite phone.[48]

Why might the blackout help the government? Jacob and Akpan quote a colonel in the Nigerian army on the effect of the blackout:

> The moment we shut down communication, there was a lull in [Boko Haram] operations. We had alternative means of communication and they didn't. The moment we shut down [mobile] communication, we were able to carry out successful raids and cordon and search operations on so many Boko Haram camps. We caught them unawares. Using mobile phones to coordinate their activities made it look as if they were everywhere. But they are not everywhere, they communicate to people from different camps (or cells) where they have people. When they want to carry out an attack, they call their members within that location, muster them together and they face a particular town. When they want to go out on a wide offensive, they normally use mobile phones to bring themselves together and carry out their attack. I can tell you the mobile phone shutdown was successful. During that period their attack was reduced to a minimum.[49]

According to military statistics, the period of ICT blackout coincided with a spike in the number of insurgents killed or captured (1,956 over two months versus 734 in the previous three months) and a dip in the number of Boko Haram operations.

While officials attributed this success to the disruption of Boko Haram communications, Jacob and Akpan point out that other factors could have contributed to that spike, including a troop surge and an increase in the number of checkpoints. If the blackout prevented militants from planning attacks, did it not also prevent the government from listening in on those plans? That was, after all, the reason that Boko Haram had attempted *its own* blackout. Furthermore, the authors report that the action had detrimental effects on the local economy, citizens' feeling of safety and well-being, and their links to the rest of the country. One citizen the authors interviewed said, "We were cut off from life and from everyone and everything else in Nigeria."[50]

Ultimately, Jacob and Akpan conclude that "while the mobile phone blackout helped checkmate Boko Haram in the short term, it forced the group to develop new coping strategies and to evolve."[51] The group established a stronghold in the remote Sambisa forest, from which it carried out its subsequent operations, including the infamous kidnapping of 276 schoolgirls in April 2014. That year, Boko Haram's death toll increased 300 percent, to 6,664, briefly surpassing even IS as the world's deadliest terrorist organization.[52]

To get at the question of who was right, we can look at what was at stake for each side and the primary constraint—real or perceived—limiting their success. Boko Haram rebels were betting that the key constraint limiting their use of violence was information: phones enabled civilians to give the government information that it could use to shut them down—the father in the courtyard—or perhaps allowed the government to tap their operatives' phones. The government posited that coordinating operatives was the primary constraint holding Boko Haram back. Cell phones allowed the insurgents to coordinate, the government thought, so it was worth blacking out ICT even if that meant sacrificing both the ability to track their movements through signal triangulation and the ability to act on information gained from civilians via tip lines.

The question of who was right ultimately comes down to what was at stake on each side and the primary constraint keeping them from achieving it. When phones went down, the insurgency was indeed constrained for a period, but it survived, and the Nigerian government did not take advantage of the lull in violence to restore its relationship with the people of northern Nigeria.

WHEN DOES ICT INCREASE VIOLENCE? EVIDENCE ON MOBILIZATION

Nigerian security forces bet in 2012 that blacking out ICT would give them a net advantage by reducing the ability of Boko Haram to coordinate—so much so that it negated any loss of information flow from civilians, through tips or SIGINT. A number of academic studies support the idea that the coordination mechanism is important.

A 2013 project by Jan Pierskalla and Florian Hollenbach took the broad view, asking what effect ICT had on organized, violent protests across Africa.[53] They examined a large number of long-term, simmering conflicts across the continent and the fact that cell-phone use had risen rapidly in the years preceding the study, including coverage of many areas not previously served by landlines. They matched data on coverage from GSMA, an association of cell-phone providers, with geographic data on conflict events between 1989 and 2010. They looked at how variation over time and space in cellular coverage correlated with violence. To identify shifts in coverage driven by factors plausibly unrelated to levels of violence, they took advantage of differences in market penetration driven both by variation in competition in the cell-phone market and by differences in regulatory environments.

Pierskalla and Hollenbach showed that the introduction of new cellular coverage was associated with a 0.5 to 1 percentage point *increase* in the probability of an armed conflict event in the same 55 km^2 grid cell in any given year. The results were clear and statistically significant. The authors attributed the effect to cell phones allowing rebel groups to improve coordination. "When cell phone coverage is present," they wrote, "the likelihood of conflict occurrence is substantially higher than otherwise."[54]

That finding seems consistent with findings from the Arab Spring uprisings of 2011. Philip Howard and Muzammil Hussain collected qualitative evidence on the role of technology in the Arab Spring and concluded that "the Internet, mobile phones, and social media such as Facebook and Twitter made the difference this time. Using these technologies, people interested in democracy could build extensive networks, create social capital, and organize political action with a speed and on a scale never seen before. Thanks to these technologies, virtual networks materialized in the streets."[55]

Perhaps the most conspicuous response to ICT-fueled collective action came on 27 January 2011, at the height of protests in Tahrir Square, Cairo, when President Hosni Mubarak gave an unprecedented order that all mobile providers suspend service.[56] This was not a new tactic in the Middle East. Iranian authorities had shut down cell-phone service in Tehran in the wake of the disputed June 2009 elections in an effort to prevent protestors from organizing.[57]

Mubarak may have been tactically correct. In a recent working paper, Marco Manacorda and Andrea Tesei showed that greater cellular coverage does seem to enable small-scale political protests.[58] Like Pierskalla and Hollenbach, they used geo-referenced data on cell-phone coverage in Africa (here, 1998–2012), but while the 2013 article looked at incidents of conflict, Manacorda and Tesei looked at incidents of *protest* (compiled from newswires).[59] Manacorda and Tesei found that cell phones enabled mass mobilization but only during economic downturns; during good times protests were rare and ICT coverage didn't appear to enable them. This stands to reason: in economic downturns people might have more reason to protest.

The reader may rightly point out that we are freely mixing evidence on nonviolent protests, violent protests, and violent insurgencies. But note that the mobilization problem that cell phones help solve is similar across these three activities: you can bring together a sufficiently large group of people at a certain time and place without tipping off the authorities in advance. (The number needed is much larger for a protest than for an ambush, of course, but the coordinating role of mobile communications is the same.)

The leaders who accept the informal intuition behind those findings, that antigovernment activity seemed to be correlated with the expansion of cellular coverage, could have been making a mistake. Pierskalla and Hollenbach estimated the average effect on violent protest across Africa (where most states have lower suppression capacity than Nigeria does), while Manacorda and Tesei were extrapolating to a different kind of activity—*nonviolent* protest. Furthermore, precious little research exists addressing how ICT enables or disables *insurgent* violence (beyond what we offered earlier).

WHICH FORCE WINS OUT?

So why did Iraqi insurgents pressure providers to maintain cell-phone coverage, while Boko Haram tried to shut it down and the

Taliban demanded that providers turn off towers at night? Assuming they had a strategy, it was presumably to keep the lines open for the benefit of the insurgency (in terms of organizational ease and fusing IEDs), then to flood the tip lines with fake calls to mitigate the costs (HUMINT acquired by the Coalition). Our analysis suggests that this was a mistake. Any benefits the insurgency incurred with ICT coverage were overwhelmed by their degraded capability to produce violence—an understandable mistake, given the countervailing forces we've been considering, but a mistake nonetheless.

That mistake raises a larger question. How do we reconcile our finding, that the spread of mobile connectivity *decreased* violence in Iraq, with the evidence from Africa—Pierskalla and Hollenbach's finding that connectivity *increased* violence across African countries—and Manacorda and Tesei's that on average it led to *more* protests?

We believe that the key is to distinguish between asymmetric and symmetric warfare, as we emphasized in chapter 1. Compared to the U.S.-led Coalition, the Iraqi insurgents faced a great disadvantage in weaponry and surveillance technology. They depended on secrecy and on their ability to hide among civilians. Any information passed from civilians to the Coalition was particularly debilitating to them because Coalition forces acting on tips could target insurgents anywhere and around the clock (using either precision-guided munitions delivered by aircraft and drones or highly trained personnel delivered by helicopters that can operate day or night in almost any weather). In Africa on the other hand, during the period studied by Pierskalla and Hollenbach, the civil wars were more symmetric—typically a rebel group fighting a government with both sides employing similar weaponry (mostly small arms and some artillery) and transportation technology (mostly repurposed civilian vehicles). Recall that symmetric civil wars function like traditional interstate wars: the side with more fighters and guns usually wins, and civilians calling in tips are largely inconsequential. In such a conflict, the organizational advantage afforded by easy communication might outweigh the costs of sharing information with the enemy.

WHEN DOES CONNECTIVITY FAVOR REBELS?

Clearly there are a number of ways that ICT connectivity in a given area can either increase or decrease violence. In Nigeria in 2012, for example, a combination of factors were at play, which could have made the correct strategy unclear for rebels and governments alike. On the one hand, the Nigerian military was relatively weak and ill-equipped to fight an insurgency in 2012, and so perhaps the government was right that cellular communications would help Boko Haram kill their soldiers with IEDs without providing offsetting benefits because their intelligence networks and special operations forces were not very effective.[60] On the other hand, the government created a number of special units in 2011, so perhaps their capabilities were thought by the insurgents to be stronger than an outsider might have believed, which would have made the insurgents' strategy of attacking cellular towers a good one.[61]

Because there's no good way to collect objective data on that combination of factors across a large number of conflicts, Jake and coauthor David Siegel turned to theoretical modeling to address the issue of when connectivity will favor one side or the other. In an article published in the *Journal of Peace Research* in 2015 they extended our three-player analysis, adding different channels for the types of information exchange cell-phone coverage can facilitate.[62] A lot of factors weigh in here, such as characteristics of the citizenry, how technically advanced the government is at surveillance of mobile communications, and how much efficiency gain insurgents get from coordination over cellular phones.

That theoretical exercise is a bit too involved to cover here and would distract from our main focus, but it yielded three heuristics (rules of thumb that can dramatically simplify complex decisions) for how to think about who will benefit from connectivity:

- Do the insurgents have a strong ability to detect and punish civilians who share information in the absence of cellular coverage, which is negated if civilians can text or call in tips at convenient times? If so, then you can expect large gains in HUMINT from the introduction of cell phones and therefore a reduction in violence.

- Does the government have significant SIGINT and/or HUMINT capacity and the tools (such as precision-guided munitions, drones, air-mobile special operations forces, etc.) to take advantage of it? If so, then you can expect reductions in violence as cellular coverage is introduced, both because people will inform more and because insurgents' use of ICT creates vulnerabilities for them.[63]
- Do the insurgents use tactics that are facilitated by cellular communications such as cell-phone-activated IED attacks? If so, it is more likely that introducing cellular coverage will lead to increased violence.

PUTTING OTHER CONFLICTS IN CONTEXT

To summarize the evidence so far, the information-centric model's predictions are borne out in asymmetric conflicts—where civilian tips matter—but they do not always carry over to symmetric conflicts. As we noted in chapter 1, knowing your war matters. Can the model help us understand other asymmetric conflicts? Let's take a look at Indonesia and Thailand.

Jemaah Islamiyah in Indonesia

In the wake of the 2002 bombings in Bali, which killed over two hundred people, Indonesia's preeminent violent Islamist movement, Jemaah Islamiyah (JI), fell into ideological infighting. Leaders already disagreed about whether violence was the right approach. Many favored proselytizing in Indonesia and supporting jihad only in the Middle East.[64] Even among those who supported violence at home, many considered assassinations to be more cost-effective than bombing foreign targets.[65] Large-scale attacks often killed Muslims and militants disagreed heatedly over Al-Tatarrus, the theological justification for spilling the blood of the faithful. The Bali bombings, which were carried out by JI members acting independently, galvanized those disagreements into divisions. A splinter group led by Noordin Mohammed Top went on to carry out terrorist attacks on the Marriott

Hotel (2003) and the Australian embassy (2004), as well as a second Bali bombing (2005). These were not endorsed by the JI leadership and seemed to lead conservative clerics to defect to more tolerant groups, which were plentiful in this ethnically and religiously diverse country. A report by the Center for Strategic and International Studies describes the subsequent shift among the Indonesian public:

> The 2005 Bali bombings and subsequent acts of violence shocked Indonesians and hardened their opinions against JI and its tactics. This shift meant that other Indonesian politicians could also pursue JI without fear of alienating their constituents. Jakarta began arresting JI members and cooperating more closely with foreign partners to dismantle the organization, without fear of provoking a negative response from Indonesians.[66]

The Indonesian government set up tip lines in 2005,[67] leading to successful raids on the more militant groups.[68] The police also carried out deradicalization programs among imprisoned jihadis, who were interested in securing assistance for their families and education for their children.[69] Once a large organization that spanned five countries, Jemaah Islamiyah was largely dormant by 2008, with many of its veterans who had been trained in Afghanistan in the 1980s and 1990s now working with the police.[70] In 2009, police acting on tips tracked down Noordin Mohammed Top in a farmhouse in Central Java. They captured several other militants and uncovered a cache of weapons and explosives. Top killed himself in a suicide blast.[71]

Separatists in Southern Thailand

In January 2004, the Thai government imposed martial law in its three southern provinces where a local Malay-Muslim population had long chafed at rule by the Buddhist-led government in Bangkok. An active insurgency quickly took root, and as of this writing more than seven thousand people have died in fourteen years of on-and-off conflict.[72]

Early in the conflict, Thai authorities feared that access to cellular networks was a boon to the insurgents. After a series of IED attacks fused with cell phones in early 2005, the government passed a law mandating new identification standards for prepaid SIM cards.[73] They hoped that doing so would reduce insurgent access to the technology and thereby hinder the rebellion.[74]

The law would go unenforced until 2015, however, and by 2006 the insurgents had begun targeting the cellular communications infrastructure.[75] They attacked 92 mobile telephone stations on 18 January of that year and have continued to do so on a smaller scale ever since, attacking telecommunications targets at least 62 times since 2004.[76] A year or so after the insurgency began attacking cell towers the Thai military noticed a trend away from cell-phone-fused IEDs and toward radio-detonated and timed ones,[77] suggesting that maybe cell phones were no longer as useful to the insurgents.

So what happened? Why did the government not enforce its requirements that SIMs be registered, and why did the insurgency begin attacking communications infrastructure? One possibility is that the government learned that it could exploit information shared through mobile phones and the insurgents developed other ways to fuse bombs. As the relative utility of the network went up for the government, it backed off anything that would impede use, while the insurgents began to target towers.

In sum, the information channel is a central liability for insurgencies. They know it—and we can see that in their actions. This gives governments a very cost-effective way to weaken insurgencies by increasing the *threat* of information-sharing. In terms of the arrows in figure 3.2, increasing the flow of services to civilians costs money, and increasing suppression efforts against rebels costs lives. But extending ICT coverage and advertising a tip line cost little. If civilian attitudes are close to indifferent between supporting and opposing the rebels, a small ICT investment can tip the balance toward the government.

TIPS AND TIPPING POINTS

As the Islamic State marched across parts of Syria and Iraq in 2013–14, the self-styled "Caliphate" invested heavily in portraying itself as a viable, service-providing government. Reports in the Western media suggested that it was succeeding. In a July 2014 story about the group's stronghold in Syria, the *New York Times* wrote, "In the city of Raqqa, traffic police officers keep intersections clear, crime is rare, and tax collectors issue receipts."[78] The article quoted citizens on how conducting business was easier because IS was less corrupt than the Assad regime. *Foreign Policy* reported that U.S. intelligence indicated that "militants are becoming as good at governing territory as they are at conquering."[79]

But as 2014 wore on, areas under IS control suffered blackouts, unsafe water, and staggering inflation, particularly in Mosul, Iraq's second-largest city, which the group had conquered in June. After months of occupation, Mosul's citizens got fed up with violence, public executions, and disintegrating infrastructure.[80] The urban environment afforded them plenty of opportunities to observe IS's movements and communicate them to the Iraqi government. In an interview, Saad Mann, the spokesman of Iraq's Interior Ministry, confirmed that the government had been receiving a steady stream of tips from within IS-controlled territory, including more than eighteen thousand emails.[81] In Anbar province, a smuggler-turned-informant described how he and his associates would use their phones' geolocation function to pinpoint targets for the Iraqi government and its U.S. allies to target in air strikes. "We open GPS on the mobile phone and leave the phone behind and get out of the place fast," he said.[82]

On 27 November 2014, IS shut down mobile communications in Mosul (as Boko Haram had in northern Nigeria), a move that caused "chaos," "paralysis," and a standstill among businesses.[83] IS attributed their ICT-related disadvantage to SIGINT (as Boko Haram had done). Using the terms "Crusaders" for American forces and "Rafidite," a pejorative term meaning "rejecters," for Shias, the statement said, "while the Crusader-Rafidite aircraft has been able to monitor the phones of the mujahideen and follow their movements, the Islamic State has decided to cut off connections and prevent their restoration."[84]

IS also acknowledged its vulnerability to tips (HUMINT). The group's Ninewah province office released a statement the day after the blackout began, asserting that *spies* were using "various devices of connection to provide the enemies of the Islamic State with information that has brought about losses to the [caliphate] of many of its knights." Two months later, the group went a step further and cut Mosul off from the Internet, declaring that anyone attempting to connect would be lashed.[85] Of course, if IS's vulnerability were to SIGINT alone, they could have simply stopped using cell phones to communicate, especially since cutting off communications would severely undercut their image as a government—a deliverer of services and stability.

The evidence we've reviewed in this chapter suggests that the group was motivated at least as much by HUMINT concerns as by SIGINT. Late 2014 was a critical juncture when the group's leaders would have been assessing the costs and benefits of ICT connectivity. ICT brought easy organizational capability via cell phones and the civilian support that service delivery could buy. On the other side were the costs: vulnerability to attacks by an informed government. As citizens' anger rose and they picked up their phones, IS had to act. In our assessment, where AQI and the earlier Iraqi insurgencies got it wrong, IS got it right.

Even the most extreme of extremists tend to act rationally in their own best interest, so sometimes the best guide to their vulnerabilities comes from observing their choices. When they move to shut down communications they reveal that their relationships with civilians have become strained (or worse, that their own operatives are leaking information). It is useful, then, for the government (and in some of the cases, the government's Western allies) to keep a finger on the pulse. How many moderate Muslims has Boko Haram killed in attacks lately? Is the Taliban adjudicating disputes among villagers or just punishing shop owners for staying open during Friday prayers? If an insurgency appears to be exceeding the threshold of suffering that a local population will tolerate, then providing cell-phone coverage—perhaps via temporary towers on police bases—might be a cost-effective way to reduce insurgent violence.[86]

Mosul remained under IS control for over two years. When the Iraqi army and Kurdish Peshmerga forces approached the city in October 2016, they brought cell-phone reception with them and used planes to fly over the city, showering residents with leaflets inviting them to share tips. A Kurdish mobile provider offered a special rate: 5 hours of talk time for about 50 cents. Mosul residents began calling the tip lines, as well as relatives and news agencies. When the front line of the Iraqi army crossed city limits on 25 October, semitrucks carrying portable cell-phone towers followed right behind. Peshmerga captain Ghazi Rashid Hasan told the *Wall Street Journal*, "It's happened for the past two years, actually. Whenever we have control of an area, they come in and fix the towers."[87]

To summarize, in this chapter we've looked at several mechanisms by which information flow can work for or against insurgents. Evidence on ICT connectivity and tips in all the asymmetric conflicts we've examined indicates that, on net, connectivity favors government, which we stated as our *Proposition 1* in chapter 3. We've also provided evidence on two corollaries: in asymmetric conflicts rebels tend to attack connectivity while governments support it, though with some exceptions. Since evidence for *Proposition 1* could alternatively be interpreted as supporting surveillance (SIGINT) rather than tips (HUMINT), we've also reported direct evidence for the tip mechanism. That distinction matters, since tips require civilian support, which in turn means that government and rebels need to be sensitive to protecting and providing for civilians, as in the information-centric model of the previous chapter.

In chapter 1 we promised to lay out a theory and then its propositions in successive chapters. Here we presented evidence on *Proposition 1*: making it safer for civilians to share information with government forces will lead to less violence. We've seen that was certainly the case in Iraq, and some circumstantial evidence suggests that it's probably the case elsewhere. Next we're going to turn to the role of services. In particular, we're going to look at how efforts to provide for citizens through development assistance—that is, aid from the central government or other countries in various forms, such as food deliveries, infrastructure projects, and welfare payments—can also make citizens more willing to cooperate with government.

5

THE ROLE OF DEVELOPMENT ASSISTANCE

> The rebuilding of Iraq's infrastructure and the provision of essential services will increase the confidence of Iraqis in their government and help convince them that the government is offering them a brighter future. People will then be more likely to cooperate with the government, and provide intelligence against the enemy, creating a less hospitable environment for the terrorists and insurgents.
>
> —United States Public Law 108–106, 108th Congress, 6 November 2003, "Other Bilateral Economic Assistance Funds Appropriated to the President, Iraq Relief and Reconstruction Fund"

Fallujah, Nasiriyah, and Erbil, Iraq, 2004-15

War creates need. Civilians are injured, displaced into refugee camps, their livelihoods disrupted and their supplies of food and services destroyed. The international community acknowledges a responsibility, now enshrined in the Geneva Conventions and International Humanitarian Law, to step in and help, by providing aid. In fact, the original international aid organization, the Red Cross, had its roots in war relief during the Franco-Austrian War of 1859.

Beyond the immediate humanitarian imperative, many in the international community also see a role for aid in stabilizing conflict environments. The $60 billion reconstruction effort in Iraq, for example, attempted to rebuild that country's infrastructure to meet human needs and also, as the 108th Congress made clear, to turn Iraqis away from terrorists and insurgents in favor of a stable government.

One specific goal of the reconstruction effort was to deliver fresh water to 90 percent of the Iraqi people. There was great need: Iraq's water supply had been safe before the first Gulf War of 1990–91, but American bombing destroyed much of it and sanitation-related disease sharply increased child morbidity and mortality in subsequent years.[1] During the 2003 war, tank-based sewage systems failed in many cities, spilling waste into the streets and contaminating rivers.

Intuitively, the treatment plants that could improve Iraq's water systems are like other purely humanitarian infrastructure projects, such as schools and hospitals. They might engender loyalty of Iraqis by demonstrating both the compassion of the United States and the strength and legitimacy of the Iraqi government. Pumping oil could be construed as an underhanded attempt to steal resources from the Iraqi people, but one might think that pumping fresh water could only be viewed as a benefit.

Was stabilization through infrastructure investment a realistic premise? Comparing three different water treatment projects offers some insights.

This first was in Fallujah—certainly a town where relations with the local population needed healing in 2004. After a mob killed four Blackwater contractors and strung their bodies from a bridge on 31 March, the U.S. Marines launched an operation to root out insurgents,[2] which swelled over the month of April, claiming civilian casualties.[3] By the time U.S. troops withdrew from the city, 600 to 800 Iraqi civilians were reported dead as a result of the operation.[4]

In June the United States awarded a contract to Fluor, a multinational engineering firm, to construct a $34 million water treatment plant over eighteen months to serve 100,000 residents of Fallujah.[5]

The project ran into trouble almost immediately. The makeshift police force the Marines had left in charge of security turned out to be staffed largely by Saddam loyalists or allies of the insurgency. It disbanded in September, allowing insurgents to take control of the city.[6] Escalating violence halted work on the water plant in November. The Second Battle of Fallujah, over November and December, was the bloodiest of the entire war and the deadliest urban battle the Marines had known since Vietnam.[7]

When construction resumed two years later, in early 2007, an optimistic Department of Defense report predicted quick completion: "About 450 Iraqis are working to get Fallujah's first sewer system operational by summer."[8] Yet over subsequent years militants kidnapped and killed staff and regularly blew up pipes leading to the plant.[9] Concerned for the safety of American contract workers, Fluor trained Iraqis to take their place, which built local skills but slowed the project. Construction was further obstructed by frequent miscommunications between the Coalition Provisional Authority and the Iraqi government, while subcontracted firms repeatedly halted operations over poor security and wage payment delays.[10]

The United States finally turned the Fallujah project over to the Iraqi government for a ribbon-cutting ceremony in May 2011, over five years late and $74 million over budget. The plant was still incomplete; it could serve only one-third of targeted residents.[11] It was doubtful that the Iraqi government had the technical expertise to run it or the political will to continue funding construction. By 2014, when the so-called Islamic State captured Fallujah, the cost had risen to about $195 million, over four and a half times the original estimate.[12]

Perhaps it is unsurprising that such a project could go terribly wrong in Fallujah, a town in Anbar province. Both of those names have become synonymous with violence (in large part because of the events described here). Yet a comparison with other projects is instructive.

Nasiriyah, a majority Shia city 250 miles down the Euphrates River, saw far less violence in the early years of the Iraq war. How did water plant construction go there?

In April 2004, the Coalition Provisional Authority contracted the same firm, Fluor, to build a larger treatment plant, to serve 550,000 people in five surrounding cities. Nasiriyah's construction site was not troubled by danger or insecurity as Fallujah's was.[13] The project was completed on time and on budget—at $277 million it was the single most ambitious reconstruction project in Iraq.[14] In a 2007 interview an American engineer said, "The local workers are also a big reason why the building of this plant has been so successful. It has created jobs and has become a source of pride for southern Iraq."[15]

However, Dr. Fuad Hussein, a high-level Kurdish bureaucrat who served as an advisor for American reconstruction planners, told a different story. In an interview, he said that the United States did not consult or coordinate with local officials or residents as it poured money into the Nasiriyah project. Speaking more broadly about the U.S. approach to Iraq, he said, "If you know nothing about the culture you're trying to control, the result is chaos."[16] The plant began to suffer breakdowns shortly after it was turned over to the Iraqi government.[17] By May 2010 it operated at only 60 percent capacity.[18] A review by the Special Inspector General for Iraq Reconstruction (SIGIR) looked at citizens' perceptions of the project as well as its contribution to the U.S. reconstruction strategy. It found that the project "fell far short of its goals."[19] When surveyed, only 3 percent of Nasiriyah's citizens believed that the United States had helped them with their water supply.[20]

For a final comparison, consider the water treatment plant built in Erbil, in the Kurdish area of northern Iraq. Here the United States could partner with an eager local ally. The Kurdish regional authority wanted to prove to its citizens that it could autonomously provide services, so from conception this was a cost-shared project (with the United States dedicating $185 million).

The Erbil plant was completed by the same contractor, Fluor, in 2006—about nine months behind schedule (far from ideal yet not unheard of for large projects, even in advanced Western countries). The same 2010 SIGIR investigation that found Nasiriyah operating at 60 percent—and still needing the help of U.S. engineers—found Erbil running at full capacity and completely in the hands of the Kurdish Regional Government. When surveyed, 85 percent of the population served by the plant reported being satisfied with water quality, and 43 percent believed that the United States had helped.

It is important to see these projects through the lens of Iraq's sectarian divisions. Whereas Fallujah was both a stronghold for supporters of Saddam Hussein and a hotbed of insurgency, Erbil is in northern Iraq, where Saddam had committed genocide against local Kurds. Not only was the Coalition Provisional Authority operating in an advantageous political climate on a project desired by the local populace, they were also partnering with a friendly local government.

Projects with the same goals in the same country—even using the same contractor—can succeed or fail depending on the local political and security environment. The Erbil plant met a humanitarian goal, possibly increased support for the local government, and garnered the United States some political capital. The Nasiriyah plant partially met a humanitarian goal, but the effect on civilian attitudes was either misdirected or nonexistent. Neither the Erbil nor the Nasiriyah plant reduced violence because there was no local conflict. The Fallujah plant, where an asymmetric conflict was raging, failed on all counts. These outcomes may not be surprising in retrospect, but the opposite results were expected at the outset, in 2003, when Congress allocated funds for infrastructure in the Iraq Relief and Reconstruction Fund.

- -

Could these failures have been predicted? Completing large-scale infrastructure projects on time and at budget is nearly impossible even in developed countries. And delivering big aid to countries in need is challenging even during peacetime—during war the challenge multiplies. Under what conditions *can* development assistance in conflict zones, at any scale, make residents better-off, reduce violence, improve attitudes toward the local government, and perhaps improve attitudes toward some foreign power?

AID IN CONFLICT ZONES

In chapter 3, we left a Filipino father sitting in his courtyard weighing his options. We posited that if he feels his government is doing a good job delivering services (such as potable water), he will be more likely to push "send" on a texted tip and thus reduce the rebels' ability to inflict violence on a government patrol. So in principle, public service delivery in times of war can take on strategic importance as part of a "hearts-and-minds" campaign, inducing civilians like the father in the courtyard to share tips.[21] Policymakers and strategists seek a win-win: providing aid that will serve a humanitarian purpose but will also turn the public against insurgents. After the September 11 attacks, military strategy and humanitarian aid became intertwined for U.S. policymakers, and even the European Commission put its aid budgets "at the service of Europe's security policy."[22] Perhaps the name of a series of U.S. military handbooks puts it most succinctly: *Money as a Weapons System*. Aid was no longer something that might occasionally be diverted to augment strategy; it was seen as a key tool for suppressing violence.

The U.S. Army and Marine Corps 2006 field manual on counter-insurgency gives an exclusively strategic definition of on-the-ground hearts-and-minds strategy:

> Once the unit settles into the [area of operations], its next task is to build trusted networks. This is the true meaning of the phrase "hearts and minds," which comprises two separate components. "Hearts" means persuading people that their best interests are served by COIN success. "Minds" means convincing them that the force can protect them and that resisting it is pointless. Note that neither concerns whether people like Soldiers and Marines. Calculated self-interest, not emotion, is what counts. Over time, successful trusted networks grow like roots into the populace. They displace enemy networks, which forces enemies into the open, letting military forces seize the initiative and destroy the insurgents.[23]

In this interpretation the development strategy is based not on a humanitarian objective or on changing attitudes: citizens' self-interest will lead them to support the counterinsurgency campaign. That campaign will extend benevolence not in the interest of the citizen but to obtain victory. In fairness, from a broader U.S. policy perspective, billions of dollars in aid could ultimately serve local citizens; by enabling troops to destroy insurgents it indirectly meets a humanitarian need through stabilizing a local ally who could in turn provide local citizens with governance.

An alternative view is that, strategy aside, providing aid in poor, underdeveloped conflict zones will be an unalloyed good. Regardless of the motivating factors or the strategic effects, helping people eat, providing shelter, and assisting them in finding jobs would provide a net benefit, even if only a small one, wouldn't it? Perhaps that's the thinking that motivated Congress in designing the Iraq Relief and Reconstruction Fund, which would fund the three water plants.

Unfortunately, as we will see in this chapter, providing development assistance in conflict zones *can make things worse*. If food aid gives militants something to steal, fight over, and potentially use to fuel their activities, or if reconstruction projects give them targets to destroy—and if these negative effects outweigh the friend-winning and pacifying effects of aid—then aid may indeed increase violence.

In this chapter we will examine the net effects of aid in conflict zones. We will draw insights from research by ESOC and others, in Afghanistan, Iraq, the Philippines, and elsewhere, to determine under what conditions aid projects can help extinguish rather than stoke violence and improve both well-being and attitudes toward government. Since most aid spending in conflict zones is justified as part of a broader strategy that includes a range of policies, we first sketch a history of "hearts-and-minds" counterinsurgency theory, including the variant in chapter 3. We then report on tests of that model using data from modern conflicts. Further, we use the evidence to adjudicate between variants of "hearts-and-minds" models. Finally, we employ the resulting insights to examine why the recent literature on aid in conflict zones reports seemingly contradictory findings.

HEARTS AND MINDS: A BRIEF HISTORY

The core argument of hearts-and-minds strategies is this: combining traditional military operations with interventions based on ideology, humanitarian aid, and other measures that establish government legitimacy can achieve a reduction in conflict at lower cost in lives or money than does a purely military campaign, and has a greater chance of success. This idea that winning civilian support complements military efforts rests on two beliefs: (1) how citizens feel toward one side or the other has a consequential influence on their actions; and (2) those actions can affect outcomes in a conflict where coercive force is being used. A look at the history of hearts-and-minds campaigns might suggest skepticism, and, as we will see in the recent evidence, some kinds of aid are associated with an *increase* in violence in certain places. So it's important to understand precisely what is meant by a "hearts-and-minds" strategy.

Certainly the importance of ideology as a component of conquest has been clear since Alexander the Great, but the first articulation of how it functions in a modern insurgency came from Mao Tse-tung in 1937. Mao advocated guerrilla warfare against imperialist Japan, with its superior military power and technology: "Because guerrilla warfare basically derives from the masses and is supported by them, it can neither exist nor flourish if it separates itself from their sympathies and cooperation."[24] However, Mao was conducting (interstate) guerrilla warfare against an imperialist aggressor, so he could expect a great deal of sympathy and cooperation from the people. (As we shall see, this is not always the case in today's asymmetric insurgencies.) From Mao's perspective, ideology was not critical for *recruiting* fighters, at least not during the guerrilla stage. Rather, it was critical for creating an *environment among civilians* in which the fighters could move and survive.

The intellectual roots of today's hearts-and-minds campaigns—efforts by the superior power in asymmetric conflict to win over local populations—go back to the consensus interpretation of the Malayan Emergency of the 1950s, in which British forces applied Mao's lessons to fighting communist guerrillas.[25] Widely viewed as a successful counterinsurgency effort, that campaign was led from 1952 on by British general Sir Gerald Templer, who said, "The shooting side of this business is only 25 per cent of the trouble and the other 75 per cent lies in getting the people of this country behind us."[26]

Templer's closest secretary, Sir Robert Thompson, came to be regarded as a leading expert on countering Maoist rebel tactics. His 1966 book, *Defeating Communist Insurgency*, presents his explanation of the Malayan campaign's success:

> In Malaya the government was fortunate in that the communist movement was identified with the Chinese and was therefore regarded as alien by the Malay population. . . . The main problem facing the government was to attract and win over the majority

portion of the Chinese community to its side. This was achieved by the statesmanlike approach of the leading Malays who were prepared to offer Malayan citizenship to other races on easy terms, and with it a strong political and economic stake in the country.[27]

That statesmanlike approach was advertised loudly to insurgents through propaganda. Radio broadcasts featured former insurgents enjoying Chinese New Year feasts with their families.[28] British forces carpeted the country with eighteen million leaflets proclaiming that surrendered rebels "are happier, healthier, more contented, and have peace of mind now they have left behind them the injustice, misery, sickness and uselessness of the jungle."[29]

A closer look reveals that General Templer's operation relied not only on the hearts and minds of the people but also on information flow. British counterinsurgents made generous payouts for information leading to the capture or killing of insurgents, sometimes amounting to many years' earnings.[30]

To be fair, there are other interpretations of the Malaysia case. In his recent book *Wrong Turn: America's Deadly Embrace of Counterinsurgency*, retired U.S. Army colonel Gian Gentile presents an alternative interpretation of the case. He attributes the success of the effort to Templer's predecessor in command, Sir Harold Briggs, who rounded up as many as five hundred thousand ethnic Chinese citizens and relocated them into camps called New Villages.[31] Gentile writes, "The New Villages had barbed-wire fences around them, Malayan police forces and governmental outposts in them, and the British field army conducting operations nearby to sever any remaining links between the resettled civilians and the insurgents in the jungle."[32] Gentile argues that forced relocation turned the tide and that counterinsurgency campaigns since have been misguided, mistakenly attributing Templer's victory to winning the public's trust.[33] That debate over what worked in Malaya cannot be conclusively resolved here; both arguments are consistent with the evidence in some respect. It feeds into the current debate over the importance of civilian attitudes, which brings us to evidence from Vietnam.

The counterinsurgency methods developed in the Malayan Emergency directly influenced strategy in the Vietnam War, not least because Thompson served as an advisor there, first to the government of South Vietnam and later to the U.S. command. Here, it was notably the Marines' Combined Action Program (CAP) that implemented the hearts-and-minds techniques inspired by the Malayan experience. The essence of CAP was to augment a Marine squad with local South Vietnamese soldiers—mainly those too young or too old to have been drafted into the Vietnamese Armed Forces (RVNAF)—and to charge that mixed platoon with protecting the local area. Other branches of the military used combined action as well,[34] but what distinguished the CAP was a *population-centric* approach, which emphasized building trust and winning loyalty by supporting small-scale local public goods. The third of CAP's six stated goals was "Protect the friendly infrastructure,"[35] and to that end, the Marines set up a school where CAP recruits learned local customs and picked up some local language skills.

The CAP program began just as the conflict was reaching its height in 1965 and never involved more than 2,500 U.S. men. But, as one book on the subject concludes, it "achieved results that were far out of proportion to its size."[36] In his evaluation of the CAP program, Major Curtis L. Williamson III, USMC, says, "CAP had overwhelming local successes towards achieving what 'search and destroy' never could. Combined action hit upon the true nature of the war and put in jeopardy the supporting infrastructure of Ho Chi Minh's guerrilla-based organization in South Vietnam."[37] More recently, researchers have revisited survey evidence, comparing attitudes in villages in which the Marine Corps implemented CAP to those nearby where the U.S. Army followed a more conventional approach.[38] Villages just inside Marine Corps territory had significantly more positive attitudes toward the United States and the Republic of Vietnam governments and suffered fewer attacks by communist guerrillas, suggesting that the hearts-and-minds approach was effective.

The history of the Vietnam War is subject to vastly more debate than is the Malayan Emergency. The heart of the discussion for us is this: What can we learn about strategy from a war in which America clearly failed to achieve its publicly stated strategic goals? One argument we find convincing is that the counterinsurgency campaign, with CAP as its exemplar, worked. According to this view the change in leadership from General William Westmoreland, who commanded operations from 1964 to 1968 and whose strategy depended on the heavy use of artillery and airpower, to General Creighton Abrams, who commanded operations from 1968 to 1972, represented a dramatic change in strategy. Not only did Abrams reduce troop presence, according to this view he also shifted strategy toward pacification and hearts-and-minds efforts, which was showing some success.[39] (We return to this question in the next chapter when we look at new evidence on the efficacy of U.S. bombing in Vietnam.) It was only after the American withdrawal that the South lost a conventional symmetric war (as opposed to an asymmetric insurgency) to the North.[40]

If we accept that the asymmetric conflicts of the Cold War provide evidence in favor of using aid as an instrument of "stabilization"— which we take to mean violence reduction or control of territory by the local government—that still leaves open the question of how it does so. And on that point proponents of using aid sharply disagree on the *mechanism* by which it stabilizes.

1. *Self-interest*: The model we described in chapter 3 featured a civilian weighing the implications of future control of his neighborhood by government as opposed to rebels, so that an aid project enabled by government control might sway his decision in favor of providing a tip.

2. *Gratitude*: An alternative mechanism is gratitude rather than self-interest, in which case aid enabled by government would sway the civilian to the government side, even if the neighborhood were to fall out of government control.

3. *Grievance*: Related to gratitude is a third mechanism—the very common idea that grievances about lack of services or poor economic conditions are a root cause of the conflict, so that if the grievances were treated, the insurgency would end.

4. *Labor market*: Yet a fourth mechanism works through the labor market for insurgents: aid projects hire potential insurgents away from violent activity.

Linked to these competing hypotheses about what aid does is a set of hypotheses about key resources that civilians bring to the conflict. In chapter 3 we emphasized the role of civilians in providing information in asymmetric conflicts; and in chapter 4 we provided evidence. Yet civilians could be providing recruits (as in the labor market explanation), shelter, material support, informal taxes, or other resources to insurgents, as they might do in a symmetric conflict.[41] The current U.S. counterinsurgency manual alludes to all of these mechanisms without prioritization.[42] However, as we will see, differences in mechanism matter: they dictate conditions for program success or failure.

To summarize, scholars, soldiers, and aid professionals have competing interpretations of how hearts-and-minds campaigns have functioned in the past and conflicting recommendations on how they should function in the future. The evidence we present will generally support the arguments of British major general Richard Clutterbuck, who participated in the Malayan campaign. He wrote extensively about counterinsurgency there and in Vietnam, as an academic after his retirement. Clutterbuck argued that in Malaya, the British succeeded in large part by collecting "grassroots intelligence" on Communist guerrillas, using it to disband their groups and weaken their influence on civilians.[43]

SPECIFIC PREDICTIONS OF AN
INFORMATION-CENTRIC APPROACH

The Iraq war generated not only an urgent need to figure out how aid best fits in a counterinsurgency strategy but also an unprecedented amount of data to apply to answering that question: $29 billion of reconstruction aid spent in Iraq from March 2003 through February 2009, tracked at the project level and geolocated, with reliable dates for when projects were authorized, started, and completed, allowing us to estimate the local effects of aid.[44] We analyzed these data in our

2011 article, "Can Hearts and Minds Be Bought?"[45] The predictions of that model are much more specific, though, than the broad idea that more aid will result in less violence.

Recall from chapter 3 that game theory gives us a way to predict what will happen in a state of equilibrium—meaning (roughly) that all the players are taking the best action they can, given their options, while assuming that the other players are doing the same.

To review interactions within our model: government seeks to fight the insurgency through military means and by providing services—public goods such as education and secure roads—to motivate the community to share information, which in turn enhances the effectiveness of military counterinsurgency. Rebels seek to persuade the population to refrain from sharing information by providing public goods themselves, by retaliating against those who do share, or alternatively by restraining their violence to levels the community will tolerate. Civilians share information if the benefits of doing so outweigh the costs. According to this model, hearts-and-minds campaigns attempt to increase those benefits—the ones civilians enjoy thanks to government—thereby buying government more information to enhance its counterinsurgency efforts.

What does the model predict about the relationship between development aid and violence, specifically? Now that we've sketched several competing approaches to understanding aid in counterinsurgency theory, it will help to review the relevant propositions from chapter 3 and add some predictions that distinguish between approaches.

Proposition 2: Once we control for local conditions (including preexisting attitudes), an increase in reconstruction spending that improves the welfare of local communities should *reduce* rebel violence against government. This is because, as government serves civilians, the level of rebel violence those civilians will tolerate (without informing) declines, restricting the ability of rebels to inflict violence on government.[46] That logic implies three additional sub-propositions that we can also test.

Proposition 2A: Government spending on projects and services *that the community prefers* will have the greatest violence-reducing effect. Hence, the effect of reconstruction spending will be greater when government forces have better knowledge of local community needs and preferences.

Proposition 2B: Government spending on projects implemented using more expertise (assuming that it increases the value delivered per dollar spent) will have a greater violence-reducing effect.

The logic of 2A and 2B is intuitive in the information-centric model: for a program to succeed at reducing violence, it must necessarily succeed at delivering desired services to community members. Note that these predictions are not shared by the labor-market-for-insurgents mechanism, in which a program that employs fighting-age males would reduce violence regardless of whether it delivers valued services.

Proposition 2C: The most controversial result of our information-centric model in chapter 3 is this: for development aid to be effective in reducing violence it must be conditional, in the sense that if the government loses control of the territory the aid project will stop providing services. The logic is straightforward. If the service benefits the father in the courtyard regardless of who controls the neighborhood, then it provides no incentive for him to favor the government with a tip. He gets the service either way. If, on the other hand, the service only benefits citizens if the government controls the territory, then service provision generates an incentive. For example, if the nurse in the local clinic can work safely only in a government-controlled neighborhood, then her presence in the clinic incentivizes tips. Note that this prediction is not shared by mechanisms invoking grievance or gratitude.

Proposition 3: The more security forces present in the neighborhood, the greater the violence-reducing effect of development aid. This happens because a tip is more valuable if government forces are available to quickly act on it. This prediction is not shared by the labor-market-for-insurgents mechanism.

We will briefly mention evidence on this proposition here, returning to a detailed discussion of complementarity between coercive and benign methods in the next chapter.

Finally, our model has one more implication that we only briefly mentioned in chapter 3 but that is important in thinking about evidence on development assistance and violence. There we noted that both government and rebels will provide services to civilians, and we provided qualitative evidence from several conflicts to support that proposition. (We numbered that 6; Propositions 4 and 5 will come up in later chapters.) Extending the same logic, the more valuable the information, the more services they will provide. Thus, places suffering more insurgent violence should generally have more aid spending by governments. This is not because aid attracts violence. Quite the opposite: government spends more on aid in places that are more predisposed to violence because the return on all violence-suppressing activities (including aid) is higher where there is more violence to reduce. So local conditions that enable rebels to produce more violence attract more effort by government.[47]

EVIDENCE FROM IRAQ

The key to understanding how aid affects violence is to methodically test those propositions. To do that we focused on two types of projects: projects that we knew were secure and could be implemented conditionally at a local level and larger-scale projects for which security and conditionality would be difficult or impossible. To measure the first, we separated out $2.9 billion allocated through the Commander's Emergency Response Program (CERP) and related small-scale programs such as USAID's Community Stabilization Program (CSP), about 10 percent of aid spending in Iraq.[48] CERP was designed specifically to give U.S. commanders funds for small, focused, community-based projects with the aim to increase peace and security. On average CERP spending was associated with small-scale, highly localized projects.[49]

Rather than examine violence as a whole we were interested in one particular *type* of violence: attacks on government by rebels (such as the planned ambush of the patrol in chapter 3). To isolate these, we used "significant activity" (SIGACT) reports by Coalition forces. Out of a total of 193,264 incidents over our period of focus, we used 168,730 that were specifically directed at Iraqi government and Coalition targets. Finally, we looked at the smallest geographic division we could, the district or *qada*.

To test Proposition 2—that effective development will reduce violence—we had to isolate the effect of changes in aid. We did so by looking at the statistical relationship between changes in aid spending and changes in violence. This removed elements that can affect both aid spending and violence but do not change over time. (After all, we wanted to understand what happens when things change.) Geography, for instance, doesn't change, but it can affect which side has the advantage in a conflict. The ethnic makeup of a village greatly affects attitudes and is stable over time: it can be different in different villages, and certainly influences the outcome (think of Shi'ite versus Sunni, versus Kurdish Iraq), but it doesn't change—at least not over the time span we considered. And, most important, we needed to account for trends in local attitudes to control for norms of cooperation with government forces.

Using that approach, the data backed up the proposition: CERP *spending reduced violence.* Over the span of half a year, an additional $10 of per capita CERP spending caused 15.9 fewer violent incidents per 100,000 residents. To put that estimate in context, average incidents per capita were 58.6 per 100,000 residents during the entire period, so a crude extrapolation indicates that violence could be eliminated by $37 per capita of CERP spending in an average district.[50]

We tested Proposition 2A—that aid valued by communities will reduce violence more—by appealing to an assumption. Based on many discussions with personnel running CERP projects and other aid programs in Afghanistan and Iraq we came to believe that smaller projects were more likely to be guided by consultation with local citizens.[51] (For example, when Eli and his team met with development experts [chapter 2], those experts described consultation with prospective local program recipients at a village level as a standard best practice.) Regular consultation with communities was built into a number of projects funding localized service provision in Afghanistan. USAID's Community Cohesion Initiative (CCI), which sought to strengthen ties between local customary governance structures and the national government, appears to have been effective at delivering valued services in part because projects were chosen with substantial community input.[52] By contrast, many case studies and official reports also suggest that large-scale projects often failed to respond to local needs and were, perhaps as a result, accompanied by significant corruption and worse oversight.[53] Both less consultation and increased corruption in larger projects would imply that smaller projects should provide more value to the community per dollar spent and thus be more violence reducing.

We therefore separated larger CERP projects from smaller ones (with $50,000 in spending as a cutoff), finding that the smaller ones were associated with *almost six times* as much violence reduction. Even within the CERP program (which ran smaller than average projects), smaller worked better.

In contrast, non-CERP reconstruction spending, which typically funded much larger projects ($678,000 on average, as compared to the CERP mean of $104,000), was estimated to have a small but significant violence-*increasing* effect. That violence-increasing pattern will show up again below, and in chapter 8, where we will discuss possible explanations. For now we simply note that it is easy to see how large-scale, poorly executed projects could be hard to defend, hard to make conditional, lead to anger, disrupt local politics, and for all those reasons potentially increase violence.[54]

Proposition 2B claims that among programs that do reduce violence, increased development expertise should amplify the violence-reducing effect. The basic idea is that the marginal aid dollar provides more value to a community when experienced development professionals direct project implementation.

We were able to test Proposition 2B with data on the presence of development experts.[55] Specifically, we looked at how the effect of aid varied depending on whether a district had a Provincial Reconstruction Team (PRT). The PRTs were small teams of nine to fifteen people who advised military units on how to implement development activities.[56] Once a team was in a region all military units in that district had the chance to access their expertise in planning and executing CERP and other projects. The number of teams reached twenty by the second half of 2008, each operating in a separate region. (To measure the presence of development expertise, we coded the teams' location using information gathered from a set of maps kept by the

State Department PRT office.) We also controlled for troop strength in order to distinguish benefits of expert guidance from those of security. We then looked at the average difference in violence reduction per dollar spent, comparing districts with and without PRTs present.[57]

Spending indeed reduced violence more when guided by PRTs. That was true for CERP projects (large and small) and for the small-scale CSP projects run by USAID in coordination with U.S. military units. The presence of a PRT amplified violence-reduction effects of CERP and CSP spending by 50 to 200 percent, depending on the program.[58] This amplification remains when we control for other variables, such as troop strength, which might reflect security, or project size.

The results are illustrated in figure 5.1: the left panel illustrates changes in violence plotted against changes in CERP spending for small projects (< $50,000), with each dot representing a half-year interval in a district of Iraq (and the effects of several control variables statistically removed). The slope of the lighter line indicates the violence-reducing effect of small project spending, while the steeper slope of the darker line indicates the violence-reducing effect of small project spending when a PRT is present to provide expert project advice. The right panel illustrates the analogous violence-reducing effects of spending on large CERP projects, with and without PRTs; here again the steeper slope of the darker line indicates that the violence-reducing effect of large CERP projects was amplified with a PRT present.

Proposition 2C, that conditionality is necessary for violence reduction, does not lend itself to easy testing, given practical and ethical limitations on experimenting with conditional development assistance in conflict zones. Nevertheless, four types of evidence make us think conditionality is important. First, an alternative interpretation of the greater violence-reducing effect of smaller projects is that they are more likely to be de facto conditional on government control: a small clinic will go unstaffed if a neighborhood falls out of government control, while an expensive new road is impossible to withdraw if tips stop flowing.[59] Second, conditioning development assistance on cooperation with forces is actually a directive of the counterinsurgency field manual.[60] Third, when we surveyed CERP implementers in Afghanistan, a majority (61 percent) reported that if a community

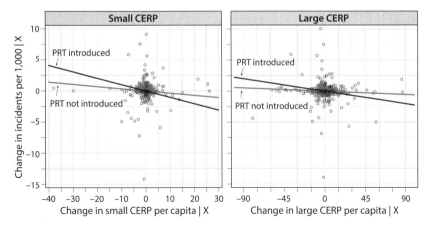

FIGURE 5.1. Effect of Commander's Emergency Response Program (CERP) spending on combat incidents by Provincial Reconstruction Team (PRT) presence. Each dot represents a district of Iraq for a six-month period. CERP spending data from Iraq Reconstruction Management System (IRMS) database. Conflict events from MNF-I SIGACT-III Database.

failed to cooperate with security forces, they would use CERP conditionally.[61] Fourth, when Joe and colleagues interviewed staff who implemented a cash transfer program in the Philippines that appeared to reduce violence (which we discuss in detail in the next section), the staff reported that recipients perceived that the transfers were conditional on cooperating with the government.

Our third proposition was that development spending would be more violence reducing if secure (for instance, if conducted in places with more counterinsurgent forces present). We describe the test in detail in the next chapter, when we discuss optimal combinations of coercive force and aid programs. Briefly, the presence of an additional maneuver battalion of U.S. troops *doubled* the violence-reducing effect of aid spending.[62]

Proposition 6, which states that government will spend more where tips are more valuable, implies that it will spend more where the risk of violence is greater. (Evidence on Propositions 4 and 5, which do not concern development spending, will come in later chapters.) For government to spend more on areas that they believe are at greater risk of violence they must be able to predict that violence. Our analysis confirmed that violence is indeed predictable, based on a range of factors: the history of such violence (perhaps obviously), the percentage of minority Sunni votes in a district (since sectarian violence was rife), and economic indicators such as changing inequality. Thus Coalition commanders could plausibly target aid at districts that they perceived were prone to future violence, and they could have justifiable confidence in that prediction.

The data support Proposition 6: districts of Iraq with foreseeable violence did indeed receive higher CERP spending. Districts that saw an additional insurgent attack per 1,000 population in a half-year period (approximately an additional attack every fourth day in a median-sized district) received an additional $21 in CERP spending per 1,000 population over the same period (approximately $180,000 in a median-sized district). As we would expect if that relationship reflected predictable traits of an area (such as its topology, proximity to major roads and resources, or political attitudes), that predicted level of spending is halved once we control for linear time trends and community ethnicity (which strongly predicted attitudes toward government and Coalition forces in Iraq during U.S. involvement).

In sum, though the majority of aid to Iraq had no violence-reducing effect at all, small, focused community programs did—and this effect was heightened if the aid was guided by development expertise and secured by more troops.[63] That evidence has a strong implication for program design: certain aspects of aid entirely within government control—keeping projects modest and well informed—will help reduce violence locally, even as large-scale aid often *increases* violence. These findings were consequential, as they constituted the first direct evidence of the importance of project scale and other design features in reducing violence. Additionally, these findings—which were among our first discoveries— were important for us as researchers: they validated our approach to modeling and demonstrated the promise of the information-centric approach as an analytical tool for understanding asymmetric conflict.

EVIDENCE FROM THE PHILIPPINES

Proposition 2 (modest, secure aid programs reduce violence) seems to be borne out for the conflict it was designed to explain, the insurgency in Iraq. Does our model work in other asymmetric conflicts?

For evidence let's return to the Philippines, and a study by Joe and two of his coauthors, Ben Crost (University of Illinois at Urbana-Champaign) and ESOC alumnus Patrick Johnston (RAND Corporation), on the effects of conditional cash transfers (CCTs) using the remarkable data on individual conflict incidents introduced in chapter 2 and village-level measures of insurgent influence.[64]

CCT programs distribute cash payments directly to poor households that meet a number of prerequisites (hence "conditional"), such as vaccinating their children or keeping them in school. Over the past decade CCTs have become a staple of development aid, with many studies showing positive effects on the well-being of the poor. A 2009 World Bank report on the spread of CCTs found "strong evidence" that CCTs reduced child labor, increased school enrollment, and reduced gender gaps in education. Furthermore, certain CCTs improved nutrition: "households that receive CCTs spend more on food and, within the food basket, on high-quality sources of nutrients than do households that do not receive the transfer but have comparable overall income or consumption levels."[65] CCTs successfully incentivize mothers and children to undergo regular health checks and induce women to give birth in safer environments (at clinics or with a professional attendant at home).[66]

The Philippine government, through its Department of Social Welfare and Development (DSWD), runs the country's largest CCT. The Pantawid Pamilya program gives cash to poor households if their children attend school and get regular health checks. It also has a maternal health component: to qualify for the grants, expectant mothers must get regular checkups, attend family development education sessions, and use health professionals at childbirth.

To allow World Bank researchers to rigorously evaluate the effects of the program, the government rolled it out by *randomized controlled trial* in part of the country. Of a sample of 130 villages, a treatment group of 65 received the program in 2009, while a control group of equal size was held back, not receiving the program until 2011. The World Bank study provided evidence that this CCT made successful progress toward its specific development targets.[67] Day care enrollment rose 11 percentage points (to 76 percent in treatment villages as compared to 65 percent in control villages), school attendance rose to 95 percent relative to 91 percent (among controls), antenatal care was received by 64 percent of new mothers versus 54 percent, and so on.

This World Bank program offered a unique opportunity for Joe and his team to determine whether a program clearly valued by community members reduced violence (Proposition 2). They piggy-backed on its randomization, comparing changes in violence before and after the program started (in 2009) for villages in the treatment group to changes over the same period for the controls ("difference-in-differences" with randomization, in the jargon of empiricists).

Both treatment and control villages experienced an upswing in vio-lence over 2007–8. However, during the first nine months of the CCT program in 2009, treatment villages experienced nearly 50 percent fewer reported conflict events than did control villages. These conflict measures started to even out in the second year of the program, but Joe and his coauthors still found that the program generated a statisti-cally significant reduction in violent incidents up to eighteen months after it arrived. The study comes with some caveats: the villages se-lected for the World Bank study were not in the most violence-prone areas of the country, and these results were based on a limited number of reported incidents. However, anecdotal evidence also supported these findings. So, on balance, the research team is confident that the CCT program did in fact lead to a reduction in violence in the areas studied, as predicted by the proposition.

Joe and his coauthors were able to go a step further and exam-ine the effect of the CCT on local insurgent influence (as opposed to violence).[68] This distinction is important because rebels can depress the local economy, undermine the rule of law, and oppress a village's citizens without resorting to armed conflict. Insurgent groups may recruit villagers away from productive activities or tax them—in some villages, the New People's Army (the armed wing of the Philippine Communist Party) delivers services and charges "revolutionary taxes"—and create uncertainty that dissuades firms from doing busi-ness, all of which can hinder prosperity, as we will discuss at length in later chapters. So a program that weakens the rebel group's influence may be more consequential in the long term than one that reduces its incentives to fight temporarily. The research team's analysis indicated that insurgent influence did indeed decline substantially in treated villages during the experimental period, 2009–10, by approximately one-third, though this result was not statistically significant.

Why did the CCT program reduce violence and the local-level influence of rebel groups? This study could not statistically identify the channels (as it lacks measures of tip flow, or conditionality of implementation), but Joe's familiarity with the context did allow some good guesses. One possibility was that the cash transfers allowed households to pay off rebels through "revolutionary taxes," and as a result extractive violence declined. This seems unlikely since the logic of extortion (and evidence presented below) suggests that violence *increases* with the value of resources available for capture. Another was that the money improved the economy and raised opportunity costs for would-be rebels so that citizens were more likely to work for pay than join the rebellion (the rebel labor-market mechanism). This too was unlikely; treatment and control villages were close enough that citizens and insurgents could move back and forth to work and recruit, so that mechanism would have decreased violence across the whole sample, not just in treatment villages.

The third possibility, which Joe favors, is that the CCT made the population more likely to provide information on insurgents to government forces, better enabling them to capture or kill insurgents and reduce attack rates, as well us undermining support for rebellion and reducing its influence at the local level.

If so, what about Proposition 2C? Was the CCT program *conditional* not only on compliance with education and health behavior but also on cooperation with government (which would induce government control), as the logic of the information-centric model implies? Formally, the answer is negative: the CCT had no such requirement. Nevertheless, a senior government official responsible for program implementation recounted to us a case from the volatile Basilan Province in the southern part of the country. Wives from families participating in the CCT program pressured their husbands to turn in their firearms, lest these be considered incriminating evidence of affiliation with a rebel group and, as such, threaten the family's continued eligibility for cash transfers.[69] So anecdotal evidence suggests that the program was *perceived* as conditional on compliance with the government counterinsurgency program among families who received the CCT.

Another study that piggybacked on the World Bank's randomization supports the notion that the program increased support for government, though in another dimension. Looking at the results of local elections, Julien Labonne of Oxford University showed that the vote share of incumbents was 26 percentage points higher in treatment villages (i.e., villages that received the CCT) than in control villages.[70] This suggests that the CCT did increase trust in government. (Whether local incumbent politicians deserved credit for a randomly assigned program is a separate issue, which we revisit in chapter 9.)

EVIDENCE FROM AFGHANISTAN

The Pantawid Pamilya program of conditional cash transfers paid directly to beneficiaries, often electronically, decreased violence. That finding is consistent with the second proposition and with our findings from Iraq. Three studies from Afghanistan by other authors report findings that are also consistent with the second proposition, in the sense that development assistance improved *attitudes* toward government in that asymmetric conflict as well.

In a 2013 article, Jan Rasmus Böhnke and Christoph Zürcher used surveys in northern Afghanistan (a relatively peaceful area during their survey period) to focus not on actual levels of violence but on citizen attitudes.[71] They separated the effects of aid into three distinct outcomes: citizens' beliefs about their own security, their attitudes toward foreign actors such as the United States, and the legitimacy and strength of the state. The authors show that aid was not correlated with citizen beliefs about their own security or with their attitudes toward foreign actors. Aid was correlated with their faith in the state. As the authors point out, bolstering state legitimacy is a central goal of the hearts-and-minds campaigns, so this is encouraging evidence for the second proposition.

In a 2012 study, Andrew Beath, Fotini Christia, and Ruben Enikolopov were able to work with Afghanistan's rural development ministry on a rigorous evaluation of the National Solidarity Program (NSP), which, at a cost of over $1 billion, was the country's largest development program.[72] In this version of a community-driven development (CDD) program, NSP allocated funds according to the number of households in the village. Villages, in turn, nominated councils to decide on infrastructure projects. Because of a funding constraint affecting 74 districts (2,000 villages), the ministry was able to implement the program in only 40 villages per district. This presented an opportunity for a *randomized* rollout, the gold standard of program evaluation: the team selected 10 of those districts (that were safe enough to work in), then randomly selected 250 out of 500 villages to receive the program. They found that citizens in villages randomly assigned to receive CDD were "more likely to hold positive perceptions of their economic situation and exhibit positive attitudes towards the government."[73] The program also reduced the incidence of violence— though only after a year or more of implementation and only in regions where initial levels of violence were moderate, not high.

Beginning in 2012, USAID contracted a third-party development research firm, Management Systems International, to conduct an impact evaluation of USAID programs that sought to increase stability in Afghanistan. The Measuring Impacts of Stabilization Initiatives (MISTI) evaluation implemented five waves of surveys over 3.5 years, covering 36,000 to 41,000 households each, to determine whether perceptions of stability and support for the Afghan government differed between villages with USAID programs and those without.[74] It found only minor differences in stability overall. Most citizens supported neither the government nor the Taliban. Using observational methods (as opposed to the randomization performed by Beath et al. to evaluate NSP), the MISTI study reported that estimated effects of USAID project activities on stability were highly dependent on local context. They reported improvements in three measures of respondents' perceptions: government capacity, provincial government performance, and quality of life. When researchers broke down the results geographically, they saw that the estimated effects of projects on stability were more positive in zones with greater Taliban control (where the Taliban may have expropriated the aid, or at least taken credit for it, and used it to entrench their control; see below). On the other hand, projects seemed to increase violence in government-controlled areas (perhaps because conspicuous USAID projects made these communities targets for the Taliban and other insurgent groups; more on this below, and in chapter 8). A peer-review report found flaws in MISTI's quasi-random approach and in its ability to identify villages receiving projects,[75] yet we view the MISTI results as grounds for cautious optimism: stability-enhancing programs may achieve some improvements in trust while also improving beneficiaries' quality of life. The MISTI program also exposes a challenge: How to ensure that the government paying for the aid actually gets credit for it?

This evidence is all quite consistent with the idea that aid might earn goodwill for governments. Yet for students of conflict (and game theory), that evokes the problem of strategic response. Goodwill for governments works against insurgents, so building projects when security is poor may invite increased violence rather than suppress it.

WHAT ABOUT EVIDENCE THAT AID CAN MAKE CONFLICT WORSE?

One of the challenges in taking a data-driven approach to testing theories of conflict is that the world is complex, so not every result lines up with the theory. This is particularly true when comparing results across different conflicts. In this section we examine cases in which, unlike CERP and Pantawid Pamilya, aid *increases* violence. At first glance, that appears to be a contradiction. Yet that evidence will reinforce our understanding of the necessary elements of program design for violence-reducing aid.

Aid Can Also Increase Violence

So far, we have presented *good* news from the Philippines. But when Joe, Patrick, and Ben studied another Philippine development program, this one delivering public works, they found a more disturbing result.[76] Specifically, they looked at the effect of a large CDD program—KALAHI-CIDSS, the Philippines' flagship development program—on civil conflict fatalities and found that the program led to increased violence. This contrast was especially informative, as the CDD was implemented in overlapping periods with the Pantawid Pamilya CCT program, in similar geographic regions, and by the same government agency: the Department of Social Welfare and Development. Thus many potentially confounding factors are held constant.

A CDD program works like this: the government gives communities block grants for small infrastructure improvement projects that villagers themselves propose. CDDs are unique in that, with certain monitoring and grievance redress systems in place, they typically transfer both the funds and the administrative responsibilities to the community. They have become a popular form of development assistance around the world, including in conflict-ridden countries. For example, the NSP in Afghanistan, which we described above, is a World Bank CDD. In 2012, the World Bank supported 400 CDD programs in 94 countries, valued at close to $30 billion.[77]

KALAHI-CIDSS was a particularly large CDD, implemented in 184 municipalities, which are county-like administrative districts containing roughly 20 villages apiece. Recipients lived in the poorest areas of the Philippines—in the average participating municipality less than 40 percent of households had access to electricity or running water. Grants per municipality averaged about 7.5 million Philippine pesos ($150,000)—equivalent to about 15 percent of the annual municipal budget.

There are big challenges in estimating the effects of a large-scale government program like this with the rigor that we require. The best way to estimate a program's causal effects is to do what the Philippine government did with their CCT: run a randomized controlled trial. This was not the case with KALAHI-CIDSS. The government simply implemented CDD in municipalities that met a specified poverty threshold.

However, that threshold allowed Joe and his coauthors to use a *quasi*-random estimation method called Regression Discontinuity (RD). RD designs (i.e., methods of estimation) are based on the idea that the population immediately above and immediately below some arbitrary threshold can be considered otherwise identical. The random element (which, again, allows us to shut out noise and put our finger on the effect of treatment) is whether a municipality just barely qualified or just barely missed out.

To digress for a moment about the method, a good example of an RD design is a 2009 study by Andrew C. Eggers of Oxford University and Jens Hainmueller of Stanford.[78] They wanted to estimate how much wealth British Members of Parliament (MPs) obtained by wielding political influence. Just looking at the net worth of MPs' estates (at death) and comparing them to estates of non-MPs won't work, since so many other factors contribute to whether someone becomes rich or poor over a lifetime, and many of those factors are plausibly correlated with winning office (e.g., coming from a rich family). Yet by comparing politicians within the same party who *barely* won their seat to those who barely lost, the authors were able to show that serving in Parliament doubled the wealth of Conservative MPs but had no effect on that of MPs from Labour.

Returning from enriched Tories to poor Philippine villagers, aside from being just above or just below the income threshold, the municipalities in our sample showed no major differences in measured variables before treatment, which is consistent with the idea of *as-if* random treatment. Moreover, the threshold calculation formula was complex and opaque enough that communities near the threshold could not have predicted which side they would fall on (and somehow prepare for violent behavior before receiving the program). Joe and his coauthors looked at 222 municipalities—94 eligible and 128 ineligible—and matched their participation in KALAHI-CIDSS with the detailed violent incident data we described earlier.

The study provided strong evidence that CDD led to *increased* hostilities in communities that received it, significantly *raising* casualty rates. Initially, violence was simmering at a low level, with 0.94 casualties per municipality per year, on average. Over the three years of the program, the just-eligible municipalities in our sample experienced about twice the violence experienced by the just-ineligible: 85 to 110 percent more casualties, depending on the statistical method used.[79] Assuming that this effect size can be extrapolated to all 184 municipalities that received the CDD (remember, the estimate comes from data on a smaller set of communities near the eligibility threshold),

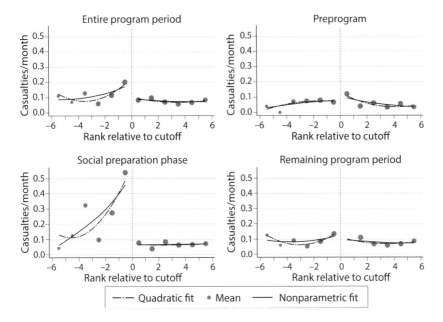

FIGURE 5.2. Effect of Kalahi CDD eligibility on casualties.

Relationship between casualties during the program period and the distance between a municipality's poverty rank and the provincial eligibility threshold for the program. Casualties are from
Armed Forces of the Philippines incident data as coded in the ESOC Philippines Database. Scatter
dots represent means within rank bins. Dashed lines are quadratic fits, separately estimated on
both sides of the eligibility threshold. Solid lines are nonparametric fits from a local linear regression separately estimated on both sides of the eligibility threshold. Dot size proportional to
number of villages in the bin.

the program would have caused 550 to 930 excess casualties over the
three years.

These spikes in violence did not exist before the program was implemented, and other observable characteristics do not explain the
effect. And as we see in the top-right panel of figure 5.2, there was
previously actually a bit *less* violence overall in places just below the
eligibility threshold (which received the program) than in those just
above (which did not).

Revealingly, violence preceded program implementation. The effect of receiving the program on violence occurred only during the
"social preparation" period, after a community knew that it would
get the program and was working to set it up. That's when treated
communities suffered a large increase in violence relative to those that

fell above the threshold and remained untreated (as illustrated in the bottom left panel). During the subsequent period when the development program was actually implemented, there was no difference in incidents between eligible and noneligible villages.

Why attack development projects only before implementation? One possibility is that insurgents were trying to demonstrate strength, as would plausibly explain any number of other attacks by Philippine rebels on government targets.[80] But that's inconsistent with the timing: casualties were mostly inflicted early in the aid program's life, *before* a signature project was there to be destroyed or the funds were even disbursed.

Another possibility is that insurgent groups aimed to sabotage state-sponsored projects out of fear that their successful implementation would shift popular support in the government's favor, undermining their own influence. That's consistent with a number of features of the attacks. First, the timing: during that social preparation period municipalities decided whether to participate, and the government determined which municipalities to drop. Indeed, the largest increase in violence was suffered by municipalities that ended up *not participating* in the program—so if deterring participation was the intent, it may often have succeeded. Second, violence was unleashed by groups with strong ideological motivations—the communist New People's Army and the Muslim-separatist Moro Islamic Liberation Front—but not by others, notably "lawless elements," armed criminal groups who lack a clear political motivation. Third, the New People's Army made no secret of opposing the KALAHI-CIDSS program—they issued several statements denouncing it as "counterrevolutionary and anti-development."[81]

The very clear evidence that this CDD program sharply increased violence for a short period is open to multiple interpretations. The interpretation consistent with our information-centric model is that successful development projects are perceived as a threat by insurgents (since they undermine civilian support and increase tips to government), so projects—and even plans to build them—risk increasing effective attacks on rebels initiated by the state's security forces. An alternative interpretation is predatory violence, with the aim of extorting some of the project's value—a mechanism we discuss in detail in chapter 8. Note that this result is inconsistent with gratitude or grievance motivations for violence, inasmuch as they would predict that the government's intention to provide services would be welcomed—rather than violently opposed.

Notably, AFP officers whose Area of Responsibility included CDD projects commented on a lack of coordination between this World Bank–sponsored CDD program's implementers and the military forces tasked with securing these areas. One of Joe and his coauthors' recommendations was to encourage the military to proactively provide greater security in CDD project areas in anticipation of greater risk of attacks.

Feeding Insurgencies: Fighting over Food

Food aid is conspicuous—it is bulky, it usually travels long distances in convoys of big trucks to remote villages, and its arrival must be publicized in order to alert intended recipients, who typically must come to the village center to receive it. That high profile makes food aid especially vulnerable. Militants can post checkpoints and extort aid deliveries, extracting bribes in the form of cash or food in return for letting a convoy pass.[82]

Reports abound from numerous conflicts of food aid funding and feeding militants. Linda Polman cataloged these in her 2010 book, *The Crisis Caravan: What's Wrong with Humanitarian Aid?*[83] She documented extortion of aid at rates ranging from 15 percent (in 2002 by warlord-turned-Liberian president Charles Taylor, now jailed for war crimes), to 25 percent (by Sri Lanka's Tamil Tigers after the 2004 tsunami), to 30 percent (by Serb armed forces during the 1998–99 Kosovo War), to one-third (by the Taliban in 2006).[84]

In the Nigeria-Biafra civil war of the late 1960s, rebel leader Odumegwu Ojukwu manipulated Western media to publicize a food shortage, then restricted aid entering areas under his control to that shipped on his planes. He used the transport fees he charged aid agencies to buy arms, which he often shipped in the same planes. The food he skimmed off the top allowed him to feed his army.[85] Polman argues that the same type of manipulation occurred in Ethiopia and Sudan in the 1980s, and again in the Darfur region of Sudan in the 2000s.

Food aid also played a prominent role in the conflict in Somalia, which began in 1991. After repeated raids by warlords, the United States and United Nations sent in troops in 1992 under Operation Restore Hope, specifically to protect aid shipments. Later, eleven thousand jobs sprang up around humanitarian and nation-building efforts; money flowed to the warring factions, fueling the conflict. There were familiar scenes of warlords extracting rents for access to starving communities.[86] In his book on the "disaster relief industry," Alex de Waal writes, "The struggle to control Mogadishu in 1991–2 can be seen in part as a struggle to control the keys to foreign aid. Factional leaders mobilized their troops by promising future reward (through looting and aid), not by tangible political reform or economic welfare."[87] More recently, aid workers in Iraq in 2015 reported that IS soldiers required transit fees for trucks carrying food and medical supplies to pass.[88]

Does systematic data analysis back up this anecdotal evidence of aid causing extortionary violence? And if so, why is food aid different from CERP or CCT, which reduced violence?

Economists Nathan Nunn and Nancy Qian looked at exports of food aid from the United States from 1971 through 2006 and its effects on violence across recipients.[89] As in some of the other studies we've discussed, to disentangle the effects of one variable on another (here, food aid on violence) the researchers needed a source of *exogenous* variation in food aid—that is, variation in food aid related to violence only through its effect on conflict, as opposed to food aid that occurred because of violence or because of some confounding variable, such as poor governance, that resulted in both violence and food aid. (In the Philippine CCT example, randomization ensured that exogeneity.)

Nunn and Qian found an exogenous force: variation in U.S. wheat production. Wheat is the largest component of U.S. food aid, constituting 58 percent of total assistance over the study period.[90] The share of U.S. food aid donated to different countries is politically determined, but the level of overall food aid in any given year is dictated by excess U.S. production. Thus the amount of food aid countries get over time depends on U.S. weather, which year-on-year is independent of local conditions in the receiving country, providing exogenous variation they could use to estimate the effects of aid on violence. (The authors used statistical controls to exclude the possible effect of a recipient country's weather correlating with that of the United States.)[91]

A pronounced effect emerged when the authors distinguished civil wars from interstate wars: U.S. food aid had a large, positive, statistically significant effect on deaths in civil conflict but none on interstate conflict. The distinction we drew in chapter 1 between symmetric and asymmetric conflicts can help us understand this finding. Interstate conflicts, when they persist at all, are symmetric, so that territory behind the front lines is secure. Food aid delivered in that territory should not provoke violence. In contrast, at least some civil wars in that study would have been asymmetric, typified by insecure spaces in which non-state groups (rebels and gangs) use violence to extort and capture resources, including food aid.

Three more important aspects of Nunn and Qian's findings inform our discussion: first, the violence-heightening effect of aid was stronger in small civil conflicts, those with 25–999 combat deaths; second, the effect appeared only in countries with civil conflict in their recent history; and third, while aid had no significant effect on the onset of conflicts, it significantly prolonged their duration. In short, this cross-national study showed that food aid's primary effect on violence was to escalate and stretch out civil conflicts already in progress, especially smaller-scale ones.

These findings are broadly consistent with the anecdotal evidence Linda Polman and others report and with the CDD results from the Philippines. Food aid appears to create resources worth fighting over, resources that are not sufficient to start a new insurgency but are large enough to sustain ongoing small wars just a bit longer. Food aid, in other words, can have pernicious as well as beneficial effects, in the absence of security.

But why didn't the food aid reduce violence? It would, if gratitude or grievance were the main driving force of conflict. After all, it presumably reduced the need for people to fight in order to make ends meet. Yet in an information-centric model only aid that is secure and conditional reduces violence. Aid that shows up whether or not the government controls the territory doesn't change the incentives for civilians to provide tips, so it should not be expected to reduce violence. Indeed, the kind of unconditional food aid that Nunn and Qian study should extend conflicts if it supplies the weaker side in an asymmetric conflict with resources or incentivizes extortionary violence. The anecdotes we've looked at suggest that it does both.

Co-opted Aid

In addition to stealing and extorting aid, insurgents often rebrand it as their own and distribute it, effectively capturing any influence on attitudes the original donor might have intended. Hamas in the Gaza Strip has made a practice of intercepting international aid meant for all Palestinians and distributing it only to supporters.[92] When it started gaining territory in 2014, IS became vigilant about removing markings identifying Western organizations from aid it allowed in. "There is not a problem for us to work," reported a relief worker in Tikrit, Iraq, in December 2014, "the only problem is the labeling of the organizations that send us the aid supplies. We have to have it without labeling for IS to accept it. If they saw these labels, they wouldn't let it in and they give our volunteers trouble and they forbid the distribution of those items to the people."[93]

In February 2015, IS went one step further. Pictures surfaced on social media appearing to show them relabeling boxes from the UN's World Food Programme (WFP) and distributing them.[94] The WFP expressed that it was "extremely concerned about images circulating on social media showing WFP food boxes bearing Islamic State in Syria (ISIS) labels." Apparently these were supplies stolen during IS raids on warehouses in Dayr Hafr, Aleppo province, the previous September. "WFP condemns this manipulation of desperately needed food aid inside Syria," the statement said.[95] This was not an isolated problem according to some reporting.[96]

Beyond food and supplies, services can also be co-opted. In Eli's 2011 book, *Radical, Religious, and Violent: The New Economics of Ter-*

FIGURE 5.3. Aid packages from the UN World Food Programme, apparently rebranded with the insignia of the Islamic State.

rorism, he recounts a story that A. Heather Coyne of the U.S. Institute of Peace told at a 2007 panel discussion on development aid in Afghanistan. Early in the U.S. occupation of Iraq, an army colonel charged with controlling a poor, violence-prone section of Baghdad attempted to build support for a politically moderate local council by initiating a street-cleanup program. The U.S. Army would pay $10 to anyone who showed up one morning to help clean up the streets— a quick, simple way to provide a basic service, create jobs, and perhaps turn them away from anti-American clerics such as Muqtada al-Sadr.

Coyne described what happened next:

> The project had actually been running pretty smoothly for a while and he had the idea of going out and talking to the people who had been participating, to get their feedback. It turned out that they were just so enthusiastic about the program. They said: "We love this program. We are so happy about it. We have money in our pockets. We can care for our families. It shows concern for the communities. We are so grateful for this program.
>
> *"And we're so grateful to Muqtada al-Sadr for doing this program."*
>
> The Colonel did a double take, and said: "No, no. This is the army program, and the district local council. We're doing the program."
>
> They said: "No. Muqtada al-Sadr is doing the program."
>
> Colonel: "Why do you think that? Why do you think it's Muqtada al-Sadr?"
>
> And they said: "Because Muqtada al-Sadr told us that it was his program."
>
> Sadr agents had been infiltrating the program, going around telling everyone that this was Muqtada al-Sadr showing his concern for the community, and nobody else had told them anything different, so they believed them.
>
> So the Colonel was crushed. All credit for his great idea was going to the Army's arch nemesis.[97]

Aid capture also showed up in Afghanistan. In the fifth wave of the MISTI survey project in Afghanistan, researchers found fairly strong evidence that USAID programming in Taliban-controlled villages *increased* support for the Taliban.[98] Across this and earlier waves of the study, the researchers could see that violence was greater in closer proximity to USAID projects, as Taliban and other armed groups targeted beneficiary villages.[99] The authors concluded:

> This set of findings shows that stabilization interventions can have perverse, Taliban-supporting effects when they are implemented

in areas where the Taliban has control, as opposed to areas that are contested or under government control. In areas under Taliban control they are likely to take credit for allowing projects to take place, and use violence to ensure that interventions do not lead to increased government control of the area.[100]

To summarize, two common elements are typically present when aid fails to suppress violence.[101] The first, and most intuitive, is simply a lack of secure control of areas in which the program is operating, which invites leakage and violence. A 2005 *Washington Post* article cataloging difficult and often botched U.S. construction projects in Afghanistan recounted a typical case of corruption experienced by Shelter for Life, a Wisconsin-based relief organization that was building fifty-two schools and clinics across the country.[102] The organization had nearly completed a schoolhouse in rural Kandahar when a local commander took a shine to it and decided it would make a good stable for his horses. William Billingsley, the project director, told the *Post*, "They just basically came in and took over." It took Shelter for Life weeks, with the help of the U.S. military, to persuade the commander to vacate.

Beyond theft, relabeling is another worrisome implication of insecure projects. The information-centric model implies that rebels will not only oppose government services but also provide services themselves (Proposition 6). Better than destroying an aid program is to co-opt it. By claiming credit for aid they not only prevent aid from shifting civilian attitudes toward favoring government but also can even shift those attitudes in their own favor.

The most disturbing aspect of insecure projects is of course that they attract violence.

The second common element of failed aid programs is subtler, involving the role of incentives for civilians. In the case of food aid, the lack of a violence-reducing effect is consistent with aid being unconditional, thus not creating incentives for information-sharing.

From the perspective of our theories, these elements are not surprising. Recall that the information-centric model recommends that projects be secure and conditional. From a broader policy perspective they raise further questions.

WHY DIDN'T BIG AID REDUCE VIOLENCE IN AFGHANISTAN AND IRAQ?

A vast amount of development spending goes to large infrastructure projects, such as the example of the water treatment plants we launched this chapter with. What does all this tell us about why some water purification plants successfully delivered water and changed attitudes, some did not, and none reduced violence, the question that launched this chapter? We see five main reasons large-scale aid projects failed to achieve their desired effects.

First, the mechanism linking development spending to violence is not what funders initially assumed. Big projects sought to give potential insurgents something else to do, and they may have succeeded in displacing a few, but the insurgency probably had sufficient recruits anyway. In asymmetric conflicts, it's not labor supply (but rather information flow) that constrains rebels from inflicting violence—an idea we have touched upon repeatedly and will examine at length in chapter 8.

Second, inadequate security in Fallujah made the project a viable target for attack and extortion. Broadly speaking, aid projects can be a source of funding for the same insurgents the development aid is supposed to suppress. In Afghanistan the Taliban were able to gain resources by taxing logistics flows,[103] in Africa rebels routinely stole food aid,[104] and in several places emergency relief funds allowed violent groups to spend more on conflict because their constituents' basic needs were being met by outsiders.[105] There is little systematic evidence on how pervasive such problems are, but their existence across many conflicts suggests that aid can enable violence when projects give local fighters new opportunities to support their military budgets.

A third reason, which we've touched on already, is that very large projects are less likely to have been chosen in consultation with the local population. That might be why the local government in Nasiriyah did not build the capacity to conduct adequate maintenance, causing the plant to run at low capacity. The local Shia-dominated government, though in a well-controlled region, was also unlikely to want to advertise to its constituents a project in which it shared credit with the U.S. government.

A fourth reason is that large projects cannot really be conditional. Most of the value of a major road or massive water treatment plant serving dozens of communities will accrue to the population regardless of who controls any given village. Such projects do little to alter incentives.

A fifth reason is that large-scale projects attract corruption. There are unfortunately too many examples of how that happens. We'll present just a few.

The final report from the Special Inspector General for Iraq Reconstruction (SIGIR) published in 2013 tells how Anham, LLC, a contractor that ran warehouses and distribution facilities, overcharged for supplies: $900 for a control switch valued at $7.05 and $80 for a pipe worth $1.41. Nearly 40 percent of the company's charges were deemed questionable by the inspector general.[106] Between 2004 and 2007, U.S. Army major John L. Cockerham received over $9 million in kickbacks for contracts in Iraq and Kuwait, crimes for which he was sentenced to seventeen years in prison.[107] And there was little accountability. Local ministries spent billions of dollars from the Development Fund of Iraq with missing or nonexistent documentation.[108]

Corruption is exacerbated by insecurity, which undermines oversight and enables extortion. In Afghanistan in 2009, the Department of Defense contracted local companies to transport supplies from an airfield north of Kabul to troops across the country. Ostensibly, the Host Nation Trucking contracts would be a win-win, both outsourcing a dangerous part of U.S. operations and providing a boost to the local economy. At $2.16 billion, the deal was equivalent to 10 percent of the nation's gross domestic product.[109] However, to ensure safe passage, local contractors paid bribes to local politicians. And the security firms they hired for protection were essentially armed gangs led by warlords. A 2010 congressional report titled "Warlord, Inc." stated, "Providing 'protection' services for the US supply chain empowers these warlords with money, legitimacy, and a *raison d'etre* for their private armies."[110] Worst of all, these groups had relationships with the Taliban and colluded: *attacks were organized to justify expenditures.* Ultimately this created a situation in which, according to then secretary of state Hillary Clinton, "one of the major sources of funding for the Taliban is the protection money."[111] The Department of Defense was, in effect, funding the enemy.

Clearly corruption can negate the violence-reducing influence of aid. First, because it damages trust in the strength and legitimacy of the government and its allies, making local populations less likely to side with them and share information on insurgents. Second, because opportunities for extortion bring with them their own violence. In their firefights along the U.S. supply line, the groups contracted for security frequently killed and wounded civilians. A 2009 assessment by General Stanley McChrystal said that as a result Afghanis perceived that U.S. forces were "complicit" in "widespread corruption and abuse of power."[112]

While infrastructure (such as water treatment, roads, and electricity) is a priority for development, effective delivery of large projects seems to require a secure, stable, and relatively functional local government that can enable contracting with sufficient oversight to control corruption. Those conditions existed for the most part in the Kurdish region of Erbil where the water treatment plant was built with only a modest delay, but that effort was far from the contested regions of Iraq that actually needed stabilization.

CONCLUSION: WHAT WORKS?

The empirical evidence we've reviewed on aid projects in Iraq, Afghanistan, the Philippines, and other conflict areas indicates that not all development aid is violence reducing. There are plenty of examples like the CDD program in the Philippines, or the food aid in developing countries, where aid delivery *increases* violence.

What *does* seem to work consistently is programs that are modest (less than $50,000 per project in Iraq), secure, in the sense of being conducted where there is some local military (or perhaps police) presence, informed by local preferences and expertise, and conditional on cooperation of the local population with security forces.[113] We find the empirical evidence on modest, secure, and informed projects (Propositions 2, 2A, and 2B) pretty convincing. The results are consilient across a number of studies in different contexts. While the evidence on conditionality (2C) is indirect—mostly derived from the underlying theory and anecdotes we collected when we asked implementers what they thought was driving the results—we find little evidence against an information-centric view of how aid affects conflict. In contrast, the evidence weighs against an important role for aid in displacing insurgents into aid-supported jobs, at least in asymmetric conflicts where an insurgency needs very few cadres. And the evidence is at best neutral on grievance and gratitude mechanisms.

Others may quite reasonably be more guarded in their assessment of the evidence on development projects and violence presented so far. As we proceed through the chapters we believe that the reader will find evidence for the five propositions piling up in a convincing way. The quantitative tests are almost all single-country studies, albeit ones with what we think have credible causal identification. So far, we hope the reader will agree that the empirics are more consistent with the information-centric model than they are with alternatives and that the information-centric approach might help us understand findings from other conflicts.

The Humanitarian Dilemma

At this point we think that the evidence is strong enough to discuss a dilemma that the information-centric model implies for nongovernmental organizations (NGOs) delivering development assistance. Even if their objective is not stabilization (i.e., violence reduction) but improving human welfare, aid that increases violence may harm recipients more than it helps. On the other hand, though modest and informed are characteristics of aid programs an NGO can deliver, secure and conditional are not.

Oxfam, one of the world's foremost humanitarian organizations, offers a road map to aid provision that recognizes these trade-offs.[114] Writing in 1997 in the wake of the Rwandan and Bosnian crises, Oxfam's director, David Bryer, and Edmund Cairns approached this question using the standards of international humanitarian law (IHL)—which have evolved over centuries and were codified by the Geneva Conventions—and refugee law, which is also the product of a series of conventions by the UN and other organizations. According to Oxfam's argument, individuals have rights to both food and safety, all under the umbrella of the guiding principle to "safeguard human life." "Charity" is removed from the equation and replaced by the donor's obligation to both provide relief and judge how best to maximize the welfare it provides. "A real woman in a real conflict needs food as well as some means to stop combatants shelling her," the authors say. "If the combatants are taking some of the food aid, and perhaps even selling it to buy guns, there comes a time when the humanitarian agencies who provide that food aid must ask themselves whether it is doing more harm than good."[115]

Recognizing that aid cannot be neutral in these settings and negotiating the trade-off between help and harm are difficult and frustrating propositions for private aid organizations. Yet, as Bryer and Cairns point out, governments often depend on NGOs such as Oxfam to fill a "policy vacuum"—by dealing with difficult, remote populations as de facto ambassadors.

We have no general solution to this dilemma, but our analysis can contribute by circumscribing its scope. In a *symmetric* conflict, food aid or water treatment distributed in an uncontested space is unlikely to be captured by violence or extorted (though it may be co-opted). While aid in a symmetric conflict may not be totally neutral, it is unlikely to sway the balance significantly enough to make the NGO a target. In contrast, in an *asymmetric* conflict—in which tips make insurgents vulnerable—both sides are extremely sensitive to who delivers services to civilians, creating a dilemma for aid workers and putting recipients, and aid workers, at risk.

To summarize, in asymmetric conflicts more aid is not necessarily better. Subtle differences in implementation can lead to large differences in violence—and likely to large differences in the well-being of civilians in general. Since aid resources are scarce and many places require assistance, wasting those resources on poorly designed projects is a terrible shame. The community of donor agencies and implementers working in conflict zones owes those they are trying to help, and the brave aid workers who put themselves at risk, much more analysis of what works, where, and why. The starting point for that analysis is more systematic collection and maintenance of data on what was spent where. Without that relatively small investment in data, empirical analysis of billions spent on development assistance conflict zones will remain a quixotic task.

Referring back to the milestones we described in chapter 1, we've laid out a theory (chapter 3) and now examined two types of evidence. Chapter 4 examined evidence for Proposition 1, that making it safer for civilians to share information with government forces by expanding cellular communications would reduce violence. In this chapter we tested implications for development assistance (Propositions 2, 3, and 6). We saw that modest, secure, and informed projects generally helped reduce conflict locally. They did so, it seems, because their benefits are targeted and conditional and therefore incentivize citizens to share information. Development assistance projects that lacked those characteristics often failed to reduce violence. In asymmetric conflict settings, they even increased it. With those results in hand, the next chapter is going to look much more closely at the role of military suppression and see how it complements the effect of those small-scale aid projects.

6

THE ROLE OF SUPPRESSION

- -

In November–December 2004 two U.S. Marine Corps Regimental Combat Teams fought the Second Battle of Fallujah (Operation Phantom Fury), reinforced by U.S. Army mechanized infantry and heavy armor battalions, Iraqi Security Forces, and supporting elements. After twelve days of intense urban combat with insurgents, the approximately 13,500-strong assault force successfully cleared and secured Fallujah, a large town of about 275,000 located forty miles west of Baghdad. After the battle, six maneuver battalions—infantry and armor units with 600–800 Marines or soldiers each—remained to hold the area. These forces held violence down to approximately 100 attacks per month in January–February 2005. But by June 2005 insurgent attacks had again increased by 50 percent, and would rise to a peak of 387 attacks in December 2006, more than 10 attacks daily, against the five maneuver battalions then remaining in the district. Then something remarkable happened. Over the following year, U.S. forces managed to reduce insurgent violence to fewer than 50 attacks per month, while shrinking force size to only four battalions.

How did four battalions manage to bring violence down more than 85 percent in a twelve-month period when a larger force could not previously provide similar levels of security? Part of the answer surely lies in the massive political changes commonly termed the "Anbar Awakening." Between early 2006 and mid-2007, tribal leaders across Iraq realigned their militias *against* al Qaeda and began cooperating with U.S. and (sometimes) Iraqi forces in suppressing insurgent activity. The reasons for the "Awakening" are debated to this day, but what is clear is that in different places at different times the local politics of the insurgency shifted dramatically. In the context of our model the key reason would be a significant shift in civilians' attitudes about who should control the territory.[1] Civilians became less tolerant of insurgent violence and more willing to share information with Coalition and Iraqi forces. This rapid shift in community attitudes suddenly enabled a successful counterinsurgency effort.

The fact that similar levels of suppressive effort can lead to such different levels of violence raises the question of what effect troops have on insurgent violence. When do government security actions spark revolt, or smother it, and how do they interact with other policy choices? What background conditions matter the most? Following on the previous chapter, we will start by looking at the relationship between troop strength, aid spending, and insurgent violence. We will then turn to a more thorough examination of the relationship between local attitudes and violence reduction.

AID SPENDING AND SECURITY: THE AFGHAN CASE

In the previous chapter we discussed conditions under which small aid projects could be violence reducing. One of those was adequate security. Intuitively we know that in order to implement development projects well (in the sense of providing the intended service at a reasonable cost) you need to be able to visit the site repeatedly: at the planning stage to make sure the project is actually what the village wants (e.g., the current well really isn't drawing, so the village needs a new one) and again during and after implementation to make sure the project is carried out properly and with high quality. What happens when the site is too dangerous to visit? Let's consider as an example: Commander's Emergency Response Program (CERP) spending in Laghman province, Afghanistan.

In 2010 the Special Inspector General for Afghanistan Reconstruction (SIGAR) audited CERP projects in the province.[2] The inspectors chose Laghman because it showed the highest CERP spending in eastern Afghanistan. Laghman may have warranted high spending for a few reasons. First, although this small province of lush valleys and high mountain passes had a pro-American governor and a relatively secure capital, its remote areas still served as strongholds for the Taliban— and CERP money was intended to be used as a "nonlethal weapon,"[3] spreading goodwill among citizens so that they would turn against local insurgents.[4] Second, the province was underdeveloped even by Afghanistan's standards. Laghman's adult literacy rate was 26 percent to the nation's 32, and the infant mortality rate was 190 per 1,000 live births to the nation's 84.[5] Third, since Laghman contains the trade route between Kabul and Jalalabad (and on to Pakistan), repairing its roads was critical to the economy. Those roads were in dire need of repair: a 2002 *New York Times* report on Afghanistan's "diabolical roads ... with potholes large enough to topple even the largest trucks" quoted a man whose job was to ferry goods between Laghman and Kabul: "If we could have roads that are even 100 times worse than America's, we would be the happiest of men."[6]

Repairing roads is expensive, and CERP spending reflected this. The SIGAR audit covered 69 projects conducted over the previous two years at a cost of $53.3 million; of those, 11 road-construction projects accounted for 84 percent of total spending.[7] All had been performed by Afghan contractors and managed by U.S. field commanders, primarily in the local Provincial Reconstruction Team (PRT).

The SIGAR's findings were grim: "$2 million was obligated (4 percent of the projects we selected) for 19 projects that had generally successful outcomes; however, about $49.2 million was obligated (92 percent of the projects we selected) for 27 projects that are at risk or have resulted in questionable outcomes."[8]

Those are discouraging numbers—all the more so because insecurity prevented SIGAR from *assessing* all projects. Of the 69 projects selected, SIGAR was able to assess the outcome of only 46. Why were 23 projects missing from the analysis? Five were in too early a stage for evaluation and three had been terminated before completion, but the other 15 could not be evaluated "due to security concerns or remoteness of the site."[9] Reading the short write-ups for these projects—dams, school improvements, and boundary walls costing over $1.4 million—two sentences crop up again and again: "We did not attempt to inspect the project site due to security concerns" and "The project file contained minimal evidence of work performed and no evidence of quality assurance reviews conducted"—which probably suggests a site too dangerous for the PRT to visit.

Now consider another ratio: of the 46 projects that SIGAR *did* assess, inspectors could visit only 36—again, largely because of security concerns. To audit the remaining 10, the auditors depended solely on the PRT's records. The report described one of these projects, which spent $5.3 million to improve a 25-kilometer stretch of road: "we traveled briefly along the road but were unable to inspect the road due to security concerns." The PRT's records report that "a section of the road is beginning to deteriorate; several places are easily disturbed by digging the heel of a foot into the road surface." If the service the father in the courtyard wants most from his government is a passable road, then the troops had better provide at least enough security to allow construction.[10]

The SIGAR report captures the irony of the situation. It cites the army field manual on counterinsurgency as suggesting that "CERP projects should help promote stability in insecure areas" before stating that auditors did not attempt to assess projects on that criterion in part because they were unable to visit dangerous areas.[11] In other words, some of the highest-value projects were sited in areas where lack of security could prevent their effective completion—and hence be of lower value to local civilians. In fact, we may never know for sure whether some projects were completed; if local contractors can't securely operate there, neither can the inspectors charged with monitoring them.

Lack of security has been a key factor in the failure of many development projects in Afghanistan; Laghman's roads are one example, while school construction presents a longer-running tragedy. A rush beginning in 2002 to build or refurbish 1,000 schools and clinics before the September 2004 presidential elections produced only 100 completed projects.[12] In October 2004 Patrick Fine, who was serving as the third head of USAID's Afghanistan program in a year, wrote a scathing internal memo that was later leaked to the *Washington Post*. He wrote that the reasons for project failure—lack of competition in awarding contracts, poor contractor performance, minimal monitoring and quality assurance—were exacerbated by "deteriorating security conditions in a majority of areas where work is being done."[13] Eventually there would be many success stories in school construction in Afghanistan—there are far more children, particularly girls, attending school today than in 2001. However, in 2015 a team of investigative journalists acquired GPS locations of all the schools funded by USAID since 2002. They spot-checked 50 locations across seven battle-torn provinces and found that *at least 10 percent of the schools* "no longer exist, are not operating, or were never built in the first place."[14]

In certain cases, U.S. reconstruction spending in Afghanistan perpetuated the violence it sought to end. Contractors, who were often warlords themselves, colluded with insurgents to extort money from the development effort.[15] Karolina Oloffson of Integrity Watch Afghanistan—an Afghan NGO that works to increase transparency, integrity, and accountability in government programs—described the complex mix of benevolent and malign actors engaged in reconstruction spending in Afghanistan in evocative terms: "It has all messed up into one big soup."[16]

Missing schools and clinics are often not only a humanitarian failure. They constitute a counterinsurgency failure as well, if the absence of security in areas of great risk makes it likely that service delivery will fail to win support of civilians. If so, perhaps *adding* security will increase the potential of service delivery to change attitudes, and thus reduce violence. This logic is captured by our information-centric model as a *complementarity* and forms the basis of Proposition 3 in chapter 3, which stated that the more security government forces can give to service providers, the more effective services will be in reducing violence. In this chapter we will define the concept, discuss the complexities of measuring its effects in real conflict environments, and then explore quantitative evidence of the complementary relationships that the presence of force has with other variables within our model.

SUPPRESSION + SERVICES, OR SUPPRESSION × SERVICES?

Will the effects of security and the provision of public services be the sum of their parts or something more? Economists speak of the difference using the terms "additively separable" and "complementary." If X and Y are additively separable inputs then an additional unit of X will have the same effect on output no matter how many units of Y there are. If X and Y are complementary inputs, then a unit of X will have a greater effect on output if there are more units of Y in place. (If the reader remembers high school calculus, the distinction is between the cross partial derivative of output with respect to X and Y being zero or positive.)

One example of complementarity is between information technology and education. While computers and the Internet allow almost all workers to be more efficient in doing their jobs than they once were, the gains are larger for skilled workers than they are for unskilled. For instance, engineers or scientists can use a computer-assisted design program, or a word processor, to complete a task much faster than they did a generation ago, making them more productive (increasing demand for an hour of their work and driving up their wages). A less educated worker, like a barber, is generally not complemented by information technology in his work. So he is about as productive as he would have been about a generation ago (and as a result earns about the same income).

Examples abound. Eggs are worth more to you in the presence of frying pans, and vice versa. The same is true of basketballs and hoops or soccer balls and goals. Fried chicken has a complementary relationship with mashed potatoes and gravy because you'll enjoy more of the two together than of either one alone.[17]

Security and services complement each other in the information-centric model we sketched in chapter 3. According to that model the services that government provides citizens (which we can call *g* for "public goods" and which corresponds to one of the arrows from government to the civilian population in figure 3.2) and government suppression of rebels (or *mitigation, m*) should be complements. Government services will be of more value in a secure environment where projects can be completed successfully—as the roads example illustrates—and where people are unafraid to move about and use them.

Conversely, security will be easier to provide if civilians provide tips that enable precisely targeted operations against insurgents, which is more likely if valuable government services are provided to them. One way to think about it is this: tips provided by civilians are of more value to government if it has sufficient force strength to act on them. In the setting we described in chapter 3, knowing the location of the planned ambush is of more value to government forces if they have a squad available to capture the insurgents. So tips complement suppression. Because government services increase tips, as we argued in the previous chapter, those services complement suppression as well, making a fixed amount of suppressive force, a battalion, say, more effective.[18] Referring to the question we began this chapter with, one possible reason that it took fewer forces to control Fallujah in 2007 and 2008 could be that during the later period service provision was an explicit part of the strategy, alongside the use of force.[19]

In shorthand, the violence-reducing power is not simply $g + m$ but closer to $g \times m$. This is because the model assumes *diminishing returns*, as is common in economics. The idea is that successive units of some input are of declining value (per unit). For instance, the second scoop of ice cream gives less pleasure (per scoop) than the first. Going from zero to one teacher in the school has a greater effect on education than going from one to two teachers; or, going from no daily patrols to one has a greater effect on security than does going from one to two (a negative second derivative, from that high school calculus course). An implication of complementarity in the presence of diminishing returns is that if security and service provision are both reasonably affordable, they are most effectively provided together: for instance, rather than incurring the expense of adding another battalion to go from two to three patrols of a neighborhood per day, it may be more effective to spend those funds on a complementary (first) development project.

In the previous chapter we saw demonstrations of insecure aid programs not only failing but being attacked and captured by insurgents. We can think of that as the inefficiency of g without m. Here we are arguing that m without g is also inefficient: that would be a battalion constantly ambushed and surprised by insurgents for lack of tips from the civilian population. Perhaps for that reason, even some of the most suppression-heavy counterinsurgencies in history made some efforts to provide g.[20]

To understand the substantive intuition for why g complements m, think of residents of three villages in Colombia.[21] In the first, a father is converted to supporting the government by a program that provides welfare payments and school vouchers. He may want to help the government take control of his village, but that is difficult because the only guns he sees in the streets are in the hands of FARC guerrillas. A tip is unlikely, because he can't imagine what the government forces would do with it.

In the second village the government spends the same amount on troops, rather than on welfare and schools, so an elderly woman sees government forces moving in, somewhat replacing the FARC. She could give them the location of the guerrillas' forest hideout, but why would she take that risk? What has the government ever done for her? At least the FARC has kept a degree of law and order in this village, which Bogotá seems to have forgotten about.

Now imagine a third village, where the government incurs the same costs as in the first two but splits the budget between welfare payments *and* troops. Parents in that village see both services and the troops as necessary to act on tips and will favor that government with much higher tips flow than the first or the second. That's the logic of Proposition 3.

SUPPRESSION + ATTITUDES, OR SUPPRESSION × ATTITUDES?

Attitudes toward government and suppression are also complements, though that can sometimes be masked when we look at data. The reason for complementarity is this: when attitudes shift, say, toward government, the probability of a tip increases, which in turn increases the effectiveness of suppression (i.e., troops) since they are much more likely to catch insurgents with a tip than without one.[22] That effect alone should lead the government to increase troop strength when attitudes shift in its favor.

At the same time, if attitudes shift toward government, insurgents will respond by reducing violence. Why? Because the increased probability of tips reduces the level of violence that the public will tolerate, so insurgents' efforts will more likely be wasted—and get their operatives captured or killed.

So a shift in attitudes toward government reduces violence for two reasons: the increased propensity of civilians to tip both increases suppression at a given level of insurgent violence and decreases insurgent violence at a given level of suppression. In the new equilibrium, violence will be lower, perhaps much lower, as a result of the shift in attitudes toward government. That complementarity between attitudes and suppression is an implication of the model (just as Proposition 3 is, though we did not list it as a proposition in chapter 3 because we lack data to test it).

The underlying reason for this complementarity is worth thinking through. Suppression and attitudes are complements for the same reason that suppression and services are complements, because information makes suppression so much more effective and efficient. With tips and enough forces the government can almost always win the village, but without one or the other the government's chances are much worse. Importantly, the expectations of such complementarities are particular to the information-centric approach; they are not an implication of alternative models of asymmetric wars: grievance, gratitude, or labor market for insurgents, the mechanisms we listed in chapter 5.

Returning to a shift in attitudes toward government, as in our motivating discussion of Fallujah, in the new equilibrium the level of suppression *could be higher or lower* than it was with the old attitudes. The reason is that with insurgents choosing less violence, all that suppression may not be necessary.

For a reader who remembers some economics, this logic is analogous to the ambiguous effect on price of a simultaneous reduction in both supply and demand. (A reader who skipped economics might *not* find this next figure a complement to the text.) Figure 6.1 shows the best-response functions of government and insurgents, with suppression (m) on the horizontal axis and insurgent violence (v) on the vertical. A best-response function is just the mathematical expression of the behavior we described in explaining equilibrium in chapter 3: make your best choice, given what the other party is doing. The best response in choosing violence, v, for rebels to each level of suppression by the government, m, is the curve labeled v^*. Note that this curve is downward sloping in m, which simply means that if government chooses more suppression, rebels will optimally choose less violence (as they are more likely to get caught). The optimal choice of suppression for government, m^*, is upward sloping in v because government is increasingly sensitive to violence. When we plot best-response functions in two-player interactions the equilibrium is the point where they cross, that is, the point at which both sides are doing the best they can given the other side's choice, and no further adjustment of choices is necessary.

The point labeled A in the figure shows equilibrium levels of violence and suppression when local attitudes favor the rebels. If attitudes shift against the rebels, then both curves shift down to lower levels of violence—the rebels because now the population will tolerate less violence before informing and the government because they will get more information at a given level of violence—with their new intersection represented by point B. Note that the effect of a change in attitudes on m in equilibrium is ambiguous; suppression has become more effective (the shift of the curve m^* to the right) but also less necessary (the shift along the curve to the left).[23]

That scenario of shifting attitudes is very attractive to counterinsurgents (who typically have the flexibility to increase troop strength in reaction to a change in attitudes). The reverse scenario (from B to A in the figure) would be very attractive to insurgents: if attitudes shift in their favor they will optimally increase their use of violence, and, though government will optimally increase suppression at any given

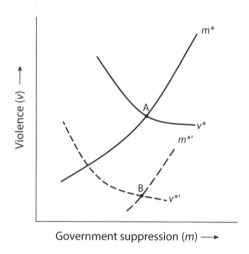

FIGURE 6.1. Suppression and insurgent violence when attitudes shift toward government.

level of violence, the reduced effectiveness of suppression means the net effect of the attitude change on suppression is ambiguous. So increased violence due to a shift in attitudes toward insurgents may go largely unchecked by government forces.

Both scenarios are a challenge for an empirical study of conflict, since the strategic reaction of insurgents and government makes tracing the underlying cause of a change in equilibrium violence difficult. Fortunately, the ways that military force is used in practice make it possible to see what happens net of that strategic reaction.[24]

HOW IS FORCE APPLIED IN THE REAL WORLD?

If we are going to study the effects of suppression, it is important to understand how it moves in the real world. You may have a perception that military commanders move units from one place to another seamlessly—in old movies generals stand over a map of Europe moving miniature tanks and infantry divisions back and forth along a front. If the movement of troops perfectly follows strategic decisions, then researchers will have a hard time sorting out the effect of suppression alone or in combination with other programs, as forces shift in equilibrium in response to changes in attitudes and other conditions. In other words, if suppression follows services closely enough, the two will serve as proxies for each other and researchers will be unable to disentangle their effects.

Say you're going to build a water treatment plant in a volatile area. You are likely to send ground troops to protect it. If violence declines, is that because you are successfully winning tips with service provision or successfully suppressing rebellion with those added security forces? There are many ways in which m follows g (to protect the lives of those building the plant, say, or to protect the population from the plant being used as barracks for insurgents) or that m and g have some other reason to be in the same neighborhood at the same time (an area ravaged by insurgents will be a magnet to both suppression and relief efforts). And if you can't sort one from the other, there's no chance of estimating how they work in concert.

Examples from Iraq support the notion that suppression follows services—in particular services provided by the U.S. military as aid. A prominent case is the rebuilding of oil pipelines.

At peak in the 1970s, Iraq produced 3.7 million barrels of oil per day. Production had dropped to 2.6 million before the war began in 2003 and sank below 1.5 million after the war.[25] There were at least 400 attacks on pipelines in 2003–7.[26] With the world's fifth-largest proven oil reserves, Iraq promised to be capable of funding its own social programs once the oil infrastructure was restored. So the United States prioritized rebuilding it and protecting pipelines from being tapped or destroyed by insurgents.

The pipeline connecting Iraq's rich northern oil fields to a refinery in Baiji 60 miles (95 kilometers) to the west was both critical and vulnerable, since it was mostly above ground.[27] The Coalition budgeted $227 million in fiscal year 2006 to develop a Pipeline Exclusion Zone and assigned a U.S. Army maneuver unit to patrol it.[28] This and other repair and security efforts helped increase Iraq's oil output to 2.1 million barrels per day by July 2007; in its audit, SIGIR (the equivalent of SIGAR for Iraq) considered the Pipeline Exclusion Zone a success.[29] During the Iraq war, the U.S. government spent a total of $1.76 billion, along with innumerable man-hours, to restore and protect the country's oil and gas sector. Yet there was no rigorous evaluation of the effect of those expenditures on oil production—much less on their impact on attitudes, information flows, or violence suppression. Our main point is this: had there been an evaluation, it would have been difficult for researchers to disentangle the effects of fixing the pipelines from the direct effect on violence of the troops assigned to protect the projects.

In the presence of such confounding factors, what is an empiricist to do? It is outright unethical to experimentally vary troop strength just to see how suppression works in combination with the delivery of services. If commanders have any ideas about where forces could do the most good, then randomization would imply depriving some reconstruction teams of protection their leaders deem necessary. Furthermore, a simple head count of troops is not always a perfect representation of force: units vary tremendously in the equipment they bring to bear, the training of their soldiers, and how they are employed. One can easily imagine a commander sending one battalion to each district but sending the most effective and experienced battalion to the district where the water treatment plant is being built. While we will argue that such experience-based allocations are unlikely in practice, those kinds of tactical decisions are usually kept secret, so it is hard to be sure. Altogether, a challenging environment for empirical research.

In short, if the level of force is very responsive to predicted violence, then we cannot separate the effect of force on violence from the effect of violence on force. To be able to sort out the different effects, we need some *stickiness* in force levels—meaning a slowness of response or otherwise erratic application—so at a given point in time t, m is constrained to be larger or smaller than the optimal level government would choose if it could predict violence (v) and respond perfectly.

In fact, however, finding such situations is not hard because the level of m is quite sticky. Troops cannot be redeployed in a fully flexible way in response to short-run fluctuations in violence. Modern military forces in long-term counterinsurgency operations are subject to dozens of constraints unrelated to the day-to-day or even week-to-week progress of conflict. And knowing which units will perform well is an almost impossible task. Let's consider the qualitative evidence for these claims, before getting into an analysis that assumes force allocations are not perfectly adaptive to local conditions.[30]

Moving large mechanized battalions around Iraq required weeks of planning by the entire command staff. The unit had to simultaneously set up security at the new site and maintain security at the old, which was tricky because it entailed spreading combat power across two locations and temporarily degrading their ability to conduct offensive operations. The unit had to move all supplies to the new location—fuel, ammunition, repair parts, food—under tight security. They had to take down and reassemble the entire communications infrastructure, including antennas, radios, computers, and cables; if the whole battalion was moving, this could take a week and a half. The medical staff had to establish new procedures for the destination base, including landing zones for helicopters and evacuation routes, with the goal of being able to transport injured soldiers to the main base within sixty minutes—the crucial "golden hour" during which lives are saved or lost.

All this was just for a partial or temporary move. Establishing a new base for an entire battalion required more effort and attention to a larger set of considerations. The location had to be accessible by supply lines for ammunition, fuel, food, and water. Engineering support needed to establish a safe perimeter around the base with sandbags, concrete barriers, and HESCO bastions (collapsible wire mesh barriers filled with earth, sand, or gravel). Contractors had to build kitchen and sanitation systems. Troops needed to conduct patrols and get to know the area, which again drained combat power from offensive operations in their prior location. Transferring a heavy, mechanized unit with M1 tanks and Bradleys was slower, more involved, and more prone to fall under attack than was a light infantry or an airborne unit—especially if the move was over more than ten miles. Long moves required air lifts, which needed to be arranged in advance and were subject to weather conditions and terrain (including the location of landing strips), not to mention competing requests for these scarce assets from other units.

Finally, relationships with local partners had to be considered. Over time, a unit builds personal relationships with indigenous military and/or police forces, as well as influential local figures, such as tribal leaders, imams, and political officials. These relationships had to be created or transferred, which was usually a protracted process. Bringing along local enablers such as interpreters and translators could also be difficult, as their safety in one location versus another had to be achieved.

For a publication on how the citizens respond to harm (which we will discuss in chapter 7), Jake and his coauthor needed to find out how different *types* of brigade combat teams were sent to patrol an area—infantry units with few heavy vehicles versus mechanized ones that had tanks and other armored fighting vehicles. They asked Douglas Ollivant, who, as Chief of Plans for Multinational Division-Baghdad from October 2006 to December 2007, was the lead Coalition force planner for the development and implementation of the Baghdad Security Plan, in coordination with Iraqi Security Forces. Ollivant told them that there was no deliberate effort to match more mechanized units to more violent areas.[31] Instead, he described myriad other considerations commanders must take into account when moving forces around: troop rotation schedules, an organizational interest in maintaining unit cohesion (and developing local knowledge), staffing, logistics constraints, and even factors as far afield as the timing of when units can leave U.S. shores.

Ollivant also said that the planners didn't have access to information on the quality or expertise of troops, thus alleviating our concerns from a methodological perspective (in Iraq, at least) that the most expert troops might be charged with providing security for the most important aid projects. That view was subsequently confirmed in many further conversations with planners in Afghanistan and the United States. Commanders at the battalion level have some ability to assign their most capable subordinates at the company and platoon levels to certain missions and operational responsibilities within their area of operations. Which battalion is assigned where, when, and for how long, however, is determined by a vast set of considerations beyond anticipated battlefield performance.[32]

In short, it was just not feasible to add *m* to a district in response to short-term fluctuations in violence (or at least the cost of doing so was too high to justify outside of a handful of critical places). Military planners do not enjoy full flexibility, so force levels in long-running asymmetric conflicts are not immediately responsive to threat levels.[33] There will always be delays, frictions, and compromises. This is surely a source of frustration for commanders. After setting up a base in Afghanistan, if the neighboring district started to heat up, it would be to their advantage to immediately shift troops over. But unfortunately they couldn't.

In this case, the strategist's loss is the researcher's gain. Constraints in deployment generate variation in how much suppression is applied, which interacts with the variation in how the other programs are applied, be they a particular type of aid or a new strategy. Researchers can exploit those different types of variation to cut through the data and examine how suppression works in combination with other factors.

QUANTITATIVE EVIDENCE THAT AID SHOULD BE MODEST AND SECURE

On 10 January 2007, President George W. Bush announced reinforcement of the U.S. presence in Iraq, together with a new commander and a new doctrine. Roughly thirty thousand soldiers were added to the forces in Iraq. Now famous, the "surge" provided an influx of troop numbers in each of many local conflicts, allowing us to check if the extra m the troops brought complemented existing small, community-based development projects under the CERP program discussed in the previous chapter.

When we consulted the data we saw that, compared to an estimated violence-reducing effect of CERP that was statistically zero in the initial period, the post-2007 coefficient represented *a dramatic improvement* in program effectiveness.[34] In theory, there are two potential explanations for that sudden increase in program effectiveness, both flowing from propositions of the information-centric model. The first is that the violence-reducing effect of service provision will be enhanced when services are those that the community prefers (Proposition 2A). Under "surge" tactics of dismounted patrols circulating among civilians, CERP would have been better informed about community needs, increasing the violence-reducing utility of the projects. The other explanation is that suppression and projects are complements (Proposition 3) and that additional troops in Iraq during this period provided better suppression.

We conducted a further test with fine-grained data to measure how suppression heightened the violence-reducing effect of small-scale aid. To measure force levels we used data created by then Stanford PhD student Carrie Lee Lindsay, who had coded press reports to compile a data set identifying the number of maneuver battalions present in a district for each month from February 2004 through December 2008.[35] As a measure of violent events we again used SIGACT data.[36]

We found that on the whole, small-scale spending and force levels complemented each other, as predicted by Proposition 3. Figure 6.2 illustrates evidence of this complementarity. It plots the estimated violence-reducing effects per dollar of spending of three kinds of projects—small CERP, large CERP, and USAID's Community Stabilization Program (CSP—which also funded small-scale local projects)—each according to the number of maneuver battalions present.

As we saw in the previous chapter, CERP spending was violence reducing on average (as measured on the vertical axis) and more so for small than large projects. That finding is replicated for spending on the CSP program as well, which was done in small projects administered in consultation with local forces.

Figure 6.2 illustrates that the size of the violence-reducing effect increases with troop strength, which is measured by the count of maneuver battalions on the horizontal axis. With a higher concentration of security forces, project spending had a more pacifying effect: for every additional maneuver battalion present in a district, the violence-reducing effect of small CERP projects increased by approximately 80 percent. In the context of Iraq in 2007, an additional dollar per person in small-scale CERP spending for a median-sized district (roughly 171,000 people) would lead to roughly 4.5 fewer attacks over a six-month period if there was one maneuver battalion present, but 8.6 fewer if there were three battalions. While these numbers seem exact, there's a fair amount of uncertainty around them (the vertical interval between the dashed lines shows the range of effects that are

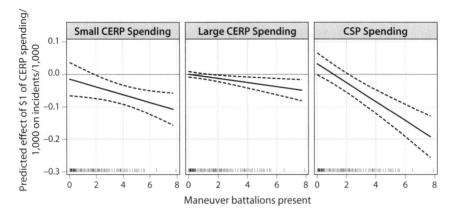

FIGURE 6.2. Marginal effect of different kinds of aid spending on violence depending on force levels.

Incident data from declassified data from Multi-National Force–Iraq SIGACT-III database. Spending from Iraq Reconstruction Management System data. Force levels from Carrie Lee, "Battalion Dataset Codebook" (working paper, Stanford University, 2011), Order of Battle Data. Dotted lines represent the 95 percent confidence interval. Rugs at the bottom of each panel show the density of observations at different Coalition force levels.

consistent with the data). What the exercise highlights is not the exact returns; rather it shows that modest amounts of spending on services and development projects can act as a force-multiplier. Or, likewise, the presence of forces complements development spending.

Does Proposition 3 hold in other conflicts? Research by Renard Sexton suggests that it did in Afghanistan.[37] Like us, Sexton looked at CERP spending. For data on conflict incidents, he combined military records on more than 46,000 security incidents that were reported by the International NGO Safety Organization (INSO) in Afghanistan from May 2008 through December 2010. For data on suppression, he used the positions of ISAF Forward Operating Bases (FOBs) and larger military installations. Finally, for the element that would allow him causal identification, Sexton used what he calls "the chaos of the CERP procurement process" according to which the arrival of CERP funds was plausibly random. To strengthen this approach, he compared districts only to themselves, over time.[38]

Among Sexton's findings was that civilian aid reduced insurgent violence only when implemented in districts where the United States had military bases. It *increased* violence in other districts.[39] The effects varied by the type of violence. For bombings, $100,000 of aid spent in a week resulted in an increase of 1.1 incidents in a district without a base but did not increase them in a district with a base. For live-fire attacks against pro-government forces, that same $100,000 increased these incidents by 0.6 in a district without a base and *decreased* them by 0.4 in a district with a base.[40]

Interestingly, Sexton found that while aid in districts without bases increased insurgent attacks against government, it reduced another type of violence, "non-insurgent political violence," for example, between citizens in land disputes. Why would ISAF aid ease conflict *among citizens* in areas the Taliban controlled? Sexton interprets this as the Taliban attempting to counteract government intervention (in the form of CERP aid) by providing governance, for example, dispute resolution and law enforcement, which in turn reduced violence among citizens. This is an effect that we might expect to see in contexts where the insurgency enjoys a degree of legitimacy among the public and is able to deliver some services, but not in Iraq in 2003–9. Sexton found that aid in districts with bases made this type of noninsurgent political violence increase, perhaps because it gave actors more to fight over.

Returning to insurgent violence, Sexton's findings are consistent with our own, and with Proposition 3: security provided by a military base allowed CERP projects to reduce violence in Afghanistan, while CERP actually increased violence in insecure districts. That complementarity of security and service provision echoes what we found during the 2007 surge in Iraq, where the presence of troops enhanced the violence-reducing effects of CERP projects. The data from both Iraq and Afghanistan indicate that suppressing rebellion with troops in the presence of government services is like skilled labor in the presence of the Internet—far more powerful in combination with its complement than without.

TESTING THE SURGE

Can complementarity explain the puzzle we began this chapter with, how four battalions managed to largely pacify Fallujah where fifteen had failed?

As is becoming clear, when researchers try to establish causal pathways between different variables in the study of conflict, we hit major obstacles around suppression. We must depend on the haphazard application of programs (the inconsistent assignment of mechanized troops in Iraq, the vagaries of CERP spending in Afghanistan) and on advanced statistical methods to ferret out causal relationships. When it comes to the other complementarities our model posits—between force and community attitudes, for example—the best approach may be to lean more on theory and qualitative evidence: compare the different possibilities, make predictions about each, and gather as much evidence as possible that will prove or disprove them. This is what Jake and coauthors Stephen Biddle and Jeff Friedman did in a 2012 article titled "Testing the Surge: Why Did Violence Decline in Iraq in 2007?"[41] They used two main sources of evidence: a database of 193,264 SIGACTs from February 2004 through December 2008 and 70 structured interviews with Coalition officers who had fought in the 2006–8 campaign and observed its conduct firsthand. They supplemented these sources with data from Iraq Body Count (IBC), a nonprofit organization that tracked civilian casualties.

This publication differs from the others we've discussed so far, not only in methodology but also in the approach it takes to the question of complementarities. We have been following two threads, aid and attitudes, and watching how they behave once intertwined with another, suppressive force. Now we will look at the larger tapestry and ask how the different threads contributed to the entire cloth. That requires taking a step back.

As we said, the surge in 2007 deployed a 30,000-soldier reinforcement of troop numbers in Iraq. It also entailed a shift in doctrine. Before the surge, the U.S. military operated from large, fortified bases and conducted patrols with convoys of armored vehicles, largely depending on Iraqi security forces to protect citizens. With the increase in troops, the new commander of Multi-National Force-Iraq (MNF-I), General David Petraeus, initiated a practice of *population-centric counterinsurgency*—that is, operating out of smaller, dispersed bases, conducting patrols on foot, and using U.S. forces to provide security for threatened Iraqi civilians.

The surge corresponded with the reduction in violence we cited in opening this chapter. Monthly civilian fatalities fell from more than 2,800 in May 2007 to under 1,000 in December, then to a monthly average of around 500 over the years 2008 to 2011.[42] That's about one-sixth of the rate for the latter half of 2006. U.S. military fatalities declined from 131 in May 2007 to 25 in December, then to a monthly average of around 12, from 2008 through 2011.[43]

The surge was one of the most discussed military events in recent memory. The reasons behind its success were hotly debated in the 2008 presidential race, and the doctrine that underlay it made its way into counterinsurgency manuals.[44] In popular and scholarly discourse, a few theories emerged attempting to explain why the surge had worked. Primarily, the disagreement centered on whether the reduction in violence was due to suppression itself or to a Sunni uprising that coincided with the surge, termed the "Anbar Awakening."

These competing accounts emerged quickly—each was in print before the surge had ended—but there was little effort to test their relative merits rigorously. Explaining the reasons for reduced violence matters, as the answer will inform how the United States and our allies can best conduct asymmetric conflicts—which, as we saw in chapter 1, is a generational challenge. Jake and his coauthors looked at the competing hypotheses and conducted a process of *elaboration*, listing the theory's observable implications and asking if the qualitative and quantitative evidence would support or reject them.

Surge

Let's start with the "surge thesis"—the idea that the troop surge alone caused the reduction in violence. This view was popular with hawks in Washington. In a *Wall Street Journal* op-ed published exactly a year after Bush announced the surge, Senators John McCain and Joe Lieberman said, "In Congress, opposition to the surge from antiwar members was swift and severe. . . . In fact, they could not have been more wrong." The coauthors went so far as to construct a counterfactual, what the world would look like absent the policy: "And had we heeded their calls for retreat, Iraq today would be a country in chaos: a failed state in the heart of the Middle East, overrun by al Qaeda and Iran."[45] A range of scholars and military writers backed up this conjecture.[46]

If the surge-only thesis were correct, Jake, Steve, and Jeff observed, then one of two components or a combination of both would have been sufficient to cause the reduction in violence. The first component was troop numbers: 30,000 troops were necessary to do what Coalition forces didn't do before, which was to secure and hold critical sections of western and central Iraq that they had cleared previously but had fallen back under insurgent influence. The second component was the shift in doctrine: it took Petraeus's theaterwide movement of U.S. forces out of bases and onto the streets to reduce violence.

Real-world facts refute the surge thesis. The surge entailed only a marginal, temporary increase in troop density: about 30,000 U.S. troops to a pre-surge Coalition strength of about 155,000 foreign and 323,000 Iraqi soldiers. This amounted to less than a 15 percent overall increase, perhaps 20 percent in U.S. strength.[47] Half of the increase was in Iraqi forces who could not have fully adopted the new methods in the time frame in question. To believe that a reinforcement of this magnitude was decisive, you must accept that previous troop density lay just below some critical threshold that happened to be within 20 percent of the pre-surge value: possible, but quite a stretch. According to the evidence, the surge alone, without other shifts, would have improved security temporarily but would not have broken the insurgency. The rebels would have returned after the reinforcements went home, just as they had after previous suppression efforts.

Awakening

If it wasn't the surge alone that caused such a reduction in violence, could it have been the Anbar Awakening alone? Over 2006 and 2007, leaders of a number of Sunni tribes formerly allied with AQI became weary of that group's extremely violent methods, their criminal activities, and their dependence on smuggling to fund their operations. In one district after another, tribal leaders changed sides, realigning with the government. Their militias accepted U.S. payments of $300 per fighter per month to become "Sons of Iraq" (SOI) and promise a cease-fire. The idea that the Anbar Awakening was primarily responsible for the reduction in violence is implicit in a broad series of articles. Austin Long wrote, "Fully embracing a tribal strategy for internal security in Anbar has been successful to date and expansion of this strategy over the rest of Iraq could provide real short-term security gains in at least some areas," before warning of a possible backfire in the medium term.[48] Soldier-turned-scholar Daniel R. Green argued that a synchronized effort "along security, political, and development lines along with a robust tribal effort" reduced violence but "was insufficient to defeat the insurgency by itself absent the population's decision to turn against the insurgents."[49] And *New Yorker* staff writer Jon Lee Anderson warned "it is unclear whether the gains can be expanded upon—or even sustained—with fewer troops, but further increases alone will not win the war."[50]

But if the reduction in violence was primarily due to the Awakening, then why hadn't previous attempts by Sunni tribal groups to turn against AQI caught hold in 2004–6? There had been at least four such failed attempts; the story of the final one, which Jake and his coauthors constructed from their interviews and secondary sources, is instructive. Seventeen tribal elders mostly from the Fahad tribe organized the "Anbar People's Council"—its leaders and many of its members insurgents from a prominent Sunni guerrilla faction called the 1920s Brigade. On 28 November 2005, they decided to break with AQI and support the Coalition, directing tribesmen to join the police for local security duty. Revenge was swift: in January 2006, al Qaeda bombed a police station during an Anbar Council recruitment drive, killing 70. By late January, AQI had killed almost half the founding elders. Although initially resilient in the face of this violence, the Anbar People's Council could not hold out indefinitely, and by the end of the month it had disbanded.[51]

The failed realignment of the Anbar People's Council was notable for its similarity to the later, successful Anbar Awakening movement: it had a wide popular base (much broader than that of the tribe that eventually catalyzed the Awakening), it included a substantial number of disaffected insurgents, and its leaders and foot soldiers accepted significant personal risk to combat AQI. Yet, like the other attempts before it, the Anbar People's Council was unable to defend itself from counterattack; it shut down within weeks. Pre-surge, the Coalition accepted recruits from Sunni tribes but was not in a position to protect them from attack—not only for lack of troops but because the pre-surge doctrine called for insulating U.S. forces in large bases and mounted patrols. This made it difficult for tribesmen to communicate with U.S. troops without being spotted and difficult for troops to be present to stop AQI operatives from infiltrating tribal groups or killing tribesmen or their families. According to this evidence, the Anbar Awakening would probably not have spread fast or far enough without the surge, and sectarian violence would likely have continued for a long time to come.

Synergy

In the judgment of Jake and his coauthors, a "surge-Awakening synergy" thesis was the strongest explanation for the success of the surge. This theory stated that while both the surge and the Awakening were *insufficient* on their own to bring violence down to the level seen in 2008–11, they were both *necessary*. There was a political desire among Sunni tribesmen to realign loyalties from AQI to the government, but it remained latent until sufficient suppression capacity arrived to protect them from the counterattack by their former allies. U.S. reinforcements and the shift in doctrine under General Petraeus provided this protection. Once the Awakening caught on, it radically weakened the enemy, not only because it took most of the Sunni insurgency off the battlefield as opponents but also because it provided the United States with crucial information on remaining holdouts, and especially on AQI. With U.S. troops more interspersed in the community, there were far more chances to receive and act on this information. This created a positive feedback loop—a complementarity between information and suppression, if you will.[52]

But how can you prove it?

The timing with which the Anbar Awakening spread offered a quantitative test. In the autumn of 2006, Sheikh Sattar and his Albu Risha tribe worked out an arrangement to assist U.S. forces under Colonel

Sean MacFarland in exchange for physical protection against coun-terattack. Gradually, different leaders announced that their tribesmen would stand as Sons of Iraq—the announcements coming both before and after the surge began in early 2007.

From their interviews, Jake and his coauthors were able to deter-mine the timing of SOI stand-up in 38 areas of operations (AOs), as well as the boundaries of each AO (which interviewees drew for them on maps). They compared the stand-up dates with the time span of the surge and to microdata on local violence. You can see a visualization of this process in figure 6.3. The graphs show the monthly count of com-bat incidents for each AO from January 2005 through December 2009, while the dashed vertical lines show the date a local SOI unit stood up.

At first glance these data look quite confusing. Each of the 38 AOs shows a slightly different pattern. This is where some simple statistical analysis is useful; it helps isolate the deeper trends masked by all the local detail. In this case, Jake and his coauthors did something very simple: they asked if violence declined faster after SOIs stood up than before.

The answer to that question is positive: in 24 of the 38 AOs, vio-lence trended downward more sharply after SOI stand-up than before. The difference was large: across all 38 areas, before SOI stand-up the average decline in violence was 2.5 percentage points per month; af-terward it declines by 5.8—more than twice as fast. Furthermore, SOI stand-up had bigger effects in more important areas of operations: in areas where SOIs stood up prior to August 2007 (when fighting was generally heaviest), the decline in violence was faster after stand-up in 78 percent of cases. Violence had been increasing in each of these areas, but it reversed and plummeted after SOI stand-up, falling by more than 8 percentage points per month on average.[53]

In short, change was happening very slowly under the surge alone but turned on a dime when the tribes changed sides. When the re-search team considered what a violence profile would look like under the competing theories, 24 out of the 38 AOs considered (63 percent) showed results strongly consistent with the synergy thesis, eleven showed ambiguous results, and only three supported the surge-alone theory unambiguously.

In terms of our model, v (violence) dropped fastest when there was a change in n (attitudes) with sufficient m (suppression) present. Once Anbar was secure, the increase in troop strength was in fact not necessary in the new equilibrium, since the shift in attitudes reduced violence in equilibrium, allowing the surge troops to be redeployed elsewhere in Iraq or sent home. That pattern is consistent with our theoretical discussion of suppression-attitude complementarity.

THE DIRECT EFFECT OF SUPPRESSION

In our research we've been forced to assume without testing that suppression by government forces (m) reduces insurgent violence. That seems like a reasonable assumption. Both governments and insurgents certainly behave as if it is true. Reliable direct estimates are rare, though; the use of force is generally correlated with unobserved factors, some of which are generated by the conflict and some that are hard to measure such as civilian attitudes, both of which confound estimating how much forces reduce violence. Without an experiment that involves random deployments (ethically unacceptable), how can we know its independent effects? We know of two cases in the literature where quirks in how coercive force was used to counter insurgency allow causal estimation of their effects on subsequent attacks. Though we have serious concerns about these as military strategies, we'll look at them and discuss the results.

In a working paper, Melissa Dell and Pablo Querubín exploit the fact that the U.S. government used an algorithm to choose targets for certain kinds of air strikes during the Vietnam War.[54] Based on 169 characteristics measured in monthly surveys, many of which were inconsistently measured,[55] villages were given "security ratings," which were rounded to the nearest number on a scale of 1 to 5. Targets were chosen based on that number. Rounding errors in this process and inconsistencies in how the characteristics were coded for each village allowed the researchers to compare villages that were similar in all important respects except that some were just above the cutoff, and therefore more likely to be bombed, to those just below, and therefore less likely to be bombed (a "regression discontinuity" design like

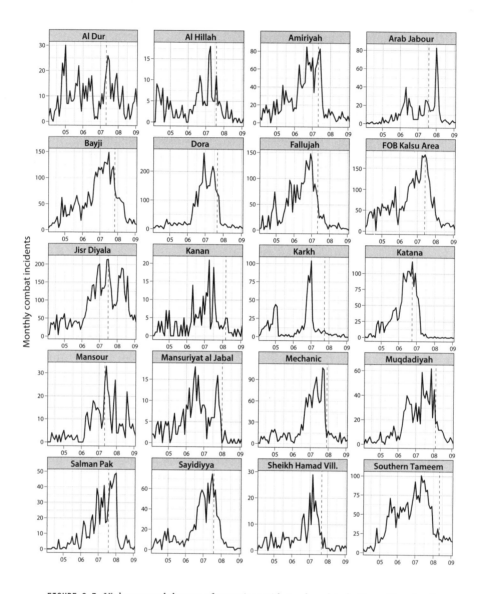

FIGURE 6.3. Violence trends by area of operations with stand-up date for Sons of Iraq (SOI).

Area of operation boundaries and SOI stand-up dates from author interviews. Dashed vertical line shows month of first SOI stand-up. SIGACT counts based on declassified data from Multi-National Force–Iraq.

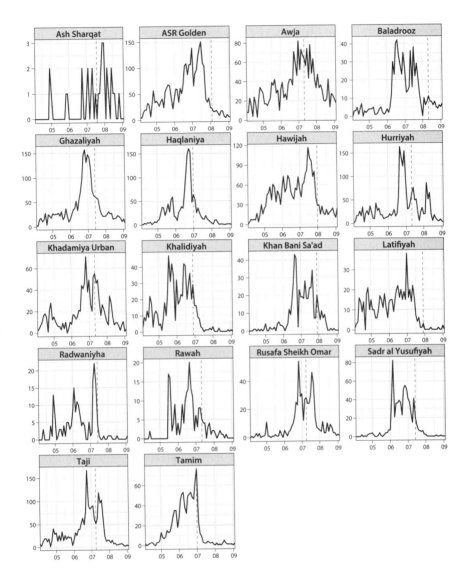

the one Joe and coauthors used for the Philippine CDD results in the previous chapter).[56]

The authors' estimates revealed that U.S. air strikes significantly *increased* insurgent activity: a village that went from zero strikes to the sample average experienced a 24 percentage-point increase in the probability of having an active local Viet Cong unit and a 9 percentage-point increase in the probability of an insurgent attack.[57] Bombing also had other adverse effects, such as damaging the local governments' ability to collect taxes and reducing civic engagement among citizens.

Dell and Querubín also contrast the army's air-strike approach to the Marines' community-based methods that attempted to win hearts and minds (e.g., the Combined Action Program [CAP], which we discussed in chapter 5), which, they say, plausibly reduced insurgent attacks, improved attitudes toward the U.S. and South Vietnamese governments, and led to a number of development benefits that surfaced over time.

In a separate study, Jason Lyall discovered another setting where attacks were just about randomly assigned. From 2000 to 2005 Russian troops in Chechnya followed a policy of "harassment and interdiction," which explicitly called for shelling villages at random times and at arbitrary levels, unrelated to insurgent activity.[58] Additional unplanned shelling seemed to result from Russian troops' drunkenness and indiscipline. Lyall's results clashed with Dell and Querubín's from Vietnam—and with the preponderance of the literature. He found that experiencing an indiscriminate attack was associated with a more than 50 percent *decrease* in the rate of insurgent attacks in a village—which amounts to a 24.2 percent reduction relative to the average.[59] Furthermore, the correlation between the destructiveness of the random shelling and subsequent insurgent violence from that village was either negative or statistically insignificant, depending on the exact statistical model.[60] While it's not clear how civilians subject to these attacks interpreted them, what is clear is that in this case objectively indiscriminate violence by the government reduced local insurgent activity.

Both of these studies are of asymmetric conflicts, and while the settings differ in important ways, each provides evidence that is not obviously consistent with the model. When we look deeper, however, we believe that both are consistent with the arguments about the use of suppressive force in our model. In the Vietnam study, increases in suppressive effort not driven by changes in local attitudes led to increases in insurgent violence. This is a puzzling result insofar as insurgents' best response (i.e., their optimal reaction to a given level of government suppression, in figure 6.1) is to produce less violence when government increases suppression. We suspect that what is going on in this setting is that the bombing shifted local attitudes against the government (perhaps because large-scale strikes with gravity bombs put civilians at risk), as suggested by Dell and Querubín's analysis of the survey data. That shift would lead to more insurgent violence, as we will discuss in the next chapter.

In the Chechen case, indiscriminate artillery shelling was met by decreased violence, which would be consistent with the model if the shelling did not significantly shift local attitudes and if the insurgents took the shelling as an indicator that there would be greater suppression in that area in the future. In Chechnya there were no survey data to check whether the random-fire missions failed to shift attitudes, so it is ultimately unclear whether we should interpret that study as confirmatory.

These results suggest that targeted application of force can be violence reducing or increasing, depending on how it is applied and perhaps on how it is interpreted by civilians. Note that the application of suppressive force we described when sketching the model in chapter 3 was typically discriminate. It was applied in the context of a military that controls territory by patrolling, providing services, and gaining information that informs suppressive efforts—the Marines' approach in Vietnam and U.S. doctrine since the 2007 surge in Iraq. The examples from the U.S. Air Force in Vietnam and Russian artillery in Chechnya are much less informed or discriminate, to say the least. A possible explanation for the Vietnam results is that air strikes were perceived as indiscriminate and turned local attitudes against government forces, giving the insurgent Viet Cong more latitude to attack without fear of tips. The Chechen results are harder to reconcile. We therefore return to them in the next chapter when we report evidence on how civilian attitudes and behavior respond to civilian casualties.

SUMMING THE PARTS

The model of asymmetric conflict as a three-player game that we laid out in chapter 3 predicts that suppression will have strong complementary relationships, both with aid that augments government services and with civilian attitudes toward government. The result of applying suppressive force in concert with aid, or with an improvement in attitudes, will be greater than the sum of the parts, in the sense that the violence-reducing effects will be greater.

The nature of suppression efforts—the costs in terms of lives and the secrecy it requires—makes it very hard to measure its direct effects. And the direct estimates we have come from settings that are not obviously applicable to the type of military strategy we're thinking of, which applies force in a discriminate manner, subject to rules of engagement. However, when the complementarity between suppression and aid in violence reduction is estimated in Iraq and Afghanistan, the results validate Proposition 3 of the information-centric model. This is good news for governments with limited resources looking to create stability, as it allows an option of combining coercive and benign tools—including those provided with international support.

The complementarity the model predicts between attitudes toward government and suppression does not lend itself to quantitative testing, but it is consistent with the evidence from Iraq. An increase in available "surge" troops, combined with an increased willingness of Sunni tribes to work with Coalition and Iraqi forces, as part of the Sons of Iraq program, indicates a synergy not evident when those elements occurred in isolation. Complementary relationships represent chances for big gains in efficiency: every insurgent who became a Son of Iraq represented far more than one fewer insurgent to fight—he also represented a gain in U.S. intelligence and a reduction in Iraqi Shias' need for protection by violent militias. In both Afghanistan and Iraq, places where suppression worked best to reduce violence were the ones where these complementary factors were present.

We started this book by arguing that asymmetric conflicts have dynamics involving a third party: civilians. This distinguishes them from symmetric, interstate wars that we are used to thinking about. As the 1st Infantry Division pushed the front back across Europe at the end of World War II, the factors that determined its success were additively separable units—troops, tanks, and artillery. Success was measured in territory gained and casualties inflicted. In today's asymmetric conflicts the fronts are harder to define and success harder to measure—and with an imbalance in force come complementarities with information about the identities and location of insurgents. Access to that information is subject to decisions made by civilians. That information is key: the greater the force imbalance at the local level, the more we can expect actions that influence information-sharing to be consequential.

Overall, a clear picture is beginning to emerge, as we promised in chapter 1. In chapter 4 we saw how expanding cellular coverage made it safer for civilians in Iraq to share information with government forces, which in turn led to less violence, and we talked about why that wasn't always the case. In chapter 5 we looked at how certain kinds of development projects seem to help reduce conflict locally, which we attributed to the ability of the projects to make people more willing to share information with government forces. In this chapter we looked at Proposition 3, the complementarity between traditional military efforts (i.e., combat operations and the presence of troops) and those small-scale aid projects. Once again most of the findings align with the theory: aid is more effective when paired with sufficient forces, and additional forces make a bigger difference when they coincide with political shifts. In the next chapter we will look more directly at another broad implication of the information-centric model, probing evidence on how the consequences of combat for civilians shift their attitudes and behavior.

7

HOW CIVILIANS
RESPOND TO HARM

Having been on the other side, I know that if you harmed one innocent civilian in an area, that whole area will become your enemy. For instance, in one village, you accidentally bomb and kill a child, the whole village will become your enemy.

—Victor Corpus, one-time communist rebel who became a general in the Armed Forces of the Philippines

Helmand province, Afghanistan, January 2010

In January 2010 a rumor spread through the villages of Garmsir district, in the famously volatile province of Helmand, Afghanistan: a U.S. Special Forces soldier had stabbed a Koran with a knife during a night raid. Local Afghan men took up makeshift weapons and headed to the District Center of Hazar Joft, home to the American-backed Afghan government.

Carter Malkasian, advisor to the Helmand Provincial Reconstruction Team, was stationed there. In his book *War Comes to Garmsir*, he describes the ensuing riot:

People swarmed around [the local police chief] and stoned him. Struck twice in the head, he bravely stood his ground but to no avail. As the crowd entered the bazaar, Taliban fighters, who had been hiding in the mosque, got on the loudspeakers and called for an uprising. Two climbed on top of the mosque to shout orders.

The crowd pressed to the governor's compound and police station. They lobbed rocks over the three-meter wall but did not try to breach the gate, behind which the police and a handful of Marines crouched ready to fire.[1]

Those eight Marines, members of the 2nd Battalion, 2nd Marines, held their fire as shots rang out and stones and bricks rained down. A backup unit attempted to come to their aid, but a crowd pelted their armored vehicles with stones and bullets. One soldier said later, "My gunner kept yelling he had definite targets, people shooting at us, but he couldn't fire back because there were unarmed people around them."[2] The unit withdrew.

Under the standing rules of engagement (ROE) the Marines were clearly permitted to open fire in order to protect themselves, but they understood that doing so could have a long-term downside. Six months earlier, General Stanley McChrystal had issued a Tactical Directive that called for ISAF troops to dramatically limit the use of lethal force when it placed civilian lives at risk. While the directive did not change the ROE, the language was unambiguous about the value of restraint: "We must avoid the trap of winning tactical victories—but suffering strategic defeats—by causing civilian casualties or excessive damage and thus alienating the people."[3] The directive was controversial among many of the troops and the public—a discussion we introduced with Radha Iyengar's ISAF briefing in chapter 2. McChrystal urged the troops to practice "courageous restraint" in order to protect civilians, which at times meant holding their fire or avoiding the employment of certain types of weapons and munitions—perhaps at personal risk—to avoid alienating civilians and to attain an eventual strategic advantage.

The crowd in Garmsir burned several vehicles and a recently built school. After it had moved on from the District Center the Afghan police regrouped and opened fire on the protesters. When the smoke cleared, three Afghan police had been killed by protesters.[4] Six to eight protesters were also killed (including one who had been armed).[5]

The next day local mullahs led an even larger protest in Mian Poshtay, a town ten miles away. A crowd numbering over a thousand surrounded a much smaller group of U.S. Marines and Afghan National Security Forces. This time, U.S. military leaders were able to take the mullahs aside to negotiate. But still the crowd rushed the troops. Though there were several injuries on both sides, the mullahs were able to calm and disperse the crowds without anyone being killed.[6]

The protests soon petered out. The report of the stabbed Koran turned out to be a rumor planted by the Taliban.

What allowed a provocative rumor to catalyze violent riots? One contributing factor was the strained relationship between the local population and what they perceived to be foreign occupiers. For example, ISAF night raids, while sometimes necessary in order to capture Taliban operatives and confiscate weapons caches, greatly angered local citizens. Pashtun social code, the Pashtunwali, dictates that a man must protect his home from intruders and traditionally forbids that women interact with male strangers. A night raid, however, would often violate the code on both counts since it typically entailed forced entry into a compound without notice. As Malkasian put it, "Raids pushed people toward the Taliban."[7] Taliban operatives were extremely canny in their misinformation campaign; they knew when to execute it and how to play on local attitudes and on reverence for the Koran.

In the end, the Marines successfully avoided the trap. By exercising "courageous restraint" and refusing to be baited by the Taliban into retaliating against the volatile crowd of angry local citizens, they prevented a dangerous situation from escalating to cause even more loss of life, in both Hazar Joft and Mian Poshtay.[8]

As commander of ISAF's Counterinsurgency Advisory Assistance Team (CAAT), Joe frequently visited Helmand at the time. In discussions with forces there he learned that following those protests and the restraint displayed by that unit, the Marines in Garmsir enjoyed one of the highest success rates in theater in locating and defusing IEDs. Senior leadership recognized their battalion for its ability to gain tips from local Afghans, revealing the locations of those deadly bombs.

While many factors combined to drive those IED finds, the leaders of the Marines in Garmsir at the time agreed that having a good relationship with Afghans in their area of operations provided their best protection.

CIVILIAN CASUALTIES, MINDS, AND HEARTS

In this chapter we focus on what happens after unintended deaths, injuries, and loss of property due to hostilities in asymmetric conflicts. (For simplicity we will call these civilian casualties—death and injury—though the same logic will apply to loss of property.)

Why would the Taliban provocation strategy work? Neutral, unarmed noncombatants in Helmand can't possibly know whether those heavily armed Marines in body armor and sunglasses are friend or foe to their particular tribe. Given the long history of animosity between Pashtuns and foreign invaders, most recently the Soviets, foe would be more likely than friend.[9] If the Taliban could goad those Marines into endangering civilians when threatened, they could then claim to have revealed that the Americans disregard Afghan civilian lives. Provocation would then make the fearsome combat capacity of U.S. troops into a liability.

Restraint, on the other hand, undermines that claim, showing that even when threatened, the troops value the safety of Afghan civilians. This problem is familiar in law enforcement. In chasing a car thief speeding down a crowded street, how much risk should police expose bystanders to? In suppressing a race riot, when attacked with rocks or even bullets, police face a trade-off between preserving public order (and defending themselves) and protecting innocent civilians. In Helmand, as in any community where armed representatives of the state strive to maintain order on behalf of an unpopular government, citizens watch and decide on their attitude toward those in uniform.[10]

Attitudes matter, since, as we argued in chapter 3, tips from citizens will decide who ultimately will control the neighborhood, and choosing the side with loose trigger fingers could be a fatal mistake for those civilians.[11] So citizens observe how combatants behave, update their attitudes, and act accordingly—in Garmsir, apparently by sharing information with ISAF on the location of IEDs. In that sense a citizen observing how mindful troops are in preventing civilian casualties is like the father in the courtyard in chapter 3.[12] Indeed, the importance of how citizens interpret combatants' actions shows up in many studies of asymmetric conflicts, from Huw Bennett's brilliant analysis of the Mau Mau revolt in Kenya in the 1950s through more recent books on the wars in Afghanistan and Iraq.[13]

Naturally, citizens' attitudes will also be tempered by politics (coethnicity, sympathy for the goals of one side or the other, etc.), but we believe that their shifts in attitudes and their resulting actions can be measured and understood in terms of our model of conflict as a three-sided game. With that model, we can use data to test whether our interpretation of the anecdotal evidence (such as the Garmsir episode) plays out broadly across conflicts. We can test where and under what conditions it does, and then use our conclusions to inform actions that will reduce violence.[14]

We often distinguish between intended and unintended harm to civilians as a matter of ethical and legal importance. When a rebel group exacts reprisals upon the local population for not paying "protection fees" or for cooperating with government, that harm is intentional as part of the group's strategy, and we would call it extortion, or even terrorism. Similarly, intentional harm of civilians by state forces is properly characterized as extortion or state terrorism (and prosecutable under international law). In contrast, if a rebel group's roadside bomb targets government soldiers but kills civilians instead, those deaths would be unintentional. Both rebels and governments generate unintended harm in their operations; history is full of tragic instances.[15] Our focus here is not on ethical or legal aspects of that harm but on how civilians perceive combatants based on their observation of civilian casualties and how careful combatants are to prevent them.[16]

So what does our model predict specifically about the relationship between civilian casualties and attitudes, violence, and information-sharing? Recall the Filipino father sitting in his courtyard, in chapter 3. He hated that the rebels endangered his family and neighbors by placing IEDs near their homes but remembered that government forces *also* endangered civilians. Thinking through his decision leads to one general proposition about how combatants will behave given our assumptions about how people respond to harm in asymmetric conflicts, and to three more specific ones about how attitudes and support will shift when combatants harm civilians.

Proposition 4: Combatants (even the most vicious), aware that hurting civilians can shift civilian attitudes against them, will endeavor to restrain the harm they cause.

Proposition 4A: Civilians in conflict-affected places should dislike groups causing harm, and those who suffer civilian casualties should express less support for those groups. Harm to civilians provides information about how they will be treated if one side or the other controls the area, and that information is reflected in the attitudes people hold.

Proposition 4B: An increase in support for rebels due to government-caused casualties should allow rebels to increase attacks, while rebel-caused civilian casualties should have the opposite effect. This is because rebels correctly anticipate that after the government hurts noncombatants, civilians will tolerate more rebel violence before deciding to inform; the opposite will happen after rebels hurt civilians.

Proposition 4C: Civilian casualties caused by rebels will lead to a short-term increase in tips to government forces.

When rebels cause more civilian casualties than would be expected given how intense combat is in a given area, they have effectively exceeded what the father and his neighbors will tolerate, and some citizens will decide to inform. Recalling that the citizen's decision cycle is quicker than that of combatants, this response will be a short-term one: once the rebels realize that local attitudes have shifted, they will restrain their violence to prevent further tips.

RESTRAINT AND MITIGATION

Let's begin with Proposition 4. Combatants in asymmetric conflicts often act in ways that are mindful of civilian casualties, urging restraint and attempting to mitigate damage that civilian casualties do to their prospects. Here are three examples, two from insurgent leaders operating in Iraq and another from the experience of U.S. forces in Iraq and Afghanistan.

In 2004, Jordanian extremist Abu Musab al-Zarqawi aligned his Iraq-based insurgent organization with al Qaeda and renamed it al

Qaeda in Iraq (AQI). The group turned from attacking primarily foreign military targets to targeting Iraq's own Shia population. Zarqawi's goal was to provoke sectarian conflict and thereby radicalize Iraq's moderate Sunnis, to draw them into jihad. Those attacks drew a sharp critique from Ayman al-Zawahiri, al Qaeda's second-in-command, who operated out of a hidden location, likely deep in a tribally controlled region of Pakistan. In a July 2005 letter (which, at over six thousand words, is something of a manifesto) Zawahiri wrote, "If we look at the two short-term goals, which are removing the Americans and establishing an Islamic emirate in Iraq, or a caliphate if possible, then we will see that the strongest weapon which the mujahedeen enjoy—after the help and granting of success by God—is popular support from the Muslim masses in Iraq and the surrounding Muslim countries. So, we must maintain this support as best we can, and we should strive to increase it, on the condition that striving for that support does not lead to any concession in the laws of the Sharia."[17] Zawahiri's point was that needlessly killing Shia civilians (along with other brutal tactics such as broadcasting executions of hostages) would deplete civilian support, a precious resource.

A second example follows on the first, a few years later, shortly after Zarqawi was killed in a targeted U.S. precision air strike. AQI had succeeded with one of its goals—sparking sectarian conflict—but in the process had fulfilled Zawahiri's prophecy. The group had suffered a backlash, as its brutal tactics had induced several Sunni tribes to publicly disavow AQI in September 2006, commencing the Anbar "Awakening" that we analyzed in the previous chapter. In a 2009 publication by the Combating Terrorism Center at West Point, Brian Fishman describes this rupture among Iraqi Sunni militants.[18] The leader of the Islamic Army of Iraq said that Muslim blood was the "red line" that should not be crossed: "All things of a Muslim are sacred for his brother-in-faith: his blood, his property, and his honor."[19] In an online video, a speaker with apparent links to another group, the 1920s Revolution Brigades, condemned AQI for "attacks on the very livelihoods of Muslim Sunnis—they planted charges in front of houses, schools, and hospitals, and under electric generators without any consideration for the importance of [these facilities] for the society." He also decried AQI's practice of Al-Tatarrus, a theological justification for killing fellow Muslims in the pursuit of infidel casualties: "They also went too far in the issue of *Al-Tatarrus*, exceeding all limits."[20] Apparently AQI's competitors witnessed the mistakes the group had made and were eager to assure civilians that they would not cross the same lines.

Our third example of combatants' concern with how civilians interpret their actions is of mitigation, that is, their damage control *after* a civilian casualty. The U.S. military, like others, has a history of compensating civilians for unintended harm. It has a few different ways of doing this. Under a 1942 law, foreigners harmed by U.S. troops can claim compensation up to $100,000, though not for losses during active combat.[21] Since the Korean War the military has developed additional methods for its forces to extend payments as a gesture of condolence for combat-related losses (without admitting fault), often called *solatia* payments.

While solatia is not modeled explicitly in our information-centric framework, the logic of it is clear: a costly gesture of condolence or apology should mute the negative effect of a civilian casualty on civilian's attitudes (Proposition 4A) by reinforcing the idea that the harm was in fact accidental. Extending that causal logic, it should mute the increase in insurgent violence (4B) and the decline in tip flow (4C) as well.

The ground rules for solatia are determined anew for every conflict, with very different policies followed in Iraq as opposed to Afghanistan. In Afghanistan there seemed at least initially to be little consensus on the value of these payments. The war began in 2001 and authorized compensation payments to civilians did not start until 2005.[22] The guidelines for payments were similar to those provided by U.S. forces operating in Iraq: up to about $2,300 for a fatality, $470 for a serious injury, and $230 for property damage. However, total disbursements per event were far lower and amounted to less than $400,000 in 2006.[23] As we will see, ISAF may have paid a price in terms of the attitudes of civilians for not using solatia earlier and more consistently.

In Iraq implementation began more quickly and payments were more frequent. The war in Iraq began with the U.S. invasion in March

2003, and compensation payments started in June of that year. They varied in terms of the procedures required, whether they were called "condolence" or "solatia" payments, and where the money came from—the Department of Defense or USAID. The upper bound on compensation was $2,500, and while commanders exercised broad discretion in disbursing the funds, they generally paid $2,500 in the case of a death and less for property damage.[24] In fiscal year 2004 around $5 million was paid out, but that number jumped to $19.7 million in 2005 as a result of increases in both the tempo of operations and the frequency of payments.[25] In 2006, an allowance raised the maximum condolence payments to $10,000 in extraordinary circumstances.[26]

General Petraeus, as commander of Multi-National Force–Iraq in 2007, spoke of the effectiveness of the policy as an instrument of counterinsurgency. "Solatia payments, as they're called, these condolence payments are very much a part of the tradition and culture certainly of Iraq and I think throughout the region," he said. "And the quicker you can do it, the more responsive you can seem to be. And of course the more concerned you are, the more valuable it is, and the more helpful it is to your operation."[27]

To summarize, in Iraq and elsewhere, combatants on both rebel and government sides acknowledge in their statements and deeds that civilian casualties can have consequences beyond the human tragedy, and recognize in many cases a strategic benefit in limiting civilian casualties or mitigating the damage they cause to military campaigns. We turn now to the rest of Proposition 4, on the effects of civilian casualties, for which we have quantitative evidence as well as illustrative anecdotes.

CIVILIAN CASUALTIES AND ATTITUDES: SURVEY EVIDENCE FROM PAKISTAN

Before we ask how exposure to harm affects civilians' actions, we will consider how it affects their attitudes (Proposition 4A).

We begin with evidence from a survey of 6,000 Pakistani citizens that Jake and coauthors Christine Fair and Neil Malhotra conducted in 2009 and analyzed with help from Graeme Blair. Their purpose was to measure citizens' attitudes toward insurgent groups—including al Qaeda, sectarian militias, militants fighting against India in Kashmir, and the Afghan Taliban—but the first hurdle was getting an accurate answer from surveys. Most survey techniques, which underpin the numbers we see quoted in newspapers and magazines, by Gallup or Pew for instance, aren't applicable in this context: they don't give reliable information because when asked questions about sensitive topics, people tend to decline to answer, say they don't know, or claim to have no opinion. When respondents *do* answer sensitive questions, we know from a large body of literature that their responses may well be skewed toward what they believe is acceptable to society or to the surveyor. (A lot can be inferred from the surveyor's appearance, name, or, in the case of phone interviews, accent.)

In conflict zones it gets worse; respondents may think that certain answers will put them or the surveyor in danger. They may be right: our survey teams in Pakistan often came into contact with militants. For some context on the atmosphere in 2009, the year of the survey, the month of March alone saw gunmen fire on the Sri Lankan cricket team in Lahore, a mosque bombing kill as many as seventy in Jamrud, and attackers dressed as policemen kill several students and teachers at a police academy, again in Lahore.

To get accurate answers to sensitive questions, researchers increasingly employ indirect survey methods including *endorsement experiments*, which Jake and his team chose. The underlying idea is that, in such a charged atmosphere with a variety of militant organizations active, people are more likely to answer—and answer truthfully—questions about their like or dislike for a *policy* than for a group. Comparing support for policies endorsed by specific groups to support for the same policy when not endorsed indirectly reveals support for the endorsing *group*. This approach relies on a basic psychological principle: we evaluate things more favorably if they are associated with groups we like.

To implement this idea Jake and his team divided respondents into treatment and control groups. The control group was asked for their opinions on four policies deemed uncontroversial in a preliminary survey. The treatment group was asked the same questions after being told that one of four militant organizations supported one of the policies in question. The researchers randomly shuffled which organization was associated with which policy. Since the only difference between the treatment and control conditions was the stated endorsement by an organization, comparing the average level of approval for a policy between the treatment and control groups yielded an indirect but fairly accurate idea of actual support for that organization.[28]

Jake and coauthors had enumerators conduct the survey face-to-face, using six mixed-gender teams, women surveying women and men surveying men, in keeping with the Pakistani norms.[29] Of the people approached, 71.8 percent agreed to take the survey (which is pretty high) and the endorsement technique succeeded in providing a better response rate to delicate questions within the survey. For example, when asked directly if they thought the actions of al Qaeda were effective, 22 percent of subjects declined to respond; when we asked about a proposal for Frontier Crimes Regulation reform that had been endorsed by al Qaeda, declined responses dropped to 8 percent, and even lower for other militant groups. Arguably, this study constituted the first valid, national measurement of attitudes toward militant groups in Pakistan.

A surprising result of this study was that *poor Pakistanis disliked militants more* than did middle-class citizens. This evidence was fairly conclusive and merits a closer look, which we will give it in chapter 8, when we examine how economic conditions affect support for insurgents.

The natural next question was "Why?" When we broke responses down by area, distaste for militants was strongest among the urban poor: the gap in support between low-income and middle-income respondents was larger in urban than rural areas. This turned out to be consistent with the hypothesis that violence suffered by civilians generates antipathy for insurgent groups among the poor.

To see why, we needed an observation by Christine Fair, coauthor on all the survey-based studies ESOC carried out in Pakistan. Christine has been working in Pakistan since the mid-1990s and knows the country quite well. Her years of fieldwork suggested that the burden of militant violence fell particularly on the urban poor. An IED set off on a city street threatens far more people than one that explodes on a country road. Rural areas are also relatively insulated from the negative *economic* effects of attacks. Few attacks we know of in Pakistan destroyed enough infrastructure to hinder agricultural supply chains.

In contrast, if a terrorist attack depressed commercial activity in an *urban* area (such as a street market) for weeks or months, it was *poor* people selling wares or working in the surrounding area who would be most affected, both by the sense of insecurity and by the loss of income. Middle-class Pakistanis are more likely to receive salaries from firms or the government, so urban terrorism poses less of a threat to their livelihoods. The middle class can also avoid the dangers of shopping for themselves, since most have domestic employees who run such errands. In contrast to the urban poor, the lives of many of the rural poor are dictated by forces less sensitive to terrorist attacks: agricultural production is dictated by seasons, and because people are more spread out, the number who would directly observe the disturbing effects of any given attack is much smaller. So it is the urban poor who are most likely to suffer the effects of violence, through enhanced threat, depressed markets, and visibility.

To recap, in accordance with Christine's observations, the research team found that the gap in support for militants between low-income and middle-income respondents was about twenty times larger in urban areas than rural areas. Moreover, the size of that gap in attitudes correlates with the experience of violence; antipathy to militant groups was nearly three times stronger among the poor living in districts that had experienced violence in the previous year. Given the controls used in the analysis, it is hard to imagine anything other than civilian casualties causing those large effects, which would make this supportive evidence for Proposition 4A.[30]

So the 2009 survey provided strong grounds to think that the reason poor urban Pakistanis disliked militants more than their middle-class countrymen did was that they suffered more from militants' attacks. But we did not have direct causal evidence for that proposition until we experimentally tested how perceptions of violence affect attitudes in 2012. We will discuss that direct evidence in chapter 8.

CIVILIAN CASUALTIES AND ATTITUDES: SURVEY EVIDENCE FROM AFGHANISTAN

More direct evidence that civilian casualties reduce civilian support for the perpetrator (Proposition 4A) comes from another endorsement experiment, this one conducted by Jason Lyall, Graeme Blair, and Kosuke Imai in Afghanistan.[31] The authors asked how damage caused by ISAF affected civilian attitudes differently from that caused by the Taliban. Working in 2011, they surveyed 2,754 male citizens in 204 villages in five Pashtun-dominated provinces of Afghanistan—areas strongly supportive of the Taliban—obtaining a very high response rate (89 percent).

The authors added an important note of complexity. A large literature from social psychology documents that people favor members of their own group, whether group membership is based on nationality, ethnicity, or tribe, or even constructed arbitrarily in laboratory settings.[32] Lyall and his colleagues hypothesized that civilians would be more tolerant of damage at the hands of "in-group" members than "out-group" and assumed that citizens saw the Taliban as their in-group and ISAF as the out-group. They tested for that asymmetric effect.

Before turning to results, there is an interesting wrinkle to this study's data. When surveyors asked these village men whether they had been "victimized" by ISAF or the Taliban, response rates were very high (98–99 percent), but their responses correlated poorly with ISAF-recorded violent incidents. While ISAF recorded that 89 percent of incidents were Taliban inflicted, the survey self-reports spread blame much more evenly between the two combatants. Part of the difference is in definitions: ISAF recorded violent incidents comprehensively but only tracked casualties (death or wounding), whereas the self-reports included damage to property. But the disparity in blame also indicates a broad gray area in perceived responsibility for violent acts. The researchers therefore used the citizens' self-reports as their measure of harm. This allowed them to include property damage in their study and to allow for the possibility that citizens misattributed harm a fair amount of the time.

The authors measured approval and disapproval in terms of "latent" preferences, ranging on a five-point scale from "strongly agree" to "strongly disagree." They then used the endorsement experiment method described in the previous section to measure attitudes.[33] If a person's position on a given issue was neutral, and endorsement by the Taliban was estimated to move it one standard deviation toward approval, then the authors scored that as 1. If Taliban endorsement caused it to move one standard deviation toward disapproval, then that was coded −1.[34] Using that method to set a baseline, the study found that while the population generally disliked both combatants, they disliked ISAF more than they did the Taliban: ISAF endorsement reduced approval of policies by 0.62 standard deviations, while Taliban endorsement reduced approval by only 0.29 (which, assuming that the Taliban *were* the in-group, is consistent with the hypothesis that the in-group suffers less anger from the perception of perpetrating a given level of harm than does the out-group).

The effects of harm were consistent with Proposition 4A, though asymmetric in their magnitude. Respondents who recalled being harmed by ISAF alone showed 0.89 less approval of ISAF, while those who recalled being harmed by the Taliban alone showed only 0.40 less approval of the Taliban. And, while harm by ISAF translated into increased support for the Taliban (by +0.27), it didn't go the other way—harm by the Taliban did not translate into increased support for ISAF. Moreover, respondents who perceived themselves to have been victimized by both ISAF *and* the Taliban were more supportive of the Taliban (by +0.15). Those asymmetries are all consistent with the authors' in-group/out-group hypothesis.

Another interesting aspect of the study is the analysis of solatia payments and analogous compensation by the Taliban. As described earlier, solatia fit in our information-centric approach as a method of influencing attitudes. The same logic that applies to ISAF forces also applies to the Taliban, so it should not surprise us to see them use compensation as well. Lyall and his colleagues showed efforts by the Taliban (as well as by ISAF) to provide payments in order to mitigate the shift in attitudes (in terms of approval) toward the other side caused by civilian casualties, a finding consistent with Propositions 4A and 4B.[35]

These findings are important for U.S. policy. As the authors put it, "Experience with ISAF victimization alone is associated with a positive effect on support for the Taliban. Yet if aid has been provided by ISAF, the result is a large negative effect on Taliban support."[36] The difference was large and statistically significant, and while it is important to bear in mind that it was not increased support for ISAF but, rather, increased *dislike* for the Taliban, the result still makes a strong case for the United States to invest more in mitigation, and more consistently. In this context the United States provided mitigation (one-off solatia payments of 100,000 Afghani or about $2,300) to only 16 percent of self-identified victims in the study, while the Taliban reached out (usually with small monthly pensions, food staples, and symbolic gestures such as speeches at funerals) to 60 percent of theirs.[37] In the Kolenda et al. study cited earlier, the authors make a complementary strategic point:

> We assess with high confidence that civilian harm by US, international, and Afghan forces contributed significantly to the growth of the Taliban, particularly during the crucial periods 2002–04, and 2006–08, and undermined the war effort by straining US-Afghan relations and weakening the legitimacy of the US mission and the Afghan government. We also assess with high confidence that the reforms made by ISAF were successful in reducing civilian harm, while not impeding strategic aims and not undermining force protection. The most important factors in reducing harm were leader emphasis, training, and data collection-analysis-feedback loops. The reforms, however, were too late to reverse the strategic damage.[38]

A nagging question keeps us from putting too much weight on these studies. Did harm affect the attitudes, or did attitudes coincide with some unobserved factor correlated with harm? When surveys rely on retrospective questions, our concern is that memories of harm are more easily recalled if they align with current attitudes, creating a correlation with an unobserved factor—in this case the current belief. The fallibility of memory is well documented: false memories are easily implanted;[39] an interviewer's characteristics can affect responses;[40] recall improves when people return to the original state in which the memory was formed (state-dependent memory);[41] and recall improves when we are in the same mood as when the memory was formed (mood-dependent memory).[42] Importantly, information *confirming* our beliefs is better remembered than information *opposing* beliefs.[43]

That's a problem: we don't know if harm led people to dislike of a group, or if dislike led them to better remember harm previously caused by the other side, or if it made people more likely to attribute (ambiguously caused) harm to the disliked group. It certainly looks like harm sways civilians' hearts away from the perpetrators, especially when you consider that the poor were most ardently anti-insurgent in areas with recent insurgent-caused deaths. Yet there could well be some share of both truth and recall bias in the results. Unless we surveyed the population before and after the harmful event, how can we say for certain? We will give some experimental evidence on this question in chapter 8. We turn now to more concretely measured aspects of Proposition 4: the effects of civilian casualties on combat outcomes (4B) and their effects on tips (4C).

THE EFFECT OF CIVILIAN CASUALTIES ON COMBAT OUTCOMES, IRAQ

While attitudes of civilians are important in their own right, our model implies that the effect of civilian casualties on attitudes has a critical operational implication: the side that turns civilians against it by perpetrating harm will suffer more attacks itself. For government that would mean that the flow of information from civilians will wane (about the location of rebels and of deadly IEDs), emboldening rebels and increasing attacks. For rebels it would imply the opposite: hurting civilians would result in well-informed government raids and disarmed IEDs. So far the evidence indeed indicates that casualties sway attitudes and that solatia mute that effect. We turn now to ESOC research on rebel attacks on U.S.-led Coalition forces in Iraq and how civilian casualties affected those attacks.

Starting in 2008 Jake and Luke Condra decided to conduct what seemed like a fairly straightforward test of Proposition 4B using Iraqi data: Did civilian casualties caused by Coalition forces result in blow-back, in the form of increased attacks by rebels on those troops?[44]

Accessing microdata on civilian casualties proved a challenge. A nonprofit website called Iraq Body Count (IBC) used press coverage to record civilian casualties and coded some attributes of the individual incidents but not with the specificity Jake and Luke required.[45] For instance, IBC often recorded location according to the Baghdad neighborhood where a death had occurred or by listing a nearby landmark. That didn't always allow Jake and Luke to match the location of those events to their district-level data on violence. Also, it was particularly important to obtain data on *who* was responsible for the civilian casualty.

Fortunately IBC was an outstanding partner in seeing the value of the research. Over eighteen months Luke brought in experts on Iraq and worked with them to pinpoint the location of incidents using satellite imagery and maps.[46] Working with IBC personnel, he developed rules for coding more types of information from the press reports into the database. They also disaggregated data from Baghdad morgue reports to identify timing and location of incidents whenever possible. These activities—along with some other improvements—added almost 4,000 incidents to IBC's data (a 23 percent increase). When complete, 87 percent of incidents were successfully coded down to the district level (and made available to researchers and the public).

The data enhancement effort paid off in a clear substantive finding: Coalition-caused casualties led to *increased* insurgent violence against Coalition and Iraqi forces in the short term; insurgent-caused casualties had the opposite effect.[47] The effects were statistically strong, providing evidence for Proposition 4B, though substantively small. A one-standard-deviation increase in the number of civilians killed by insurgents compared to the previous week (approximately 3 fatalities) led to a 2 percent drop in the number of insurgent attacks on troops.

Conversely, a one-standard-deviation increase in the number of civilians killed by Coalition forces (approximately 8 fatalities) predicted a 1 percent increase in insurgent attacks.

Jake and Luke provided two strong arguments for a causal interpretation of those coefficients (i.e., "led to" rather than "predicted"). First, the change in civilian casualties happened *before* that in violent incidents, but the opposite was not true: there was no systematic change in the number of violent combat incidents in the week before civilian casualty events. Second, to a large extent *chance* determined the deaths of bystanders caused by an IED or a stray bullet. By this we mean, for example, that whether a roadside bomb targeting troops harms Iraqi civilians depends on the timing of the cars that happen to be coming in the other direction, a matter of chance: good luck or bad. As described in chapter 2, a random element serves as a kind of strainer for the data, sifting out other omitted variables that might generate the outcome in question.[48]

Analysis using a different statistical method, one that matched weeks with casualties to those without—using their history of combat as a matching criteria—corroborated this result. The substantive idea behind the approach was that combatants in places with a given level of violence and a given set of trends toward one side or the other would have similar unobservable incentives regarding the treatment of civilians. Using this approach Luke and Jake found that each additional civilian killed by Coalition forces predicted approximately 0.16 additional attacks per 100,000 people in the following week. The effect estimated this way was larger than that estimated using the previous method. It implies that for an average district in Iraq (277,000 residents) a Coalition-caused incident resulting in two civilian deaths (the average) would cause roughly 0.9 extra insurgent attacks on Coalition forces in the subsequent week.

Jake and Luke also used this matching method to estimate the effect of insurgency-caused civilian casualties. Though this effect was statistically weaker than in the previous analysis it still yielded a large estimate: an average insurgent-caused incident killed 3.7 civilians, implying that it led to roughly 1.5 fewer insurgent attacks on Coalition forces in an average-sized district.

In short, both methods of examining the evidence yielded support for Proposition 4B.

To see whether the mechanism driving those results was indeed informational, as opposed to grievances or gratitude, they examined three further implications: (1) the effect would be strongest in mixed areas where the populations had a more heterogeneous set of attitudes, so they included more civilians who might be swayed to tip by civilian casualties; (2) the effects should be stronger in urban areas where there were more civilians present to observe insurgents' activities, making it harder for insurgents to wield a credible threat of retribution against informers; and (3) because IEDs and direct-fire ambushes are more easily rendered harmless with operational intelligence, they should be more sensitive to civilian tips than are indirect-fire attacks.

To test the first hypothesis Jake and Luke separated the data by the sectarian mix of the district, coding districts as mixed if no ethnic group had more than 66 percent of the population and otherwise coding the district as Sunni, Shia, or Kurd. The reprisal effect against insurgents was indeed strongest in mixed areas: there, a one-standard-deviation increase in the number of insurgent-caused civilian casualties predicted approximately 0.5 fewer attacks in the next week in mixed districts. This amounted to a 12 percent drop, relative to the average number of attacks.

Next, they looked at the data separately for urban and rural districts.[49] Urban districts indeed drove the results on anti-Coalition reprisals—in fact, the anti-Coalition effect was absent in rural districts.

Finally, they looked at the type of attack: civilian casualties increased direct fire and IED attacks more than they did indirect fire or suicide attacks. This is consistent with civilian harm inducing tips locally. Indirect-fire attacks use weapons such as rockets or mortars that can be fired far from their target, so attackers face less risk of exposure during setup and none during the incident, making them less vulnerable to tips. Suicide attacks are typically very resistant to exposure during setup, so they will be less likely to vary in intensity as the propensity of locals to share information shifts.[50]

Jake and Luke's evidence from Iraq supporting Proposition 4B has an interesting parallel to research we mentioned in the previous chapter by Efraim Benmelech, Claude Berrebi, and Esteban Klor on the effects of house destructions by the Israel Defense Forces on suicide attacks emanating from the Palestinian Authority.[51] During the Second Intifada (2000–2005), Israel Defense Forces (IDF) conducted two different types of home demolition as part of their counterterrorism strategy. In the first type, termed "punitive house demolitions," they destroyed the homes of suspected perpetrators of attacks and others involved in planning attacks or providing assistance. In the second type, "precautionary demolitions," IDF destroyed homes for reasons unrelated to activities of the owners or occupants but instead to meet purely military objectives, usually to create "no-go areas" that would assist IDF in preventing attacks (e.g., a location on high ground threatening a vulnerable settlement or road). Supporters argued the demolitions would deter and prevent attacks, while opponents claimed that they fostered hostile attitudes toward Israel, which in turn provided justification for suicide bombings.

To conduct empirical analysis, Benmelech and coauthors combined data on home demolition assembled from an Israeli NGO with data on suicide attacks compiled from a number of sources.[52] After controlling for economic and demographic conditions, estimates of the number of civilians affected, and other counterterrorism efforts running concurrently (e.g., curfews), the researchers found two effects running in opposite directions: punitive demolitions indeed suppressed attacks, while precautionary demolitions *increased* attacks.

The resulting effects were large. A one-standard-deviation increase in punitive demolitions (about two homes demolished per district-month) caused a 12 percent decrease in the number of suicide terrorists originating from that district—effects that were not only large but also statistically significant. The reduction was immediate, starting within a month of demolition. It dissipated over both space (not affecting neighboring districts) and time (mostly fading away after a month or so). By contrast, demolishing homes in the second type of operation—preemptive—*increased* the number of suicide attacks. A one-standard-deviation increase (about eight homes demolished per district-month) caused a 49 percent increase in the number of suicide terrorists originating from that district.

These results indicate that terrorist attacks are influenced by non-combatants, since the harm was to civilians rather than directly to the attackers (usually deceased) or their organization. The evidence on punitive home destruction shows that anticipated damage to the property of immediate family can deter suicide attacks, a mechanism outside our model, with the opposite prediction. By contrast, the results on preemptive demolitions evoke Proposition 4B, as a failure to mitigate harm to noncombatants (presumably unrelated to the attackers) seems to give local terrorists an operational advantage, allowing them to carry out suicide attacks. The source of that operational advantage is not revealed by the research, though the result is consistent with the predictions of an information-centric model, in which people share less information if they think the security services act unjustly or are not mindful of their interests.[53]

TIPS: EVIDENCE ON MECHANISMS FROM IRAQ

We turn now to direct evidence for the characteristic that distinguishes the information-centric mechanism from other population-centric models: tips. In keeping with what practitioners have long claimed, Proposition 4C states that civilian casualties perpetrated by government forces decrease the flow of tips to government, while those caused by insurgents increase tip flow.

When we conducted our early research on aid, attitudes, and complementarity, we had only suggestive evidence that those effects occurred through information flow, as we lacked data on tips. But that changed. In a 2016 working paper, Jake and coauthor Andrew Shaver provided the missing link—the first direct quantitative evidence that civilian casualties affect the number of tips that citizens give the government.[54]

The breakthrough was enabled by a boon to empirical social science, the U.S. Freedom of Information Act (FOIA). In early 2015, Andrew filed a series of FOIA requests to U.S. Central Command and the Joint Chiefs of Staff to acquire data on tips the Coalition received during the Iraq war. The initial response was that the raw tips data were impossible to locate. However Multi-National Corps units had assembled a number of briefing slides based on that now-lost information, some so detailed as to include tip figures at the province-week level. You can see one such slide in figure 7.1. Andrew ran these graphs through a digital extraction program to recover estimates of the underlying tip counts—roundabout but still fairly accurate. The resulting data were not the volume of calls received (which would not really measure information flow because of the insurgents' efforts to flood the line with fake tips) but instead the number of tips classified by Coalition and Iraqi operators as *valuable*. U.S. Central Command voluntarily helped out, providing a number of supporting documents describing the data. Much of this was classified before Andrew's request and would not have been released otherwise.[55] Andrew's initial success was followed up by the subsequent release of information by the British government regarding tips called in to a line in Basra in southern Iraq, data that were critical to his results on the value of tips to counterinsurgents, which we discussed in chapter 4.

The resulting data set spanned the thirteen provinces in Iraq where over 99 percent of the violent incidents occurred, over a sixty-week period from June 2007 through July 2008. For civilian casualties, Andrew and Jake used IBC data described earlier.

While citizens shared tips in a few different ways, most made calls to an anonymous hotline—either the central one that Coalition forces established in January 2005 (handed over to Iraq's Ministry of Interior in November 2007) or one of several regional ones. During the period of the study, tips flowed in at a good rate: the Coalition received twenty-four useful tips in the median province-week.[56]

As Proposition 4C predicts, civilian casualties perpetrated by Coalition forces in a given week were associated with small but statistically significant *decreases* in the number of tips supplied the following week. Insurgent-caused casualties were associated with corresponding *increases*. Specifically, an additional Coalition-caused death predicted roughly 0.8 fewer tips the following week. An additional insurgent-caused death predicted an increase of about 0.5 tips the following week.[57]

This effect of civilian casualties on tips faded pretty quickly; it was not statistically meaningful more than a week or two after the event.

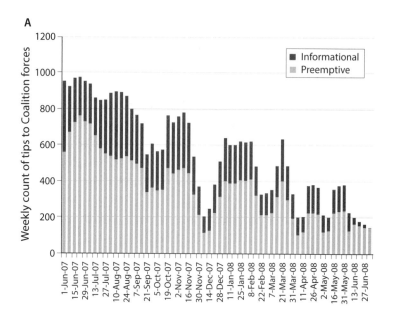

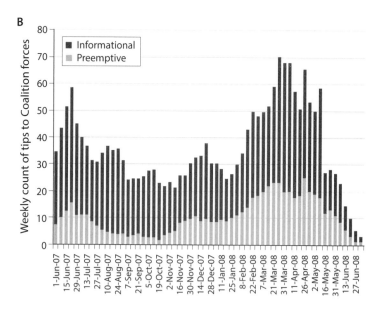

FIGURE 7.1. Total informational and preemptive tips reported for Diyala (A) and Salah-al-Din (B) provinces between June 2007 and July 2008. Source: Multi-National Corps—Iraq. Date (of containing report): 21 July 2008.

Notably, the effect was asymmetric (like the effect on attitudes and the effect on subsequent attacks discussed above): government forces incurred a higher cost for causing casualties than did insurgents, insofar as the drop in tip flows following a single government-caused casualty was roughly 60 percent larger than the increase following a casualty perpetrated by insurgents. Although this difference is modest in statistical significance, it corresponds almost directly to the in-group advantage that Lyall and colleagues observed in Afghanistan. Such consilience, not just in the direction of results but also in their relative magnitudes, is very unusual in conflict research and suggests to us that this asymmetry in response may be a general phenomenon.

The variation in tips due to civilian casualties was large enough to be consequential. In the median week in which insurgents caused civilian casualties, they killed four civilians, predicting two additional tips to Coalition forces. That is a substantial number (roughly 10 percent of the weekly mean); single tips often resulted in raids that led to the capture of both large numbers of weapons and prominent insurgents.

With direct evidence on civilian casualties leading to tips added to the stack of evidence, the scales start to tip. Civilian casualties predict attacks, and the tips as intermediating mechanism are vouched for by evidence that casualties and other forms of harm predict both attitudes and tips. This evidence faces the same limitation as that from other observational studies: it's always possible that some unobserved and uncontrolled-for factor is haunting our inference. Yet the parallel pattern of asymmetry and the fact that predictions are consistent with the model's implications across time, space, and different data sources combine to make what we think is a compelling case for the information-centric model. Moreover, in a setting in which experimental evidence is unlikely and would require grossly unethical initiatives, we would argue that preponderance of observational evidence is a reasonable and feasible approach to validating a model.

That conclusion has implications for restraint and mitigation, which we will return to presently. But first let's look at the Afghan experience with civilian casualties, which provides some reinforcing evidence and some potentially richer interpretations.

THE EFFECT OF CIVILIAN CASUALTIES ON
COMBAT OUTCOMES IN AFGHANISTAN

Courageous restraint was, quite understandably, a controversial topic at ISAF command when Joe took the helm of the Counterinsurgency Advisory Assistance Team (CAAT) in Afghanistan in 2010. By that time, Jake, Joe, and Luke Condra had collaborated with Radha Iyengar of the London School of Economics to look at Afghan data on the effect of civilian casualties and subsequent attacks for the period from January 2009 through March 2010.[58] Again the team used SIGACT reports to measure attacks but this time could link them with civilian casualty data from the ISAF Civilian Casualty Tracking Cell (CCTC). This was the office responsible for reviewing ISAF unit reports and collecting data on civilian casualties—deaths *or* injuries—that occurred at the hands either of ISAF or the Taliban.[59] This data set contained 4,077 civilian casualties from 2,118 incidents, 10 percent of which involved women and children. During this particular stretch of the war, over 86 percent of civilian casualties were perpetrated by insurgents. The relationship between civilian casualties and subsequent insurgent violence in these data is the research Radha presented to General McChrystal and the ISAF leadership in the briefing we described in chapter 2.

The estimated effect of those civilian casualties provides mixed support for Proposition 4B. Civilian casualties attributed to ISAF led to *more* attacks over the following six weeks. This finding was robust to a number of controls, including comparing districts only with others with similar previous trends in violence. These effects are substantive: if one ISAF-caused incident were eliminated (two civilian deaths or injuries on average), then in an average-sized district there would be *six fewer combat incidents* between ISAF and insurgents over the next six weeks. A different statistical method using the same data but a longer time frame found that this effect of ISAF civilian casualties was enduring, peaking sixteen weeks after the event.

But when it came to civilian casualties cause by the insurgents, we found evidence that contradicted 4B: civilian casualties caused by the Taliban *also* seemed to *increase* violence directed against ISAF, though the effect was small. This contradiction is an anomaly in our findings on civilian casualties. One possible explanation is that the attribution of the Taliban as perpetrator by the CCTC (based on ISAF unit reports) was not what local civilians perceived. Another possibility is that events which were recorded in the data as Taliban-caused civilian casualties were not mistakes but intentional retaliation, which if successful would embolden the Taliban by deterring tips. (In this respect the data differ from those we used in Iraq, where we could better separate intentional targeting of civilians from casualties that were the accidental consequences of combat.) We return to retaliation in the next chapter, when we discuss studies of Naxalite violence that have more accurate data.

So what should we make of the fact that half of our findings from Afghanistan are consistent with those from Iraq, though over a longer time frame, and half are not? We will revisit this apparent contradiction later in this chapter, when we discuss the differences between Afghanistan and Iraq. For now, recall that our approach is to assemble results and tell you how they inform the overall picture. In social science results rarely line up perfectly, and so what we look for is what most of the data agree on—the "central tendency" in our jargon.

Important evidence in locating that central tendency comes from Jason Lyall, who has results on Proposition 4B in a working paper on the effects of a solatia-like program in Afghanistan.[60] Recall that Lyall was one of the authors of the study examining the differential effects of ISAF- and Taliban-caused casualties and solatia, discussed above.

The Afghan Civilian Assistance Program II (ACAP II) was implemented from 2011 through 2013 to assist civilians harmed in conflict between ISAF and the Taliban. Characteristics of program implementation enabled Lyall to estimate plausibly causal effects on civilian attitudes and subsequent violence. Unlike solatia, the program provided relief whether the damage was caused by ISAF or by the Taliban—if Taliban-caused damage was in operations due to local ISAF presence. USAID funded the program but ISAF determined which incidents met that criteria. Villages deemed eligible received food aid and shelter construction, amounting to about $300 on average per villager. Within those villages, individuals directly affected by the violence could also receive medical and psychological assistance, livestock, business grants, and so forth, amounting to about $4,000 on average per beneficiary.

What would we expect the effects of this program to be? The information-centric model of chapter 3 predicts that solatia should mute the negative effects of civilian casualties on attitudes and subsequent rebel violence, as we discussed earlier, in line with Propositions 4A and 4B. The model makes no prediction for effects of humanitarian assistance in response to Taliban-initiated violence, though grievance or gratitude arguments would predict that they would sway attitudes toward ISAF and government, and perhaps reduce Taliban violence as well.

In estimating the effects of ACAP II, Lyall had two levels of "as-if" randomization to work with. First, he leveraged the haphazard implementation. Whether or not a village was included depended on the inner workings of ISAF rather than on characteristics of the village itself, Lyall argued, and he performed a number of tests to show this was the case. Bureaucratic delays and implementation challenges led to ISAF actually dispersing funding to only 592 of the 1,061 incidents investigated; nearly all of the other cases went undecided. Second, he took advantage of individual-level variation driven by the fact that only certain people within those "treated" villages receiving the program were injured and thus eligible for the (far more generous) individual-level grants. Shrapnel and stray bullets behave in a plausibly random way, as Luke and Jake argued in their Iraq work. This is not an ironclad research design—the difference in eligibility coincides with a strong secular trend in violence, but that trend seems unlikely to fully account for the differential effects that remain over very small time differences.

Lyall surveyed over 3,000 people in treatment and control villages, using endorsement experiments to measure their level of support for the Taliban, the Afghan government, and the United States.[61] The delivery of individual aid *did not induce* a statistically significant improvement in attitudes toward ISAF. If anything, the ACAP II grants *increased* support for the Taliban, when violence was perpetrated by the Taliban. Recall that our model makes no prediction about how non-solatia assistance should affect attitudes, though a gratitude model would have predicted the opposite. In any case, Lyall read it as evidence of aid capture (as discussed in chapter 5), concluding that citizens in areas controlled by the Taliban actually gave credit to the Taliban for allowing aid to reach them.[62]

Turning to effects on violence (Proposition 4B), comparing villages that received ACAP II to those that were eligible but did not get the program suggests that it likely reduced attacks against ISAF. Announcement of ACAP II assistance predicted a reduction in insurgent violence by about 17 percent a month later. When Lyall separated ISAF- from Taliban-caused events, he found that while both were associated with decreased insurgent attacks, the results were *only statistically significant for ISAF-initiated events*, with announcement generating a 30 percent reduction. He saw a similar pattern on effects after aid was distributed (as opposed to announced): the reduction in insurgent attacks is large and significant when ACAP II payments follow ISAF-initiated civilian casualties but not when they follow those initiated by the Taliban.[63]

If interpreted as a test of a grievance or gratitude model, these results reveal a puzzling asymmetry in response to assistance. That thinking likely motivated the program—eligibility criteria did not include all victims of all violence, as a purely humanitarian motivation would have implied. Yet in the context of an information-centric model, the results on violence make sense: assistance as an apology for civilian casualties, to correct a perception that harm might have been deliberate (the intent of solatia), should lessen the damage to attitudes and therefore reduce insurgent violence. Assistance that does not carry that message, extended in response to violence by others, would have no such effect in an information-centric war.

TIPS: EVIDENCE ON MECHANISMS FROM AFGHANISTAN

Thanks to the efforts of Luke Condra, Andrew Shaver, and Austin Wright, we can now augment evidence on the effects of civilian casualties with direct evidence on Proposition 4C, which implies that casualties caused by insurgents in Afghanistan would lead to more information-sharing.[64]

Like many ESOC projects, this one draws on years of relationship building and painstaking work to get data declassified. In this case Luke, Andrew, and Austin worked through the results of a series of successful FOIA requests, from 2014 to 2016, to compile nearly complete information on more than 270,000 individual incidents recorded by Afghan, U.S., and NATO forces from 2003 through 2014 in Afghanistan. These geo-coded and time-stamped data include insurgent activity (mostly attacks on Afghan government and NATO forces), harm to civilians, and provision of local intelligence to security forces. With the help of Kyle Pizzey—who worked with these data in theater for many years—and others, they developed a rich understanding of various biases in the data and also of how they could be used to test whether insurgent-caused harm to civilians induced more civilian tips. These data cover a much broader geographic and temporal range than any prior analysis.

Andrew, Austin, Jake, and Luke took two approaches to testing Proposition 4C. First, as in Andrew and Jake's work on Iraq, they looked at how harm to civilians due to accidents of combat affected subsequent information-sharing. Their approach was to control statistically for a range of factors that might influence the propensity of individuals to share tips, including: district fixed-effects to account for the aspects of local politics that do not change over time (e.g., ethnic composition); time fixed-effects to account for seasonality and broad trends in the war; and measures of the intensity of insurgent combat operations in a given district-week to account for how violent a given location was predisposed to be.[65]

Second, they used what is called an instrumental variables approach. The idea is to find some factor that would influence information-sharing only through its effect on harm to civilians. By isolating the changes in harm due to that factor (the *instrument*) and then looking at how those changes relate to information-sharing, the instrumental variables approach estimates the causal effect of civilian casualties. In this case that other factor was changes in nighttime luminosity—

moonlight—due to the combination of the lunar cycle and cloud cover. Insurgents planted more IEDs on darker nights when drones and satellite imagery were blocked by clouds, so weeks with darker nights averaged more civilian casualties caused by insurgents. It was as if the clouds were conducting a randomized experiment for research, generating variation in civilian casualties they could use to estimate causal effects on tips. If cloud cover is indeed independent of other confounding factors that might affect tips—as the authors claim—then this is as good as an experiment in discovering the effects of civilian casualties.

Both approaches show the same result: more insurgent-caused harm to civilians led to more tips. It is hard to be sure of the exact magnitude because the data did not record how many civilians were killed in any given incident, but district-weeks with civilian casualty events (above and beyond what one would expect due to the level of combat) clearly averaged more informing. Using the first approach, Jake and coauthors find that district-weeks with one additional insurgent-caused casualty event saw a roughly 50 percent increase in informant reports over the weekly average. The instrumental variables approach yielded an even larger estimate, suggesting that following an incident of civilian harm caused by insurgents, information-sharing at least triples over the weekly average, inducing roughly two more tips per week in small districts and over 65 more in large districts. These effects are substantively large and statistically quite strong, even if the exact magnitude is a bit uncertain, yielding more evidence in support of Proposition 4C.

THE EFFECT OF CIVILIAN CASUALTIES ON COMBAT OUTCOMES ELSEWHERE

Outside of the wars in Afghanistan and Iraq, most of the evidence that often informs debates about civilian casualties comes from research focused on tactics used by various armed forces, not directly from measured harm to civilians. Excellent work has been done on the consequences of indiscriminate uses of force, for example, though studies in different contexts arrive at different conclusions, as we saw in the previous chapter. Lyall's work on Chechnya showed that villages targeted by indiscriminate use of artillery strikes saw less insurgent violence than those not targeted.[66] Dell and Querubín's research on Vietnam showed that uses of indiscriminate air power led to increased insurgent attacks.[67] These studies did not focus primarily on the effect of civilian casualties, controlling for other kinds of combat activity; instead the treatment effects they measure precisely are attributable to the use of a particular kind of violence, not its consequences. In Chechnya Lyall comes close, by looking within only shelled villages at how the count of civilians harmed and other measures of damage affected subsequent rates of violence. He found the correlations were mostly weakly negative and statistically insignificant.[68] As we discussed in the previous chapter, that result is consistent with the theory if the casualties caused by the shelling did not shift local attitudes. In a setting in which civilians were already implacably opposed to the Russians, further evidence of malevolent and indiscriminate shelling might do little to convince civilians—who might be already so opposed to Russian control of their neighborhoods that information-sharing would have been unthinkable.

DIFFERENT INSURGENCIES, DIFFERENT RESULTS

Recall that civilian casualties in Iraq changed insurgent violence from week to week. This, and the other supporting data, suggests that the information mechanism was in play. In Afghanistan, the impacts of civilian casualties were longer lasting, operated most strongly for ISAF-caused casualties, and were in the opposite of the hypothesized direction for Taliban-caused casualties in one analysis. Yet we find that the information mechanism clearly operated in both places, in the sense that we reported clear evidence that tips responded to civilian harm. So why the differences?

One possibility is that what we measured as Taliban-caused civilian casualties are actually targeted retaliations. More likely, we suspect, is that it boils down to differences in the geographic and political environment in which the insurgencies operated, their different organizational structures, and the nature of the constraints they faced.

Before we explain those differences, let's take a step back and revisit our epistemology. When we see different results in different places, what social scientists like to call *heterogeneous treatment effects*, we think that's potentially informative. Researchers see this kind of ambiguity as an invitation to look closer, and a reason to compare results across many studies, because the differences could tell us something about other factors our theories need to consider.

One such factor is cultural context and how people respond to events that harm their friends, families, and neighbors. In a setting where family honor and vendettas are important social institutions it is easy to imagine that civilian casualties caused by government could increase the willingness of civilians to tolerate insurgent activity and therefore lead to more subsequent violence.

Is Afghanistan such a society? Probably, at least in the parts of the country where most of the insurgent violence took place. Pashtuns make up close to half of the population of Afghanistan and up to 95 percent of Taliban membership.[69] Pashtun social code (the aforementioned Pashtunwali) calls for the biblical "eye for an eye," and the region has a tradition of blood feuds that, according to some soldiers and scholars, makes it a particularly hard place to wage a counterinsurgency campaign.[70] Pashtun men may be more willing to enlist in the Taliban if they are under pressure to settle a score against the Afghan government or its allies.[71]

But then how do we explain the fact that civilian casualties caused by the Taliban were associated with a small but statistically significant *increase* in subsequent attacks against ISAF? Shouldn't the same social mores that pushed people to punish ISAF for casualties it caused have operated in the opposite direction when the Taliban harmed civilians? The short answer is that we are not sure. One possibility is that the way incidents were recorded in the CCTC data was not how the people in an area understood them. In particular, it is possible that the Taliban public-relations machinery successfully blamed ISAF for civilian casualties caused by Taliban actions, or that people reasoned that deaths caused by Taliban IEDs would not have happened had ISAF forces not been around.[72]

That possibility is consistent with the evidence we reported in chapter 5 about how the Taliban successfully claimed credit for U.S.-funded development projects, with Lyall's findings discussed earlier, and with a range of qualitative reports.[73] But it is not consistent with the evidence on tips in Afghanistan, which clearly shows a reaction *against* the insurgency after Taliban-caused violence. Perhaps Taliban-caused casualties led *some* people to call in tips, but were also blamed on ISAF by others, and therefore shifted community norms leading insurgents to increase their attacks (or leading more fighters to join). Could that explain the anomaly of the increase in attacks after Taliban-caused casualties?

Maybe. First, let's consider the spaces in which the insurgencies operated. In Iraq, conflict occurred largely in an urban environment. The country's greater population density made insurgent activity easy for civilians to observe and this, combined with a high density of Coalition forces, meant that the insurgents really had to rely on civilians keeping their mouths shut. In Afghanistan, by contrast, the Taliban operated in a wider and more rural area, against a sparser deployment of counterinsurgent troops. Fewer civilians observing insurgent activities meant fewer potential informers—and those civilians encountered fewer troops pressing for information. So the sensitivity of Taliban operations to informing might have been lower in Afghanistan.

Second, consider the organizational structure. While the Iraqi insurgency was largely decentralized, with subgroups vying for political and social influence, the Taliban were (and remain) more centralized and coordinated—a structure that allowed them to engage in sophisticated information operations. For instance, recall the tactics the two insurgencies used to combat tip sharing. In Iraq, when the government advertised a hotline for anonymous tips, insurgents had an ad hoc, crowd-sourced response: men called in insults and death threats, while women called to flirt with the operators and waste their time. In Afghanistan, the insurgency took a different and more sophisticated approach to prevent villagers from calling in tips. The Taliban used its power to force mobile companies to turn off cell-phone towers at night so that tips could not be called in while insurgents were moving about. (At the same time they did not destroy the towers in many areas, as doing so would have angered the population.) It seems more likely that the Taliban could blame ISAF than that the less-organized Iraqi insurgents could blame the Coalition.

Finally, consider the different competitive political landscapes the groups faced. In Iraq many competing insurgent organizations often fought each other, even as they were fighting American and Iraqi forces. Additionally, because the insurgency took place primarily in urban settings there were many sources of information on any given event. In Afghanistan, by contrast, there was only one major insurgent organization during the period of Jake's study with Luke and Radha. If an organization is to cast blame for its activities on the other side, it requires a coordinated response targeted at key areas with few alternative sources of information. This is only possible in a consolidated, noncompetitive insurgency like the Taliban. A rural setting helps.

Overall, then, most of the evidence is consistent with an information-centric view of how people will respond to civilian casualties. The anomaly is the Taliban's apparent—and quite remarkable—ability to exploit civilian casualties that the Taliban itself caused. We suspect that this is due to effective public relations, but we cannot be sure.

Shifting to the counterinsurgent perspective, information flows should be considered a critical component of operations in high-population-density, urban conflicts. This is augmented by the kind of advanced technology the Coalition enjoyed in Iraq, because to act on tips effectively requires a quick, precise response. In more rural insurgencies, the counterinsurgent must work harder to make sure it can credibly attribute blame when insurgents harm civilians, which may require establishing a reputation for sometimes acknowledging mistakes and accepting blame. In either setting, the evidence from Propositions 4A, 4B, and 4C on civilian casualties caused by *government* forces indicates that limiting those mistakes should be viewed not just as an ethical obligation but also as a way to reduce future attacks.

THE BULLET NOT FIRED

The evidence on civilian casualties supports our approach: asymmetric civil wars in which noncombatants are consequential actors. Civilians update attitudes quickly, informed by constantly changing information in deciding which combatants it is less dangerous to cooperate with. They do so in ways that are influenced by preexisting partisan loyalties to be sure, as is true of how people interpret all manner of information relevant to attitudes in settings with partisanship.[74] Their decisions affect violence, including attacks directed against the state and its allies. They are active participants who protect their lives and interests, punishing or rewarding combatants by sharing information, or not—which is often their only recourse.

Stepping back to our larger argument, the evidence on how civilians respond to harm caused by one side or the other in Afghanistan and Iraq is largely consistent with the three-player game-theoretic model presented in chapter 3. When insurgents hurt civilians and thereby downgrade the population's perception of how they will fare under rebel control, civilian attitudes turn against them, tips increase in the short term, and insurgent attacks decline. The opposite appears to happen when government forces cause harm. We've found direct evidence for these shifts in cooperation in both Afghanistan and Iraq and reviewed circumstantial evidence for them elsewhere. Once more our core argument is consistent with a broad array of relationships in the world. Not all the evidence points in the same direction, but the preponderance surely does. Either way, we have tried to capture the nuances and explain why we interpret this evidence as we do.

Deciding which model applies to civilians in small wars matters because innocent civilians so often are trapped in these conflicts. In Syria alone over 200,000 civilians have been killed since that conflict began in 2011 (through the end of 2016).[75]

Turning to policy, much of the discussion of civilian casualties within the defense community attempts to weigh between two options. Should we ask soldiers to risk their lives and forgo local tactical victories over insurgents in order to keep civilians safe, perhaps winning the hearts and minds of those civilians in the process? Or should we apply greater force, ensuring tactical victory but placing civilians at greater risk—regrettable but perhaps serving them in the long run, from a utilitarian perspective, by hastening government victory and an end to insurgent influence?

The studies we've described in this chapter reveal that this is often a false dichotomy. A reduction in civilian casualties is powerfully associated with a reduction in insurgent violence, an implication of the consequential role of civilian decisions in asymmetric civil wars. Restraint—holding fire or opting to apply it more discriminately in order to protect civilians—has tactical value in the pursuit of the military objective: suppressing insurgent influence.

This is the same conclusion some military leaders arrived at, not via analysis and empirical testing but through long experience in fighting insurgents. As we noted earlier, General McChrystal encouraged the practice of "courageous restraint" in his 2009 Tactical Directive in Afghanistan. British major general Nick Carter, whose command included Helmand—the location of the riots we described to begin this chapter—went as far as advocating for a medal recognizing ISAF soldiers and Marines who exercised restraint in battle when appropriate. According to Carter, restraint and tactical patience should be viewed as an "act of discipline and courage not much different than those seen in combat actions."[76]

The responses to General McChrystal's Tactical Directive indicate a struggle to internalize the lessons of an information-centric approach to countering insurgency. Both in the military and more broadly, opposition quickly arose to any tactics that appeared to endanger troops or "tie their hands." Many military members focused on the dangers associated with McChrystal's strategy shift to the exclusion of its intended goal, to reduce insurgent violence.[77] More restrictive rules of engagement in some cases spurred anger that McChrystal seemed to be placing the safety of Afghans, or even perceived political favors to then president Hamid Karzai, above troops' welfare.[78] At least one soldier even publicly called for McChrystal to be fired.[79] Some in the press also responded, citing complaints from within the military and questioning the efficacy of prioritizing civilians' safety.[80] Even the U.S. House of Representatives became involved—somewhat uncharacteristically—in the regulations governing tactical engagements, passing a provision in the 2012 defense authorization bill that called for loosening rules of engagement.[81]

News that the U.S. military was considering a "courageous restraint" medal incited anger. A U.S. Army review of military award policies noted that "the response to this proposal was almost entirely negative even though its premise is entirely consistent with both reward theory and counterinsurgency doctrine."[82] The same publication went on to describe vociferous opposition in the media, including Rush Limbaugh's outrage at what he said "would be the Yellow Heart medal."[83] Veterans of Foreign Wars and the American Legion were also quick to condemn the proposal, the latter claiming that "too much restraint will get our own people killed."[84]

Part of the controversy over restrictive rules of engagement (and unconventional awards) is likely due to the challenges in communicating the linkage between tactics and strategy. That's true both when the audience is the lower echelons of the military and when it's an American public rightly concerned about the safety and welfare of young men and women in uniform. Interviews with soldiers and Marines at the battalion level and lower—those immersed in the tactical fight—indicated that the details and intent of McChrystal's strategy often failed to penetrate the ranks, down to those obliged to make critical heat-of-the-moment decisions regarding the application of firepower in the small-unit combat that characterized operations in Afghanistan.[85] A study of British counterinsurgency practices in Helmand, for example, found a wide variety of interpretations of the 2010 ISAF Tactical Directive among combat units. It concluded that these differences were due to divergent beliefs held at different levels of command and across different commanders in the field.[86] General McChrystal himself reportedly acknowledged that his directives were at times misinterpreted on their way down the chain of command.[87]

On the ground in Afghanistan, a priority mission for ISAF's CAAT during Joe's tenure in command was to help communicate and explain the commander's intent to troops in the field and help them appreciate how their actions at the tactical level could affect achievement of strategic objectives. Closing with and destroying the enemy remained a core mission of combat units in the field. The Tactical Directive issued by General McChrystal did not lose sight of this, nor did it prevent ISAF members from defending themselves.[88] But understanding where and under what conditions the gains from enemy attrition (captured or killed) in the near term might be outweighed by the downside risks to the mission if attrition harmed civilians was critical in the complex, varied, and dynamic threat environment in which ISAF operated in Afghanistan. The challenge was *not* convincing troops to take risks in order to achieve a mission—which was well understood—but instead convincing them that exercising restraint in order to limit harm to civilians in some cases would indeed *help them achieve* the mission.

The argument for recognizing courageous restraint with a medal was this: "We routinely and systematically recognize valor, courage, and effectiveness during kinetic combat operations. . . . In a COIN campaign, however, it is critical to also recognize that sometimes the most effective bullet is *the bullet not fired*."[89] Our analysis and empirical testing provide some validation for that argument.[90]

Referring to our outline in chapter 1, we can now take stock. We've assembled evidence on the information-centric theory piece by piece. In chapter 4 we saw that making it safer for civilians to share information with government forces led to less violence. In chapter 5 we examined the role of development assistance and saw how project design was critical: projects that were modest, secure, informed, and conditional can enable information flows and help reduce conflict locally. Chapter 6 looked at two complementarities that our model predicts—between military suppression and those small-scale aid projects, and between suppression and civilian attitudes. In this chapter we've reported a number of findings, most of which align with the theory: combatants make efforts to avoid harming civilians and to mitigate the consequences when they do (solatia); civilian attitudes shift against those causing them harm; violence drops after rebels cause civilian casualties and increases after government forces do. Finally, we report evidence that the mechanism by which civilian attitudes affect outcomes is through the flow of tips, which increases after rebel-caused civilian casualties.

In each of these chapters we've seen how different causal relationships line up with different expectations of the theory. In the next chapter we're going to do something slightly different: instead of presenting positive evidence for our theory, we will show how the data on the relationship between economic conditions and violence in *asymmetric* conflicts do *not* support prevalent assumptions based primarily on evidence from *symmetric* conflicts. Then we will examine how evidence contradicting those assumptions can deepen our understanding of asymmetric wars.

8

ECONOMIC CONDITIONS AND INSURGENT VIOLENCE

Afghanistan, 2006-11

The Local Governance and Community Development program (LGCD) was one of USAID's flagship programs in Afghanistan from 2006 through 2011. Its goal was to *stabilize* communities by training and supplying local officials and to fund small infrastructure projects that would employ community members. LGCD paid men to dig irrigation canals, build footbridges, and shovel snow to clear paths to markets and health centers. The intent was to help the Afghan central government "extend its reach into remote districts, encourage local communities to take an active role in their own development, and create incentives for stability in critical border provinces"—which would keep communities from sliding back under Taliban influence.[1] By the program's end in 2011, LGCD had spent $109 million on community-stabilization projects.[2]

Stabilization seems a worthy goal. Though the term is often used ambiguously, a necessary component of any definition would surely be low levels of insurgent violence.[3]

Figure 8.1 illustrates how violence in LGCD-treated districts diverged from that in other districts from the program's start date in early 2006.[4] The average LGCD district was a bit more violent than others before the program started. But afterward *violence worsened faster* in districts with LGCD in operation than in districts without, surely a cruel surprise to the intent and predictions of both USAID and the Afghan government.

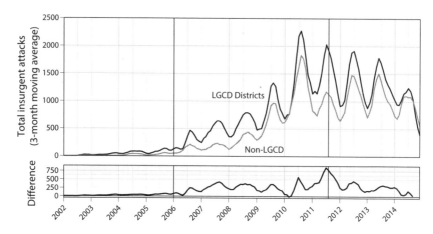

FIGURE 8.1. Trends in conflict in Afghanistan, LGCD versus non-LGCD districts, before, during, and after LGCD country-wide operational period.

Average insurgent attacks per district, January 2002–December 2014. Vertical bars denote start and end dates of LGCD spending. Attack data from ISAF Combined Information Data Network Exchange (CIDNE). LGCD districts identified in USAID program documents.

What happened? LGCD certainly put people to work. In fact it exceeded program targets on both job creation and training.[5] It also trained local government officials and provided Internet connectivity to enable them to communicate with their superiors in provincial capitals and in Kabul.

One possibility is that LGCD targeted districts in which deteriorating security was correctly anticipated. Perhaps if there had been no program, things might have been far worse.[6] Lacking an evaluation design that can capture trends and generate counterfactuals—as we have done for Commander's Emergency Response Program (CERP) in chapter 5, for instance—we can't know for sure.

USAID was less generous. Its final review, based on site visits and interviews, concluded that the program had *failed to foster stability*.[7] A SIGAR audit reached a similar conclusion.[8]

This raises another possibility, that in asymmetric conflicts job creation and development programs do not decrease violence but instead stoke it, as we saw in Joe's analysis of a community-driven development program in the Philippines in chapter 5.[9]

We're not surprised that a program like LGCD might fail to reduce violence, and perhaps by this point the reader is not either, given the evidence we've offered in support of the information-centric model. If that's an appropriate way to think about development programs in asymmetric small wars, then LGCD projects failed to meet (at least) two necessary conditions for violence reduction discussed in chapter 5, security and conditionality.

Yet *others are surprised* that LGCD failed, and perhaps for good reason. Our evidence in chapters 4–7 supports the information-centric model but does not preclude some other approach to understanding insurgency. Perhaps not all of asymmetric conflict is a father in a courtyard with a tip to offer? Maybe those alternative theories prescribe a different, or less stringent, set of conditions for designing aid programs that can achieve violence reduction?

The idea that employment—and economic growth in general—will pacify is the conventional wisdom among practitioners and is shared by many academic development economists and many scholars studying insurgency. It has been used to justify huge volumes of development spending over the past few decades in many fragile states, states in which conflict is most likely asymmetric.

The argument for employment reducing violence is often shored up by the common observation that higher-income countries (and even regions within countries) tend to have less insurgent violence. It also draws support from broadly accepted theories linking unemployment and poverty to recruitment and support of rebellions.

Following that line of reasoning, gainful employment and a route out of poverty should reduce violence—because poor, unemployed, disaffected young men make up the recruiting pool for insurgencies. If these men were given jobs, a shot at prosperity, and a place in society, the rebellion would weaken. President George W. Bush articulated this position in 2005, referring to Iraq: "Unemployment is high, which fuels popular dissatisfaction and may generate sympathy for the insurgency . . . [and] makes some Iraqis more vulnerable to terrorist or insurgent recruiting."[10] President Barack Obama echoed this sentiment ten years later, in broader terms: "There are millions, billions of people who are poor and are law-abiding and peaceful and tolerant. . . . But when people—especially young people—feel entirely trapped in impoverished communities . . . that feeds instability and disorder, and makes those communities ripe for extremist recruitment."[11]

- -

In this chapter we will examine the literature that informs such thinking, reviewing the evidence base: a wide variety of studies on economic conditions and insurgent violence. In doing so we will be attentive to "knowing your war," checking whether intuition drawn from symmetric conflicts can reliably inform design of aid programs in the asymmetric conflicts we generally find ourselves in today.[12] Those aid resources have alternative uses. Moreover, practitioners, and perhaps recipients, are put in harm's way in the process. So let's look carefully.

ECONOMIC CONDITIONS AND CIVIL WARS: THE CROSS-NATIONAL CORRELATION

Poorer countries *are* more likely to experience civil war. ESOC affiliate James Fearon confirmed this for 161 countries between 1945 and 1999, comparing income per capita and the frequency of civil war outbreaks over time. (Here, civil war includes both symmetric conflicts like that between Nigeria and secessionist region Biafra, 1967–70, and asymmetric.) If you look at any given point during that half century, only about 1.5 percent of the richest one-fifth of the countries would suffer a civil war erupting within the measured five-year intervals. Among the poorest fifth, the corresponding figure is 14.3 percent. In fact, Fearon stated, "per-capita income is the single best predictor of a country's odds of civil war outbreak, empirically dominating other factors that one might have expected to do better, such as level of democracy, degree of ethnic or religious diversity or nature of ethnic demography, or level of income inequality."[13]

But *why* do poor countries experience more civil war than do rich ones? Poverty and unemployment feeding recruitment is intuitive, but perhaps the logic is reversed and governments in higher-income countries have more resources to spend on suppressing rebels. Fearon argued that this argument misses something too: high income in rich countries also creates more motivation for rebels, as there is more to gain from overthrowing the government, which could nullify that suppression effect. So, though poor countries are at higher risk of civil war, that single cross-country correlation is clearly open to multiple interpretations. Let's look carefully at the conventional wisdom and expose it to *subnational* data.

PARSING THE CONVENTIONAL WISDOM

Relative Deprivation

When Presidents Bush and Obama asserted that "popular dissatisfaction" and poverty fuel rebellion, they followed a prevalent and well-articulated argument in political science, that deprivation breeds rebellion. However, their argument raises an important question: would the poor rebel if there were nothing to gain? The answer comes in the form of the slightly more nuanced concept of *relative deprivation*.

In his seminal 1970 book, *Why Men Rebel*, Ted R. Gurr theorized that an individual's propensity toward violence resulted largely from his or her relative deprivation, defined as his "perceived discrepancy between value expectations and value capabilities."[14] This gap between where someone thinks he is and where he thinks he should be will be exacerbated if others' position improves while his stays the same (i.e., the rich get richer, or the neighboring country throws off a dictator while his remains under an oppressive regime) or if his position worsens while others' stays the same (if his property is destroyed by a drone, or if he becomes unemployed). That sense of relative deprivation then leads to frustration, which, through a well-documented psychological mechanism, makes people more aggressive and thus easier to motivate to fight. Gurr therefore concludes that "the potential for collective violence varies strongly with the intensity and scope of relative deprivation among members of a collectivity."[15] The idea that relative deprivation stokes insurgency is widely accepted; we imagine that unemployed people—mainly young men—become so frustrated with their actual (versus their ideal) capabilities that they turn against the state.

Grievances are often cited in the literature as drivers of insurgency. Relative deprivation is one type of grievance, but for clarity in this chapter, we'll use the term "relative deprivation." Analogously, gratitude is sometimes cited as a mechanism by which development programs reduce violence. If a development program reduced violence by creating gratitude for the relief of relative deprivation, we'll call that a relative deprivation mechanism as well. All three variants will have the same testable implications in this chapter, so for empirical purposes we will treat them as one.

Opportunity Costs of Time

A second mechanism linking economic conditions to violence is more practical: unemployed people have less to lose from participating in an insurgency.

The basic concept of an opportunity cost is simple (though economists can make it more complex). It refers to the choices one makes given limited resources and the opportunities one passes up, in terms of time, capital, or even difficult-to-measure variables such as "mental bandwidth." We can measure opportunity costs in dollar amounts or in lengths of time—or we can speak more abstractly about the opportunity costs one imagines for a given choice, how they compare to actual costs, and how this influences behavior. The opportunity cost of buying stock in Amazon is the payoff to other uses of the money, perhaps the dividends and capital appreciation you would have earned if you had invested that money in a mutual fund or the fun you would have had spending the money on a lavish vacation. The opportunity costs a woman in a traditionalist society faces when she quits school to marry early and start a family include the wages she would have earned if she had finished high school and entered the labor force. They can even take into account the lost lifetime earnings, net of the support she'd receive from her children in old age.

In the case of unemployed potential insurgents, the opportunity cost of time spent rebelling is the money that could be earned if that time were spent working, which would be weighed against the risk of injury or death, and perhaps the social connections it might imperil, and so on. We assume that because the unemployed aren't passing up wages that their opportunity cost will be lower, making them more likely to rebel. In contrast, the employed are less likely to rebel because they face greater opportunity costs.

To summarize, the cross-country evidence of insurgency-prone countries being poor, combined with the appeal of the deprivation argument, and the very intuitive opportunity cost mechanism have been influential among policymakers and practitioners, convincing them that development assistance can be used to combat insurgency. As we have seen, there are other possible explanations for the cross-country pattern of low insurgency in more prosperous countries. The information-centric model predicts that if prosperity is conditional on cooperation with government, then the same pattern will be found. Or, the causal direction might be reversed: conflict-cursed countries suffer lower prosperity—perhaps because markets are disrupted and investments are unsafe, including investments in education and health. Distinguishing between those explanations is critical to designing development programs and even to deciding whether to run them at all. To decide on the broad relevance of relative deprivation and opportunity cost arguments we need to figure out their specific testable implications and see if the facts can help adjudicate between models. We'll do that now, starting with relative deprivation.

RELATIVE DEPRIVATION: ARE THE POOR MORE LIKELY TO SUPPORT INSURGENTS?

If our mental picture of rebellion is *Les Misérables*, the Russian Revolution, or Che Guevara riding his motorcycle through the hills of Latin America, then we might believe that poor people support insurgencies because they have legitimate grievances against the government and the most to gain if it is overturned. Of course, poor people also occupy the most tenuous position in society, so their well-being is most vulnerable to the chaos that accompanies violent political change—just as they are most vulnerable to natural disasters and financial crises, and more so in the insecure contested areas that asymmetric conflicts generate. That might make them *less* likely to support violent insurgents.[16] On net, which force wins out?

In chapter 7 we described an endorsement experiment that Jake and coauthors carried out among six thousand Pakistani citizens; it showed that, contrary to expectations, *poor Pakistanis disliked militants more* than do middle-class citizens. This difference was not small: the poor were up to twenty-three times more negative about militants than their middle-class counterparts. This held true even as they controlled for a wide range of potentially confounding factors (i.e., gender, education, etc.) and regardless of what policies the organizations espoused. When broken down by area, the distaste for militants was strongest among the urban poor: the gap in support between low-income and middle-income respondents was about twenty times larger in urban than rural areas. We used that contrast as evidence that exposure to harm by rebels explained the difference, as the reader might recall.

In more recent work in Iraq, we have seen similar patterns. Surveys show that expectations among the poor of future progress were more sensitive to short-term fluctuations in violence than were those among the wealthy.[17] Furthermore, the survey Jason Lyall and coauthors conducted among 2,754 male respondents in the heart of the Afghan insurgency (which we discussed in the previous chapter) also showed that income was weakly *positively* correlated with support for the Taliban.[18]

It seems that in these asymmetric conflict settings poorer people are *less* likely to see militant groups as a solution to their grievances and perhaps more likely to see them as a source of threat and disruption. Yet, as informative as this research is, it does not tell us whether the support-reducing effect of exposure to violence is direct or indirect. By *direct*, we mean that poor people's dislike of violence comes from the direct effects violence has on income and personal safety. (The relationship could be subtler but still direct: studies have shown that poverty is associated with a general withdrawal from politics and disaffection with political figures, so it could be that poor people are simply less engaged politically with rebels than are richer people.) By *indirect* effects, we mean psychological effects: if people gauge themselves as poor and view rebel violence as putting the poor at a disadvantage, this might result in an antipathy for insurgents. Indirect effects could take the form of an "us versus them" mentality: the insurgent team hurts the poor team, so as a member of the poor team, I am against insurgents.

Determining whether the relationship is direct or indirect is important, because if it is indirect—if it depends on psychological links rather than direct experiences—then it can be altered by changing perceptions.[19] A rich literature in psychology as well as economics has shown that our perceptions of our own economic standing depend on reference points, in particular on comparisons to others, as well as on our absolute economic standing. Yet, despite the very influential standing of the relative deprivation hypothesis among scholars of conflict, in 2012 it had not previously been tested in a large-scale survey experiment with respect to support for violent organizations.

Jake and his colleagues tested the relative deprivation hypothesis by conducting a large-scale face-to-face survey experiment, which included 16,000 subjects in four Pakistani provinces, as well as in the remote and undergoverned Federally Administered Tribal Areas (FATAS).[20] They used the endorsement survey technique explained in the previous chapter.[21]

The key to the experiment was manipulating how subjects felt about their own relative position—poor or not, living in a violent place or not. On poverty, surveyors asked respondents, "What is the approximate monthly income of your household?" and showed them one of two scales featuring six brackets of income. One of these scales had a much wider lowest-income bracket, such that 39.3 percent of respondents would be placed in that poorest category; the other had a narrower lowest bracket, so only 4.4 percent were classified among the lowest income. This gave the team a large crossover population of respondents with similar actual incomes, some of whom were labeled "relatively poor" and others of whom were labeled "relatively rich." Because the brackets respondents experienced were randomized across individuals, differences between the groups could experimentally estimate the effect of being made to feel relatively poor (unconfounded by other characteristics, which randomization would average out).

To measure the effect of feeling like Pakistan was unusually violent (as opposed to feeling relatively deprived) they formulated a question about the current challenges facing Pakistan. They mentioned recent floods, oil prices, and the economy. The question posed contained a comparison with another South Asian country, but here again there were two versions: one said, "Pakistan has also suffered from instability and violence. On average, Pakistan suffers from more extremist violence than Bangladesh." The other ended with, "Pakistan suffers from less extremist violence than Afghanistan." Similar to the relative-poverty intervention, this question created at random two populations, one of which was told that their country was relatively more violent than its neighbor, and the other that it was less.

In terms of Gurr's theory, the researchers experimentally increased respondents' feelings of *relative deprivation*—once of wealth and once of peace and stability (though without deceiving subjects).

The team also used endorsements (a method introduced in previous chapters) to better estimate attitudes, but in this case they included, in addition to four Pakistani militant organizations, an endorsement by Abdul Sattar Edhi, a well-known humanitarian. This provided a benchmark to compare the other endorsements against, since Edhi was uncontroversial and his endorsement of a policy would encourage broad approval. Among respondents who reported little support for Edhi, his endorsement had very close to a zero effect. Across the entire sample it increased support for a policy by 1.7 percent, and among strong Edhi supporters, by 3.1 percent. This gives us a benchmark of 3.1 percent to compare to other endorsement effects for which we do not have direct questions for comparison.

First, Jake and his coauthors replicated the key finding from their earlier survey: using a measure of actual poverty the poorest individuals held the most *negative* attitudes toward militant groups.

Next, the team examined whether changing people's *perceived* poverty affected those attitudes. It did. Among those placed in the "relatively wealthy" category, the endorsement experiment revealed no increased dislike of militants. However, being put in the "relatively poor" category *decreased* support for militant groups by 5.2 percent. That's about 67 percent greater than the Edhi benchmark of 3.1 percent—strong evidence that part of the observed correlation between poverty and opposition to militant groups stems from psychological feelings of relative deprivation.

Turning to perceptions of violence, respondents perceiving Pakistan to be a relatively violent country had an even greater effect in *reducing* support for militant groups. Telling people Pakistan was relatively *less* violent may have made them slightly more approving of militants, but as this effect was not statistically significant, we can't say with confidence if it was really different from zero. Yet telling them Pakistan was relatively *more* violent did have a statistically significant effect, decreasing support for the groups by 10.7 percent—nearly 3.5 times the Edhi benchmark. As you might expect, subjects exposed to both treatments—told both that they were relatively poor and that Pakistan was relatively more violent—showed the *greatest* drop in support for militants, at 14.6 percent. Furthermore, these effects were stronger among middle-class and wealthy Pakistanis (exactly the people who should be most affected, as they are not used to feeling poor) and among Pashtuns and FATA residents, those who were more likely to have experienced violence in an asymmetric small war.

ESOC scholar Andrew Shaver has analyzed a survey of over 175,000 Baghdadis during a violent period of the insurgency in 2005–6, which is consistent with the relative deprivation result.[22] Iraqi citizens were strongly opposed to the presence of Coalition forces in Iraq, and the unemployed were no exception. When asked about violence, however, interesting differences emerged. Half of the unemployed said they supported the use of violence against Coalition forces, which would seem high were it not the case that students, housewives, and retirees were slightly *more* supportive of violence than the unemployed. Strikingly, those employed full-time supported violence at a rate 10 percent higher than that of the unemployed. Shaver noted a similar pattern when asked about optimism concerning a range of things from conditions in the city to family life. The unemployed were relatively less optimistic; women, students, and retirees slightly more optimistic; and the employed significantly more so.

If we consider these survey results alongside findings in the psychology literature that unemployment causes depression and anxiety,[23] it begins to make sense that job loss might discourage, rather than encourage, participation in insurgency. Rebels are goal oriented— optimistic, in their way. Shaver's results are still preliminary, but they give us food for thought.

To summarize, in addition to survey evidence refuting the deprivation hypothesis in an asymmetric conflict, we also have strong experimental, microlevel evidence *reversing* Gurr's relative deprivation hypothesis in an asymmetric conflict setting. The evidence favors a vulnerability hypothesis that pushes in the opposite direction: *in asymmetric conflicts, the poorer you are—and not only that, the poorer you feel—the less likely you are to support insurgents.*

That finding has some interesting implications for policy. Using the media to inform and mobilize the poor, and to advertise the violence that militants cause, may reduce support for them. We return to policy in the following chapter and move on now to evidence on opportunity costs and the inner workings of insurgent organizations.

INSURGENT LABOR: DEMAND AND SUPPLY

The opportunity cost explanation for the negative correlation of income and violence draws on the logic of standard labor markets: if raising income increases demand for labor in regular jobs outside of insurgency then it should pull fighters out of insurgency and into regular jobs.[24] Recent research reveals several unusual aspects of the labor market for insurgents that challenge the relevance of that logic: extensive use of part-time and casual fighters, the small labor requirements of insurgencies, their very low wages, and an abundance of insurgents willing to accept those low wages despite high risk.

Let's begin with part-time insurgents. They pose an empirical challenge to the opportunity cost justification for an LGCD-like program, since they can shovel snow or clear canals by day and still have time to plant IEDs at night.

In general, part-time employment among insurgents varies a great deal by conflict, and sometimes over time within the same conflict, but in many places *a majority of insurgents are in fact part-timers.* In some cases it is useful to go beyond the full-time/part-time division among insurgents to include "casual" soldiers—those who participate only when there is a local need—a kind of guerrilla national guard. The People's Army of Vietnam functioned in this way. While data are patchy, it appears that the full-time Main Force made up a very small percentage of fighters early in the war—4 percent, compared to 44 percent in the part-time Provincial and District Forces and 51 percent in the "casual" Village Defense Forces—in 1958. The Main Force swelled to 28 percent when the war entered its most destructive phase in 1966, still a minority of fighters.[25] In Peru, at the peak of the Shining Path insurgency in 1990, it had only 3 percent full-time members versus 20 percent part-time and 77 percent casual soldiers.[26]

In a number of insurgencies, the percentage of full-time members seems to hover around only 15 to 30 percent. At the height of the Party of the Poor's insurgency in Mexico in the early 1970s, full-time members made up 26 percent of the movement and part-time 74 percent.[27] A report from the Philippines in 1985 had the government and the New People's Army (NPA) agreeing on 12,000 armed militants, but NPA leaders claiming an additional 20,000 part-time and casual soldiers available.[28] The FARC, too, complemented its activities with part-time militias embedded in communities.[29] In his book on Chechnya, Robert W. Schaefer points out a geographic division as well, with the 500 full-time insurgents based in rural areas and 600 to 800 urban-based members who could "rally to conduct operations as needed in either urban or rural environments."[30] The Naxalite insurgency in India, which we discuss below, has an estimated 38,000 part-time fighters out of 46,000 (83 percent).[31]

In Iraq the structure of the insurgency looked a lot like many nonviolent grassroots organizations, with some full-time members and many part-timers. According to some reports, al Qaeda in Iraq (AQI) preferred that most of its members have full-time jobs outside of the insurgency. Other rebel groups in Iraq seemed to offer a spectrum of part- to full-time work. The Taliban in Afghanistan seemed to work similarly. A 2007 report in *Der Spiegel* estimated that of 10,000 available soldiers, only a core of 2,000–3,000 were committed full-time insurgents, while the rest worked part-time.[32] Anecdotally, participation among these part-timers was seasonal: they would plant crops in the spring, fight over the summer, then leave the insurgency to harvest.

As the numbers indicate, not only are the majority of insurgents part-time workers in many places, but *insurgencies use very few fighters*. In countries with many millions of fighting-age males the labor requirements of an insurgency (part-time and full-time together) are well below 1 percent of the recruitable population.

None of that evidence contradicts the idea that increasing wages will raise the opportunity cost of insurgency for this small group, making them more expensive as recruits. But it does challenge the relevance to suppressing violence. With such a small portion of the population serving as full-time insurgents, could employment creation programs like LGCD possibly reduce the number of fighters enough to make an appreciable difference? Given that insurgencies sustain with very few fighters, the Taliban could counteract the labor market effects of an LGCD-sized program (costing over a $100 million) by giving those few (perhaps one in a hundred) a small raise, at very low cost.

How big a raise would it take? IS fighters, like almost all soldiers worldwide, are paid a wage. The wage structure of that insurgent organization provides some surprising patterns, which further challenge the logic of drying up the recruiting pool of insurgencies with job creation programs.

Data on the inner workings of insurgent organizations were not easy to come by. Not only do the organizations themselves closely guard their communications—for obvious strategic reasons—but when governments uncover internal records they tend to keep them classified. An exception, since 2005, is the Harmony Program at the United States Military Academy's Combating Terrorism Center (CTC)—an effort Joe and some of our team members have worked on—which has campaigned to release relevant documents for analysis. The scholars at the CTC reason that making documents available to scholars outside the military will enable deeper analysis that, in the end, outweighs any strategic risks (presuming that those scholars augment an asymmetric advantage the United States has over insurgents and terrorists in data analysis). As of 2015 the Harmony collection contained over a million electronic and paper documents gathered during operations in Afghanistan, Iraq, and elsewhere.

Focusing on the pay scale of AQI—the insurgent organization that would later metamorphose into the Islamic State of Iraq and then into IS[33]—Jake, Radha, Patrick (whose work with Joe we read about in chapter 5), and coauthors analyzed a cache of documents. Those included 21 large spreadsheets, 20 reports with a mix of narrative content and small financial tables, and 112 documents that provided context. They gave us information on 3,799 payments to at least 2,080 members across three provinces in 2006 and 2007, which we reported on in a 2013 article and later in a book.[34]

In some ways AQI operated like most organizations: they needed to balance expenditures against revenues and make payroll every week. Comparing AQI documents to an array of documents recovered from other groups, we see that organizational templates are very persistent over time, suggesting that even radical groups do not readily adjust to changing circumstances.

But similarities with familiar organizations end when it comes to wage structures. AQI followed an egalitarian salary structure, relatively flat among fighters of different rank. The monthly salary (as listed in a manual found in Anbar in 2007) was 60,000 dinars (IQD), about $41. This was pretty low by Iraqi standards, near the bottom of the pay scale for unskilled labor, less than *half what the average illiterate male reported earning*, and about a third of what a bricklayer would earn.[35] This low wage is puzzling given the risk: in Anbar in 2005 and 2006 the mortality risk for AQI fighters was over 47 times that of males aged 18–48 in the general population.[36]

Moreover, there were competing insurgent groups, so a zealot who was committed to waging jihad could choose which to join. In most markets, that competition would drive wages *up*, yet insurgent groups apparently managed to recruit and retain fighters at these very low wages for years, suggesting an ample supply of willing fighters to go around—who were willing to endure *high risk at low wages*.

In addition to wages, the manual specified that a fighter got an additional 30,000 dinars for each of his dependents and that payments would continue if he was killed or captured. Our data reflected this in practice, with a large percentage of payments going to families of fighters who had been killed or captured. Across eleven spreadsheets that labeled a large number of the salary payments, only 56 percent went to active fighters.

On average, the data showed that salaries stayed relatively constant across provinces. But salaries were supplemented with compensation for living expenses, which seemed to be determined on a more ad hoc basis (we saw letters requesting payment for this or that expense) and which did fluctuate by area. So while salaries varied little by region, a fighter's total compensation could vary quite a bit, depending on where he was stationed.

One might think that if compensation varied across regions, more dangerous postings would provide more compensation (what economists call a "risk premium" or a "compensating differential"). Surprisingly, the opposite was true: fighters facing greater danger seemed to get paid *less*. Of the three provinces we looked at, Anbar was by far the most violent, with 94.5 combat incidents per 100,000 inhabitants, versus 41.7 in Diyala and 21.7 in Ninewa. When we created a "riskiness ratio" for the types of activities the average fighter carried out, leaving out activities that wouldn't put him at greater risk (indirect fire, IED explosions), we came up with 0.50 for Anbar versus 0.37 for both Diyala and Ninewa. And yet fighters in Anbar had the *lowest* average monthly wage: 93,302 dinars versus 96,406 and 98,097. If we considered the median wage—which may be more telling, as it gave less weight to extremely high or low salaries—Anbar was still the lowest. And while some of this could arise from compensating fighters for family size (those in Anbar had fewer dependents), our statistical analysis showed that this could not fully account for the difference. At the province level, there was a negative correlation between pay and combat: *more dangerous postings paid less.*

We confirmed these findings in a more recent study that analyzed 157 more documents and a longer time frame, 2005–10.[37] These showed that revenue for AQI, and later ISI, came from domestic activities such as extortion, looting, vehicle theft, and selling oil on the black market, rather than from rich donors abroad (as is commonly believed). In fact AQI leaders resisted depending on donations in order to maintain autonomy. Another 89 documents that recorded 9,623 payments to ISI members showed the same *low wages, flat wage structure, and puzzling correlation of lower wages with higher risk*.[38]

A number of organizational practices could explain these patterns. The de facto life insurance created by the policy of supporting martyrs' families could have compensated for low wages. Alternatively, AQI might have used low wages to screen new members for loyalty.

A simpler possibility is this: the *supply of willing recruits far exceeded their tiny demand*, so AQI could pay subsistence wages, regardless of demand from competing organizations. Moreover, AQI could pay lower wages when risk was high, indicating that, at least among Iraqi rebels, nonmonetary rewards (such as the chance to fight—or even to be a martyr for a worthy cause) were much more important to these young recruits. Perhaps this is unsurprising; after all, it is hard to take a traditional view of risk in a group that highly values martyrdom. All of this, however, poses a challenge to the opportunity cost logic of job creation programs as a solution to insurgency. The idea that increased labor market could possibly drive up wages enough to deprive AQI of the small number of risk-seeking fighters it needed to remain viable seems unlikely.

Foreign fighters pose another challenge to the opportunity cost argument for an LGCD-like job creation program. When AQI (by then calling itself IS of Iraq, or ISI) was rapidly losing personnel to raids and arrests in 2007, it increasingly opened its ranks to foreign fighters. ISI officials methodically collected, organized, and stored information on new recruits' skills and other characteristics, such as "desires martyrdom," to match them to the group's requirements.[39] The new foreign fighters tended to be less educated and less likely to have battle experience (though more likely to have received military training). ISI apparently didn't waste extra training on those designated for suicide missions. Meanwhile, a growing proportion of revenues went to payroll and to compensating families. ISI and its parent organizations had long desired members with education and battle experience, but increasingly ISI accepted many uneducated and inexperienced foreigners. There were several possible reasons for this, but one was that, like low wages, the high price of travel to Iraq allowed the organization to screen out those who were financially motivated and attract instead a pool of committed jihadists. The main point is simply this: for the foreign fighters in ISI local wages outside the insurgency—the labor market opportunity cost—would be irrelevant; they had come to fight.

In summary, pulling together what we know about the organization of insurgencies indicates that they *demand* very little labor and only for short periods of time. The two youths planting an IED and setting an ambush in chapter 3 would typically have day jobs. Would it be harder for an insurgent cell to recruit those two if the economy were booming and wages were high? Perhaps. But the insurgency only needs to recruit a few per village. At the same time, AQI/ISI data indicate an *abundant supply* of potential recruits available, locally and abroad, who are willing to work at wages well below market, without even requiring a risk premium. These individuals augment what appears to be a devoted core of full-time fighters, whose motivations are ideological or political, or the appeal of fighting or even of martyrdom, and for whom the opportunity cost in market wages would be largely irrelevant.

EMPLOYMENT, UNEMPLOYMENT, AND VIOLENCE

To recap, so far we've established that there is reason to be skeptical that the cross-country correlation of low income with civil wars holds any insight relevant to development programs like LGCD in asymmetric conflicts. Empirical evidence also casts doubt on the logic of applying relative deprivation or opportunity cost reasoning.

What happens when we look at subnational data—that is, data within countries—on employment rates and insurgent violence in asymmetric conflict settings? That's critical evidence in any discussion of economics and insurgency, since both the relative deprivation hypothesis and the opportunity cost hypothesis make the clear prediction that raising employment rates should reduce insurgency by starving it of recruits and making current cadres hard to retain.

In *symmetric* civil wars, where neither side has an overwhelming military advantage, existing research suggests that these mechanisms (it's hard to distinguish which one) work more or less as expected. Postwar survey data from participants in the Rwandan genocide and the Sierra Leone civil war show that a lack of economic opportunity predicted participation in violence.[40] Similarly, Klaus Deininger used data from Uganda to show that communities with fewer economic opportunities were more likely to experience civil strife.[41] Other researchers have used weather-driven variation in employment rates (i.e., weather as an instrument for—driver of—labor demand) in agricultural economies to understand how economic conditions affect violence.[42] These studies generally find that conflict is *more* likely during periods of *low* rainfall, suggesting that when traditional employment is less profitable, people are more inclined to engage in violence.

Yet, as we have seen now in many contexts, asymmetric conflicts can function very differently from symmetric ones. In a symmetric conflict it is critical to recruit as many fighters as possible, so they generate plenty of labor demand, making the opportunity costs of regular employment relevant. In an asymmetric conflict, the framework we presented in chapter 3 suggested no particular role for employment rates in influencing whether the father chose to call in a tip (unless employment were tied somehow to government or rebel control of the neighborhood). In particular, how economic conditions affected the recruitment of the two youths setting the IED, or retention of troops in the patrol for that matter, was not examined, as we didn't think it was critical to the outcome. The evidence in the intervening chapters has supported that information-centric approach, but we haven't examined whether that neglected recruitment channel is *also* important in our asymmetric setting. We now turn to subnational evidence on that question.[43]

Do Working Men Rebel?

So, does unemployment feed violence by providing recruits to insurgencies? Fortunately, thanks to the perseverance of Joe and others, by 2010 we could examine that question empirically, using microlevel data sets from *three* asymmetric conflicts: Afghanistan, Iraq, and the Philippines. These data allowed us to measure nearly all violent acts perpetrated against government and/or allied forces over many years. Two of the data sets, from Iraq and the Philippines, allowed us to look at civilian fatalities as well. We could examine both employment levels and violence nationwide, with unprecedented geographic precision: 398 districts in Afghanistan, 104 in Iraq, and 76 provinces in the Philippines. In Afghanistan we used two databases that recorded a range of violent incidents for six separate months spread over 2008 and 2009; for Iraq we used 148,546 incidents recorded by the Coalition and 49,391 recorded civilian deaths from 2004 to 2007; and for the Philippines 22,245 security incidents reported by the Armed Forces of the Philippines from 1997 to 2006. We compared all incidents to employment data for the same time periods and subjected our findings to a range of controls.[44] The results are reported in a 2011 article we wrote with ESOC member Michael Callen of UCSD titled "Do Working Men Rebel?"[45]

The answer to the question "Are higher employment levels associated with low insurgent violence?" is an emphatic *No*. On the contrary, in all three conflicts, higher employment rates predicted *more* violence, not less.

We initially found this result surprising, steeped as we were ourselves in the conventional wisdom about employment, deprivation, and violence. We first saw the positive correlation of employment rates and violence in Iraq and subjected it to every robustness test we could think of—which it survived—then set it aside as an anomaly, taking it seriously only when we could replicate it in two other asymmetric conflicts, Afghanistan and the Philippines.

The estimates are statistically precise, so the probability that we would find that positive correlation between employment and violence *in all three places*, and with so much data, if the true relationship were the opposite, is vanishingly small (about five one-hundredths of 1 percent).[46]

To think about what the estimated magnitudes entail in Iraq, for example, a 10 percent increase in employment rates is associated with 0.75 more attacks per 1,000 inhabitants per district over a three-month period. If we narrow the scope to Baghdad alone, the increase is over twice that large, at 1.96 more attacks per 1,000 people, roughly 40 more attacks in a midsized district, per quarter. This may not sound like much, but in a highly volatile atmosphere (in terms both of employment and violence) that would constitute a meaningful reduction in casualties. In the Baghdad governorate with its 9 districts, for example, it would imply roughly 6 more U.S. casualties per quarter.[47]

A positive correlation between employment rates and violence is consequential, as *it soundly refutes the two mechanisms* that motivate most development assistance programs in asymmetric settings: *relative deprivation and opportunity costs.*

Wait, So Working Men *Do* Rebel?

We don't think so. The result creates a theoretical puzzle that our information-centric model cannot solve: the model is mute on the employment-violence relationship, so *no effect* of employment rates on violence would be easy to explain. Why do the data insist that working men are associated with *more* violence?

A first possibility is that the cause and effect don't actually run from employment to violence but the other way around. Take, for instance, the successful campaign to curb sectarian violence in Baghdad conducted by (then) Lieutenant Colonel Jeff Peterson, one of the most successful practitioners of "surge" strategy (and, as it happens, a PhD social scientist). His approach to reducing violence between Sunni and Shi'ite groups was to construct massive concrete barriers between their neighborhoods. This created homogeneous zones for Sunni from Shia residents, each with their own shops and mosque. And it succeeded in limiting violence.

However, building walls between neighborhoods is like building them between countries—impeding movement slows trade, which in turn reduces economic activity, and typically reduces employment.[48] In general, barriers and checkpoints make it hard to get food to restaurants and merchandise to shops. The drag that puts on the local economy is well documented in the case of the Palestinian territories, in research by ESOC affiliate Alexei Abrahams, and others.[49] The presence of American troops, and the attacks they attract, may also dissuade people from going to markets. We call this the "*reverse causality*" explanation, as suppression of violence reduced employment.

A second possibility is an information-centric type of explanation. As local economic conditions deteriorate, the *price of information* (purchased tips) falls, and government forces and their allies can buy more intelligence on insurgents, undermining insurgent operations. Conversely, as economic conditions improve and employment rises, information becomes more expensive, favoring insurgents over government forces and allowing more insurgent violence. In our discussion so far civilians provided tips for free. In terms of the model in chapter 3, a price for information provides another tool available to government forces but otherwise does not change the workings of the model much. In the next section we'll provide some evidence that a market for tips exists.

A third and related possibility is *retaliatory violence*, which we didn't seriously pursue as a hypothesis in the 2011 article but which new data reveal to be important. That is, insurgents use violence against civilians to prevent tips. When incomes fall and the price of tips falls with it, insurgent violence against civilians (not government) may therefore increase as well, as insurgents become more vulnerable. But insurgents have limited resources, so in order to increase attacks on civilians they must reduce attacks on government forces, generating a positive correlation between income and attacks on government. That mechanism emerges clearly in research by ESOC affiliate Oliver Vanden Eynde on the Naxalite insurgency in India.[50] We will dig deeper into it shortly.

A fourth possibility is that as the economy improves and employment rises, there are more chances for insurgent groups to squeeze local businesses for taxes or "protection" payments. With more extorted funding, they might be able to produce more violence, or they might use more violence to implement the extra extortion. We saw evidence of this mechanism in chapter 5, in food aid and in the CDD program in the Philippines. We'll explore more evidence for this "*predation*" effect later in this chapter.

In the next few sections we will explore how tips, retaliation, and predation could plausibly explain the positive correlation of employment levels and violence that we found in the Philippines, Afghanistan, and Iraq. Before we do that, it's worth pausing a moment to reflect on refuted mechanisms.

The relationship between employment and violence in asymmetric insurgencies appears to be more complex than had been commonly assumed—by practitioners, scholars, and even American presidents. What we can say for sure is that *the expected relationship based on intuition from symmetric conflicts is exactly reversed* in three asymmetric conflicts: Afghanistan, Iraq, and the Philippines. It's hard to refute the proposition that opportunity costs and relative deprivation exist in asymmetric conflicts, but if they do, they seem to be dominated by some stronger forces that tie high employment to high violence.

We shift now to a more disturbing possibility: if we put aside the reverse causality explanation, the other three mechanisms suggest that the *typical* effect of an LGCD-like program would be to *increase* violence. We examine them in turn, starting with a brief introduction to the market for tips.

THE INFORMATION MARKET

In a 2002 article Kumar Ramakrishna described the effort—first by the British colonial authority, then by the Malayan federal government —to conduct a psychological war against a communist insurgency during the Malayan Emergency of the 1950s.[51] Ramakrishna saw this as a dual effort, including "pull" techniques, such as advertising leniency for those who gave themselves up, as well as "push" techniques—efforts to create an atmosphere within the insurgency that would push low-level players out. The propaganda campaign we described in chapter 4 represented an essential element of the "pull" technique: radio broadcasts of former insurgents enjoying New Year's feasts with their families, and eighteen million leaflets air-dropped over the country advertising the benefits of leaving the jungle. A key "push" technique was offering citizens—members of the insurgency and nonmembers alike—rewards for information leading to the capture or killing of a terrorist.

Two years into the conflict, in 1950, an officer who had formerly been a journalist with the BBC, Hugh Carleton Greene, established the "Emergency Information Services" office, with himself at the helm. Greene believed that stronger than the power of fear was the power of "greed" (today he might say "incentives") and established a schedule of payments for information; it ranged from $60,000 for the capture or killing of the secretary-general of the party to $2,000 for a low-level terrorist. Soon Greene realized that live insurgents were worth more than dead ones, as they could also provide valuable information, so six months into the effort he published an amended schedule: $80,000 for information leading to the *capture* of the head of the party to $2,500 for the lowest-rung member. If they were brought in dead, the old rates applied. Later, Greene created a schedule of payments for insurgents' weapons as well, from $500 for machine guns to $20 for hand grenades to 25 cents per round of ammunition.[52]

After Greene left Malaya, a later administrator discovered a perverse consequence: high-level insurgents flaunted the price on their heads as a badge of honor. He tamed and simplified the payment schedule; now there were only four levels of reward for information on rebels, ranging from $20,000 to $1,500.[53] By the end of 1956, just before mass defection of members led to the collapse of the insurgency, a typical informant earned $12,000 for a tip that led to the ambush and killing of three terrorists. This sum, Ramakrishna calculates, "represented 17 years' pay at the average rubber-tapper's salary of $100 a month."[54]

In short, this adjustment of prices based on a back-and-forth negotiation between information customers (the government) and vendors (whether citizens or turncoat rebels) follows familiar market patterns.

Ethically, it's questionable: Ramakrishna points out that one rebel caught driving a supply truck could be tried and sentenced to death, while another who had killed government soldiers but surrendered could, due to well-funded "push" and "pull" campaigns, end up with thousands of dollars or a government job. From a purely utilitarian perspective, though, these campaigns helped end the war quickly and in favor of a government that will presumably do a better job providing services, so perhaps on balance they were ethically defensible.[55]

The Malayan Emergency is long over and, as an example of psychological warfare, may be extreme. What about the asymmetric conflicts the United States and its allies have been involved in in recent decades? Traditionally the U.S. military only allowed commanders and their designees to make payouts for information and kept the rewards structure confidential. But in 2008, U.S. Central Command (CENTCOM)—the military command covering the Middle East and central Asia—began to authorize regular forces and their allies to pay for tips and, as a result, released guidelines to the public.[56] The program, called the Department of Defense Rewards Program, was laid out in a strategy handbook unsubtly titled "Money as a Weapon System."[57]

The strategy created the role of Rewards Authorization Officer (RAO) to authorize payments of up to $10,000 for individual pieces of information and to establish rewards criteria. In Iraq, all Brigade Combat Team (BCT) commanders were designated RAOs. The strategy also suggested how to determine these criteria: for instance, to take into account the number of personnel or weapons captured and their importance, and "the number of intermediate steps required by us forces between receiving the information and making the capture."[58] And leaders at lower levels also received funds through the program. In 2009, for example, $1,000 was made available to each company for "micro-rewards" of $500 or less apiece per event (which could be increased up to $10,000 upon RAO approval). Micropayments were authorized for on-the-spot use. In-kind rewards of food, cigarettes, and vehicles were acceptable; cash payments should be in dinars; dollars should be used in special cases only.[59]

A higher class of "small rewards" between $500 and $10,000 were "intended for High Value Individuals (HVI—i.e., terror cell leaders, terrorist financiers, and smugglers) or weapons caches." And a top class of "large rewards" above $10,000 were strictly "for the capture of HVI, large weapon caches that significantly reduce the effectiveness of a terror cell, and other pre-approved rewards of similar significance (i.e., the capture of foreign fighters or the abductor of a us service member)." These large rewards called for a two-step administrative process, where "pre-nomination" paperwork was filed before the capture or killing of an insurgent, a legal review was sometimes conducted, and a funding request with proper signatures was made "after capture/kill." All in all, the payment procedure for large rewards was lengthy. In practice, it could be used to reward informants for HVI already in captivity, but the document warned that "this process takes a few weeks, so units are encouraged to pre-nominate targets before the HVI is captured in order to streamline the payment process."[60]

The document reflects a fascinating process of trial and error perhaps similar to the British experience during the Malayan Emergency. It acknowledged that putting very high prices on the heads of lead rebels was counterproductive for a number of reasons: first, informants generally used the money to leave the country; second, a large sum might increase the danger to them or their families; third, large rewards might mark an insurgent as important and well connected, thus increasing the possibility of reprisals and effectively deincentivizing citizens from turning him in; and fourth, as in Malaya, the rebels might see a large price on their head as a mark of distinction (the document called this the "Jesse James effect"). For these reasons, "very little is paid out over the $10K threshold."[61]

The Department of Defense deemed the Rewards Program a success. In reporting on its 2014 budget for Operation Enduring Freedom, the office of the Secretary of Defense said that in 2013 the program had paid out 367 rewards in 15 countries. In Afghanistan, Iraq, and the Philippines this resulted in "the removal of over 100 high-value individuals, interdiction of over 300 improvised explosive devices, capture of hundreds of weapons and ammunition caches, disruption of enemy plans, and recovery of missing personnel and sensitive equipment."[62]

To summarize, for our purposes three facts are important: tips often have prices, that price can increase with the value of information, and customers (the demand side) have some flexibility to respond to market conditions. For the informant, the reward for the tip must be weighed against the possibility of retaliation, which we turn to now.

RETALIATION

Until now we've interpreted all violence initiated by insurgents against civilians as accidental. We can now do better, using new data that detail who initiates violence against whom, and sometimes even why. What if insurgents could identify informants, or narrow down the source of information to a particular family or street, and deter future tips by attacking them? For instance, insurgents might attack civilians in a government-controlled shopping center in an area known to be populated by government sympathizers (would-be informants). These new data allow us to measure *retaliatory violence against civilians*.

How would retaliation respond to a general improvement in economic conditions (as distinct from a project like CERP, which is conditional)? In the simple version of the information-centric model we outlined in chapter 3, it wouldn't matter, as that model had no price for tips and there was no wage for insurgents, so incomes and wages had no influence. Oliver Vanden Eynde describes a more complex setting, with active markets for tips (and other forms of cooperation with government), expanding a model like that in chapter 3 to allow economic conditions to matter, in order to study the Naxalite insurgency.

As background, Naxalites are Maoist insurgents who have fought the Indian government in very poor peripheral rural communities in the east and southeast states of India, the "Red Corridor," since 1967. Violence has been particularly intense since 2004, when Naxalite groups unified to form a single Communist party. That conflict claimed 5,500 lives between 2005 and 2011.[63] The conflict is asymmetric but much less so than those we've discussed so far. The states use police to conduct counterinsurgency, with little federal assistance and no international assistance, so that government forces have less technological capacity and training than do ISAF forces in Afghanistan or the Philippine military. Instead, security forces are mostly police, who make use not only of civilian informants but also of vigilantes and conduct an active campaign to bribe Naxalites into defection. Naxalites respond with retaliatory violence against civilians. One of the tragedies of the conflict is that over one-third of the fatalities are civilian.

Carefully coding data from the South Asian Terrorism Portal (SATP), Vanden Eynde assembled incident data for analysis covering the period 2005–11.[64] The SATP data are extremely useful because they identify both the initiator of the violence (government security forces or insurgents) and the victim (security forces, insurgents, or civilians). One remarkable dimension these data provide is the *purpose* of insurgent attacks on civilians: two-thirds are retaliation for collaboration, of which the leading categories are retaliation against police informers (31 percent) and against individuals carrying out political activity in mainstream parties opposed to Naxalites (26 percent), with smaller categories being retaliation against members of vigilante groups (7 percent) and surrendered Naxalites (2 percent). Of the rest, 26 percent are untargeted, only 2 percent are for failure to pay "taxes," and 2 percent are as punishment for crimes. The conflict data were even detailed enough for Vanden Eynde to see that the large majority of victims belonged to *the specific groups of civilians* who typically collaborated with the Indian government against the rebels. This type of retaliatory violence has gone largely unstudied in the recent empirical literature, for lack of large data sets and variation that lends itself to estimating causal effects. It is more common in earlier, more qualitative research, such as Stathis Kalyvas's classic study of the Greek civil war.[65]

In order to rule out reverse causality (violence affecting economic conditions), Vanden Eynde studied the consequences of variation in income generated by variation in rainfall; this is a very strong relationship in rural India, which has a highly localized pattern of monsoon rains affecting crop yields within regions and within years.[66] Decreases in income generated by weak rainfall *increase* violence initiated by insurgents, which might seem at first glance like evidence for relative deprivation or opportunity costs—except that the increased violence is *not directed against security forces but against civilians*.

Vanden Eynde offers retaliation as a more likely explanation. He describes a setting in which the government bids against insurgents for support from civilians, offering payments for tips, as well as for political and vigilante activity. When crops fail due to low rainfall, both the civilians and Naxalites suffer lower income—Naxalites tax (extort) farmers—but the government does not (as crops are not taxed). Civilians, who are subsistence farmers, face lower income (and presumably lower wages) when crops fail and become more willing to accept payment for supporting the government (in return for information, political support, vigilante activity, or even defection from the insurgency). So when the harvest is weak, the price of civilian support for government has effectively declined, so the government buys more of it. Insurgents respond by attempting to deter this loss of civilian support by allocating more resources to violence against civilians.

This is in a sense an opportunity cost mechanism but with an important twist on the conventional wisdom: civilians with poor market opportunities are recruited to support the *government* side, not the rebels. The Naxalite organizational structure is much like those of other insurgent organizations we described earlier. They are not particularly responsive to changes in local labor income because they are small, and the vast majority of fighters are low-wage local farmers working part-time; so the organizational wage bill is not large. Moreover, the core leadership are urban and middle or upper class, so local weather would be uncorrelated with their opportunity wages. Thus, it's probably *on the government side that an opportunity cost mechanism is relevant*. "This finding," writes Vanden Eynde, "is consistent with the idea that rebels use violence against civilians to counterbalance the increased appeal of collaboration after scanty rainfall."[67]

This interpretation is consistent with evidence from another recent study of Naxalite violence as well, by Thiemo Fetzer of Warwick. Fetzer asks how the effect of income on violence changes after a guaranteed work program is introduced. The National Rural Employment Guarantee Scheme (NREG) is the world's largest poverty reduction program, benefiting over fifty million households annually. It guarantees India's rural poor one hundred days of labor per year at minimum wage.

Fetzer uses the same design as Vanden Eynde did to estimate effects of changes in income induced by changes in rainfall and indeed finds that in a region without NREGS increases in income reduce Naxalite violence. Again, the effect is mainly driven by reductions in *violence by insurgents against civilians*. Once NREGS is in place, rainfall-induced income ceases to change local wages, and ceases to change violence, again, mostly because *the effect on violence against civilians is muted.*[68] So this effect of droughts on violence against civilians, which we know from the incident reports is mostly retaliatory, can be reduced to a statistical zero by providing income support.

When Vanden Eynde turns to the type of violence we've been concerned with so far, insurgent violence against government forces, he finds a statistically insignificant *increase* when rainfall (and thus income) is high, as we found in Afghanistan, Iraq, and the Philippines. Interestingly, that effect is muted in areas where Naxalite insurgents have access to revenue from extorted mines. (The increase is statistically insignificant, but the contrast between the responses of the insurgents in agricultural and mining areas is statistically significant.) His explanation is tied again to the cost of maintaining civilian support: when civilian income increases, the price of cooperation with government rises (in tips, political activity, or vigilante activity), so the government buys less cooperation. Insurgents both have more income to spend (from extorting farmers) and can afford to allocate fewer fighters to retaliate against cooperating civilians, so they devote more to attacking the government. This mechanism is weaker and perhaps even reversed in mining areas, where rainfall affects civilian income less, and where income of insurgents gained from extorting mines makes them less dependent on taxing agricultural income.

Now let's return to the program that motivated us, LGCD. If economic conditions were improved through an unconditional job creation program then they might affect violence as rainfall does. Vanden Eynde's version of the information-centric model would predict a reduction in retaliatory violence by insurgents—as fewer civilians turn to government for payments—and an increase in insurgent violence against security forces. Alternatively, if those improvements in income were due to increases in government service provision, optimally delivered (i.e., modest, secure, informed, and conditional—as small CERP projects were in chapters 5 and 6), then our model from chapter 3 has clear predictions. We expect an *increase* in suppressive violence by government, through the complementarity of suppression and service provision (chapter 6), as government will use the information to increase its suppression of rebels. The likelihood of insurgent retaliation against citizens will also *increase* in response to the extra service provision, as rebels react to becoming more vulnerable.[69] This corresponds to the retaliation arrows, which point from rebels toward the civilian population, in figure 3.2. As in chapter 5, we would also predict a reduction in violence against government.

Another study on the Naxalite insurgency backs up some of these predictions. A recent article by Gaurav Khanna and Laura Zimmermann examined the effects of the same NREGS program on Naxalite violence.[70] The way the government rolled the program out across districts at inception in 2006–8 gave the authors leverage to estimate causal effects. Each state used an algorithm to select its poorest districts to receive the program first; however, the threshold varied by state. That meant the authors could apply a regression discontinuity design, as Joe and coauthors did in the CDD paper in the Philippines (chapter 5), and compare places just above one state's threshold to those just below another's, and claim with confidence that they have no other discernable difference that would confound estimating a causal effect.

In that first phase of rollout, the *arrival of NREGS led to an increase in fatalities*, of about 0.55 to 0.75 deaths per district per month—about a 125 percent increase. Similarly, the number of affected persons increases about 56 percent and the number of incidents, 70 percent. Across all the districts, that amounted to about 785–1,071 more fatalities in 314–385 more incidents in the year after NREGS arrived. In some respects the evidence from India is particularly strong for an information-centric view of asymmetric conflict because the Naxalites claim to be fighting largely to redress economic grievances—the alternative hypothesis. If there is any asymmetric conflict where we should see strong effects from providing employment, the Naxal conflict is it. But we see the opposite.

As in the other studies based on SATP incident data, the authors could measure *who* inflicted violence upon whom. That increase in violence was mainly by government against Naxalites, *and by Naxalites on civilians—retaliation*, as our model in chapter 3 predicted for a conditionally implemented program. That's speculation on our part, as we don't know that NREGS practiced conditionality, and the authors have no direct evidence on tips. The authors also found a smaller, but statistically significant, increase in Naxalite attacks on government, which contradicts the predictions of the information-centric model and might be interpreted as predation—if the presence of government forces prevented extortion of income related to NREGS. Alternatively, if we measure violence by fatalities (rather than by incidents), the largest effect and the only one that is statistically significant is the increase in Naxalite fatalities due to a rise in government-initiated attacks, again consistent with the predictions of the information-centric model in chapter 3.

Interestingly, Khanna and Zimmermann observed that the burst of violence was concentrated in the first seven months after NREGS' arrival, when plans were announced but typically not yet implemented: compared to the next seven months, the number of affected persons was 1.6–2.2 times higher and fatalities, 1.4–1.6 times higher. This led the authors to extend inference beyond the predictions of our model (which is static). After that initial burst of violence (information leads government to suppress rebels, and rebels retaliate against citizens), suppression efforts will start to work, and overall violence will recede. This is consistent with the finding of another paper on the conflict that analyzes a longer time frame.[71]

The authors conclude that there are two possible explanations for their results. The first is a "citizen-support" channel, which encompasses tips (as in chapter 3) but also other forms of citizen cooperation with government forces (as in Vanden Eynde's work). The second is predation, which we will turn to in the next section.

Taken together, these three studies of the Naxalite insurgency add a new set of important insights to the literature. First, they provide direct evidence of retaliation by insurgents. Second, they push the recent empirical literature into a setting that is more symmetric, with a government side that is less dominant in capacity, technology, or training, and relies on civilians who are more easily identified for retaliation by insurgents and less protected, sadly. Third, they provide a model by which increased income can reduce retaliatory violence. That model has the advantage of not relying on an opportunity cost mechanism of insurgent recruiting that is hard to reconcile with what we now know about the demand and supply of insurgents. Instead, they argue, increased income has a price effect on tips and other forms of citizen support *for government* that lead rebels to use violence to control civilians.

Further, if we are willing to assume that civilians perceived NREGS as conditional on cooperation with government, then the model in chapter 3 does a pretty good job of explaining the major findings of increased violence by government and Naxalites, even if it fails to explain why Naxalite violence against government forces increased. It also does an impressive job in answering a question the Naxalite findings raise: Why does an unconditional increase in income (caused by rainfall) induce no increased suppression by government, while a conditional increase in income (NREGS) induces a large increase?

We turn now to predation, our final candidate explanation for the (Afghan, Philippine, and Iraq result of a) positive correlation of employment rates and violence.

PREDATION: A BIGGER PIE INVITES MORE VIOLENCE?

What if you see that improved economic conditions are accompanied by more violence in some regions but less violence in others in the same asymmetric conflict? That was the case in Colombia, as reported in a 2013 article by Oeindrila Dube and Juan F. Vargas.[72]

Colombia's civil war had been going on in one form or another since the 1960s, with levels and locations of violence, and relative power of different groups, in constant flux. Left-wing guerrilla groups FARC and ELN jockeyed for power against right-wing paramilitaries (originally founded to protect the interests of landowners and drug cartels) and, of course, the government.[73] The FARC especially was a large and powerful insurgent group, with around 10,000 fighters in 2105, down from 16,000–20,000 at its peak.[74] By some estimates it was the richest insurgency in the world. At times the FARC had flirted with becoming a legitimate political party; that, and its stated purpose to fight for the poor, gave it powerful recruiting appeal. The paramilitaries also had huge resources, as they drew funds from the cocaine trade and by siphoning oil to sell on the black market. (Colombia's main pipeline is said to have so many holes, it is nicknamed "the flute.")[75]

Using conflict data from 978 municipalities over eighteen years, Dube and Vargas showed that changes in world prices for Colombia's two largest exports, coffee and oil, had opposite effects on violence. For coffee, as the price went *down*, violence went *up*: "the 68% fall in coffee prices over 1997 to 2003 resulted in 18% more guerrilla attacks, 31% more paramilitary attacks, 22% more clashes, and 14% more casualties in the average coffee municipality, relative to non-coffee areas." However, for oil, the relationship was opposite, as prices went *up*, violence went *up*: "The 137% increase in oil prices over 1998 to 2005 led paramilitary attacks to increase by an additional 14% in the average oil producing municipality." These changes were differential, meaning the more the economy of a district depended on the commodity, the stronger the effect.[76]

The difference, the authors argued, comes down to how labor-intensive a product is. Coffee is labor intensive so the preponderance of citizen working hours in coffee-producing regions are spent in its production. When the price goes down, the authors argue, so do wages and with them opportunity costs, making citizens more likely to join the insurgency. As mentioned earlier, this is the pattern we see in symmetric conflicts. Oil, on the other hand, is not a labor-intensive product. A rise in oil prices does not mean a rise in wages in oil-producing regions, but it does cause an increase in tax revenues and municipal budgets. In Colombia this led to guerrillas in oil-producing regions extorting greater rents from locals and increasing political kidnappings. So for such "capital-intensive" products, the predation effect rules. Dube and Vargas went on to analyze other labor-intensive and capital-intensive products in Colombia from bananas to gold and showed that the contrast between predation and labor costs effects on violence held true across many products.

The authors' interpretation of the opportunity cost effect is plausible, but given the other evidence we've presented from similar asymmetric settings, we remain skeptical. An alternative is that when coffee prices decline, the FARC shifted their attention to coca production and distribution systems, which are labor intensive themselves and entail violence in contract enforcement. Perhaps that's why they run an unusually labor-intensive insurgency, unlike IS, the Taliban, or the

Naxalites.[77] Nevertheless, this remains the strongest evidence for an opportunity cost mechanism in the literature. The study also provides the best evidence yet that the predation effect is particular to the source of revenue, not to the character of the insurgency.

PREDATION AND TAXATION

In 2000, a Japanese development bank loaned the Philippine government $215 million to modernize a commercial port facility in a former U.S. Navy base on Subic Bay, about sixty miles northwest of Manila. The region until then had a small but persistent Maoist rebel presence, but with the development, rebel-initiated violence began to rise. A Japanese firm broke ground on the port in 2004; in that same year, government-initiated incidents spiked. These included violence at the hands of special operations teams, combat troops, intelligence operations, and police, and resulted in twenty-one fatalities. In subsequent years incidents declined to a relatively low level, but still with government initiating more incidents than rebels. By 2007 the region was safe enough for a Korean firm to be building ships and operating a cargo port in the facility, which was planned to expand to be the fourth-largest dry dock in the world. The episode at Subic Bay can be read as evidence that a very large local investment invited both predatory violence by rebels and suppressive violence by the government.

In 2013 Eli and Joe circulated a working paper with Ethan Kapstein and Erin Troland, expanding the model in chapter 3 to allow for investment by firms, predatory rebels, and government taxation.[78] The expanded model had some additional propositions, predicting that *both rebels and government would initiate violence* in response to investment, under certain conditions.[79]

To test the propositions, we matched investment data[80] to the Philippine incident data for eighty provinces between 2002 and 2008. Investment was high in the areas around population centers such as Manila and low in conflict-ridden areas. That was no surprise. Importantly, *increases* in business investment were positively correlated with increases in rebel violence, as a predation mechanism would predict.

While Eli, Joe, and coauthors did not establish causality, their results were the first we know of to link investment to predatory rebel violence in nationwide data.

The most novel finding had to do with violence inflicted *upon* rebels by the government. Government-sponsored violence *also increased with private investment*—a second avenue through which increased private investment can cause violence. If the government sees investment as an opportunity for income through taxes, it may move to protect its financial interests by cracking down on predatory insurgents in the area, as it seemed to be doing around Subic Bay.

In a variant of this logic, the government's motivation to protect investment may not be taxation. In Colombia private companies took a more active role, actually subsidizing government forces to protect their interests. Working with the same political landscape as Dube and Vargas, Austin Wright (one of Jake's graduate students now at the University of Chicago) argued that when local economies improve, and the government and civilians reap the benefits, insurgent groups shift from regular to irregular warfare—in essence switching from insurgent tactics to criminal operations such as kidnappings and drug trafficking.[81] Moreover, Wright documented that at times during the 1990s British Petroleum and Occidental Petroleum simply paid the Colombian army to protect their pipelines and machinery.[82]

CONCLUSION

The development assistance prescription that flows from the information-centric model is empirically validated (or so we've claimed) but organizationally demanding. For a project to be modest, secure, informed, and conditional in an asymmetric conflict setting it ideally requires a responsive local government, a disciplined and thoughtful battalion, and some valiant development practitioners. Failing that, two of those three elements must be unusually talented or well trained. So we began this chapter with a question: Is there some alternative theory in the economics and conflict literature that suggests less restrictive conditions and is itself empirically validated in an asymmetric conflict setting?

This chapter has surveyed that literature and found no such theory. The conventional wisdom supporting projects such as LGCD is based on inference from cross-country correlations where most of the conflicts are symmetric. Drawing evidence from those wars and applying it to asymmetric ones appears to have been grossly misleading. The implications of relative deprivation and opportunity costs theories are usually refuted in asymmetric conflict settings. Worse, much of the evidence flowing out of countries with asymmetric conflicts indicates that improvements in economic conditions often *increase* violence, either by rebels or by government, or both.

In this light, USAID's experience with the LGCD program in Afghanistan may be more comprehensible, in having increased employment but also violence. Perhaps USAID's revised evaluation of its own program puts it best. This is how the Special Inspector General for Afghanistan Reconstruction put it, when comparing USAID documents over the life of the program:

> The original LGCD task orders emphasized the importance of development and employment projects in achieving success with stabilization activities. For example, they stated that short-term stabilization involves identifying and engaging populations that are vulnerable to recruitment into militant groups, such as alienated, uneducated, and unemployed youth, and that violence linked to a lack of development had created an environment of generalized instability. The task orders offered examples of activities that the contractors could undertake to promote stability, including using development projects as an incentive for different groups or tribes to negotiate truces or ceasefires and employment activities for at-risk young people. A 2011 USAID presentation, however, appears to call into question the value of these activities in contributing to stability. Specifically, the presentation states that the idea that "economic development and modernization foster stability" and that "more jobs means less support for insurgents" are "myths."[83]

Our research would hazard a more general conclusion on development programs in conflict zones: know your war. In chapter 1 we told the story of how the 1st Infantry Division in Baghdad learned that lesson, retooling themselves from the symmetric conflict they had trained on, where resources and firepower mattered most, to the asymmetric conflict they were in, where information flows were critical.

Development professionals face an analogous challenge. They are trained to work in relatively secure spaces where people and property are safe, and often arrive with vast experience in those settings. Even in a country cursed by civil war, if that conflict is *symmetric*, in the space behind the front lines an implemented program will be safe enough to bring value to a community. It may even generate some extra taxable resources that can be applied by the government to help win the war. The water treatment plant in the Kurdish area of Iraq, which we discussed in chapter 5, is a good example. The lessons of the Marshall Plan's astounding success in rebuilding postwar Europe might fully apply to a symmetric conflict where governance behind the battle lines is strong enough to support markets.

In an *asymmetric* conflict, though, the consequences of a ubiquitous insurgency turn an economist's usual intuition on its head. In settings where people and property are not safe enough to support markets, increasing economic activity can just as easily stoke predatory violence as it can alleviate deprivation by increasing incomes: development programs can be captured or even make things worse when they set off a fight over new resources—or induce retaliatory violence. Moreover, alleviating deprivation may serve no military purpose, as it has at best no effect on information flow, or may even bid up the price of information. At the same time, drying up the pool of fighting-age unemployed males by providing jobs and bidding up wages can be a fool's errand. The tactics of asymmetric insurgency require only a few fighters, perhaps one for every hundred jobs created. They often work part-time, and the supply of the full-time cadres and the foreign fighters is likely not responsive to local wages.

Having reviewed the literature on economic conditions and violence in asymmetric conflicts, we have found variants, but no substitutes, for the basic model with the father in the courtyard considering his options. We can only conclude that modest, secure, informed, and conditional projects of chapter 5 are by far the best bet. If someone says "Marshall Plan" or "ambitious infrastructure project," direct them to the exit; if that fails, run for it yourself.

This news is relevant not only to development practitioners but also for scholars of economic development whose research guides program design. As formerly low-income countries graduate to middle-income status, the residual recipients of development assistance will become almost entirely fragile states (or regions thereof) with large swaths of territory cursed by conflict, most of it asymmetric. Development economists could do a much better job of understanding how economic conditions can best improve in places where people and property are unsafe. The guiding insight of modern economics, the efficiency of markets, is largely unavailable in those conditions, if contracting is precluded by an absence of security—or from forces who will happily loot resources generated by any kind of economic development. Can scholars do better than recommending some CERP, with an expensive battalion to guard it?

In the next chapter we will start to answer that question, offering evidence from a range of settings on specific interventions that seem to improve information flow, sometimes at very low cost. Before we do, we should step back and review where we are. In chapter 3 we told you the story of a father deciding whether to call in tips. Chapter 4 offered evidence that making it safer for him to do so would lead insurgents to avoid his neighborhood, or at least to plant fewer IEDs there. Chapter 5 demonstrated that modest and conditional aid seemed to motivate information-sharing. Consistent with those findings, chapter 6 provided evidence of strong complementarities between efforts to suppress violence and some kinds of aid spending. In chapter 7 we reviewed a range of evidence that civilians punish combatants for harming them by sharing more or less information with the government, so that combatants had best be mindful of civilian casualties. Now we have seen that the broad evidence base on links between economic conditions and conflict in asymmetric conflicts is generally consistent with an information-centric interpretation, while the alternatives that inform conventional wisdom are generally refuted. The next chapter looks at some practical, non-obvious interventions that can take advantage of these insights.

WHAT WORKS? LEVERAGING THE INFORMATION MECHANISM

- -

In 2006, Colin Supko deployed to Iraq as a Platoon Commander with SEAL Team 5. He was responsible for a sparsely populated area south of the Euphrates River stretching from the outskirts of Fallujah to the outskirts of Ramadi, Anbar's capital and largest city, thirty-five miles to the east. It was a volatile area: more than 30,000 people had been killed across Anbar since the beginning of the war in 2003, making it Iraq's most violent province outside of Baghdad.[1] The Awakening we described in chapter 6 would eventually stabilize Anbar, but when Lieutenant Supko arrived that movement was only beginning to stir in Ramadi. Meanwhile sixty miles away in Baghdad, roving Shia death squads—some staffed by soldiers from the national army—were kidnapping and torturing Sunnis in retaliation for suicide attacks.

The Awakening hadn't reached Supko's rural area of operations yet, but the insurgents it displaced had. As Sunni leaders in Ramadi aligned with the Coalition, their former allies in al Qaeda in Iraq (AQI) flooded the countryside. Supko's men had to work with the Iraqi army, which was largely Shia, in conducting "direct action missions"— mainly nighttime raids intended to capture or kill insurgents. That put them at odds with the local population and in particular with the police, who were largely Sunni. According to Supko, "Night raids were [generating] an undue negative influence, and fear among the people." With distrust high and miscommunication frequent, it was essential that Supko start winning the trust of civilians if the wave of Sunni Awakening was to spread. "We weren't going to defeat insurgency with just bullets," Supko said, "we were going to have to demonstrate to the people that things were getting better and not worse."[2]

At the center of Supko's territory lay a Coalition airbase, Camp Habbaniyah. It had long held strategic importance, situated next to the main transit route between central Iraq and Syria—its airfield had served as a key stop on the supply route from Britain to the USSR during World War II. Camp Habbaniyah was made up of hundreds of brick barracks and hangars dating back to the 1930s, many of them unoccupied and strewn with old papers and broken machinery.

Supko worked for a special forces task unit based at Camp Habbaniyah, headed by another recent arrival, Lieutenant Commander Ryan Shann. His job was to maintain security along the road between Fallujah and Ramadi. The towns along the road lacked many important services, including communications. Insurgents had bombed a cell-phone tower on a bluff overlooking Camp Habbaniyah two years prior, knocking out service to a wide area.[3] Although one mobile provider, MCI, had restored cellular service to Coalition forces and some senior Iraqi leaders, the public remained without ICT service and had little hope of being reconnected.

Supko and Shann agreed that they could ease tensions with the local Sunni police if they could phone them at key junctures to inform them of Iraqi army troop movements or steer them away from the location of U.S. missions. This required restoring cell-phone service, but as Shann told us, "Coalition Forces, Iraqi government, and Iraqi Army entities in the area had accepted that bringing cell phone service west of Fallujah was beyond their capability."[4]

Then Shann realized that one of his intelligence officers could help: Andrew Montalvo was a Naval Reservist who had volunteered for a tour of duty in Iraq. Back home in Texas he worked for Southern Bell Company. He had started as a POTS ("plain old telephone service") repairman, working with analog "tip and ring" lines before becoming a line crew supervisor. "I arrived at Camp Habbaniyah in August, 2006," Montalvo told us. "Within 20 days of arriving, Commander

Shann called me in and said, 'I need you to figure out how we can get cell service going.'"[5]

The first task was to see just which Iraqi company held the license for the area. With an interpreter, Montalvo sat down at the base's MWR computer—the one meant for "morale, welfare, and recreation," that is, writing home—and googled "mobile service in Iraq." A company called Iraqna came up, then its Egyptian parent company, Oriscom. A few phone calls put Montalvo in touch with an Iraqna official who, Montalvo was surprised to discover, passed him on to an American in Baghdad.

"Then it got strange," Montalvo said.

He endured some bumping up against various U.S. intelligence agencies and military branches, but Montalvo was eventually able to secure the backing of Iraqna. Commander Shann told us, "Task Unit Habbaniyah was able to bypass astonishing amounts of bureaucracy on both the Iraqi civilian and Coalition military sides." After several meetings in Baghdad, they had a deal.

The next challenge was getting the Iraqi technicians and all their equipment from Baghdad to Camp Habbaniyah safely. The engineers were justifiably wary of being seen assisting the Americans, but the team hatched a plan that would provide these civilians with a cover story. A SEAL unit drove to Baghdad, met the technicians at a planned location, and then made a show of pulling over their vehicle, forcing them to the ground, handcuffing them, and driving them away. Meanwhile, a convoy of Iraqi soldiers left Baghdad heading westward on leave. Embedded among their armored vehicles was an Iraqna truck carrying the equipment.

For two months Montalvo worked with the engineers at Camp Habbaniyah. In most mobile phone networks, fiber optic cables link towers to the network, but not on Iraq's ICT frontier. Instead, the technicians used microwave transmission to connect the Habbaniyah tower to the company's switches in Kuwait. That required climbing an old radio tower, attaching a line-of-sight microwave receiver much like the satellite dishes people have on their roofs, and pointing it with precision at the next tower, in Fallujah. The Marines contributed a generator to power the system. They also provided protection. (Montalvo told us that the project would not have been possible off base where the technicians would not have been guarded.) And they mollified the Iraqi base commander, who complained about not getting a cut. "His cousin was looking for the contract to maintain the generator and provide the fuel," Montalvo explained.

In spring 2007 the line went live, and people south of the Euphrates between Fallujah and Anbar had access to national and international networks for the first time in two years. Since the project had enlisted a private-sector firm in return for a chance to profit, the Coalition had spent zero dollars.

The project succeeded beyond its original goals. The team's impetus had been to improve communication with the local police to avoid incidents in which task unit forces might get into firefights with local law enforcement. Indeed, Montalvo told us, "policemen's lives were saved because the unit was able to call the chief of police's phone to prevent them from going to places where they shouldn't." However, the effects of restoring service surpassed everyone's expectations. The number of significant activity (SIGACT) incidents declined. Chiefs from outlying villages started calling and asking if they could have towers put up in their areas.

This represented the first time local tribes had seen a positive result from American intervention, and Supko maximized the political capital gained by praising the local police and giving them credit for the project. This led to joint operations. Supko was able to shift from night raids conducted with the distrusted Iraqi army to daytime operations conducted with the Sunni local police. Eventually a local antigovernment militia shifted allegiance, joining the Coalition-affiliated Sons of Iraq. After a couple of months, Supko was able to turn his attention to water systems, school-building projects, and the founding of the first Iraqi police academy in the area.

Shann summarized the impact: "Restoration of cell service had a profound effect on quality of life throughout the area, and had a more significant impact than any offensive mission conducted. Coordination between the Iraqi government, army and police, tribal and Coalition leaders became possible. Tip lines were immediately established and the intelligence gathering and passing capabilities of the anti-insurgent movement improved dramatically." The team had created the conditions where a concerned father like the one we described in chapter 3 had the option of providing a tip to help reduce violence in his community. And his community got connectivity back. Shann added that further and more profound effects occurred, which remain classified.

Camp Habbaniyah's geographic position, with cities to the east and west, and being situated on the main road, made it a natural communications hub. Hence, a functional tower established a link to other towers deeper into Anbar's western hinterlands.[6] Shann and his team helped move this process along by erecting another tower in an outpost on the other side of the Euphrates River valley. Their efforts set an example that broke the Iraqi telecoms' refusal to work in this volatile area and created a framework for reestablishing service throughout the rest of western Anbar province.

In the end, the task unit's accomplishment garnered praise from high-level military and civilian leaders who had been attempting to restore cellular service for over eighteen months. General Petraeus emailed personally to express his congratulations and thanks. Supko gives Shann the real credit for pushing the project through: "Ryan took the risk—it was his ass."

Ryan Shann would not be stationed at Camp Habbaniyah long enough to observe and document the effects of providing ICT to the civilians of Anbar. By coincidence, he would feel vindicated five years later when, as a student in Princeton's master's of public policy program, he attended one of Jake's lectures. Jake related findings from the studies described in chapter 4 on the information mechanism. When they looked closely at what happened around Camp Habbaniyah Shann saw hard evidence of how his efforts had contributed to a broader pattern.

Why such high returns on such a modest investment? Remember, at the same time a massive water treatment plant just fifteen miles downriver was costing tens of millions of dollars and failing to win over the populace. Apparently, in this case, a small act was able to cause a big improvement in local security trends, probably because concurrent with having reasons to support the government, Iraqi citizens received the means to act at low risk: by passing information on insurgent activities to the Coalition via the tip line. Cellular technology and the anonymity it provides exemplify how simple, low-cost innovations can go a long way in reducing violence.

Is this potential for small changes to have large effects a general principle of asymmetric conflict? We believe it is, for two reasons. First, the logic of information-sharing by civilians implies that at any given time there might be a large number of consequential tips, whose potential can be activated by a small improvement in incentives. Second, we've seen many examples of modest and inexpensive policy changes that lead to big effects. Those examples provide rich intuition for thinking creatively about what kinds of policies are likely to help governments reduce violence in asymmetric conflicts.

- -

In previous chapters we have built out the logic of the information-centric model and laid out evidence by testing general propositions. In this chapter, we focus on specific examples: practical things governments can do to make information flow more readily, including how to reconfigure forces and how to shift community norms in their favor. The examples we describe have one thing in common: they demonstrate that modest policy changes can have large effects. This general principle is implied by the information-centric model. This chapter provides evidence from various settings.

We begin with force configuration, examining how an organizational change in the Philippines—getting locally recruited militias involved in the counterinsurgency effort—led to significant gains for government forces. We then turn to evidence on policies that can shift attitudes, beginning with research showing that successful disaster response earned citizen support in several conflict-affected countries. We then look at some simple, cheap interventions in Afghanistan and Pakistan that had meaningful effects when done well. Can simply providing small amounts of information shift attitudes? The answer is "yes" in a number of examples, including one from Bangladesh and another from Uganda. And there are even more profound effects from small improvements in governance, as we see in a remarkable result from Afghanistan. All in all, this eclectic mix of evidence shows there are many different kinds of small-scale, locality-specific policy decisions that have the potential to improve information flow and are more difficult for insurgents to counter than are large development projects. While this chapter won't provide a one-size-fits-all finding, it should provide intuition for the kinds of microlevel policies and interventions that can have large-scale impact.

THE POWER OF WORKING WITH LOCAL FORCES

In chapter 2 we told the story of how Joe discovered a data trove and managed to get it compiled into a comprehensive microconflict data set.

The unique political landscape of the Philippines—long-running insurgencies of three distinct types (separatist, Communist, and extremist), as well as various government approaches to address these threats across groups and over time—made these data particularly conducive to testing hypotheses on how best to conduct a counterinsurgency campaign. In a working paper written as part of his PhD thesis and later published, Joe developed a taxonomy of the qualities and configurations of security forces best suited to address an insurgency, drawing on the literature, his own research, and his years in Special Forces advising foreign militaries: "(1) superior small unit level leadership who can accurately assess and respond to ever-changing local conditions; (2) troops with high quality training emphasizing tactical readiness; and (3) doctrine and command-and-control measures that facilitate rapid adaptation and innovation, and the application of flexible responses and tactics."[7] These are not new ideas; many military strategists had long acted on them. The innovation was Joe's ability to use the detailed, geolocated incident data to quantify the advantage units with those characteristics had over others.

Joe used the available coded data from the Philippines, which at the time covered 21,000 conflict-related incidents from 2001 to 2008. He complemented these data with information pulled from more than 2,000 interviews with combatants—both government soldiers and former rebels—along with multiple large-scale surveys of the AFP at all levels. He developed a broad typology to describe military units in terms of their differences in quality and readiness: *high quality*, meaning the highly trained and well-led special operations forces (SOF) consisting mainly of Scout Rangers and Special Forces; *medium quality*, the regular infantry forces; and *low quality*, the part-time, locally recruited soldiers known as Citizen Armed Forces Geographical Units (CAFGUS), which had relatively weak training and poor overall equipment compared to regular infantry and SOF. With these broad categories defined and the government units participating in reported incidents coded accordingly, Joe compared select indicators of counterinsurgency effectiveness across levels of troop quality.

A standard measure of military effectiveness in battle is the Loss-Exchange Fraction (LEF)—the number of casualties inflicted on rebels by government forces divided by the total number of rebel and government casualties. It is presented visually on the left side of figure 9.1. High-quality units inflicted over three times more casualties on their rebel opponents than they suffered themselves. Medium-quality units inflicted slightly more casualties on rebels than they incurred, and low-quality units were far more likely to perish at the hands of rebels in conflict episodes they participated in, making up two-thirds of the total casualties when these local forces engaged rebels in operations. In conflict episodes led or directly supported by specialized intelligence units (represented by the black bar), four out of five of casualties were suffered by the rebel side.

Joe also wanted to measure and compare the average rate of civilian casualties caused by counterinsurgency forces, as a proxy for effective counterinsurgency, in the spirit of an information-centric model. To do this he invented the metric "Discriminate Lethality"—the number of civilian casualties incurred per rebel killed in government-initiated incidents. The *ability to apply force discriminately and avoid civilian casualties is a powerful indicator* of military effectiveness in counterinsurgency, as we discussed in chapter 7. High-quality units from the Philippine military's special operations forces inflicted, on average, 8 civilian casualties for every 100 rebels killed, medium-quality regular infantry units 24, and lower-quality local forces 35—an approximately 50 percent higher rate than medium-quality and four times

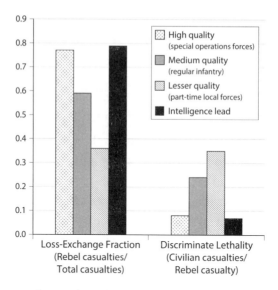

FIGURE 9.1. Force performance by quality: Philippines.

Figures from ESOC Philippines Database data from 1999 to 2008. See Joseph H. Felter, "Sources of Military Effectiveness in Counterinsurgency: Evidence from the Philippines," in *The Sword's Other Edge: Tradeoffs in the Pursuit of Military Effectiveness*, ed. Daniel Reiter (New York: Cambridge University Press, 2017).

higher than high-quality units. In incidents led or augmented by specialized intelligence units, comparatively fewer civilians were killed—7 per 100 rebels. Other outcome indicators proxying for military effectiveness—rebels captured and government firearms lost per incident—followed this same pattern: superior performance of higher-quality troops.

Joe's theory of military effectiveness identified access to local information as a critical component of effective counterinsurgency operations. He hypothesized that the *interaction* of accurate local information from local CAFGU with high-quality troops would be the most effective—and most efficient—combination at the small unit level. While this hypothesis is consistent with counterinsurgency theory— and might seem like common sense to practitioners—it does not always guide force configuration and could not have been tested previously for lack of data. Joe and his team's investment in collecting fine-grained incident data, laboriously coding it, and matching it with information on combatants and outcomes could now achieve its first returns.

Joe's empirical tests indicated that counterinsurgency effectiveness and efficiency could be measurably improved. For example, in certain cases, high-quality Philippine SOF were augmented with part-time citizen soldiers drawn from the local area to serve as guides. *That facilitated information flows from the local population* and otherwise increased situational awareness in the area where the SOF troops operated. In qualitative data and preliminary data analyses, Joe saw that the combination of a few highly trained individuals working with local forces resulted in even better performance on multiple outcome measures than SOF units operating alone. This could not have been due to tactical proficiency of the local forces—these were members of the low-quality units who could well have been a liability in combat situations. Joe believed (as did many AFP officers he interviewed) that knowledge of community and access to information channels created synergies within these hybrid units that led to performance advantages in the aggregate. Those advantages outweighed the inherent risks of operating with lesser-trained local soldiers.

To be clear, Joe's hypothesis on the advantages of mixing local and highly trained forces invokes information mechanisms beyond tips from civilians, recalling our discussion of citizen support in countering the Naxalite insurgency in the previous chapter. Anecdotal evidence *did* suggest that local civilians were more likely to share information with local troops, but local troops also brought to bear better knowledge of local topography and social conditions, beyond their advantages in access to civilian tips.

Interestingly, patterns similar to Joe's results from the Philippines also show up in the Russian campaign against the Chechen insurgency.[8] During that campaign Russian forces and their local allies conducted "sweep" operations in which they would control access into and out of a village for several days while going house to house to look for weapons and check people's identification documents. Jason Lyall, whose study on Chechnya we discussed in chapter 6, collected data on both sweep operations and combat incidents from 2000 through 2005 using press reports, government and rebel websites, and reports from human rights organizations. His data indicated whether the sweeps were conducted by Russian forces, pro-government Chechen militias, or a mix of the two. Using these data Lyall looked at whether the number of insurgent attacks declined from the 90 days before an operation to the 90 days afterward in places swept by different forces. Specifically, he identified 145 pairs of villages that were closely matched in terms of pre-sweep levels of insurgent violence, number of individuals abused during the operation, number of prior sweep operations, prior extrajudicial killings, and large-scale thefts (to proxy for economic motivations for sweep operations).[9] Within these villages attacks in the 90 days after a sweep increased very slightly (7 percent) in villages swept by Russian forces but dropped by almost a third in villages swept by Chechen forces. It also took significantly longer for the first post-sweep attack to happen in villages swept by the local militia. Unlike in the Philippines, however, the value of mixed units was absent. Joint Chechen-Russian sweep operations did no better than purely Russian ones. We suspect this is because the relatively low-skilled Russian soldiers could not take advantage of information provided by the locals in the same way that SOF in the Philippines could.

Returning to the Philippines, detailed information on the types of units participating in the reported operations provided an opportunity to learn more about how incorporating intelligence and information could improve counterinsurgency effectiveness. Joe was also able to observe a different type of troop augmentation: "intelligence leads." Like many militaries confronting internal security threats, the AFP had intelligence professionals on staff down to the battalion level, as well as specialized intelligence units deployed in the field to assist in operations.[10] These cadres were trained in opening information channels—usually through traditional human intelligence (HUMINT) methods such as recruiting informants from the community or the insurgency itself, as well as extracting information from interrogations of captured and surrendered insurgents. They then passed that information to commanders for rapid integration into operational plans. Joe's team coded which operations had been led or directly supported by these intelligence professionals and operatives—approximately 5 percent of all incidents during the period he analyzed. Comparing these to other operational incidents, he found that operations led by or directly augmented by intelligence professionals saw three times fewer government forces killed, a third more rebel fatalities, and *ten times* fewer civilian casualties than operations conducted without direct support or augmentation from intelligence assets. Additionally, over three times more rebels were apprehended and over 50 percent more rebel firearms recovered in incidents with specialized intelligence assets in direct support.

These findings amounted to strong observational evidence on the importance of information of all types to counterinsurgency campaigns. And at the same time they presented a challenge—as well as an opportunity—in assembling the ideal counterinsurgency unit. On one hand, SOF achieved better outcomes than local units on all indicators of effectiveness, but the nature of their mission (working on assignments across a wide geographic range) meant that they were especially challenged in gaining access to local intelligence. On the other hand, locally recruited and employed units with part-time, lesser-trained soldiers had preferential access to information since they were operating in areas where they lived and among populations they knew intimately. However, this also meant that they were liable to become involved in feuds, grudges, and other personal conflicts inconsistent with government objectives, which raised the specter of misinformation. And they would have to be protected from retaliation.

A promising method emerged to capitalize on the strengths of both types of units while mitigating the risks: deploy hybrid groups of local and SOF personnel. Deploying professional, highly trained, and disciplined SOF elements such as Special Forces cadres with local forces greatly improves their expected performance. Joe compiled significant anecdotal evidence to this effect, both from the Philippines and from his time spent working with U.S. Special Forces advising Afghan Local Police (ALP) efforts in Afghanistan. This enhanced supervision that SOF provides local forces appears to be an efficient way of raising the level of expected performance while mitigating many of the associated downside risks of employing local forces. The numbers back this up.[11] When acting alone local troops suffered about three fatalities per ten incidents but only one when operating in hybrid units with SOF—a reduction mainly driven by lower casualties among local troops. Hybrid SOF-local units were more effective: killing an average of four rebels per ten operations—a slight increase over when SOF engaged on their own but over double the average lethality of local troops acting alone.

This logic of optimal force configuration from the Philippines evokes parallels not only in Afghanistan but also in Iraq. Note the similarities between this synergy of high-quality and local forces and the complementarities we discussed in chapter 6. First, much of the reduction in violence in Iraq following the surge appeared to be due to increased information and collaboration gained as a result of the Sunni Awakening. Second, the gains from the surge came not only from the increase in U.S. troop strength. They also resulted from a change in troop employment, which provided greater situational awareness by deploying smaller units away from large forward operating bases to combat outposts and by increasing dismounted foot patrols.

So, in a counterinsurgency where information from the local population is critical, one way to work the information mechanism seems to be to configure forces in a way that mixes in local troops, who can better access local information. That might reduce violence at lower risk to security forces as well as civilians, and at lower cost.

HELPING IN TIMES OF CRISIS CAN WIN PEOPLE OVER

One way a government can win support is by proving to people that it cares enough—and has the capacity—to provide relief in a crisis. For outsiders seeking to help governments win over their people through service provision, improving crisis relief capacity is a very tractable challenge. Outsiders can provide behind-the-scenes logistics support when disaster strikes and can help with planning, training, and exercises to improve response capacity.

To investigate how service provision affects civilian attitudes, researchers have studied responses to natural disasters. The idea behind such work is that natural disasters create plausibly exogenous variation in the interactions between citizens and government. People inside the tornado's path need saving while people just outside of it don't, and because the tornado does not take into account political preferences, we can compare those hit to those just missed and examine the political consequences of being hurt and then getting help.[12] Natural disasters serve as natural experiments.

Evidence from India suggests that when governments step in to help they can gain substantially in one measure of attitudes: electoral returns. Shawn Cole, Eric Werker, and Andrew Healy, for example, looked at state elections in India—21,000 of them spanning nearly twenty-five years—and used district-level variation in monsoon rains as an exogenous shock to citizen welfare.[13] They found that citizens punished government for bad weather. Incumbents lost more than 3 percent of the vote for each standard deviation that rainfall deviated from the optimum level for agricultural production. The authors went further by gauging governments' response (measured as state-level spending on disaster relief) and, in turn, voters' response to that action. They found that incumbents fared better when they responded to a crisis with emergency relief, but they recovered votes equivalent to only one-seventh the loss of votes associated with having the bad luck of serving during a bad rainfall period in the first place.

You could say voters were acting rationally in bumping up vote shares for state-level incumbents who provided disaster relief—since Indian states are the bodies mainly responsible for that type of spending—they just didn't do so at anywhere near the level that would outweigh their (irrational) punishment of incumbents for the weather event itself. Furthermore, voters had short memories—they rewarded governments for relief only in the year leading up to the election. And, in a finding that warrants cynicism, Indian government officials appeared to respond to voters' short memories: providing higher levels of relief for disasters that occurred in election years.

Of course, there are different types of disaster relief, and perhaps there is something unique about floods. We suspect not, and one important piece of evidence comes from a series of surveys used to measure attitudes in the wake of the devastating wildfires that swept across central Russia in the summer of 2010.[14] A year after the event researchers visited 34 affected villages and 36 that had been spared. They asked residents about their experience with the relief effort, their attitudes toward government figures at different levels, and how they planned to vote in the next election. Having been exposed to wildfires was associated with dramatically higher support for governmental figures at all levels—by (a statistically weak) 9 percentage points for village leaders, and by (a statistically strong) 13 percentage points for governors. Residents of affected villages showed higher support for the ruling United Russia party by 15 percentage points, for Vladimir Putin by 19 points, and for then president Dimtry Medvedev by 22. And it appears that it wasn't pure gratitude for aid: people who observed the aid but didn't receive it themselves (i.e., people in affected villages who didn't lose property) showed similarly higher support for authorities.[15] The authors interpret this as a *demonstration effect*—"the impact of signaling government presence and competence."[16]

Service Provision or Clientelism?

Higher relief spending can cause higher support for incumbents—particularly local ones—through more channels than just the demonstration effect, especially in contexts where corruption is rife. A study by Jorge Gallego of Universidad del Rosario in Bogotá used the 2010–11 rainy season in Colombia, which caused catastrophic flooding and landslides, to examine effects of aid spending on local elections.[17] About 8 percent of the country's population was affected by the disaster, and the government allocated around $3.5 billion in aid spending to provide food relief and infrastructure repair. Gallego found that incumbent mayors benefited from the disaster in an election later in the year. A village where the whole population was affected was 23 percentage points more likely to reelect its mayor than an untouched village, and that percentage rose in villages that received more aid.

Gallego's data allowed him to disaggregate food relief from infrastructure aid. Villages receiving more food aid per capita were *more likely to reelect the incumbent* party while those receiving more infrastructure aid were not. He interpreted this as evidence of clientelism (i.e., buying votes with services): it is easier to buy an individual's vote with a personal bag of flour than with infrastructure such as a road, which is shared by other voters. Why? It is easier to exclude an individual from getting the flour than from using the road, which makes conditionality possible. Clientelism and CERP-like development programs have that ability to withhold benefits in common.[18]

Although we must keep in mind the vast political differences between India, Russia, and Colombia, a pattern emerges. Government assistance in the wake of a disaster influences whether citizens will reward them at the polls, and this effect is rooted at the individual level.

Trust in Foreigners

Returning to our broader question: What does it take to move citizen attitudes in conflict-ridden countries to be more supportive of government? In our countries of focus, the governments were working with Western allies to restore order. So it is worth introducing the question of perceptions of foreign allies into our discussion of natural disaster response.

In 2005, an earthquake struck a poor, remote region of Pakistan, killing as many as 100,000 people and leaving over 3.5 million homeless. In the aftermath, Western aid workers flooded into the area. How did contact with foreigners change people's attitudes toward them? To find out, Tahir Andrabi of Pomona College and Jishnu Das of the World Bank used a survey of 4,670 citizens in 126 randomly selected villages in earthquake-affected areas, four years after the earthquake.[19] They slotted the names of a number of different groups—including people in general, family members, clan and caste members, and American and European foreigners—into a concrete scenario: "Imagine you are walking down a street and dropped a 1,000-rupee note without noticing. [A member of the group] was walking behind you without you knowing and picked it up. What is the likelihood that they would return it to you?"

Andrabi and Das found that rural Pakistanis' trust in each other was surprisingly low, according to this measure. On average 16.9 percent believed that someone from the same region would return the money to them, and that number rose to 29.7 percent for members of their own caste or clan (*qaum* or *biradari* in Urdu).[20] Their trust in foreigners was higher: on average, 48.7 percent believed that Europeans and Americans would return the money to them. Surveyors also

asked whether they believed people of different religions, nationalities, and races could work together for a common cause and found
that on average 40 percent of respondents felt this ability was "high"
or "very high."

The authors then turned to how exposure to foreign aid workers
affected trust. Estimating casual effects was tricky here, because it
required that proximity to the 2005 earthquake fault line be correlated
with exposure to aid workers but not to other factors that might influence trustfulness. Poorer people, who tend to be less trustful, might live
in more dangerous, earthquake-prone areas, for example. The authors
found that proximity to the fault line *did* predict exposure to foreigners
and that citizens living near or far from the fault line had *no* observable differences pre-earthquake in poverty rates or other demographic
measures. Proximity to the fault line thus provided variation in exposure to foreigners that was plausibly independent of attitudes.

The effects of exposure to foreigners coming in to help were dramatic. Trust in foreigners increased steeply closer to the fault line,
from 30 percent 40 kilometers away (here, trust in locals was higher
than trust in foreigners) to 45 percent 20 kilometers away, to 60
percent in the immediate vicinity.[21] Meanwhile, trust in family and
countrymen was relatively constant across distances from the fault
line. Measured differently, going from exposure to no foreigners to
exposure to 100 foreigners increased trust in them by 37 percentage
points.[22] The belief that people of different backgrounds could work
together for a common cause showed a similar pattern: it increased by
3 percentage points with every 10 kilometers of proximity to the fault
line. But none of these results were sustained far from the fault line.

The authors interpret this as evidence that their results "together
with those from the conflict literature (Berman et al., 2015), suggest
that aid can have an impact on attitudes, but local presence, rather
than government-to-government aid, is arguably what matters."[23]

SMALL-SCALE LOCAL SERVICES CAN WIN PEOPLE OVER

So far we have seen that when governments (domestic and foreign)
effectively deliver relief to mitigate the effects of diseases and natural

disasters they can win support to varying degrees. What about the more modest, workaday functioning of government? Can the delivery of basic services improve attitudes toward government, and does performance factor in here as it does with the delivery of emergency aid?

Our own studies suggest that it does, and by a surprising amount. In 2012 Jake began a project with Ali Cheema and Farooq Naseer, then of the Lahore University of Management Sciences, and Asim Khwaja of Harvard to improve and evaluate a program in Punjab, Pakistan, that sought to enhance the employment prospects of the poor by giving them vocational training. A central goal of the research was to understand a gap between supply and demand: potential trainees told surveyors they wanted to enter training programs but then failed to enroll when they had the chance, even at low or no cost. For women access to training centers was a major reason: social norms prohibited them from traveling long distances alone or with a male stranger, making it difficult to get to training centers, even if transportation was provided. So the research team brought the program to the women, placing training centers in villages and measuring the effect on take-up. This was a long-term research engagement and results are still coming in as we go to press, but there is already one surprising result.

One arm of this study evaluated a program that provided training in basic stitching skills to rural women through small-scale training centers located in their villages. This was clearly branded as a public good brought to the village by the provincial government, which was dominated by the PMLN, the center-right party in Pakistan's two-party system. The placement of training centers in villages was randomized to measure the effect on take-up on training, and that randomization also enabled Jake and his coauthors to assess the effect on attitudes and beliefs.

Looking at subsequent village council elections, villages that had the training centers installed were much more likely to have a candidate from the PMLN place in the top two positions. The odds of a PMLN candidate either winning or being runner-up rose by 10 to 20 percentage points (depending on the statistical model). While other studies have shown that provision of public goods can sway attitudes, the effect is not usually so large. Remember, the training was funded and was going to be provided anyway.

On the other hand, villages where vouchers were distributed for training elsewhere—making them less useful to men and virtually unusable by women—saw no increased support for the PMLN. It looks like simply providing a public good can pay huge political dividends, but it must be done in a smart way, applicable to people's needs and conforming to people's customs.

These findings from Pakistan echo some of the effects of the National Solidarity Program (NSP), Afghanistan's large-scale community-driven development (CDD) program we described briefly in chapter 5. There, funds were allocated to villages and the community nominated councils to determine which local infrastructure projects would go forward. Limited funding prevented the government from implementing the program across the country, which gave researchers a chance to *randomize* implementation to 250 out of a sample of 500 villages and then study its effects on citizens' attitudes, among other outcomes.[24]

Citizens in NSP villages reported economic improvements: the percentage of those saying that they were better-off than the year before and optimistic about the future jumped from 11 to 18 percent.[25] When asked about the Afghan government, NSP villagers were more likely to express approval. The magnitude of the change ranged from 8 percentage points for Members of Parliament to 4 percentage points for the Afghan National Police.[26] The study also found that receiving the NSP program caused villagers to feel that the local security situation had improved, though they did *not* report a reduction in actual security incidents. This evidence is particularly convincing because of the randomization of treatment and the scale of the program: it shows a clear and significant change in civilian attitudes brought on by a development program.[27]

It is important to note, however, that these positive effects of the NSP were found only in secure areas of Afghanistan. Development spending caused no change in attitudes among civilians living in areas facing high levels of violence—a finding in line with the prediction of our information-centric approach (and validated by evidence in chapter 5): the complementarity between suppression efforts and the provision of benign public goods implies that public goods will be most effective when security is adequate.

A LITTLE INFORMATION CAN GO A LONG WAY

Perhaps we should not be surprised that sending aid to populations in crisis wins the support of local citizens and that service delivery can do the same. What does surprise us is the *scale* of the attitude change—sometimes very large, and for small interventions. We now turn to the most modest efforts that can sway attitudes—simple informational interventions. Here, especially, a little effort can reap a large reward.

In the previous chapter, we presented causal evidence that mere exposure to information can change attitudes. Our survey experiments in Pakistan found that not only does being objectively poor (having slow income) correlate with lower support for insurgents, but experimentally being made to *feel* relatively poor (by being shown income brackets that label you as such) also decreased support for those groups by about 5 percent. And being made to feel like you live in a violent country decreased support for insurgent groups by even more: about 11 percent.[28]

Small amounts of information can not only decrease support for insurgents; they can also *increase* support for foreign donors. Simone Dietrich of the University of Essex, Minhaj Mahmud of BRAC University in Bangladesh, and Matthew Winters of the University of Illinois conducted a survey experiment among 2,294 respondents across Bangladesh and showed that presenting information on charitable clinics—and noting that USAID funded them—raised respondents' (already high) estimation of U.S. influence in their country.[29] One of the authors, Winters, and Kate Baldwin of Yale University replicated that result for aid in Uganda.[30] Ninety percent of survey respondents who were aware of local infrastructure projects such as schools and water systems were unaware that they were funded by Japan, despite the work sites being strongly "branded" with the Japanese flag. Surveyors told a random subsample of respondents that Japan had funded the project, which induced among those respondents a (statistically) significant more favorable opinion of Japan.

Referring to the model in chapter 3, the objective of local interventions (including informational ones) is to increase support for *local* government, as opposed to foreign governments—whose presence is typically temporary (in the postcolonial era). Implementing externally funded interventions so that they generate support for local governments is often challenging, as USAID's Afghanistan Stabilization Initiative (ASI) demonstrates. ASI was intended to build trust and confidence in local government officials, including by supporting local government efforts to provide necessary services in a timely manner. According to a USAID Inspector General report, however, while most of the projects met community needs and improved local governance, foreigners often got the credit:

> Projects were not perceived as Afghan Government efforts. According to an independent third-party monitoring and evaluation report of ASI-SR activities, for 9 of 15 projects reviewed, intended beneficiaries did not believe that the Afghan Government was involved in the projects. Rather, beneficiaries credited "foreigners" or provincial reconstruction teams (PRTs) with implementing the projects. Afghan Government branding of project sites could help create stronger perceptions of Afghan Government involvement in ASI-SR projects.[31]

Drawing on findings like this, it is sometimes argued that foreign funding of local projects will *undermine* the legitimacy of local governments. But this is not always the case. Recent research results indicate the opposite in many settings. *Local politicians manage to capture credit* for foreign and nationally funded programs even when they clearly don't deserve it. That's what Julien Labonne found in his study of the Philippine CCT program (chapter 5), which increased voting for local incumbents who were simply lucky in the random assignment of World Bank funding across villages. It's also what Cesi Cruz of the University of British Columbia and Christina Schneider of UCSD found for the World Bank's KALAHI program, where the allocation rule was not random but used a fairly arbitrary and opaque poverty threshold, yet local incumbents nevertheless managed to benefit in vote share.[32] Raymond Guiteras of North Carolina State

University and Ahmed Mobarak of Yale report on an experiment in Bangladesh, where undeserved credit is captured by local incumbents for a randomly assigned sanitation program funded by an NGO, but that the effect was eliminated when an information intervention made the randomization transparent to residents.[33] To summarize, a non-local funder may not want to take credit, but if they do, they should count on local competition. Local politicians seem to be quite adept at messaging to claim credit, a low-cost intervention that really does sway attitudes.[34]

The Effects of a Small Improvement in Governance

Some of the most compelling qualitative evidence on how small, informational interventions can have big effects comes from experiments conducted during elections. The information enhances transparency, which in turn can shift behavior and attitudes.

This story begins with the 2010 Afghan parliamentary elections, only the second to take place since the Taliban had been ousted in 2002. Citizens were heading for the polls at a time when the Taliban was gaining ground and President Obama had announced an imminent drawdown of U.S. forces. Inspiring confidence in the government was a clear priority, but the presidential election a year earlier had been widely regarded as illegitimate by the Afghan public. Electoral fraud had been rife, election-day violence high, and turnout low, and Hamid Karzai had been declared the winner only after his main challenger, Abdullah Abdullah, had refused to participate in a runoff because, as he put it, "a transparent election is not possible."[35] General Stanley McChrystal, in an August 2009 memo to President Obama, reported "a crisis of confidence among Afghans—in both their government and the international community—that undermines our credibility and emboldens the insurgents."[36]

In this context, ESOC member Michael Callen and coauthor James D. Long set out to measure election fraud and test a method of cutting into it.[37] Of the many ways to manipulate an election, Callen and Long looked at one in particular: altering vote counts at polling stations or in centralized counting. Before the election, they devised a simple monitoring method based on a combination of high- and low-tech communications technology: smartphones and paper documents posted for public view.

In Afghanistan, as in elections in other countries, when voting at a particular polling station was completed, staff posted the vote count, usually as a physical poster outside the polling station. This document was called the Declaration of Results (DOR), and every Afghan polling station was to have produced one. Copies of the DOR were to be sent to the Provincial Aggregation Center and tallied over the following month. (The actual ballots stay behind, in storage.) This system allowed Callen and Long to check if the enumerators—usually officials with political connections working in government centers—conducted aggregation fraud (i.e., reported a fake count from the provincial center, as opposed to registering fake votes at the polling station). They had volunteers use smartphones to take pictures of the DOR at polling stations, then they compared the pictures to the final vote tallies. If there was no fraud, the numbers would be identical.

The informational intervention was a simple message. Callen and Long delivered a letter to managers at a randomly selected 238 polling stations out of the study's sample of 471, announcing that DORs would be photographed at that location by the monitoring group. The hypothesis was that managers who received the message, aware that fraud in the form of vote tampering could be observed, would reduce it.

Using these methods, Callen and Long found ample evidence of fraud: there were differences between reported DOR returns and final tallies in 78 percent of locations. Additionally, in 62 percent of the sample polling stations, candidates' agents damaged election materials, destroying the DOR, for example, or stealing election materials in order to manipulate vote counts.[38]

Yet the most striking finding was the effect of the information intervention. Polling stations randomly assigned to know that their DOR was being photographed *experienced about 20 percent less fraud.*

Fraud was also somewhat predictable: using a qualitative measure of political connectedness, they found that connected candidates got a big boost from fraudulent votes: about 13.7 percent higher vote totals than the polling station average. This stands to reason, as an incumbent with friends in Kabul would be more likely to be able to call in favors from enumerators than would his upstart challenger. The informational intervention particularly cut into votes for those politically connected candidates, who were the ones most likely to influence the polling station manager: they suffered a 25 percent reduction in votes in voting stations treated with the intervention. This effect was larger for candidates who had connections in the aggregation center specifically.

These reductions in fraud came at low cost: the authors' intervention reached 471 polling centers for just over $100,000. In contrast, the largest foreign mission during the same election reached just 85 polling centers for $10 million.[39] Mike and James interpret their findings as evidence that cheap, crowd-sourced, information-based interventions may be able to quickly cut fraud and improve the functioning of elections in weak states.[40]

These are encouraging results, but for our purposes we are interested in what happened next. Did those gains in transparency and accountability influence civilian attitudes?

Remarkably, they did. In December 2010, three months after the Afghan election and shortly after the Independent Election Commission certified the results, Callen and Long, this time with Eli and Clark Gibson of UCSD as coauthors, commissioned a survey of 2,904 citizens living around the polling stations where the experiment had been conducted.[41] Surveyors asked respondents multiple questions designed to measure different dimensions of attitudes toward government. Four of these are indicative of the general findings. The first two measured respondents' faith that the state could conduct processes fairly: (1) Do you consider Afghanistan a democracy? (2) Whom do you trust to resolve disputes, "head of family, police, courts, religious leaders, *shura*, elders, ISAF, or other?" The second two questions measured whether respondents trusted the state to deliver outcomes: (3) Whom do you consider responsible for delivering services in your neighborhood (from a range of options including government bodies and religious/ethnic leaders)? (4) "In your opinion, how important is it for you to share information about insurgents to the Afghan National Security

Forces (ANSF) (for example, pending IED attacks or the location of weapons caches)?" Naming government bodies as service deliverers and saying it was "very" or "somewhat important" to share information with ANSF indicated a citizen's trust that government institutions could deliver services and security to citizens.

The survey showed that in districts where the information intervention had experimentally decreased electoral fraud, *citizens subsequently reported improved attitudes toward government—both on processes and outcomes*. People also became more likely to say Afghanistan was a democracy, though these findings were not statistically significant. The three other measures gave clear and statistically precise results: perceptions that Members of Parliament were responsible for providing services increased by 5 percentage points, reporting that informing on insurgents is important increased by 3 percentage points, and reporting that police should resolve disputes increased by 4 percentage points. Aggregating over an index of measures (which also included attitudes toward taxation, and a belief that voting improves the future) provided a consistent message: the antifraud intervention increased citizens' belief in state legitimacy.

What's remarkable is not so much the size of the changes in attitudes but that they changed at all, considering the modest scope of the intervention and the timing. Recall what it entailed: delivering a note to polling station managers that DOR would be recorded and monitored. This low-cost program changed citizens' view of government, even though most would not have witnessed the intervention,[42] and the survey was conducted months after election day. Yet attitudes really did shift on core attributes of the perceived relationship between government and citizens.

Callen, Long, and coauthors performed a similar experiment in Uganda where electoral fraud was similarly rife and a majority of polling stations did not comply with the law requiring that a DOR be posted. In a sample of over 1,000 polling stations, the team found that sending a mix of different types of letters cut the number of unposted results by 5.6 percentage points across the entire sample and by nearly 11 percentage points in a geographic majority. They found reductions of similar levels (5–11 percentage points) in another measure of fraud, sequential numbering of ballot counts. (Psychologists have shown that when people fake numbers, adjacent digits appear more frequently than they do when generated at random. So, by examining whether the last two digits in the winning candidate's vote total were adjacent, researchers got a rough idea of how many had been fabricated by a corrupt enumerator.) Furthermore, depending on the district and the statistical method employed, treatment also lowered the vote share of the incumbent president—indicating that the information mechanism protected citizens (a little) from political elites using their connections to cook results, as in Afghanistan.[43]

Development economists have recently experimented with similar transparency-enhancing interventions to improve service quality in many contexts, ranging from schools in Kenya to clinics in Pakistan.[44] Examples in asymmetric conflict zones are rare, but one exception is an experimental evaluation of a community monitoring program by Integrity Watch Afghanistan, which improved the quality of road construction paid for by the World Bank, again at very low cost—as the monitors were volunteers.[45]

Compared to the many examples of dizzyingly expensive programs that have failed in the same task, these results are a remarkable demonstration of how small informational interventions—telling the truth of course—can reduce fraud and sometimes even shift attitudes.

WHAT WORKS? RECONFIGURING WITH INFORMATION FLOW IN MIND

Where does this leave a government attempting to gain a tip from a father sitting in his courtyard at night with valuable information? Chapters 3–7 laid out general principles and tested them proposition by proposition. The previous chapter looked at theories that might support other approaches and came back with no consistent alternative principles not refuted by evidence in asymmetric conflicts. In this chapter we've tried to get more specific about methods proven to be effective in changing attitudes and enhancing information flow.

Reconfiguring security forces with information flow in mind seems to work. In the Philippines one example is mixing SOF who can effectively use information with local forces and intelligence units. The example from Iraq that launched this chapter started with that same motivation; recall that the original reason to restore cell-phone coverage was to enable the SEALs to communicate with local police. Establishing flexible structures to pay for information, which we discussed in chapter 8 in contexts ranging from Malaya to Iraq, is another example.

Enabling cell-phone service is an act of governance that will likely require resources from security forces in the context of an asymmetric conflict, as our motivating vignette pointed out (and subject to the caveats in chapter 4). Disaster relief is an act of governance that also typically requires resources from the military and police but that seems to reliably change attitudes by helping citizens when they are the most desperate.

Most important, reconfiguring governance to meet the needs of local citizens in conflict zones is the central theme we keep returning to. Modest, informed programs such as the job training example in Pakistan and the NSP in Afghanistan really did shift attitudes, as measured by voting in the Pakistani example and by surveys in the Afghan one.

The antifraud intervention in Afghanistan was particularly cost-effective, as it was informational. One caveat is that attribution of credit is often confused in the minds of local populations. So if one aim of an intervention is to improve attitudes toward government (as distinct from improving welfare), then an information operations (i.e., marketing) component may be necessary. A second caveat is that we have no direct evidence that voting or reported attitudes on surveys actually predict tips. The evidence we've presented in this chapter is entirely indirect. Nevertheless, small interventions often seem to be able to generate consequential improvements in information flow, as cellular service in Anbar did.

Government winning support by providing services—if that sounds familiar, it might be because that's how responsive democracies function and those are the governments the authors are most familiar with. So we should emphasize three important distinctions. First, one innovation that seems to work is reconfiguring forces so that they can more effectively draw operationally relevant information, by mixing high-quality and local troops, on an operation-by-operation basis. Some of that information might come not from civilians but from rebels, through infiltration and capture.

Second, succeeding in a counterinsurgency operation may require only a few tips, in contrast to an election that requires a majority (sometimes a plurality) of votes. That is, the government can win territorial control by buying off the support of a small subpopulation (as long as that group is not so small that the tip reveals its identity and enables retaliation). That's one reason why small interventions can have large local effects.

Third, sometimes the "services" supported by outsiders are part of the problem, not the solution, as we saw in earlier chapters with development programs that disrupted local politics. This recalls a story one of our researchers brought back from a remote valley in western Afghanistan, where U.S. Special Forces asked some friendly local villagers why they endured a small Taliban presence walking down the main street. To paraphrase their response, "We need a few of them," they answered casually, "to protect us from the local police." We return to broader questions of longer-term governance quality in the next, final, chapter.

Before we turn to that concluding chapter, let's quickly evaluate our own performance, relative to the agenda we promised. Chapters 1 and 2 argued that asymmetric wars are the major concern moving forward, for both military and development reasons, and that they are fundamentally different from symmetric wars. We then used chapter 3 to lay out a highly stylized theory of how asymmetric wars work, focusing on the decision of a father in a courtyard. Chapters 4–7 tested propositions implied by that information-centric approach, mostly weighing costs and benefits for that father, the civilian, of calling in the tip. Chapter 8 examined alternative theories that inform the conventional wisdom on designing development programs and military practices, finding that in an asymmetric setting they were generally refuted by recent empirical results in the scholarly literature. It then reported on how this evidence, provided by ESOC researchers and others, pushes us to enrich the basic theory developed in chapter 3 by adding retaliatory violence, a market for tips, and a market for civilian support more generally. This chapter focused on practical interventions that seem to enhance information flow and discussed their underlying logic.

If the reader has found the discussion so far convincing, then the next chapter should be of interest. It attempts to take what we've learned and see how it can inform the larger discussion of insurgency, terrorism, and development among policymakers and scholars.

10

THE ENDURING IMPORTANCE OF UNDERSTANDING ASYMMETRIC CONFLICT

On both political and moral grounds, it was impossible for the United States to take a decisive military role in another nation's civil war, and the average Marine on postwar duty in China found himself an uneasy spectator or sometimes an unwilling participant in a war which he little understood and could not prevent.

—Henry I. Shaw Jr., "The United States Marines in Northern China, 1945–1949"

- -

As the Empire of Japan suffered defeat after defeat in the Pacific near the end of World War II, the 50,000 U.S. Marines of III Amphibious Corps (IIIAC) conducted training exercises in Guam, anticipating an invasion of Tokyo.

Then came the events of August 1945. The United States dropped an atom bomb on Hiroshima on the sixth and on Nagasaki on the ninth, and on the fifteenth, Emperor Hirohito addressed his nation by radio in a reedy, aristocratic voice, announcing a negotiated surrender. It was the first time his people had ever heard that voice.

Within forty-eight hours, IIIAC had a new destination: northern China, where hundreds of thousands of Japanese were stranded following their long occupation, and where Chinese Nationalists and Mao's Communists were struggling for control. In the postwar chaos, these American soldiers would play a completely different role than they had expected or prepared for: they would work with China's Nationalist government under Chiang Kai-shek to conduct an orderly repatriation of over six hundred thousand Japanese and Korean soldiers and civilians from areas formerly held by Japan. This operation, code-named "Beleaguer," was America's first postwar intervention.[1]

IIIAC received a hero's welcome at Tianjin, Beijing's harbor, in October 1945, then got to work. They had little trouble securing the surrender and cooperation of Japanese soldiers. But their second objective proved to be more complicated: they were to help the government assert control in areas where Mao's influence had spread during the war and, at the same time, "avoid participation in any fratricidal conflict in China" (in the words of the directive issued by General Albert Wedemeyer, the IIIAC commander).[2]

Avoiding participation proved to be impossible. Ground troops encountered unmanned roadblocks and land mines. Units traveling by rail screeched to a stop where sections of track had been torn up, then fought off ambushes by Communist guerrillas. American pilots were under strict orders to return fire only when certain criteria were met, including "The target was in the open and easily defined" and "Innocent people were not endangered."[3] During a prolonged skirmish in November 1945, the Marines called in air support, but pilots could not fire on Communist insurgents without endangering civilians, so they withdrew. In an incident in December, American troops came under fire from guerrillas who then disappeared into a village. The Marines called on the villagers to turn them in, but there was no response. So they fired mortars outside the village walls—an act that later drew criticism from the U.S. press.

As the mission wore on into 1946, it expanded to include protecting humanitarian relief deliveries for Chinese citizens and enforcing cease-fires between Nationalists and Communists. By autumn 1946 the repatriation of Japanese and Korean citizens was largely complete. A reduced contingent of Marines stayed to protect U.S. installations, but most of IIIAC headed home to join the victory celebration a year late. The last of the troops had left by the time Chiang Kai-shek fled to Taiwan and the People's Republic of China was founded in 1949. Over the course of Operation Beleaguer, thirty-four Marines were killed and forty-two were wounded in action.[4]

ASYMMETRIC CONFLICT: THE CONTINUING STORM

While Operation Beleaguer may have been just a coda to the war in the Pacific, it was an overture to a long series of engagements that would see Western soldiers wrestling with new challenges: Should I fire dangerously close to villagers? Is the next roadblock a trap? How can I mediate disputes in languages I do not speak and in cultures I barely understand? For their commanders these engagements posed a broader challenge: How do we win and go home?

Since World War II, a clear priority of foreign policy in developed nations has been to bring order to countries that have fallen into conflict. Many early interventions were expressions of Cold War competition or aftershocks of colonialism, but since the end of the Cold War, the United Nations, NATO, and other regional bodies continue to intervene in asymmetric conflicts. These recent interventions are taking longer to resolve. In Iraq and Afghanistan, for instance, U.S. military presence does not appear to be ending any time soon, at least at this writing. And overall, *the number of accumulated interventions in asymmetric conflicts is growing.*

Figure 0.2 illustrated that increase in accumulated interventions by year since 1976 for both the United States and NATO. That figure made clear the extent to which the West is willing to intervene in non-state conflicts, but it didn't explain why. Over the course of this book, we've touched on what led to some of the overseas interventions the United States and its allies have conducted over the past quarter century— mainly the longest and costliest ones. But what about the others? In table 10.1, we've randomly drawn ten interventions from the list: six by the United States alone and four by NATO, half of which involved significant combat. We lay out the background for each, as well as the ultimate outcome in terms of peace and stability.

The particular causes of crises that require military intervention vary but provide no reassurance that new interventions by developed countries will decline significantly in the future. The motivation from a Western point of view is often all too familiar: contain a crisis, prevent a smaller conflict from becoming a catastrophe, such as Syria, Somalia, or Libya, where collapses into civil war have caused hundreds

TABLE 10.1. OUTCOMES FROM SELECTED MILITARY INTERVENTIONS BY THE UNITED STATES AND ITS ALLIES

LOCATION	COUNTRY	START DATE	END DATE	BACKGROUND	OUTCOME
Democratic Republic of the Congo	US	19 May 78	31 Aug 79	The US provided air support to French and Belgian troops in response to an invasion by an approximately 3,000-strong force from the Front for the National Liberation of the Congo rebel group.	The Front for the National Liberation of the Congo massacred more than 800 people, 93 of whom were French or Belgian expatriates, prior to their forced retreat to Angola.[1]
Honduras	US	7 Dec 86	20 Mar 88	Operation Golden Pheasant—In response to conflict between the Contras and the Nicaraguan army that crossed the Nicaraguan-Honduran border, the US dispatched several infantry, airborne, and parachute regiments to Palmerola Airfield, Honduras.[2]	Nicaraguan troops withdrew. Following negotiation of a truce between the Sandinista (Nicaraguan) government and Contra leaders in March 1988; US troops were withdrawn.
Philippines	US	01 Dec 89	09 Dec 89	Operation Classic Resolve—President Aquino requested US support to quell an ongoing coup attempt by Colonel Gregorio Honasan and 3,000 troops. The US responded by deploying two aircraft carriers, engaging in the evacuation of American citizens, and conducting air patrols above rebel bases.[3]	US fighter jets prevented rebel planes from taking off, successfully undermining the coup attempt militarily, though at high political and economic cost for the Aquino government.[4]
Haiti	US	19 Sep 94	31 Mar 95	Operation Uphold Democracy—With authorization from the UN Security Council, a US-led force invaded Haiti to remove a military regime established in the 1991 Haitian coup d'états. US objectives included restoring democracy and reducing the number of displaced persons fleeing to the US.[5]	Authority was restored to democratically elected president Jean Bertrand Aristide. The United Nations Mission in Haiti (UNMIH) was established to oversee peacekeeping, though a rebellion in 2004 saw the return of UN presence (MINUSTAH).[6]
Iraq	US	17 Jan 91	28 Feb 91	Operation Desert Storm—In response to Iraqi military buildup (and later invasion) on the Iraq-Kuwait and Iraq-Saudi Arabia border, the US deployed ground and air forces to defend American interests in the area. This action was followed by similar responses from other countries.	After diplomatic efforts failed, the US and allies began a large ground offensive followed by a sustained air campaign followed by a large ground offensive. The Iraqi army surrendered and the Kuwaiti monarchy was restored to power.[7]
Kuwait	US	8 Oct 94	24 Dec 94	Operation Vigilant Warrior—In response to consistent buildup of Iraqi military force on the Iraq-Kuwait border, the US ordered 36,000 troops to support the	UK, France, Oman, Bahrain, and the United Arab Emirates also provide ground, air, and naval support. Iraq withdrew its forces, though the US maintained a sizable

Location	Actor				
Albania	NATO/ Coalition	1 Sep 99	1 Apr 99	Operation Allied Harbor—NATO's humanitarian operations sought to provide relief to refugees fleeing the conflict in the former Yugoslav Republic of Macedonia and to promote stability in the region. These operations included several thousand metric tons of food aid and a 12,000-troop deployment of NATO forces.[10]	Operations oversaw the distribution of food and services to refugees fleeing the conflict as well as the construction of refugee camps, various infrastructure projects, and transportation.
Afghanistan	NATO/ Coalition	28 Dec 14	20 Dec 01	ISAF—the International Security Assistance Force, led by NATO, was initially authorized to secure and maintain Kabul and provide assistance and training to the national government and military of Afghanistan. In 2003, this mission was expanded to include all of Afghanistan.[12]	Following a decade of sustained combat, ISAF disbanded in 2014, leaving behind approximately 13,000 troops to conduct training, advise the government of Afghanistan, and conduct counterterrorism operations (Resolute Support Mission).[13]
Bosnia and Herzegovina	NATO/ Coalition	20 Dec 95	12 Apr 93	Operation Deny Flight—164 NATO aircraft were authorized by the UN Security Council to enforce a no-fly zone over Bosnia and Herzegovina.[14]	NATO aircraft shot down several warplanes and conducted several air strikes on Bosnian Serbs. Under Implementation Force (IFOR), airspace enforcement became Operation Decisive Edge.[15]
Pakistan	NATO/ Coalition	31 Jan 06	6 Nov 05	Following an earthquake that killed approximately 80,000 individuals, NATO responded to Pakistan's request for assistance by implementing an airlift of supplies and later deploying engineers and medical personnel.	NATO flew approximately 3,500 tons of supplies to Pakistan, which included tents, blankets, stoves, heaters, medical supplies, and food. NATO helicopters assisted in the evacuation of victims and distribution of supplies. Engineers supported repair and construction operations, and medical personnel treated approximately 5,000 patients.[16]

Note: Observations provided are a random sample of military interventions from the IMI data set stratified between US (6 observations) and NATO (4 observations). Half of each involved combat. Dates are from the IMI data and include the period of time for which the US was militarily involved in the conflict, excepting the observation in Afghanistan, which was ongoing at the time of the IMI data collection.

1 Alan Cowell, "At Zaire Massacre Site, the Scars and Fear Live On," *New York Times,* 20 August 1981, http://www.nytimes.com/1981/08/21/world/at-zaire-massacre-site-the-scars-and-fear-live-on.html, accessed 8 February 2017.

2 Marjorie Miller, "1,000 Troops Ferried Close to Nicaragua: U.S. and Honduran Soldiers Deployed in Show of Muscle," *Los Angeles Times,* 21 March 1988, http://articles.latimes.com/1988-03-21/news/mn-1013_1_honduran-soldiers/, accessed 8 February 2017.

3 Jim Mann, "Coup Launched in Philippines; Bush OKs Aid to Aquino: Rebellion: The Presidential Palace Is Bombed, Two Military Garrisons Are Taken Over; the Airport Is Closed," *Los Angeles Times,* 1 December 1989, http://articles.latimes.com/1989-12-01/news/mn-138_1_presidential-palace, accessed 8 February 2017.

4 Davide Fact-Finding Commission, *The Final Report of the Fact-Finding Commission (Pursuant to R.W. No. 6832),* 3 October 1990, http://www.gov.ph/1990/10/03/the-final-report-of-the-fact-finding-commission-october-1990/, accessed 8 February 2017.

5 David Bentley, *Operation Uphold Democracy: Military Support for Democracy in Haiti,* Strategic Forum No. 78 (Washington, DC: Institute for National Strategic Studies, National Defense University, 1996).

6 United Nations, "MINUSTAH Mandate—United Nations Stabilization Mission in Haiti," http://www.un.org/en/peacekeeping/missions/minustah/mandate.shtml, accessed 8 February 2017.

7 William J. Taylor Jr. and James Blackwell, "The Ground War in the Gulf," *Survival* 33, no. 3 (1991): 230–45.

8 Michael R. Gordon, "At Least 46,000 U.S. Troops Going to Gulf in Response to Continued Iraqi Buildup," *New York Times,* 9 October 1994, http://www.nytimes.com/1994/10/10/world/threats-gulf-military-build up-least-46000-us-troops-going-gulf-response.html, accessed 8 February 2017.

9 W. Eric Herr, *Operational Vigilant Warrior: Conventional Deterrence Theory, Doctrine, and Practice* (Montgomery, AL: Air University, Maxwell Air Force Base, School of Advanced Airpower Studies, 1996).

10 NATO Joint Force Command Naples, "Operation Allied Harbor," https://www.jfcnaples.nato.int/page632744/17-operation-allied-harbour, accessed 8 February 2017.

11 United Nations Security Council, "Resolution 1386 (2001)," 20 December 2001, http://www.un.org/ga/search/view_doc.asp?sym bol=S%2FRES%2F1386%282 001%29, accessed 8 February 2017.

12 United Nations Security Council, "Resolution 1510 (2003)," 13 October 2003, http://www.nato.int/isaf/topics/mandate/unscr/resolution_1510.pdf, accessed 8 February 2017.

13 NATO, "Resolute Support Mission in Afghanistan," 13 October 2016, http://www.nato.int/cps/en/natohq/topics_113694.htm, accessed 8 February 2017.

14 Frances M. Doyle, Karen J. Lewis, and Leslie A. Williams, "Named Military Operations: US Military Operations from January 1989 to December 1993," *Armed Forces & Society* 23, no. 2 (1996): 285–98.

15 Steven R. Bowman, "Bosnia: US Military Operations," Congressional Research Service, Library of Congress, 2001.

16 NATO, "Pakistan Earthquake Relief Operation," 27 October 2010, http://www.nato.int/cps/en/natohq/topics_50070.htm, accessed 8 February 2017.

of thousands of casualties, generated large, tragic flows of refugees, and helped incubate international terrorism.

The United States and NATO are not the only players attempting to restore order. Australia, for example, has intervened in the short but turbulent history of its island neighbor Timor-Leste. Australia first sent troops to contain armed conflict that sprang up among factions on either side of the province's 1999 referendum on independence from Indonesia. Australia then led the subsequent UN operation, which oversaw the transition to a democratically elected government in 2002. In 2006 Australia sent in troops again when a conflict within the East Timorese military escalated into a coup attempt. Along the way, Australia has been the largest contributor of development aid to Timor-Leste,[5] which continues to struggle economically.[6] Another example is the European Union's intervention in Somalia, a country that has endured civil war in various forms for the past quarter century. Since 2010 the EU has conducted a training mission for Somali government troops (located in Uganda because of the tense security situation in Somalia itself), and the EU Naval Force has provided commercial ships with protection from pirates off of Somalia's coast. Between 2007 and 2016 the EU contributed over €1 billion ($1.3 billion) to AMISOM, the African Union's peacekeeping mission in Somalia, and billions of euros to the Somali people in development aid.[7]

Other examples abound: from the United Kingdom's October 2000 intervention in the Sierra Leone civil war, to France's December 2012 deployment to combat Islamist extremists in northern Mali, to UN forces' ongoing mission to bring order to remote regions of the Democratic Republic of the Congo, many nations and groups of nations have intervened abroad to restore order.

The future likely holds even more interventions, as the consequences of internal wars in far-off places are felt in even the most peaceful regions of today's highly interconnected world. For instance, the refugee crisis and terrorism caused by the civil war in Syria—and in particular by the Islamic State, which was itself a product of the Iraqi insurgency—have set off a wave of isolationism in Europe that will make future interventions even more difficult politically. Every powerful nation or alliance that intervenes abroad in such conflicts risks entering an asymmetric conflict. Hence the urgency of better understanding this type of war, so that new outbreaks can be evaluated, prevented, or at least contained.

Asymmetric conflicts are not just a challenge for Western interveners. India is fighting insurgencies in the "Naxal belt," as we saw in chapter 8. Pakistan is fighting extremist organizations in the Federally Administered Tribal Areas on its border with Afghanistan, and African Union troops are engaged in counterinsurgency to support the nascent national government in Somalia.

The forces taking on such missions need a doctrine and training appropriate for these kinds of conflicts. Equally important, political leaders need to understand what can and cannot be accomplished militarily, in support of broader political strategies.

Gaining that knowledge requires a fresh perspective because, as we have seen, asymmetric conflicts are fundamentally distinct from symmetric interstate conflict. Classic theories of international relations argue that military effectiveness in conflict is mostly a function of capacity to raise and employ military forces, which are in turn dependent on a state's wealth and resources. But these theories—major works by Waltz, Morgenthau, Mearsheimer, and others, and even military doctrine developed for symmetric conflicts—break down when applied to predicting outcomes in the "information-centric" asymmetric conflicts we've studied here.[8] State resources remain important, but the evidence we have presented makes clear that what's much more important is *where* and *how* material resources are applied, the sequencing of these activities, the degree of collateral damage incurred in that process, and how they set the stage for a political settlement.

It is also vital to achieve a better understanding of how *nonmilitary* tools function and can complement military-led activities in asymmetric conflicts—especially how such tools can help reduce violence in one locality after another—thereby providing opportunities for settlement of today's small wars. It would be an error to think of any intervention on the list in table 10.1 simply as soldiers marching in like police breaking up a loud party; instead most entailed engagement of what U.S. government officials call the *elements* of national power. The

U.S. State Department and various foreign ministries apply diplomatic tools; USAID, bilateral donors, and NGOs provide emergency relief; UNHCR organizes evacuations and resettlements; private firms implement reconstruction contracts; intelligence and law enforcement agencies such as the CIA and DEA collect intelligence and pursue nonstate threats such as terrorists or drug cartel leaders; and the list goes on. Interventions in asymmetric conflicts always have important political and development components, all of which require coherent guidance. As we've seen in each of the previous chapters, guidance and doctrine informed by the conventional wisdom about development projects in peaceful places, or even in the wake of symmetric conflicts, are a poor fit for asymmetric conflicts.

In particular, as we saw in chapter 8, development agencies and NGOs are hampered by legacy notions of program design that are inappropriate for the insecure spaces that asymmetric conflicts generate.

That mismatch between design principles and operational environment is a significant problem because large-scale official development assistance (ODA) is now brought in as a regular component of interventions to suppress insurgency and terrorism. The strategic logic underlying doing so is laid out in the World Bank's 2011 World Development Report, which argues that "strengthening legitimate institutions and governance to provide citizen security, justice, and jobs is crucial to break cycles of violence."[9] Major donors have followed through with the spending which that argument implies. Figure 10.1 illustrates this fact, plotting the proportion of aid from the United States, United Kingdom, and European Commission delivered to countries in conflict (here, defined as countries experiencing twenty-five or more battle deaths in a given year according to the Uppsala Conflict Data Program [UCDP]) between 1976 and 2010.[10]

Roughly 20 to 40 percent of global ODA from these donors has gone to countries in serious conflicts in any given year since the end of the Vietnam War, with the US and the UK contributing slightly more to conflict-affected countries than the European Commission. Although overall levels of civil conflict have declined over the past four decades, aid allocation to conflict zones remains high. This is partially due to good news: relatively secure countries such as India and China are grad-

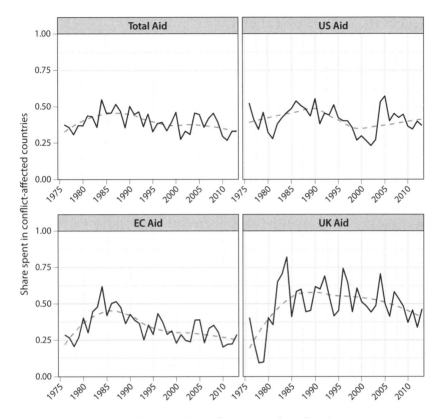

FIGURE 10.1. Proportion of foreign aid (ODA) flowing to conflict-affected countries, 1976–2010.

Conflict data from UCDP. ODA data from Development Assistance Committee of the Organisation for Economic Co-operation and Development, Geographical Distribution of Financial Flows to Developing Countries, Development Co-operation Report, and International Development Statistics database.

uating out of the need for aid, freeing up funds for poorer countries. Yet it also reflects a countervailing trend: the post-9/11 increase in the use of aid as an instrument of international security policy.

In the past three decades the international community has spent many billions on military interventions that require an economic-development component and on economic development that requires a military component. So it is of utmost importance that we better understand how armed intervention interacts with development aid and the role citizens play in conflicts between governments and insurgents. The information-centric model this volume has laid out and validated with evidence provides a deeper understanding of how aid can help reduce conflict at the local level and of why some kinds of aids that might in theory help grow the broader economy may not be relevant for reducing the intensity of conflict once it has started. We expect that as research proceeds on the longer-term economic consequences of aid in conflict zones it will yield practical lessons on which kinds of development aid best support longer-term growth and political solutions.

The need for guidance on how to grow economies in asymmetric conflicts dovetails with a larger concern of the development community. Most ODA will soon be concentrated in violence-ridden areas, even in the absence of international interventions, as those regions stagnate while the rest of the world makes economic progress. Because political violence and poor governance correlate with high population growth rates and weak economic development, the Organisation for Economic Co-operation and Development (OECD) estimates that by 2035 a full 80 percent of the world's extremely poor will live in fragile, conflicted states.[11] Thus, in order for the international community to continue to help poor people by encouraging economic growth, it will need to learn more about how to operate in places where the basic logic of economics has come unmoored, because people and property are unsafe.[12] Our results suggest that doing so effectively requires sequencing different kinds of aid to help states make the transition from conflict and stagnation to peace and growth. Many countries will have regions of conflict alongside regions of stability for long periods of time—as Colombia, India, Nigeria, and Pakistan have experienced for decades—as they bring various regions under central government control without achieving overall political settlements. Effective policy in such places will require sequencing security, aid, and governance assistance in various parts of the same country. The recommendations that flow from chapters 5 and 8 on development assistance and from chapters 4, 6, 7, and 9 on stabilization more generally can guide the critical first step in that sequence.[13]

WHY RESEARCH MATTERS MORE NOW THAN EVER

Two larger trends in Western society, we believe, make the call for careful research on conflict more urgent than ever.

Maintaining Order as the West Turns Inward

In 2016, British tabloids joined with leaders of the Leave Campaign to rally British voters to leave the European Union. At the same time another movement was afoot, orchestrated by some of the same actors. The issue was whether to uphold a commitment Parliament had made the previous year to spend 0.7 percent of national income on ODA. The right-wing tabloid the *Daily Mail* launched a petition in March calling for an end to "ludicrous funding for terrorists, palaces and despots," and by June it had gained over 250,000 signatures—far more than the 100,000 Parliament usually requires to consider a question.[14] The House of Commons debated the 0.7 percent issue on 13 June and reconfirmed its pledge; we can only wonder how that action added to the isolationist sentiment that contributed to Britons voting to leave the EU ten days later. As this book goes to press, we are witnessing a surge of isolationism in the United States, the UK, and other Western countries unprecedented in our lifetimes.

Even in more prosperous and outward-looking times, external intervention was rarely well resourced. Austere budgets in the wake of the financial crisis of 2008 have made funding even scarcer. Moreover, weariness with the long wars in Iraq and Afghanistan have made the U.S. public extremely reluctant to place "boots on the ground," preferring intervention configured with minimal risk to soldiers—or no intervention at all.

The immediate challenge is therefore clear. The academic community can make a significant contribution with research that identifies practical ways to design interventions that do more with less—less troops on the ground for the military, and less money for both development assistance and the military.

Agreeing on Facts

Implementing policies that would do more with less generally requires a public debate, which in turn requires a set of shared facts. In today's media environment agreement on what those facts *are* is distressingly lacking. Between 1998 and 2011, eighteen U.S. newspapers and two newspaper chains closed *all* of their overseas offices.[15] Most remaining foreign bureaus shrank dramatically to the point that, in 2012, of the *Washington Post*'s 16 foreign bureaus, 12 consisted of a single reporter.[16] This continues a long trend of shrinking newsroom staff from a peak of nearly 60,000 in 1990 to under 33,000 in 2015.[17] Newspapers lost subscribers as people went online: by 2016, 62 percent of American adults got news via social media, and 18 percent did so often.[18]

What is alarming is not that people are reading news on screens rather than newsprint; it is that news on social media contains less information, is subject to less careful editing, and is so much more likely to pander to the reader's preconceived notions and biases. Social media platforms do not pay for content, so they lack budgets to employ the professional foreign correspondents who are so necessary to cover and interpret international events. Moreover, since they channel via algorithm content that suits the tastes of readers, these sites, including bloggers and individuals with large Twitter followings, share and re-share information from sources that may or may not live by the canons of journalism: accuracy, objectivity, and public accountability. As a result, groups inside and outside government have an unprecedented ability to "spin" messages to their purposes and deliver them directly to readers, unmediated by editors or fact-checkers.

A *New York Times Magazine* profile of Ben Rhodes, President Obama's Deputy National Security Advisor for Strategic Communications and Speechwriting (informally, "foreign policy guru" or "unnamed senior official"), depicts how governments sell policy today.[19] White House spokespeople make policy announcements, but they don't stop there—their staff amplify their angle and spin the story by using friendly members of the digital media, who, hungry for round-the-clock content, no longer operate under the same code of ethics as traditional reporters. A successful example was the Obama administration's campaign to secure approval of the deal to lift sanctions on Iran, completed in 2015. Starting with the narrative that the 2013 election of a moderate government in Iran had prompted the deal (in fact, negotiations had actually begun in 2012 under the previous conservative regime), the White House used a constant barrage of digital media to discredit opponents and "shape" the story. Robert Malley, a senior director at the National Security Council who helped negotiate the deal, describes using arms control experts at think tanks to create an "echo chamber" of support. As Rhodes told the *Times* journalist, "I'd prefer a sober, reasoned public debate, after which members of Congress reflect and take a vote. . . . But that's impossible."

As this book goes to press, we are learning the extent to which the Russian government conducted a veiled propaganda campaign through social media to influence the 2016 U.S. presidential election.[20] Russia is not alone. Other governments are using these communication tools for political purposes in novel ways all the time.[21] Once again, the voting public is vulnerable to persuasion by veiled interest groups—including foreign governments—for lack of a clear way to distinguish unbiased analysis and facts from spin and outright fiction.

With such partisan forces working to manipulate the media, public opinion, and ultimately Congress on critical foreign policy issues, the United States desperately needs informed voices that will draw the discourse toward the "sober, reasoned public debate" that Ben Rhodes pined for. The organizations available are in many cases challenged in their ability to fill that role.

This is not the case in all areas of government: in economic policy, for instance, we have a Council of Economic Advisors (CEA), staffed by top economists, working in the White House. It traditionally draws on people and ideas from the research community, where peer review and professional reputations built by getting the facts right create exceptionally strong incentives for evenhanded, transparent analysis informed by real-world data. Outside of government, the National Bureau of Economic Research (NBER) maintains regular conferences where fresh empirical research on policy-relevant economic issues is constantly vetted and debated, testing models and trying out new methods.

Though peer-reviewed research exists on security, there is no parallel in the security policy space to the NBER or the CEA, or a research community policymakers can draw on that has at its core academics whose careers depend on conducting accurate analysis grounded in a large body of actual facts. The more easily manipulated an uninformed media and Congress are, the more we need academics to fill gaps in policy discussions with *nonpartisan research* results *informed by real-world data.*

WINNING THE VILLAGE, LOSING THE WAR?

Think back to Operation Beleaguer. It must have been confusing for a Marine in III Amphibious Corps to find himself fighting "in a war which he little understood and could not prevent" instead of marching on Tokyo. All the preparations, all the equipment, and all the doctrine had readied him for high-intensity ground combat. Instead he found himself patrolling the same places day after day, having to worry about local politics, and being caught in the middle of a decades-long political struggle—a very different mission than he had trained for. Almost six decades later, the 1st Infantry Division's soldiers, whose deployment to Tikrit, Iraq, we described in chapter 1, would arrive similarly unprepared.

That Marine's confusion is mirrored in today's foreign policy debates, which often begin with thinking about interventions as primarily military engagements but end up in much more ambiguous territory. That territory has proven hard to navigate over the past fifty years. The public is deeply dissatisfied with the outcomes of the wars in Afghanistan, Iraq, Vietnam, and elsewhere. They seem intractable and have not ended with outcomes that can be called clear victory. And indeed, the U.S.-led war in Afghanistan, which continues as of this writing, has been the longest in American history.[22] Despite these disappointing results, when pressed about what to do in a particular conflict, military leaders often confidently assert that they can bring violence down and have a record of achieving that, in the short term.

So what—really—is going on? As we hope this book shows, the strategic logic of asymmetric conflicts can be understood and acted on. There is *an approach to winning locally that works*: provide services to the population that make it worthwhile for some small number of people to share information, stage sufficient forces to take advantage of that information, and act on it—while protecting those who provided it from retaliation and minimizing collateral harm to other civilians. Doing that can win the village (or valley or district). That approach was implemented successfully in many parts of South Vietnam in the late 1960s and early 1970s, in most of Iraq from mid-2006 through 2009, and in many parts of Afghanistan in 2010–12.

Leasing Hearts and Minds

Yet winning the village does not win the war. There remains a big difference between reducing violence *locally* and ultimately reaching a *conflict-wide* political settlement, which is generally required to *end* an asymmetric war. The former can only open up space for the latter; it will not be sufficient. Simply put, the military can be effectively—and appropriately—tasked with "leasing hearts and minds"—or better yet, "leasing to own" them: providing local-level security and the critical space for follow-on development and governance efforts. But "winning" the hearts and minds of the local population—that is, securing their support and cooperation *over the long term*—requires a separate, complementary process, one convinces the population that supporting the government is a more attractive option than supporting the insurgency even after international forces depart. That process would happen conflict-wide, perhaps as a peace settlement or some more limited political deal.

Sadly, and all too often in the contemporary conflicts the United States and its allies are involved with, the hard-fought and costly "lease"—in terms of security provided by the military—runs out before a political settlement is achieved. ISAF efforts to secure the Taliban-controlled town of Marjah in the restive Nad Ali district of southern Afghanistan in 2010 provide a compelling example. In early 2010, Marjah was a center of opium production and source of income for the Talban, as well as a safe haven for hundreds of Taliban insurgents and a center for the mass production of IEDS. ISAF leadership determined that the Taliban in Marjah posed a serious threat to the region and to all of Afghanistan and developed plans for Operation Mostarek—"Together" in Dari—a 15,000-strong operation aimed to clear Marjah and its surroundings of insurgents.

Joe took over at the CAAT in early January 2010 and attended a number of the planning sessions and small group meetings with General McChrystal, the ISAF commander, where actions and phases of Operation Mostarek were discussed. The military offensive was to be followed by immediate deployment of nearly 2,000 Afghan police, government administrators, engineers, and a range of enablers, showcasing ISAF's populations-centric counterinsurgency approach. General McChrystal described this comprehensive plan to take advantage of the security space created by the military offensive as "We've got a government in a box, ready to roll in."[23]

Operation Mostarek was a hard-fought and costly military offensive that claimed the lives of over sixty U.S., NATO, and Afghan forces, but victory was declared by the end of the year, Afghan flags raised, and the rule of law under government control established. For some time it was touted as an example of the success of the "new" counterinsurgency doctrine and approach.

But follow-on development and governance efforts soon stalled and ultimately failed to establish enduring Afghan government authority and control in the longer term. In the meantime, NATO ended combat operations in 2014 and drew down forces nationwide to 13,000. While Nad Ali remained relatively peaceful (compared to 2009–10) through 2014, that stability was transient. At the time of this writing, the Taliban have returned to Nad Ali, and while the Afghan government still holds Marjah, the town and its surrounding areas are contested territory whose ultimate status is uncertain. Hard-earned gains made by the military offensive of 2010 could not be sustained without international security forces to back up the Afghan military.

Similar reversals occurred in western Iraq in 2014, when IS claimed a number of dramatic victories in Sunni-majority areas. Fallujah, the main town to the east of the region where Colin Supko and Ryan Shann helped catalyze progress in countering AQI by setting up cell-phone coverage (chapter 9), fell to IS in January of that year, followed shortly afterward by Ramadi. Tal Afar, an hour west of Mosul in northwestern Iraq, which was retaken from AQI insurgents by Colonel H. R. McMaster in 2005, in the prototypical "Clear-Hold-Build" counterinsurgency operation of the Iraq war, fell to IS in June 2014 and was one of the last major Iraqi towns retaken from the group in the summer of 2017.[24] McMaster would go on to contribute to the surge strategy, as an advisor to General Petraeus, in large part on the basis of his success in Tal Afar. (General McMaster served on the ESOC advisory board early in our development.) The counterinsurgency principle of "Clear-Hold-Build" was in practice often characterized by "Clear-Hold-Hold-Leave-Repeat."

What went wrong? One possible answer would be that Iraqi forces simply lacked the military capacity in western Iraq to hold out against IS in 2014 without the support of international troops. Yet international forces had invested heavily in building the capacity of Iraqi forces, who also benefited from the support of Shia militias, and those forces enjoyed heavy advantages over IS in manpower, equipment, and training in 2014 (as we shall see in the discussion of the fall of Mosul). And, with far less international assistance, Iraqi forces *retook* ISIS-controlled areas in western Iraq, including Ramadi, Fallujah, Mosul, and Tal Afar, in 2017.[25]

Another possible explanation is suggested by our discussion of civilian attitudes and information flow in chapters 3–9. Beginning in Tal Afar in 2005, and throughout western Iraq from 2006 through 2009, the United States and its allies mostly solved the counterinsurgency problem through a combination of shifting tactics, augmenting force strength, and making deals with the local population, including the tribal leadership. In contrast, the failure of the Iraqi government to establish an enduring political deal with their Sunni population opened the door for IS to reestablish itself in 2014 and ultimately enabled IS's takeover of large parts of the country. In this interpretation, the rise of IS in Iraq was not due to a lack of military capacity but to a lack of willingness on the part of the Shia-controlled national government to deliver enough governance to Sunni communities to win an information-centric small war. In other words, they failed in a competition to be a *less brutal government* than IS, which managed to reestablish an asymmetric insurgency, and a full-on symmetric assault by early 2014.[26]

As these cases show, there is a big difference between a tactical approach that can reduce violence locally in asymmetric wars (i.e., the combination of efforts to win small amounts of goodwill with forces that can act on the resulting information) and a conflict-level political settlement that would end an asymmetric war. While the former can open up space for the latter, as we just discussed, it cannot force a national government to make the type of sustained commitment to inclusive governance that would *sustainably win* hearts and minds in the long run.

The gap in current doctrine is not that it specifies the wrong solution to tactical challenges but that it assumes away a range of challenges involved in going from local victories to an overall political settlement, what we think of as *"the aggregation challenge."*

That difference between what it takes to win a village and what it takes to win a war matters greatly, yet it is little understood and scarcely acknowledged in policy debates. Military doctrine specifies sensible solutions to the tactical challenges of asymmetric conflict, for which we've reported considerable empirical support. So military leaders can often claim local progress. But that doctrine assumes away the complex diplomatic and political task of going from local victories to an overall political settlement. Without a clear political path from winning the village to striking a deal in the capital, policymakers will continue to fail at the aggregation challenge. Unfortunately, the current research base provides little consistent guidance on how to meet that challenge.

So we now have a rich and growing literature on what works to reduce violence, but it tells us far more about the micro than the macro—we know more about how to fix particular districts *within* broken countries than how to repair the country as a whole. For example, in Iraq our research is informative about constructive local interventions: restoring cell-phone service in Habbaniyah, providing protection and wages to sympathetic tribal militias in Ramadi, collaborating on a large-scale water treatment plant in Erbil. It doesn't inform us about how to solve the key national problem: how to induce a Shia-dominated government to reestablish service-providing governance in Sunni-majority regions.

How Does Winning the Village Help?

So how does winning the village (and any of our analysis in this book) help? Simply put, quelling violence locally can open up opportunities for larger political bargains that did not exist when the insurgency was strong. A few examples will help.

First, local successes can *reduce violence to a level society can tolerate* and grow out of. India, for example, has sufficiently contained its many insurgencies so that they do not threaten overall economic growth, even though they are generally understood to constrain development in areas affected by the Naxalite conflict or various separatist and autonomy-seeking groups in the northeast.[27]

Second, local victories may *open up political opportunities* to settle underlying issues contributing to the conflict—opportunities that don't exist when the fighting is raging. Here, Colombia is the exemplar.[28] Peace negotiations between the government and the FARC understandably broke down in 2002, a year when rebels killed 218 citizens,[29] kidnapped many others (including a senator and a presidential candidate), and forced more than 412,000 from their homes,[30] creating what was then the world's largest population of internally displaced people.[31] Álvaro Uribe Vélez capitalized on disappointment from the failed talks and won office on a hard-line campaign that initially was not very popular. In the wake of that violence the Colombian public would likely have rejected any leader who made peace with the FARC on the terms that would eventually be agreed to in 2016 (as the FARC membership would have done had their leaders offered the terms they accepted in 2016). It took sustained tactical successes by government from 2004 to 2011 to open up opportunities for the peace process that started in 2012.[32] The same tactical successes that led the FARC to negotiate also made it possible for political leaders to gain public support for the talks and, eventually, the agreement signed in January 2017. Simply put, government leaders' ability to reach a bargain grew once the FARC were pushed back to the countryside and concessions became politically palatable to the majority of Colombians. By 2016 the Colombian public could countenance a referendum on a peace deal—one that only narrowly lost (49.8 percent to 50.2 percent) with only 38 percent of eligible voters taking part—because they didn't *feel* the threat of war anymore.

In sum, getting counterinsurgency right on the local level will *never be sufficient* to create national settlements and ultimately to stabilize entire countries, though it may well be an effective—and *in some cases necessary*—step toward achieving these challenging ends.

Principals and Agents

How are *countries* (as opposed to villages) stabilized? El Salvador is often held up as an example of a successful "small footprint" intervention in which U.S. military assistance enabled a local ally to defeat an insurgency. In reality, careful analysis by ESOC member Steve Biddle along with his students Ryan Baker and Julia Macdonald reveals a more complex sequence: while military assistance was critical in preventing the collapse of the Salvadoran regime in the early 1980s, the United States subsequently failed to convince the local government to adopt a set of reforms that could have led to settlement, including making governance inclusive, professionalizing the military, and implementing land reform and other economic modernizations. The local regime chose to instead use the military as a repressive tool to maintain a grip on political power.

The conflict remained a festering stalemate until 1992. Fortunately, the FMLN insurgency (a coalition of left-wing guerrilla groups) was weakened by an external factor—loss of Nicaraguan support. Meanwhile, local elites became convinced that peace was in their interest. Those factors enabled a settlement in which, with modest U.S. political pressure, the Salvadoran military had its power limited as a political force.[33]

In a separate research project, we are working with Eli's colleague David Lake of UCSD, Steve Biddle, and other ESOC scholars to understand the challenge of managing national settlements, like that in El Salvador, using *principal-agent* theory.[34] In nine other case studies, including Iraq and Afghanistan, ESOC researchers found that the Salvadoran case is typical: most local allies (the agents) will *divert* foreign military and development assistance to meet narrow domestic political goals in the absence of very strong oversight and conditionality imposed by the foreign power or powers (the principal). Most foreign principals are slow to implement conditionality in assistance and foreign aid but can successfully implement settlements when they do, as occurred in El Salvador, South Korea, and Colombia, and briefly in the Palestinian Authority.[35]

The conquest of Mosul by IS forces in June 2014 provides a dramatic example. The Iraqi military and police, built up, trained, and equipped with extensive international assistance, had a force of about 60,000 in Mosul. Six days after being attacked it chose to retreat rather than fight in the face of a 1,500-member IS raiding party, leaving 4,000 of its own security forces to be slaughtered.[36] Our takeaway is that Iraqi security force resources were being diverted to patronage rather than training and that the Maliki government in Baghdad—if left to its own calculations—preferred not to govern Mosul. That Iraqi decision, in Mosul and across Anbar, terribly undermined the international effort to contain IS. At this writing Iraqi forces, with the support of U.S. and international partners, are engaged in completing a very costly reversal of that decision, having appropriately incentivized retraining of Iraqi security forces and coalition rebuilding with local tribes, in order to enable Iraqi reconquest of its Sunni-majority territory.

That principal-agent research on optimal intervention at the country level complements the local-level findings we've described in this book. Information-centric counterinsurgency provides a tactical approach at the local level, while the principal-agent model provides guidance on how a foreign power can induce the national government to implement both the security and the service components of the tactic—in the absence of a national settlement between local citizens and their government to provide security and services absent outside incentives. That project differs in method— lacking sufficient data to estimate casual effects quantitatively, it attempts instead a qualitative analogue by submitting to the discipline of the "analytical narrative" approach—but it is similar in seeking out evidence on a well-specified theory across a wide range of cases.[37]

Taken together, the lessons of an information-centric approach and those of an agency approach provide reason for concern about the sustainability of the 2017 reconquest of the Sunni-majority parts of Iraq. If the forces occupying Sunni-majority neighborhoods are mostly Iraqi Kurds and Iraqi Shia—who show little predisposition for inclusive governance—would a father in a courtyard with a tip really want to share it with them? Perhaps he would prefer to protect the IS fighters—they are Sunni, and Sunni forces have recovered in the past. If so, will a U.S. presence need to be indefinite, and local, in order to protect Sunni citizens from the suppressive practices of Iraqi security forces?

Is Winning Villages Even Necessary? Drones and Special Forces

On 30 September 2011 in a remote area of Yemen an unmanned aerial system (UAS), or "drone," killed al Qaeda leader Anwar Awlaki. Awlaki, a U.S. citizen, had inspired terrorists with his sermons on the Internet, had been in email contact with Fort Hood attacker Major Nidal Malik Hasan, and had reportedly helped recruit the attacker wearing the "underwear" bomb used in the attempt to bring down Northwest flight 253 en route to Detroit from Amsterdam on Christmas Day 2009.[38]

Drones are sometimes stunningly effective. The extraordinary increase in coverage and in the quality of surveillance they provide has improved actionable intelligence. They provide targeting information enabling follow-on kinetic strikes from military resources such as special forces or from armed drones themselves. Many high-value targets (HVTs)—key terrorist and insurgent leaders and facilitators—in the conflicts the United States has been fighting since 9/11 have been killed using surveillance and precision guided munitions provided by UAS from both U.S. military and intelligence sources. These strikes arguably weaken and degrade the capacity of these terrorist and insurgent groups by eliminating key leaders and other important facilitators responsible for the planning and execution of deadly violence.

In a 2016 article, ESOC affiliate Patrick Johnston and Anoop Sarbahi evaluated the effect of drone strikes in Pakistan on terrorism there. Strikes decreased the incidence and lethality of terrorist attacks on civilians and reduced successful targeting of tribal elders (whom terrorist groups view as rivals).[39]

Additionally, the credible threat of being targeted by drones constrains terrorists and insurgents and reduces the operational impact they can make. In his previous book Jake describes the trade-off terrorist leaders are obliged to make between security and control. He demonstrates that degrading the security environment that terrorist and insurgent leaders operate in—for example, increasing costs of exposure such as training and observable movement—makes it more difficult to plan and execute centrally directed attacks.[40]

So perhaps winning the villages is not necessary in order to win the war, or at least the war on terrorism. This is not the place to provide a full discussion, but we offer a brief counterargument in three parts. First, because drones and special forces cannot by themselves control territory, they *do not protect civilians* from the effects of small wars, so they cannot be expected to reduce civilian casualties or quell refugee flows. Nor do they deny terrorist entities the ability to organize and train, as the record from Iraq, Syria, Libya, Yemen, Pakistan, and Afghanistan makes clear.

Second, when intelligence fails, drone strikes *endanger* civilians. All too often a drone strike intended to target a key HVT instead targets a wedding party or other gathering of noncombatants. On 16 March 2017, for example, a 500-pound bomb dropped from a U.S. UAS platform reportedly struck a mosque in Jinah, a village in the Aleppo province of Syria, killing 46 civilians crowded inside. So drone strikes are problematic. They risk incurring civilian casualties, which generate an expected backlash and reduced popular support, which in turn reduces information flow.[41] Johnston and Sarbahi are careful to note that they cannot rule out this backlash effect.

Third, drone strikes and raids by special forces, by themselves, *cannot set up a political solution* to an asymmetric conflict the way constructive COIN does because they do not create conditions for government control of territory.

On the other hand, drones are *an effective complement* to a COIN campaign. For instance, recall that in the fictional conflict scenario in the Philippine village we describe in chapter 3, two insurgents waited on a roof to ambush a patrol. Surveillance and interdiction capabilities may have hypothetically helped government security forces locate those two insurgents. In the absence of other intelligence it could not have distinguished them from two innocent civilians sleeping on a roof, or told us whether the house was unoccupied and safe to target, so the drone by itself could not win the battle. Nevertheless, when combined with the tip and other forces, the role of UAS could be decisive. This view is commonly shared within the U.S. military. The success in Iraq in 2007 is widely understood to have been undergirded by the aggressive HVT interdiction efforts—utilizing elite SOF and drone assets.

WHAT WORKS? LESSONS FOR RESEARCH

As we hope this book has shown, there is tremendous potential in pursuing a collaborative research agenda on conflict through *engagement* with the policy community, *iterative testing* of the simplest-possible theory, and the use of modern *empirical methods*. We and our colleagues have learned a few things about the value of those approaches for both research and policy, which we think are worth sharing.

Bridging Gaps

Our unusual combined role—researchers, intermediaries, and data providers—has given us a clear view of the "research to policy" gap that exists between academia and government, along with insights on how to overcome it. The gap results from the interaction of two important institutional norms: how information is guarded on the government side and how research careers are built on the academic side.

Governments have huge military budgets and gather massive stores of information to use in formulating and implementing responses to threats, but they lack the manpower to retrospectively analyze those data and have not historically received direct or indirect analytical support from leading scholars in the academe. Governments see a need—often real, sometimes only perceived—to keep conflict data confidential. So officials tend to share data only with internal intelligence agencies, consulting firms who hold security clearances, and occasionally with think tanks. But that confidentiality gain comes at a cost. It gives consulting firms an effective monopoly on research using these data (so they can charge a premium for analysis). Furthermore, that analysis is not subject to the peer-review processes that maintain the highest-quality scholarship. Peer review typically requires that the original data be available to other researchers for replication, which security classification rules often preclude.

Meanwhile, promising young academics face daunting obstacles to conducting data-driven analysis of conflict: relationships must be built to access the data, it must then be converted into usable form, and a host of contextual information must be pulled together, sometimes including original surveys that require lengthy institutional review. All this takes time and effort with no guarantee of success; trying and failing can derail a young scholar's career. Given these risks, it is not surprising that many would-be conflict scholars go into safer fields or stick to analysis of preexisting data, which, when we started the ESOC project a decade ago, were generally only available at the cross-national level.

As a result, government officials are acting on analyses that fall short of what would be produced in a more open market, while many of the best minds are not working to understand the greatest threats to national and international security. ESOC and like-minded scholars seek to resolve this problem: as we build relationships and acquire data sets we make them openly available as fast as we can, with the intent of driving down the costs that scholars face in entering the field. That should expand the pool of researchers analyzing these data, allowing their conclusions and recommendations to be competitively cross-validated, and enhance the body of knowledge available to support decision makers. For example, we've demonstrated how useful that cross-validation can be in the discussion of new research on the economics of development assistance in asymmetric conflicts, in chapter 8.

An additional reason for lack of analytical support to security policymakers is the dearth of compelling incentives for academics working outside the realm of pure basic research. Many scholars are either unable or unwilling to support the priorities of the military and other government agencies directly. Sometimes working on research directed and sponsored by government can jeopardize career goals such as academic promotion. And, of course, some very talented scholars hold ideological views that preclude working directly for the military, intelligence agencies, or other government organizations.

Because ESOC is situated within the academy and its modest operating costs are funded by research grants, it is open to a diverse group of scholars, including those reluctant to engage directly with military and government. Since ESOC's analytical products are subject to the rigors of peer review, we are largely immune to the criticism that they are anything other than independent and objective scholarly products.

In effect, our presence creates a win-win situation. By tracking down and releasing data, ESOC effectively absorbs the fixed costs of microlevel work, enabling more talented graduate students and faculty to apply themselves to the hard theoretical and empirical problems of figuring out how to help countries emerge from conflict and move toward stability. As a result, the government and military get better information to use in making their decisions. To borrow a favorite adjective, ESOC can activate the *asymmetric* advantage the West has in research capacity by using transparency and openness to effectively crowd-source research on some of the world's most pressing security challenges.[42]

The synergy possible when you straddle these worlds is vividly illustrated by the way Jake and his coauthors acquired the data on the rollout of Iraq's cell-phone network, which we discussed in chapter 4. Recall that some initial conversations led to data sharing in early 2010 by Zain Iraq, that country's largest mobile service provider. Using those data Jake and Nils did initial analysis that Jake presented to the ISAF Telecommunications Advisory Cell in Kabul that autumn. Immediately after the briefing Lew Shadle approached Jake and later introduced him to the CEOs and CTOs of all the major Iraqi cell-phone providers, enabling Jake and Nils to figure out an econometric approach to test whether increasing cellular coverage reduced violence. More than any other study we have been part of over the past decade, this one illustrates the value of ESOC's approach. By doing preliminary research that had no chance of publication but was informative on an important policy issue, and then taking the time to share it with officials in the field, we earned the goodwill that allowed us to get the data required to generate a conclusive answer to the same research question.

Why Theoretically Grounded Microlevel Research?

Proceeding through the book, you have seen us strive to test a general theory of asymmetric conflict by evaluating its implications in as many micro-environments as possible. We seek to learn from the similarities and differences across contexts to better understand which causal relationships are generally relevant.

Clearly there are risks to conducting microlevel research on conflict. The fieldwork can be dangerous, the necessary relationships hard to build, the insights slow to materialize, and the policy audience resistant to change. On top of that, logistical and ethical concerns may rule out some methods.

Yet scholars are doing it anyway and making tremendous progress. As figure 10.2 shows, the number of microlevel studies of conflict published in leading academic journals in economics and political science rose from seven in 2001 to thirty-three in 2014, and the proportion of those using microdata has gone from 0 to 40 percent.

Testing theories against microdata can highlight areas of *consilience* where threads of new knowledge interweave with, and add detail to, patterns of other knowledge. Military practitioners long acted on the belief that giving aid in conflict zones could win hearts and minds, bring citizens in line with government objectives, and therefore lead to a reduction in violence. But rigorous research using cross-national data challenged that knowledge, as we saw in chapter 5. It showed that aid on the widest scale often stokes, rather than extinguishes, violence and contributes to instability. When we looked at microdata from Iraq, we saw that aid could help suppress violence but only when implemented in particular ways (chapter 5); otherwise, it had no effect or even increased violence. Our findings were consilient with what the hearts-and-minds practitioners in Malaysia and Vietnam wrote *and* with the findings of evidence-based researchers looking broadly at aid today—and resolved an apparent contradiction between them.

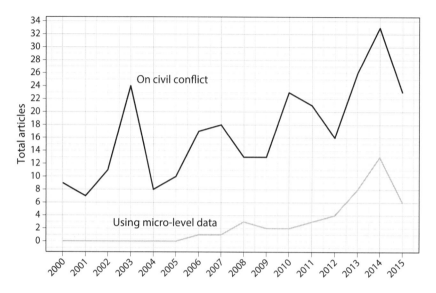

FIGURE 10.2. Conflict studies articles published, proportion using microdata.

Studies are included as part of the "micro-revolution" if they rely on (a) household survey data collected in conflict zones, (b) individual-level data on people living in places suffering from conflict, or (c) incident-level data on conflict events coded at the subnational level (either from press reports as in Jan H. Pierskalla and Florian M. Hollenbach, "Technology and Collective Action: The Effect of Cell Phone Coverage on Political Violence in Africa," *American Political Science Review* 107, no. 2 [2013]: 207–24, or from administrative data as in Monica Duffy Toft and Yuri M. Zhukov, "Islamists and Nationalists: Rebel Motivation and Counterinsurgency in Russia's North Caucasus," *American Political Science Review* 109, no. 2 [2015]: 222–38).

Today's conflict literature presents a compelling picture on its own terms, but it also validates findings from a qualitative literature, with a much longer lineage, based on historical case studies and personal interviews with combatants, ex-combatants, and civilians. The primacy of information flows, the consequential role of civilians in providing them, the ability of local efforts to yield large-scale effects, the benefits of service provision, and the cost of civilian casualties—by government and by rebels—all appear in that literature.[43] But so do other arguments, and in the frenetic discussion of the first few years, when the United States went to war after 9/11, both validated and unvalidated research from that era were thrown into the mix that guided policy.

Thanks to the efforts of a large research community, we now have far more detailed knowledge of what fans the flames of insurgency, what makes people support militants, and how programs can be implemented to save lives, create stability, and avoid wasteful mistakes.

To us, the authors of this book, this new knowledge is a source of real hope; even as militant organizations and terrorist attacks claim the headlines, we now better understand how to implement policies that would suppress violence or, better yet, implement the types of effective and inclusive governance that would induce potential rebels to choose peaceful means of advancing their political goals.

What's Next for Research?

One can think of insurgency as having four phases: onset, fighting, termination (often through political settlements though not always), and postinsurgency (i.e., helping formerly conflict-prone countries/regions become stable and prosperous).[44] The large body of cross-national work published in political science and economics in the 2000s focused heavily on the first phase, though it rarely distinguished as we do between symmetric and asymmetric wars.[45] This book summarizes research on the second phase, for asymmetric conflicts. A broad range of research has studied the third phase, a challenging topic since the outcomes of interest are mostly at the level of a conflict, and there are not that many to study (though they tend to persist for a tragically long time).[46]

We therefore see two broad priority tasks for research. The first begins with the pessimistic view that in many places the deep political solution is decades away. When outsiders intervene in such places, a precondition for successful exit is often leaving a local ally in place with the capacity to suppress the insurgent threat, as the current U.S. experience in Iraq illustrates. There, the postexit conflict remains asymmetric (in most of its fronts) and requires military assistance to enable and induce the Iraqi government to fight. Such proxy wars also require a doctrine, in order to enable success at reasonable cost. In the project mentioned above with colleagues from a number of universities we are combining game theory and historical narratives to understand better how such conflicts can be managed.[47] We hope others will bring additional work and new analytical approaches to that task.

The second research priority, and the more optimistic one, is work on the fourth phase, postconflict, which has tremendous policy relevance as countries like Liberia and Colombia transition out of persistent insurgency and conflict. One hopeful opportunity in this area is to leverage advances in machine learning and remote sensing technologies to study how peace processes play out at the local level, asking why some regions reintegrate successfully after conflict while others do not. That research will be made possible by the fact that we can now create high-resolution measures of development outcomes from space and track online political behavior to develop precise data on how attitudes and civic engagement change over time at both the individual and community levels.

WHAT WORKS? LESSONS FOR POLICY

So, what have we learned about how to effect local reductions in violence in asymmetric conflicts and spark such chain reactions? It boils down to six principles.

Information is key. When the enemy is embedded in the community rather than grouped behind a border or front line, it is essential to get information from citizens. We've seen the success that opening information channels can bring: in Indonesia, police used information from deradicalized former rebels to shut down the most violent splinter groups of Jemaah Islamiyah; in Colombia, land reforms led to both greater satisfaction among rural citizens with government *and* less violence, almost certainly by opening up information channels; and in Iraq, an ESOC study presented the first quantitative links between the number of tips received and short-term reductions in insurgent violence.

Getting more information might not be so hard. In a symmetric war, gaining significant advantage generally requires huge mobilizations of personnel and equipment to seize territory; in asymmetric warfare states can do the same with a few good tips. Winning over people on the fence may be easier than seizing territory and can provide significant benefits: in Afghanistan's Helmand province, practicing restraint during riots led to greater cooperation among citizens; in Iraq's Anbar province simply raising a cell-phone tower catalyzed a huge increase in tips; and in villages of Afghanistan where a simple intervention had cleaned up elections, citizens became more likely to say that it was important to share information with the government.

Average attitudes are important, but you only need one tip. In our theory, civilian attitudes are important as they determine how much violence people will tolerate from insurgents before changing sides. Knowing this, insurgents appear to limit violence that will offend the populace too much. But this does not mean the government needs to win over the broad mass of the population. The people who matter are the ones on the margin—the father in chapter 3 who has information on rebels and is unsure about whether to share it. Policies or political events that shift the average attitude in the population—such as the unexpected political change in Iraq when the highly sectarian Nouri al-Maliki resigned as prime minister in August 2014, dramatically improving Sunni Iraqis' views of their government almost overnight—may or may not affect the calculus of those on the margin.[48]

The mechanics of information transfer matter. One key lesson from our work is that dramatic effects can be achieved by making information-sharing safer for civilians. In western Anbar province in Iraq in 2006, U.S. forces prioritized protecting tribal leaders—that is, the local political elite who wanted to change sides—from reprisals for cooperating in the fight against AQI. Their safety played a key role in getting those leaders to share intelligence on their former allies. Across Iraq introducing cell-phone towers made it possible for people to call in tips, making sharing information safer and leading to a drop in violence. In Afghanistan insurgents shut down cell-phone towers *because* they believed that they were at risk if the average citizen could communicate about their movements. And in the Philippines the combat performance of special forces troops improved dramatically when they worked with local militias who knew the local area intimately and could therefore help them access critical information from local civilians to find and target rebels.

Keep aid modest, secure, informed, and conditional. A consistent finding across contexts in our research is that there is no clear positive relationship between how much aid is spent overall in an area and the resulting security situation. This makes sense, as flooding conflict zones with money invites corruption that can, but doesn't always, enable violence and that certainly can lose any goodwill the aid created, a logic we discussed at some length in chapter 5.

In other examples, large-scale aid projects create long-term *drivers of* instability. A notable example is the Helmand River Valley Project in Afghanistan. The story of the project is evocatively told by Carter Malkasian, who spent two years working for the U.S. State Department in Garmsir, a district heavily affected by the project. According to Malkasian, who conducted extensive interviews with local elders, this agricultural district had been quiet and peaceful during the first half of the twentieth century.[49] A balance of power existed among several players: the government, two tribes (the Alizai and Noorzai), and religious leaders. Starting in 1946, however, a massive modernization project began to disrupt that balance. The Helmand and Arghendab River Valley Project dammed the Helmand River and created a network of canals to expand arable land in the district. New roads, schools, and government buildings accompanied the project, and over three decades, British and U.S. aid agencies poured $130 million into the area, a massive sum at the time.[50] In part, this was a Cold War hearts-and-minds effort to win Afghans over to the Western model of development and thus crowd out Soviet influence.

The River Valley Project brought prosperity to Garmsir, which in turn drew a new population of landless immigrant laborers. The money, along with the disruption of landholdings, increased conflict between the Alizai and Noorzai tribes; skirmishes and assassinations began to escalate, especially upon project completion in the 1970s. Moreover, the immigrant laborers, who never successfully integrated into society, drifted back and forth over the border to Pakistan where they were radicalized. Summarizing the effect of the River Valley Project, Malkasian writes, "The immigrants and the land issues that it introduced were a permanent source of strife for the district, exploited by the Taliban. A grand plan gone awry, agricultural prosperity had been short-lived, but social discord long-lasting."[51]

The cautionary tale of the Helmand River Valley stands in direct contradiction to the idea that increasing prosperity in a given area will not only fill human needs but also increase political stability and promote peace. That view frequently motivates development projects in postconflict settings. Some of these programs have been deemed successful, such as the Siela Program in Cambodia. In the late 1990s and early 2000s, this partnership between the government and the World Bank made broad infrastructure investments—rural roads, schools, water supply improvements, and irrigation—and seemed to not only reduce poverty but also increase stability as the country emerged from decades of war.[52] Yet there are few successful examples in areas with ongoing conflict.

In those same areas we have reported strong evidence, however, that targeted small-scale programs—conditional transfers delivered directly to needy families and small-scale funds spent in coordination with military objectives—appear to decrease conflict. These projects reduce violence more effectively when augmented with development expertise and when implemented in places where there are more military forces around to take advantage of any information they generate and to keep the projects safe. To put it in starker terms: big ideas designed from afar can go badly wrong, but targeted support by outsiders can still play a constructive role.

Taken together, these patterns suggest a clear sequence to aid in conflict zones: start with small, carefully targeted projects while trying to establish order; shift into the kinds of projects the Siela Program supported once government control is robust; and avoid supporting massive infrastructure efforts like the Helmand River Valley Project that can fundamentally shift populations—unless those things are clearly desired by the local government.

Invest in administrative data, then weigh the benefits of sharing against the risks. Consider where we've learned what we have. We know more about how to best mix forces from the Philippines, rather than from Afghanistan or Iraq. Why? Because the Armed Forces of the Philippines kept immaculate records (even if they were originally on paper) and key AFP leaders were willing to share them for research purposes. We know more about how aid worked in Iraq than in Afghanistan because a central high-quality record of aid spending was kept in Iraq—but not in Afghanistan—and was never classified.

Keeping good data is no panacea. Vietnam was an asymmetric war in which the United States invested massively in collecting a wide range of microdata—on everything from combat attitudes to popular sentiment to supply flows—and ultimately still lost. Despite that obvious failure, one that has often been used to discredit the idea of quantitative metrics for conflict, meticulously collected data from the U.S. war with Vietnam remain a tremendous resource today for empirical study of a range of conflicts.[53] Collecting more and better-quality microconflict data creates a public good whose value and return on investment may be better realized outside of the here and now of the conflict where it was collected. Drawing on the earlier discussion of villages and wars, the lesson is not that data analysis did not work in Vietnam and therefore cannot work elsewhere but that when we use big data to understand small wars we should think about what it can and cannot tell us. In Vietnam—as in Afghanistan, Iraq, and the Philippines—the data were tremendously informative about the tactical question of how to best win local battles but could not help with larger strategic questions about how to make the South Vietnamese government sustainable.

Future operations should build in good data collection from the start and place a high value on consistency. Being able to track trends over time is critical for learning. Moreover, despite the risk to operational security that might come with disseminating data for research, sharing those data enables benefits that come from rigorous analysis of these complex problems.[54] Faster sharing allows more immediate application, as we saw in the successes of Joe's research team in Afghanistan. Thoughtful data collection and sharing the hard-earned information can provide returns beyond the immediate episode. These engagements may be long-lasting, and, as we've argued, new ones are likely to keep coming. In the face of that grim prospect, investing in data and research would indeed be prudent.

Negotiating the Shallows

The modern counterinsurgent faces multiple risks and constraints, like a captain navigating a ship to harbor through treacherous rocks and shifting winds, with the tide going out. Domestic public support is low in Western countries for boots on the ground or expensive long-term commitments—as Iraq and Afghanistan have become. That support will likely decline as these interventions, and others like them, predictably stretch out and stalemate because the local ally lacks the capacity or the political will to fully extend governance over hostile territory. Withdrawal runs the risk of descent into chaos: catastrophic ungoverned space spewing misery and refugees and terrorists. Drones and special forces can slow that descent but can't prevent it by themselves.

The course most likely to bring the ship home at minimum risk is charted by our information-centric approach. It can win the village using methods that domestic public opinion and the international community can support—and has done so repeatedly—albeit in wars whose strategic outcomes have been less than satisfactory (as of this writing). That course can also lead to a longer-term political solution, one that empowers civilians in their relationship with the national government of our allies. If sustained over time, those relationships can help enable the political solutions to asymmetric conflicts that we all hope to see.

DATA POINT

2010 hrs, 15 August 2011
Non-Commissioned Officer Billeting
Philippine Army Headquarters Compound
Fort Bonifacio
Makati City, Philippines

- -

It was just past 8 p.m. Joe was walking the spartan hallways of the NCO barracks facility with Lieutenant Colonel Dennis Eclarin, visiting the members of our Philippine coding team in their rooms.

Eclarin had organized a team of seasoned Philippine army noncommissioned officers to take the hand-typed accounts of Philippine internal security operations, and code the details into a database. One of the coders was Technical Sergeant Antonio "Tony" Relao, a combat-decorated Scout Ranger who had served in the storied 4th Scout Ranger Company during the height of the 2000 offensive against the

Moro Islamic Liberation Front. The company had been commanded by Eclarin—a captain, back then—and Tony had remained a loyal member of Dennis's team ever since. Now he spent his days on a different duty, not fighting insurgents but filling in spreadsheets. The first dozen or so columns included incident data: Date, Time, Location, Incident Type, Rebel Group. Moving right, the columns shifted to outcomes of these incidents: Government Killed, Government Wounded, Enemy Killed, Enemy Wounded, Civilians Killed, Civilians Wounded . . . and many more. It was long and tedious work, but it led to many of the insights in this book.

Joe stopped by the room Tony shared with Erwin Augustine, Zaldy Liban, and Brian Canedo, the core group of NCOs supporting the coding project, meaning to thank them for their efforts. He was met by the whirl of the fan and familiar greasy smell of Jollibees (the Philippine version of McDonald's) wafting through the hot and poorly ventilated space.

As Joe approached, he felt something was amiss. Tony, who had become a friend of Joe's over his multiple trips to the Philippines, was typically jovial and upbeat. But tonight he was clearly upset about something and uncomfortable with the visit. Not wanting to oblige him to "lose face" in front of superior officers, Joe thanked him quickly without asking him to explain his mood and then moved on. Tony accepted Joe's thanks graciously but without meeting his eyes.

An hour later, Joe was recapping the team's progress with Dennis over barely chilled San Miguel Light beers in a vacant room Dennis had commandeered for the purpose. Dennis told Joe, "Tony had a hard day. While he was coding, he came across a combat incident he had been involved in, where he lost a good friend."

In one painful instance, Tony did not need to read the typewritten description to code the incident because he had been there when it occurred. He had been lucky; his friend, a young Scout Ranger corporal, had not. Tony had lost touch with his friend's family over the years. But there he was in black typed ink—rank, service number, and all in the sterile paragraph associated with the incident. He had been a comrade in arms and a friend, and now he was identified as a "1" in the "Government Killed" column of a spreadsheet.

Erwin Augustine, another of the long-time ESOC Philippines incident report coders who worked closely with Tony, later told us, "Being a member of the Scout Rangers and seeing reports with the names of those who are missing—you hurt. But you must push through because you're giving them a voice. They gave their lives for the country, they sacrificed their lives for their families—and we are going to give them a voice."

All three of us—Joe, Jake, and Eli—have served in the military in times of conflict and war and have worked and conducted research in a range of conflict zones long after folding up the uniform. We are aware that many of the "data points" we work with often represent the end of a life and great pain for all who cared for them. We can go back to incident data and in a sobering, surreal moment match incidents to classmates, friends, colleagues, and, sadly, even former students. The data we work with and problems we attempt to address are real—real people with real lives cut short or forever altered because of conflict. We are convinced that conflicts can be made less costly, if not prevented, through better practices and decision-making approaches. This context helps keep us grounded in the seriousness of our chosen field of study.

Beyond active military service we've worked closely with members of the military, aid organizations, NGOs, and others risking their lives to help people caught in war zones and other conflict-affected places. We have great respect for these professionals. They are tasked with the complex challenges of bringing order to conflict areas in dangerous unfamiliar environments far from home, without the resources they truly require.

We've found that those closest to the conflict crave the actionable insights we've developed and appreciate that any opportunity to "fight smarter"—or better yet avoid conflict altogether—is worth seizing, even if it means opening the circle of trust to an academic researcher with ill-fitting Kevlar, jet lag, and a complete unfamiliarity with military acronyms. This is true from general officers to privates, from government aid workers to NGOs, and across people of many nationalities and religions.

We humbly hope that our efforts, in collaboration with an extra-ordinary range of colleagues and all the work of the conflict research community cited in the preceding chapters, have in some way contributed to an understanding of the dynamics responsible for violence—and can help mitigate its terrible costs.

This book does not have definitive answers or "magic bullet" solutions to the range of daunting challenges we address. It does, however, provide examples of the value of methodologically rigorous, evidence-based approaches to studying conflict—research conducted by individuals with passion for their subject and empathy for those suffering conflicts' effects. We don't solve these problems outright, but we believe that we have "moved the needle" and advanced our understanding. We hope the knowledge and findings compiled here can serve as a foundation, or at least an example, that both empowers and inspires further research by scholars who share our dedication and commitment to applying the research craft to bring order and peace where it is needed most.

NOTES

PREFACE

1. World Bank, *World Development Report 2011: Conflict, Security, and Development* (Washington, DC: World Bank, 2011). Also, a 2017 World Bank report on the war in Syria said, "From 2011 until the end of 2016, the cumulative losses in gross domestic product (GDP) have been estimated at $226 billion, about four times the Syrian GDP in 2010." World Bank, *The Toll of War: The Economic and Social Consequences of the Conflict in Syria* (Washington, DC: World Bank, 2017).

2. One study finds that death and disability suffered in 1999 as a result of wars fought between 1991 and 1997 were roughly equal to the death and disability caused directly by wars in that same calendar year. Hazem Adam Ghobarah, Paul Huth, and Bruce Russett, "Civil Wars Kill and Maim People—Long after the Shooting Stops," *American Political Science Review* 97, no. 2 (2003): 189–202.

3. "Liberia Country Profile," BBC News, 30 June 2015, http://www.bbc.co.uk/news/world -africa-13729504, accessed 6 November 2015.

4. United Nations Peacekeeping, "Post Cold War Surge," http://www.un.org/en/peacekeep ing/operations/surge.shtml, accessed 6 November 2015.

5. United Nations, "Peacekeeping Fact Sheet as of 30 June 2017," http://www.un.org/en/peace keeping/resources/statistics/factsheet.shtml, accessed 9 August 2017.

6. Charles C. Krulak, transcript of "The Three Block War: Fighting in Urban Areas," draft remarks for the National Press Club, 10 October 1997, quoted in James E. Szepesy, "The Strategic Corporal and the Emerging Battlefield: The Nexus between the USMC's Three Block War Concept and Network Centric Warfare" (master's thesis, Fletcher School of Law and Diplomacy, 2005), 5.

7. Charles C. Krulak, "The Strategic Corporal: Leadership in the Three Block War," *Marines Magazine*, January 1999, http://www.au.af.mil/au/awc/awcgate/usmc/strategic_corporal .html, accessed 6 November 2015.

8. C. J. Chivers, "Where the Islamic State Gets Its Weapons," *New York Times Magazine*, 27 April 2015, http://www.nytimes.com/2015/04/27/magazine/where-the-islamic-state-gets-its -weapons.html?_r=0, accessed 9 December 2015; "What Weapons Does Islamic State Have?" CNN, 8 December 2015, https://www.youtube.com/watch?v=MsIBAChh6nc, accessed 10 December 2015.

9. See, e.g., "Islamic State Crisis: Coalition Weaponry," BBC News, 3 December 2015, http:// www.bbc.co.uk/news/uk-29349918, accessed 9 December 2015; David Stupples, "How Syria Is Becoming a Test Bed for High-Tech Weapons of Electronic Warfare," *The Conversation*, 8 October 2015, https://theconversation.com/how-syria-is-becoming-a-test-bed-for-high -tech-weapons-of-electronic-warfare-48779, accessed 10 December 2015.

10. For example, in Afghanistan the number of functioning health facilities increased from 496 in 2002 to more than 2,000 in 2011. The percentage of children in school increased from 21 percent in 2001 to 97 percent in 2011 and those having access to safe drinking water improved from 4.8 percent to 60.6 percent. World Health Organization, "Country Cooperation Strategy at a Glance: Afghanistan," 2014, http://www.who.int/countryfocus/cooperation_strategy /ccsbrief_afg_en.pdf, accessed 9 December 2015; BBC, "Afghanistan: Before and After the Taliban," BBC News, 2 April 2014, www.bbc.com/news/world-asia-26747712, accessed 9 December 2015.

1   KNOW THE WAR YOU'RE IN

1. Presumably, few local civilians knew that the sounds being broadcast by American tactical deception units in World War II were actually fake. For a fascinating recent review of the operations of the 23rd Headquarters Special Troops, which conducted battlefield deceptions from June 1944 through the end of the war, see Rick Beyers and Elizabeth Sales, *The Ghost Army: World War II's Artists of Deception* (New York: Princeton Architectural Press, 2015).
2. Stathis N. Kalyvas and Laia Balcells, "International System and Technologies of Rebellion: How the End of the Cold War Shaped Internal Conflict," *American Political Science Review* 104, no. 3 (2010): 415–29.
3. Scholars actively debate the role of technology in asymmetric conflicts. See Jason Lyall and Isaiah Wilson III, "Rage against the Machines: Explaining Outcomes in Counterinsurgency Wars," *International Organization* 63, no. 1 (2009): 67–106; Niel A. Smith and Nathan W. Toronto, "It's All the Rage: Why Mechanization Doesn't Explain COIN Outcomes," *Small Wars & Insurgencies* 21, no. 3 (2010): 519–28. For a discussion of why democracies adopt relatively conventional firepower-intense strategies in asymmetric conflicts despite their poor success rate, see Jonathan D. Caverly, "The Myth of Military Myopia: Democracy, Small Wars, and Vietnam," *International Security* 34, no. 3 (2010): 119–57.
4. World Bank, *World Development Report 2011: Conflict, Security and Development* (Washington, DC: World Bank, 2011).
5. For a review of the possibilities, see U.K. Government Office for Science, "The Internet of Things: Making the Most of the Second Digital Revolution," https://www.gov.uk/govern ment/uploads/system/uploads/attachment_data/file/409774/14-1230-internet-of-things -review.pdf, accessed 23 February 2016.
6. Xin Lu, Linus Bengtsson, and Petter Holme, "Predictability of Population Displacement after the 2010 Haiti Earthquake," *Proceedings of the National Academy of Sciences* 109, no. 29 (2012): 11576–81.
7. K. Gavric, Sanja Brdar, D. Culibrk, and V. Crnojevic, "Linking the Human Mobility and Connectivity Patterns with Spatial HIV Distribution," NetMob D4D Challenge (2013), http:// arxiv.org/abs/1503.06575, accessed 23 February 2016.
8. A. S. Azman, E. A. Urquhart, B. Zaitchik, and J. Lessler, "Using Mobile Phone Data to Supercharge Epidemic Models of Cholera Transmission in Africa: A Case Study of Côte d'Ivoire," NetMob D4D Challenge, Boston, May 2013.
9. Sudha Ram, Wenli Zhang, Max Williams, and Yolande Pengetnze, "Predicting Asthma-Related Emergency Department Visits Using Big Data," *IEEE Journal of Biomedical and Health Informatics* 19, no. 4 (2015): 1216–23.
10. See, e.g., big initiatives such as the Alzheimer's disease Big Data DREAM Challenge (https:// www.synapse.org/#!Synapse:syn2290704/wiki/60828, accessed 24 November 2017) and the OECD Expert Consultation on Unlocking Global Collaboration to Accelerate Innovation for Alzheimer's Disease and Dementia (http://www.oecd-ilibrary.org/content/workingpaper /5jz73kvmvbwb-en, accessed 24 November 2017).

11. Joshua Blumenstock, Tarek Ghani, Sylvan Herskowitz, Ethan Kapstein, Thomas Scherer, and Ott Toomet, "Industrial Organization and Insecurity: Evidence from Afghanistan" (working paper, Washington University, 2017).

12. Randy Garret, interview with the author, 15 November 2016.

13. Quy-Toan Do, Jacob N. Shapiro, Christopher D. Elvidge, Mohamed Abdel-Jelil, Daniel Anh, Kimberly Baugh, Jamie Hansen-Lewis, and Mikhail Zhizhin, "How Much Oil Is Daesh Producing? Evidence from Remote Sensing" (working paper, 2017).

14. International Energy Agency, "Oil Market Report, 2014," https://www.iea.org/media/omr reports/fullissues/2014-10-14.pdf, accessed 8 January 2016.

15. "Ahram, Al Qaeda Leaves East Syria Strongholds to Islamic State," *Monitor*, 3 July 2014.

16. Ken Dilanian, "Islamic State Group's War Chest Is Growing Daily," Associated Press, 15 September 2014.

17. David S. Cohen, "Remarks of Under Secretary for Terrorism and Financial Intelligence David S. Cohen at the Carnegie Endowment for International Peace," 23 October 2014, https://www.treasury.gov/press-center/press-releases/Pages/jl2672.aspx, accessed 24 November 2017.

18. Our story gives a great degree of agency to citizens in conflict zones. In this respect we follow the tradition of both soldiers such as David Galula, who wrote about fighting insurgencies during the Cold War, and academics such as Stathis Kalyvas, who found that civilian decisions have played a key role in deciding local outcomes in many civil wars. An African proverb says, "When the elephants fight, the grass gets trampled." While citizens certainly bear the brunt when governments and insurgent organizations fight, we show that they need not—and indeed *do not*—lie down and take it. They act, and their actions help determine the outcome of the conflict.

19. We examine achieving longer-term, nation-level objectives when working with local proxies in a companion volume of research. Eli Berman and David Lake, eds., *Proxy Wars: Suppressing Violence through Local Agents* (Ithaca: Cornell University Press, forthcoming).

20. We should stress that "empirical" for us does not mean deploying quantitative measures of progress, the way that Pentagon "Whiz Kids" infamously counted bodies under Secretary Robert McNamara during the Vietnam era. "Empirical" is just short for empirical scientific research: constantly challenging a carefully elucidated model (in this case, of insurgency) with the possibility of refutation by data, using the modern methods, and exposing the results to peer review.

21. This theory differs from the way we think about terrorism, which is also information-centric but with the critical difference that terrorist organizations operate in ways that have a much lower risk of sharing crucial information with civilians, making them less dependent on civilian attitudes. Among the many definitions of terrorism, the one we find most useful is political violence that targets noncombatants to influence an audience beyond the immediate victims of any given attack. Insurgency, on the other hand, targets combatants as well and aspires to control territory. While many terrorist organizations use both strategies of political violence, they tend to occur in different settings (Eli Berman and David D. Laitin, "Religion, Terrorism and Public Goods: Testing the Club Model," *Journal of Public Economics* 92, no. 10–11 [2008]: 1942–67) and dictate different approaches to organizational form (Jacob N. Shapiro, *The Terrorist's Dilemma: Managing Violent Covert Organizations* [New York: Princeton University Press, 2013]) and to treatment of local civilians (Eli Berman, *Radical, Religious, and Violent: The New Economics of Terrorism* [Cambridge, MA: MIT Press, 2011]).

22. Eli Berman, Jacob N. Shapiro, and Joseph H. Felter, "Can Hearts and Minds Be Bought?" *Journal of Political Economy* 119, no. 4 (2011): 766–819; Eli Berman, Joseph Felter, Jacob N. Shapiro, and Erin Troland, "Modest, Secure and Informed: Successful Development in Conflict Zones" (NBER Working Paper 18674, 2013); Eli Berman, Joseph Felter, Jacob N.

Shapiro, and Erin Troland, "Modest, Secure and Informed: Successful Development in Conflict Zones," *American Economic Review: Papers & Proceedings* 103, no. 4 (2013): 512–17 (abbreviated version).

2 ESOC'S MOTIVATION AND APPROACH

1. British major general Nick Carter, commander of Regional Command South, even advocated for a "courageous restraint" medal to recognize ISAF soldiers and Marines who exercised appropriate restraint on the battlefield. This idea and McChrystal's directive in general faced resistance from ISAF soldiers and criticism from the media. Chapter 7 discusses the idea at length, presenting specific results on the relationship between civilian casualties and insurgent attacks. See also Joseph Felter and Jacob N. Shapiro, "Limiting Civilian Casualties as Part of a Winning Strategy: The Case of Courageous Restraint," *Dædalus* 146, no. 1 (2017): 44–58.
2. Joseph H. Felter, "Taking Guns to a Knife Fight: A Case for Empirical Study of Counter-insurgency" (PhD diss., Stanford University, 2005).
3. As of 2010 this database contained more than one million documents captured by U.S. and allied forces in Afghanistan, Iraq, and elsewhere. Ranging from "For Official Use Only" on up to more sensitive degrees of classification, the documents include strategic policy studies, accounting reports, membership lists, technical training manuals, draft ideological screeds, personnel memoranda, and letters between family members. Roughly a quarter have been fully translated and all are accompanied by metadata of varying quality covering the circumstances of capture and nature of the documents.
4. The report is available at https://ctc.usma.edu/posts/harmony-and-disharmony-exploiting-al-qaidas-organizational-vulnerabilities. Joe and Jake's coauthors on this project were Major Jeff Bramlett, Captain Bill Perkins, and CTC members Dr. Jarret Brachman, Brian Fishman, Dr. James Forest, Lianne Kennedy, and Dr. Tom Stocking.
5. Jake later expanded the theory and presented further supporting evidence in his book *The Terrorist's Dilemma* and several journal articles with David Siegel. Jacob N. Shapiro, *The Terrorist's Dilemma: Managing Violent Covert Organizations* (Princeton: Princeton University Press, 2013); Jacob N. Shapiro and David A. Siegel, "Underfunding in Terrorist Organizations," *International Studies Quarterly* 51, no. 2 (2007): 405–29; Jacob N. Shapiro and David A. Siegel, "Moral Hazard, Discipline, and the Management of Terrorist Organizations," *World Politics* 64, no. 1 (2012): 39–78.
6. Clinton Watts, Jacob N. Shapiro, and Vahid Brown, *Al-Qa'ida's (Mis)Adventures in the Horn of Africa* (West Point, NY: Combating Terrorism Center, 2007).
7. Joseph Felter and Brian Fishman, *Al-Qa'ida's Foreign Fighters in Iraq* (West Point, NY: Combating Terrorism Center, 2007). The CTC recently released a similar report on Syria: Brian Bodwell, Daniel Milton, and Don Rassler, *The Caliphate's Global Workforce: An Inside Look at the Islamic State's Foreign Fighter Paper Trail* (West Point, NY: Combating Terrorism Center, 2016).
8. Brian Fishman, Jacob Shapiro, Joseph Felter, Peter Bergen, and Vahid Brown, *Bombers, Bank Accounts and Bleedout: Al-Qa'ida's Road in and out of Iraq* (West Point, NY: Combating Terrorism Center, 2007).
9. In a fortuitous coincidence Multi-National Force–Iraq (MNF-I) was then under the command of General David Petraeus, who had been (cadet) Joe's instructor at West Point.
10. Lieutenant Colonel Lee Ewing MNF-I Commanders Initiatives Group (CIG) and Lieutenant Commander Jeffrey Cadman MNC-I C2 Foreign Disclosure Office provided significant liaison support in gaining approval to release these data that would be critical to multiple ESOC studies going forward.
11. In compiling and processing these data we worked with Colonel Jim Glackin at the Gulf Region Division of the Army Corps of Engineers.

12. Testing the theory with data on suicide attacks that grew out of Laitin's work with economist Alan Krueger, they produced some of the first scholarship to explain why certain kinds of groups were exceptionally good at substate violence. Eli Berman and David Laitin, "Religion, Terrorism and Public Goods: Testing the Club Model," *Journal of Public Economics* 92, no. 10–11 (2008): 1942–67.

13. This is because the AFP kept such good records and because it has been fighting insurgencies for so long.

14. For example, recently retired colonel Robert Crowley, with extensive experience in command and leadership positions within the U.S. Army Civil Affairs community, was a member of the CAAT and provided significant support to the effort.

15. Though, as we'll discuss in the conclusion, it did not remain so and was once again the scene of intense fighting by mid-2015.

16. The broad need to exercise caution when using administrative data from conflict zones is amply demonstrated by the many examples in Ben Connable's excellent *Embracing the Fog of War: Assessment and Metrics in Counterinsurgency* (Santa Monica, CA: RAND Corporation, 2012).

17. Pakistan data from the BFRS Dataset of Political Violence in Pakistan. For details, see Ethan Bueno de Mesquita, Christine Fair, Jenna Jordan, and Rasul Bakhsh Rais, "Measuring Political Violence in Pakistan: Insights from the BFRS Dataset," *Conflict Management and Peace Science* 32, no. 5 (2015): 536–58. Philippines data from the ESOC Philippines Database, which compiles unclassified details of over 45,000 individual internal security incidents reported by the Armed Forces of the Philippines from 1977 to 2008.

18. Andrew Shaver, "Employment Status and Support for Wartime Violence: Evidence from the Iraq War" (ESOC Working Paper #1, 2016).

19. You might think that *aggregation* (meaning, gathering and totaling the data) would solve this problem, but it does not and actually causes problems of its own. If you look at the macrodata—data that are aggregated over lots of neighborhoods—those other confounding factors, like the influence of intersections, might average out, but so will the presence of development programs. And the more you aggregate the more you have to deal with *ecological inference* challenges—i.e., the difficulty of saying something meaningful about relationships at the individual level based on data at an aggregated level—and aggregated regions (e.g., countries) also have different predispositions to violence and development, so you don't actually get away from confounding.

20. Two projects in particular have made valuable contributions: the Uppsala Conflict Data Program (UCDP) and the Armed Conflict Location & Event Data Project (ACLED). Their approach is markedly different from ours, however. UCDP and ACLED work on a global scale, extracting incident details from press coverage. This entails a sacrifice of precision for coverage. Meanwhile, we focus on finding the best data we can in particular places—typically high-quality administrative data sets—knowing that we cannot achieve global coverage with that approach. In academic terms, this reflects the internal/external validity trade-off: UCDP and ACLED don't achieve the high internal validity we can, but they are able to trace correlations across countries.

21. Stephen Biddle, Jeffrey A. Friedman, and Jacob N. Shapiro, "Testing the Surge," *International Security* 37, no. 1 (2012): 7–40.

22. The first RCT of a drug was published in 1948, and the first RCTs of social policies in the United States took place in the mid-1970s. Presidents Ronald Reagan and Bill Clinton used them to evaluate welfare reform, but it wasn't until the 2000s that large-scale RCTs gained wide attention by showing that some long-standing, big-budget programs (such as Head Start, the preschool program for disadvantaged children) had little or no measurable effect, as implemented. For a brief history, see David Bornstein, "The Dawn of the Evidence-Based Budget," *New York Times*, 30 May 2012, http://opinionator.blogs.nytimes.com/2012/05/30/worthy-of-government

-funding-prove-it/?_r=o, accessed 24 February 2016. For a discussion of the problems with running policy RCTs, see Angus Deaton, "Instruments, Randomization, and Learning about Development," *Journal of Economic Literature* 48, no. 2 (2010): 424–55.

The early 2000s saw a dramatic increase in the use of RCTs to test programs in developing countries. Milestones included the 2003 founding of the Jameel Poverty Action Lab (J-PAL) at MIT, which sought to promote and organize RCTs for poverty reduction (https://www .povertyactionlab.org), and the creation of an RCT registry in 2012 by the American Economic Association (https://www.socialscienceregistry.org).

Barack Obama substantially expanded the use of RCTs for federal programs, along with other evidence-based measures such as "tiered evidence" grant programs, Pay-for-Success initiatives, and the establishment of the White House Social and Behavioral Sciences Team. Tom Kalil, "Funding What Works: The Importance of Low-Cost Randomized Controlled Trials," The White House blog, 9 July 2014, https://www.whitehouse.gov/blog/2014/07/09 /funding-what-works-importance-low-cost-randomized-controlled-trials, accessed 24 February 2016.

23. Christine C. Fair, Rebecca Littman, Neil Malhotra, and Jacob Shapiro, "Relative Poverty, Perceived Violence, and Support for Militant Politics: Evidence from Pakistan," *Political Science Research and Methods* 6, no. 1 (2018): 57–81.

24. Even in our survey experiment in Pakistan we had to be very vigilant about the ethics of our actions. For instance, we did not tell the subjects lies to manipulate their perceptions or ask directly about their support for illegal groups, which might have endangered them. (We explain exactly how we did this in chapter 8.) Ethical guidelines limit what you can do with experiments on human subjects, and with very good reason.

25. Microdata have long been used to study other areas of social policy, particularly in the United States and Europe where administrative records are quite good. A notable example is Joshua Angrist's study of the effect of military service during the Vietnam era on subsequent earnings, which used variation from randomly assigned draft lottery dates. Joshua Angrist, "Lifetime Earnings and the Vietnam Era Draft Lottery: Evidence from Social Security Administrative Records," *American Economic Review* 80, no. 3 (1990): 313–36.

Observational methods used in domestic policy research, along with prominent examples, include the following.

Ecological studies compare places that implement a program with other places that do not: a 1997 study showed that cities with needle-exchange programs saw annual transmission rates 11 percent lower than cities without. Susan F. Hurley, Damien J. Jolley, and John M. Kaldor, "Effectiveness of Needle-Exchange Programmes for Prevention of HIV Infection," *The Lancet* 349, no. 9068 (1997): 1797–1800.

Natural experiments exploit a change that can be interpreted as independent from the variable in question: Helena, Montana, banned public smoking but only for six months (at which point the law was repealed) and only within city limits, allowing researchers to show that there were fewer hospital admissions for lung ailments inside the city limits than outside. Richard P. Sargent, Robert M. Shepard, and Stanton A. Glantz, "Reduced Incidence of Admissions for Myocardial Infarction Associated with Public Smoking Ban: Before and After Study," *BMJ* 328, no. 7446 (2004): 977–80.

Difference-in-differences studies are like natural experiments in that they exploit a "treatment" that is taking place in one location and not another but compare the change over time in the treatment group to that in a control group: a raise in the minimum wage in New Jersey allowed researchers to compare the effect over time on fast-food employees to a control group in Pennsylvania where the minimum wage stayed the same. The findings refuted the argument that hikes in the minimum wage cause unemployment. David Card and Alan B. Krueger, "Minimum Wages and Employment: A Case Study of the Fast-Food Industry in New Jersey and Pennsylvania," *American Economic Review* 84, no. 4 (1994): 772–93.

> *Regression discontinuity design* we discuss presently. But a famous early example of the technique was a 1960 study that showed that students who received a certificate of merit, compared to those who just missed the cutoff, were more likely to receive scholarships—but the recognition didn't affect their long-term goals. Donald L. Thistlethwaite and Donald T. Campbell, "Regression-Discontinuity Analysis: An Alternative to the Ex Post Facto Experiment," *Journal of Educational Psychology* 51, no. 6 (1960): 309–17.

For a broad sample of studies that exemplify rigorous research methods, see the Empirical Studies Index in Joshua D. Angrist and Jörn-Steffen Pischke, *Mostly Harmless Econometrics* (Princeton: Princeton University Press, 2009), 475.

26. Benjamin Crost, Joseph Felter, and Patrick Johnston, "Aid under Fire: Development Projects and Civil Conflict," *American Economic Review* 104, no. 6 (2014): 1833–56.

27. A few important exceptions include the professional literature on counterinsurgency produced largely by the military; the research of Stathis N. Kalyvas and his coauthors, defining the division between asymmetric and symmetric types of conflict and charting their relative frequency post–World War II; and the work of Roger Petersen on intrastate war in Eastern Europe and the Balkans. Stathis N. Kalyvas and Laia Balcells, "International System and Technologies of Rebellion: How the End of the Cold War Shaped Internal Conflict," *American Political Science Review* 104, no. 3 (2010): 415–29; Roger D. Petersen, *Resistance and Rebellion: Lessons from Eastern Europe* (Chicago: University of Chicago Press, 2006).

3 INFORMATION-CENTRIC INSURGENCY AND COUNTERINSURGENCY

1. Work in experimental economics has shown that people operating in familiar settings in which they have substantial experience tend to calculate utilities correctly and play a range of complicated equilibrium strategies. These findings are explored in a range of publications, including these: John A. List, "Does Market Experience Eliminate Market Anomalies?" *Quarterly Journal of Economics* 118, no. 1 (2003): 41–71; Steven D. Levitt, John A. List, and David H. Reiley Jr., "What Happens in the Field Stays in the Field: Exploring Whether Professionals Play Minimax in Laboratory Experiments" (NBER Working Paper 15609, 2010).

2. The model is laid out in detail in Eli Berman, Jacob N. Shapiro, and Joseph H. Felter, "Can Hearts and Minds Be Bought? The Economics of Counterinsurgency in Iraq," *Journal of Political Economy* 119, no. 4 (2011): 766–819. It was inspired by a model describing why communities endure, and even support, criminal gangs: George Akerlof and Janet L. Yellen, "Gang Behavior, Law Enforcement, and Community Values," in *Values and Public Policy*, ed. Henry J. Aaron, Thomas E. Mann, and Timothy Taylor (Washington, DC: Brookings Institution, 1994).

3. A typical market has supply increasing in price and demand declining in price so that there is only one equilibrium price. We call that a *unique* equilibrium as only one set of choices is the best possible response. Not all situations have unique equilibrium choices. For example, a couple could choose to spend the evening together at a movie or at a concert, each a distinct equilibrium outcome, as long as they agree.

4. Vishwesha Guttal, P. Romanczuk, S. J. Simpson, G. A. Sword, and I. D. Couzin, "Cannibalism as a Driver of the Evolution of Behavioral Phase Polyphenism in Locusts," *Ecology Letters* 15, no. 10 (2012): 1158–66.

5. Christos C. Ioannou, V. Guttal, and I. D. Couzin, "Predatory Fish Select for Coordinated Collective Motion in Virtual Prey," *Science* 337, no. 6099 (2012): 1212–15.

6. Iain D. Couzin and N. R. Franks, "Self-organized Lane Formation and Optimized Traffic Flow in Army Ants," *Proceedings of the Royal Society of London B: Biological Sciences* 270, no. 1511 (2003): 139–46.

7. We think of these attitudes as the core element of local politics in communities involved in asymmetric conflict.

8. Technically, what we mean is that actors make choices that maximize their expected utility, where the mathematical expectation is weighted by the probability of each outcome.

9. Operations researchers Vicki Bier and Kjell Hausken present a different way of thinking about the trade-off between different kinds of counterinsurgent policies (militarized ~ negative versus public goods provision ~ positive) that yields the conclusion similar to ours: there are complementarities between effort in the military sphere and effort in providing positive inducements. Vicki Bier and Kjell Hausken, "Endogenizing the Sticks and Carrots: Modeling Possible Perverse Effects of Counterterrorism Measures," *Annals of Operations Research* 186, no. 1 (2011): 39–59.

10. Savvy readers will note that less technical accounts have long had implicit testable assumptions (e.g., Mao Tse-tung's famous aphorism about the people being the sea in which the insurgent can swim and hide implies a link between civilian attitudes and insurgent efficacy). For testing purposes, however, the arguments made by Mao are open to multiple interpretation, as is historical work on the wars in Algeria, Malaya, and Vietnam, as well as in the United States Army's *Field Manual 3-24: Counterinsurgency* (Washington, DC: Department of the Army, 2006). Mao, for example, is ambiguous about exactly what influences civilians' decisions about whether to allow the insurgents to swim among them. FM 3-24 identifies many mechanisms at play, making it hard to draw precise testable implications. Another important book describes the complexity of these environments, which is wonderful for forming intuition but makes deriving testable hypotheses a challenge. Mao Tse-tung, *On Guerrilla Warfare* (1937; Champaign, IL: First Illinois Paperback, 2000). Later work, though classic, is similarly ambiguous. Those include: David Galula, *Pacification in Algeria, 1956–1958* (Santa Monica, CA: RAND Corporation, 1963); Richard Clutterbuck, *The Long, Long War: Counterinsurgency in Malaya and Vietnam* (New York: Praeger, 1966). More recent contributions include David Kilcullen, *Counterinsurgency* (New York: Oxford University Press, 2010); John A. Nagl, *Learning to Eat Soup with a Knife: Counterinsurgency Lessons from Malaya and Vietnam* (Chicago: University of Chicago Press, 2009).

11. We note here that terrorists and insurgents have worried about this very dynamic since at least the 1880s. Jacob N. Shapiro, *The Terrorist's Dilemma: Managing Violent Covert Organizations* (Princeton: Princeton University Press, 2013). See pp. 90–92 for a recent example from al Qaeda in Iraq.

12. Greg Adams, "Conflict of Interest: Military-Led Development Insights from Afghanistan for Warfighters, Development Practitioners, and Policy Makers" (thesis, MPA International Development, Harvard University, 2014); Berman, Shapiro, and Felter, "Can Hearts and Minds Be Bought?"

13. Michael Albertus and Oliver Kaplan, "Land Reform as a Counterinsurgency Policy: Evidence from Colombia," *Journal of Conflict Resolution* 57, no. 2 (2012): 198–231.

14. William Hinton, *Fanshen: A Documentary of Revolution in a Chinese Village* (Berkeley: University of California Press, 1966).

15. Lindsay Heger, "In the Cross-Hairs: Examining the Factors That Make Terrorists Likely to Attack Civilians" (PhD diss., University of California, San Diego, 2010); Jennifer Keister, "States within States: The Social Contracts of Armed Groups" (PhD diss., University of California, San Diego, 2011); Alberto Diaz-Cayeros, Beatriz Magaloni, Aila M. Matanock, and Vidal Romero, *Living in Fear: The Dynamics of Extortion in Mexico's Criminal Insurgency* (Stanford: Stanford University Press, 2014).

16. Mary Flanagan, "Nonprofit Service Provision by Insurgent Organizations: The Cases of Hizballah and the Tamil Tigers," *Studies in Conflict and Terrorism* 31 (2008): 499–519.

17. Eli Berman, *Radical, Religious, and Violent: The New Economics of Terrorism* (Cambridge, MA: MIT Press, 2009).

18. For a broad discussion, see a recent volume edited by Ana Arjona, Nelson Kasfir, and Zacha-
    riah Mampilly, *Rebel Governance in Civil War* (New York: Cambridge University Press, 2015).

4 THE INFORMATION MECHANISM

1. "Nigeria UN Bomb: Video of 'Boko Haram Bomber' Released," BBC News, 18 September
   2011, http://www.bbc.co.uk/news/world-africa-14964554, accessed 19 March 2016.
2. "Boko Haram Timeline: From Preachers to Slave Raiders," BBC News, 15 May 2013, http://
   www.bbc.co.uk/news/world-africa-22538888, accessed 19 March 2016.
3. This botched operation was clumsy at best and suspicious at worst; Nigerian president
   Goodluck Jonathan responded by firing the nation's top police officer and several of his
   deputies. "Nigeria: Terrorist Attacks Prompt Shake-Up of Police Leadership," *New York
   Times*, 25 January 2012, http://www.nytimes.com/2012/01/26/world/africa/nigeria-ter
   rorist-attacks-prompt-shake-up-of-police-leadership.html?_r=0, accessed 19 March 2016.
4. "Nigeria's Boko Haram Threatens to Attack Telecom Firms," *Business Recorder*, 14 February 2012, http://www.brecorder.com/world/africa/45736-nigerias-boko-haram-threatens
   -to-attack-telecom-firms-.html, accessed 27 February 2016.
5. "Islamist Group Claims Responsibility for Cell Phone Tower Attacks in Nigeria," *Public
   Radio International*, 7 September 2012, http://www.pri.org/stories/2012-09-07/islamist
   -group-claims-responsibility-cell-phone-tower-attacks-nigeria, accessed 23 May 2016; "Nigeria Mobile Phone Masts to Get 24-Hour Protection," BBC News, 7 September 2012, http://
   www.bbc.co.uk/news/world-africa-19524008, accessed 23 May 2016.
6. Freedom Onuoha, "The Costs of Boko Haram Attacks on Critical Telecommunication
   Infrastructure in Nigeria," E-International Relations, 3 November 2013, http://www.e-ir
   .info/2013/11/03/the-costs-of-boko-haram-attacks-on-critical-telecommunication-infra
   structure-in-nigeria/#_ednref17, accessed 27 February 2016.
7. Aminu Abubakar, "Boko Haram Kidnaps at Least 97, Kills 28 in Raid," CNN.com, 15 August
   2014, http://edition.cnn.com/2014/08/15/world/africa/boko-haram-kidnapping/, accessed
   27 February 2016.
8. Sani Tukur, "Update: Jonathan Ignores Governors, Anglican Church, ACN, CPC, Others
   to Declare State of Emergency in Borno, Yobe, Adamawa," *Premium Times*, 14 May 2013,
   http://www.premiumtimesng.com/news/134266-update-jonathan-ignores-governors
   -anglican-church-acn-cpc-others-to-declare-state-of-emergency-in-borno-yobe-adamawa
   .html, accessed 19 March 2016.
9. "ISIS Executes 262, as It Takes Ancient Syrian City of Palmyra, Group Says," CNN, 25 May
   2015, http://edition.cnn.com/2015/05/25/middleeast/isis-killings-palmyra-syria/, accessed
   23 May 2016.
10. "Hamas Executes 18 Suspected Informers," Al Jazeera, 22 August 2014, http://www.alja
    zeera.com/news/middleeast/2014/08/hamas-kills-11-suspected-informers-israel-2014
    82285624490268.html, accessed 23 May 2016.
11. "Somalia's al-Shabab Militants 'Execute Informers,'" *Al Arabiya English*, 7 January 2015,
    http://english.alarabiya.net/en/News/africa/2015/01/07/Somalia-s-al-Shabab-militants
    -execute-informers-.html, accessed 23 May 2016.
12. In India, as we will discuss in more detail in chapter 8, Naxalite insurgents increased their
    attacks on civilians in many areas when the government began providing a basic income
    guarantee through a public works program. Gaurav Khanna and Laura Zimmermann, "Guns
    and Butter? Fighting Violence with the Promise of Development," *Journal of Development
    Economics* 124, no. 1 (2017): 120–41.
13. Jonathan Miller, "Taliban Hunt Wikileaks Outed Afghan Informers," Channel 4 News, 30 July
    2010, http://www.channel4.com/news/articles/uk/taliban+hunt+wikileaks+outed+afghan
    +informers/3727667.html, accessed 23 May 2016.

14. David Galula, *Pacification in Algeria, 1956–1958* (Santa Monica, CA: RAND Corporation, 1963), reprinted in 2006: http://www.rand.org/content/dam/rand/pubs/monographs/2006/RAND_MG478-1.pdf.

15. Ibid., 89.

16. This is the equilibrium with uncertainty explained in chapter 3. Technically, what rebels know is the distribution of community attitudes but not the attitudes of a particular individual who might provide information. See Eli Berman, Jacob N. Shapiro, and Joseph H. Felter, "Can Hearts and Minds Be Bought? The Economics of Counterinsurgency in Iraq," *Journal of Political Economy* 119, no. 4 (2011): 766–819 for details.

17. Note that in equilibrium, information-sharing happens when rebels are wrong or when they've just had some bad luck—but they will move quickly to rebalance. We will see evidence of this in chapter 7 when we look at the effects of civilian casualties on tips the Coalition received in Iraq. We interpret this as the players recognizing a mistake and adjusting their behavior back to equilibrium. Thinking in terms of equilibrium makes it clear that while the *long-run* flow of tips from citizens to government will not vary much as the environment changes, in the *short term* it could depend on something quite simple: changes in the ability of citizens to phone in tips at low risk of retaliation.

18. See, e.g., reports from the states of Telangana ("Maoists Impose 'Ban' on Mobiles," *The Hindu*, 31 May 2008, http://www.thehindu.com/todays-paper/tp-national/tp-andhrapradesh/maoists-impose-ban-on-mobiles/article1267752.ece, accessed 26 February 2016) and Orissa ("Maoists Tell People Not to Use Mobile Phones," *DNA India*, 9 November 2006, http://www.dnaindia.com/india/report-maoists-tell-people-not-to-use-mobile-phones-1063051, accessed 27 February 2016).

19. "More Cellphone Towers to Be Set up in Naxal-Hit Districts," *Indian Express*, 11 February 2016, http://indianexpress.com/article/india/india-news-india/bsnl-jharkhand-more-cellphone-towers-to-be-set-up-in-naxal-hit-districts/#sthash.6Y7ZuGJC.dpuf, accessed 27 February 2016.

20. D. M. Mitra, "The Relevance of Technology in the Fight against India's Maoist Insurgency," Global ECCO (Education Community Collaboration Online) *CTX Journal* 4, no. 1 (February 2014), https://globalecco.org/277, accessed 25 February 2016.

21. Noah Shachtman, "Taliban Threatens Cell Towers," *Wired*, 25 February 2014, http://www.wired.com/dangerroom/2008/02/in-iraq-when-th/, accessed 24 May 2016; "Taliban Orders Mobile Shutdown in Afghan Province," Reuters, 21 October 2008, http://www.reuters.com/article/us-afghan-mobiles-idUSTRE49K2HS20081021, accessed 24 May 2016.

22. Yaroslav Trofimov, "Cell Carriers Bow to Taliban Threat," *Wall Street Journal*, 22 March 2010, http://online.wsj.com/articles/SB10001424052748704117304575137541465235972, accessed 27 February 2016.

23. Jacob N. Shapiro and Nils B. Weidmann, "Is the Phone Mightier than the Sword? Cell Phones and Insurgent Violence in Iraq," *International Organization* 69, no. 2 (2015): 247–74.

24. "Cell Phone Tracking Helped Find al-Zarqawi," CNN, 11 June 2006, http://edition.cnn.com/2006/WORLD/meast/06/09/iraq.al.zarqawi/, accessed 26 February 2016.

25. Kirk Semple, "U.S. Backs Hot Line in Iraq to Solicit Tips about Trouble," *New York Times*, 4 November 2006, http://www.nytimes.com/2006/11/05/world/middleeast/05tips.html?pagewanted=print, accessed 19 March 2016; Donna Miles, "Hotline Succeeding in Foiling Iraqi Insurgents," American Forces Press Service, 29 December 2004.

26. "Iraqi Insurgents Target Water and Electricity, but Spare the Cell Phone," *LiveLeak*, 5 June 2007, http://www.liveleak.com/view?i=bed_1181083522, accessed 19 March 2016; Jon Brand, "Iraqi Insurgents Target Water and Electricity, but Spare the Cell Phone," *Newshour*, 29 January 2007, http://www.pbs.org/newshour/extra/features/jan-june07/infrastructure_1-29.html, accessed 17 March 2016.

27. Rhys Blakely, "Terrorists 'Threaten' Iraq Mobile Operators," *The Times*, 22 July 2005, http://business.timesonline.co.uk/tol/business/industry_sectors/telecoms/article546896.ece, accessed 19 March 2016.

28. Zain purchased the other providers serving central and southern Iraq in 2007 and 2008, including Iraqna.

29. To be more precise, while there was a nationwide dip in tower construction at the peak of the war in 2006–7, when Jake and Nils plotted the average date of tower introduction within a district in a given year against the levels of violence in the last six months of the previous year and the first six months in that particular year, there was no consistent pattern.

30. Shapiro and Weidmann, "Is the Phone Mightier than the Sword?"

31. A standard deviation is a measure that shows how much variation a given measure displays. It is useful if one wants to communicate how much a variable typically changes, as opposed to a unit change. A low standard deviation indicates that values cluster around the mean, while a high standard deviation indicates values spread out over a larger range. Typically, in a large distribution (and in a population), there are about three standard deviations above the mean and three below. Approximately two-thirds of a population falls between −1 and +1 standard deviation of the normal curve, 95 percent between −2 and +2, and over 99 percent between −3 and +3 standard deviations. So, the greater the number of standard deviations any given data point is above or below the mean, the more significantly outside the norm it is.

32. The results at the district level are effectively a weighted average of the impact of adding towers that introduce new coverage with that of adding towers that add new towers to already covered areas.

33. Shapiro and Weidmann, "Is the Phone Mightier than the Sword?" tables 4 and 5. The magnitude of the changes is not directly comparable across these two approaches, as the treatment units are vastly different in size. The more localized approach provides greater confidence that the observed change in violence does indeed reflect the causal influence of cell-phone towers, though it precludes estimating separate effects by ethnic mix, which is unavailable at the catchment level.

34. Akerlof and Yellen, "Gang Behavior, Law Enforcement, and Community Values."

35. We thank Austin Wright for invaluable background on the history of Chicago's strategy for getting tips.

36. Chicago Police Department, "Help Fight Crime Anonymously," http://home.chicagopolice.org/community/crime-prevention/txt2tip/, accessed 24 November 2016.

37. Village of Skokie, "Text-a-Tip," http://www.skokie.org/text-a-tip.cfm, accessed 21 November 2016.

38. "Police Departments Ask Drug Dealers to Turn in Their Competition," Chicago Channel 5 News, 22 April 2016, http://www.nbcchicago.com/news/local/Police-Department-Asks-Drug-Dealers-to-Turn-In-Their-Competition-376750151.html, accessed 24 November 2016.

39. Craig Whitlock and Barton Gellman, "To Hunt Osama bin Laden, Satellites Watched over Abbottabad, Pakistan, and Navy SEALs," *Washington Post*, 29 August 2013, https://www.washingtonpost.com/world/national-security/to-hunt-osama-bin-laden-satellites-watched-over-abbottabad-pakistan-and-navy-seals/2013/08/29/8d32c1d6-10d5-11e3-b4cb-fd7ce041d814_story.html, accessed 26 February 2016.

40. Mian Abar, "Mobile Chatter Taking Toll on Terrorists," *Pakistan Today*, 21 December 2014, http://www.pakistantoday.com.pk/2014/12/21/national/mobile-chatter-taking-toll-on-terrorists/, accessed 26 February 2016.

41. In an internal document from the Islamic State of Iraq (ISI) in 2006–7 titled "An Analysis of the State of the ISI" (NMEC-2007–612449), the author writes about communications security. In a list of recommendations for "Remedial Action for Security Personnel," he includes "Pay more attention to the Thuraya phones and the use of wireless, and other

means of communications" (p. 40). Later in a list of "the needs of Mujahidin," the writer lists "To secure a mobile wireless telecommunications network." We thank Patrick Johnston for pointing out these examples.

42. "Bihar: Maoists Ban Mobile Phones among Cadres," Rediff India Abroad, 14 September 2007, http://www.rediff.com/news/2007/sep/14bihar1.htm, accessed 26 February 2016.

43. Andrew Shaver, "Information and Communication Technologies, Wartime Informing, and Insurgent Violence" (Households in Conflict Network Working Paper No. 215, University of Sussex, 2016).

44. Kirk Semple, "U.S. Backs Hot Line in Iraq to Solicit Tips about Trouble," New York Times, 5 November 2006, http://www.nytimes.com/2006/11/05/world/middleeast/05tips.html?pagewanted=print, accessed 30 March 2016.

45. Central Command, United States Department of Defense, Point Paper (U.S. Central Command, U.S. Department of Defense, 2007).

46. Shaver, "Information and Communication Technologies, Wartime Informing, and Insurgent Violence," 12.

47. Jacob Jacob and I. Akpan, "Silencing Boko Haram: Mobile Phone Blackout and Counterinsurgency in Nigeria's Northeast Region," Stability: International Journal of Security & Development 4, no. 1 (2015), 1–17.

48. "Nigerian Army Bans Satellite Phones in Borno," BBC News, 20 June 2013, http://www.bbc.co.uk/news/world-africa-22984219, accessed 27 February 2016.

49. Jacob and Akpan, "Silencing Boko Haram," 10.

50. Ibid., 13.

51. Ibid., 15.

52. Dionne Searcey and Marc Santora, "Boko Haram Ranked ahead of ISIS for Deadliest Terror Group," New York Times, 18 November 2015, http://www.nytimes.com/2015/11/19/world/africa/boko-haram-ranked-ahead-of-isis-for-deadliest-terror-group.html?_r=0, accessed 19 March 2016.

53. Jan H. Pierskalla and Florian M. Hollenbach, "Technology and Collective Action: The Effect of Cell Phone Coverage on Political Violence in Africa," American Political Science Review 107, no. 2 (2013): 207–24. Violence data geocoded by 55 km² grid cells, created by the Peace Research Institute Oslo.

54. Ibid., 220.

55. Philip N. Howard and Muzammil M. Hussain, "The Upheavals in Egypt and Tunisia: The Role of Digital Media," Journal of Democracy 22, no. 3 (2011): 35–48. See also a 2012 study in Tunisia based on 16 interviews with digital activists and 437 surveys of Internet users, which observed that social media "(1) allowed a 'digital elite' to break the national media blackout through brokering information for mainstream media; (2) provided the basis for intergroup collaboration that facilitated a large 'cycle of protest' to develop; (3) overcame the collective action problem through reporting event magnitudes that raised the perception of success for potential free riders, and (4) led to an additional element of 'emotional mobilization' through depicting the worst atrocities associated with the regime's response to the protests." Anita Breuer, Todd Landman, and Dorothea Farquhar, "Social Media and Protest Mobilization: Evidence from the Tunisian Revolution" (paper prepared for the 4th European Communication Conference for the European Communication Research and Education Conference [ECREA], 2012).

56. Matt Richtel, "Egypt Cuts Off Most Internet and Cell Service," New York Times, 28 January 2011, http://www.nytimes.com/2011/01/29/technology/internet/29cutoff.html?_r=1, accessed 26 February 2016.

57. Robert F. Worth and Nazila Fathi, "Protests Flare in Tehran as Opposition Disputes Vote," New York Times, 13 June 2009.

58. Marco Manacorda and Andrea Tesei, "Liberation Technology: Mobile Phones and Political Mobilization in Africa" (London School of Economics, CEP Discussion Paper No. 1419, 2016).

59. Another difference: Manacorda and Tesei used a statistical approach that let them identify the causal impact of expanding cell-phone coverage with greater confidence. They exploited the fact that the spread of ICT is slower in areas with frequent lightning strikes (because the strikes affect towers) as a means to isolate the relationship between changes in cell-phone coverage unrelated to political events and subsequent changes in protests.

60. The country spent only 0.5 percent of its GDP on the military (amounting to 3.5 percent of government spending), less than one-third of the 1.9 percent annual average in Africa in that year (or an average of 13.2 percent of government spending). SIPRI Military Expenditure Dataset, https://sipri.org/databases/milex, accessed 26 November 2017.

61. For a brief recent history of Nigeria's counterinsurgency campaign, see James Adewunmi Falode, "The Nature of Nigeria's Boko Haram War: 2010–2015," *Perspectives on Terrorism* 10, no. 1 (2016).

62. Jacob N. Shapiro and David A. Siegel, "Coordination and Security: How Mobile Communications Affect Insurgency," *Journal of Peace Research* 52, no. 3 (2015): 312–22.

63. These first two heuristics refine the idea of asymmetric capacity from chapter 1.

64. Sidney Jones, "Briefing for the New President: The Terrorist Threat in Indonesia and Southeast Asia," *Annals of the American Academy of Political and Social Science* 618, no. 1 (2008): 69–78.

65. A report by the International Crisis Group summarizes their logic: "The Australian embassy attack in September 2004 cost about $7,800; the assassination of the head of the Central Sulawesi Protestant Church in October 2006 cost about $20." International Crisis Group, "Indonesia: Jemaah Islamiyah's Current Status" (Asia Briefing No. 63, 2007).

66. David Gordon and Samuel Lindo, "Aqam Futures Project Case Study Series: Case Study Number 6, Jemaah Islamiyah" (Washington, DC: CSIS Homeland Security & Counterterrorism Program Transnational Threats Project, 2011).

67. Richard C. Paddock, "Police Seek Public's Help in Bali Probe," *Los Angeles Times*, 4 October 2005, http://articles.latimes.com/2005/oct/04/world/fg-bali4, accessed 29 July 2016.

68. International Crisis Group, "Indonesia: Jihadi Surprise in Aceh" (Asia Report No. 189, 2010).

69. International Crisis Group, "'Deradicalisation' and Indonesian Prisons" (Asia Report No. 142, 2007).

70. Jones, "Briefing for the New President," 71.

71. Nick Grace, "Noordin Mohammed Top Dead, Major Attack Averted," *Long War Journal*, 7 August 2009, http://www.longwarjournal.org/archives/2009/08/noordin_mohammed_top.php, accessed 29 July 2016.

72. For good background on the conflict, see David G. Timberman, "Violent Extremism and Insurgency in Southern Thailand: A Risk Assessment," Section II, USAID (2013), http://pdf.usaid.gov/pdf_docs/PA00JSJX.pdf, accessed 26 August 2017.

73. "IDs to Be Mandatory for SIM Cards," *Bangkok Post*, 19 April 2005.

74. "Will ID Requirements Deter Terrorists?" *Bangkok Post*, 25 April 2005; Nick Cumming-Bruce, "Wireless: In Thailand, on the Trail of Cellphone Terrorists," *New York Times*, 2 May 2005.

75. "NBTC Deadline for Prepaid Users," *Bangkok Post*, 21 January 2015.

76. "No One Is Safe: Insurgent Attacks on Civilians in Thailand's Southern Border Provinces," Human Rights Watch, 27 August 2007, https://www.hrw.org/report/2007/08/27/no-one-safe/insurgent-attacks-civilians-thailands-southern-border-provinces, accessed 20 August 2017. For incident counts, see Global Terrorism Database, University of Maryland, https://www.start.umd.edu/gtd, accessed 21 August 2017.

77. Zachary Abuza, *The Ongoing Insurgency in Southern Thailand: Trends in Violence, Counter-insurgency Operations, and the Impact of National Politics*, Institute for National Strategic Studies Strategic Perspectives, no. 6 (Washington, DC: National Defense University Press, 2011).

78. Ben Hubbard and Anonymous, "Life in a Jihadist Capital: Order with a Dark Side," *New York Times*, 23 July 2014, http://www.nytimes.com/2014/07/24/world/middleeast/islamic-state-controls-raqqa-syria.html?_r=1, accessed 12 April 2016.

79. Yochi Dreazen, "U.S. Intelligence Says the Islamic State Is Fast Learning How to Run a Country," *Foreign Policy*, 19 August 2014, http://foreignpolicy.com/2014/08/19/from-electricity-to-sewage-u-s-intelligence-says-the-islamic-state-is-fast-learning-how-to-run-a-country/, accessed 12 April 2016.

80. The BBC's "Mosul Diaries" documented the disintegration of infrastructure over 2014 and the corresponding dissatisfaction among citizens: http://www.bbc.co.uk/news/world-middle-east-29600573.

81. Mitchell Prothero and Susannah George, "Coalition Success Seen in Islamic State's Cutoff of Cellphone Service in Mosul," McClatchy DC, 2 December 2014, http://www.mcclatchydc.com/news/nation-world/world/article24776932.html#storylink=cpy, accessed 12 April 2016.

82. Ibid., 2.

83. "ISIS Blocks Cell Phone Networks in Mosul, Residents Say," Associated Press, 27 November 2014, http://www.haaretz.com/news/middle-east/1.628914, accessed 12 April 2016.

84. Aymenn Jawad Al-Tamimi, a fellow at the Middle East Forum, has translated this and many other IS documents and made them available on his blog: http://www.aymennjawad.org/2015/01/archive-of-islamic-state-administrative-documents.

85. Nour Malas, "Iraqi City of Mosul Transformed a Year after Islamic State Capture," *Wall Street Journal*, 9 June 2015, http://www.wsj.com/articles/iraqi-city-of-mosul-transformed-a-year-after-islamic-state-capture-1433888626, accessed 12 April 2016.

86. At the time of writing, such efforts may be on the verge of becoming much easier, as Facebook (Project Aquila) and Google (Project Loon) are engaged in a technological race to provide broad Internet access to deprived areas via drones and helium-filled balloons, respectively.

87. Ben Kesling and Ali A. Nabhan, "Iraqi Forces Seek Help by Restoring Mosul Cellphone Service," *Wall Street Journal*, 1 November 2016.

5 THE ROLE OF DEVELOPMENT ASSISTANCE

1. "Review of Major U.S. Government Infrastructure Projects in Iraq: Nassiriya and Ifraz Water Treatment Plants," Office of the Special Inspector General for Iraq Reconstruction (SIGIR), 2010, https://docs.google.com/file/d/0B2owSLV7Lgl-OUtUYTVDT0sxODA/edit, accessed 23 September 2015.

2. "Marines, Iraqis Join Forces to Shut Down Fallujah," CNN, 6 April 2004, http://edition.cnn.com/2004/WORLD/meast/04/05/iraq.main/index.html, accessed 3 March 2015.

3. Citizens were outraged by reports of attacks against mosques, the shelling of a hospital, and the use of cluster bombs and missiles against civilians. "Learning from Fallujah: Lessons Identified, 2003–2005" (Oxford Research Group, 2005), 11–12, http://www.oxfordresearchgroup.org.uk/sites/default/files/fallujah.pdf, accessed 5 March 2016.

4. Iraq Body Count, "No Longer Unknowable: Falluja's April Civilian Toll Is 600," 26 October 2004, https://www.iraqbodycount.org/analysis/reference/press-releases/9/, accessed 10 October 2015.

5. Office of the Special Inspector General for Iraq Reconstruction (SIGIR), "Learning from Iraq," March 2013, http://cybercemetery.unt.edu/archive/sigir/20131001083907/; http://www.sigir.mil/learningfromiraq/index.html, p. 81, accessed 10 October 2015.

6. National Public Radio, "Iraq Update: Fallujah Brigade Disbanded," *NPR News*, 13 September 2004, http://www.npr.org/templates/story/story.php?storyId=3915311&from=mobile, accessed 3 March 2016.

7. National Public Radio, "10 Years after Battle for Fallujah, Marines Reflect on 'Iconic Fight,'" *NPR News*, 7 November 2014, http://www.npr.org/2014/11/07/362156306/10-years-after-battle-for-fallujah-marines-reflect-on-iconic-fight, accessed 10 October 2015.

8. U.S. Department of Defense, "Iraqis Build Fallujah's First Sewer System," 26 November 2007, http://www.defense.gov/news/newsarticle.aspx?id=48222, accessed 10 October 2015.

9. SIGIR, "Learning from Iraq," 82.

10. Joel Wing, "Fallujah Waste Water Treatment Plant: A Tale of U.S. Reconstruction in Iraq Gone Wrong," *Musings on Iraq*, 29 November 2011, http://musingsoniraq.blogspot.co.uk/2011/11/fallujah-waste-water-treatment-plant.html, accessed 10 October 2015.

11. Ibid.

12. SIGIR, "Learning from Iraq," 81.

13. Contractors bragged of going 4.5 million man-hours without a single injury: Water Online, "Case Study: Water Flows in Iraq Thanks to System Automation," 28 March 2007, http://www.wateronline.com/doc/water-flows-in-iraq-thanks-to-system-automati-0002, accessed 10 October 2015.

14. Russell W. Glenn, *Rethinking Western Approaches to Counterinsurgency: Lessons from Post-Colonial Conflict* (New York: Routledge, 2015).

15. Water Online, "Water Flows in Iraq."

16. SIGIR, "Learning from Iraq," 20.

17. Ibid., 79.

18. SIGIR, "Review of Major U.S. Government Infrastructure Projects in Iraq."

19. SIGIR, "Learning from Iraq," 82.

20. SIGIR, "Review of Major U.S. Government Infrastructure Projects in Iraq."

21. The concept of "hearts and minds" goes well beyond economic aid; it typically refers to all manner of actions that can create popular belief in the legitimacy of the government/counterinsurgent and can include ideological outreach, efforts to show that the government represents the people, and delivery of a wide range of services, from public order to clean elections. We thank an anonymous reviewer for highlighting this point, which has influenced the writing of this chapter.

22. Linda Polman, *The Crisis Caravan: What's Wrong with Humanitarian Aid?* (New York: Henry Holt, 2010), 168.

23. United States Army, *Field Manual 3-24: Counterinsurgency* (Washington, DC: Department of the Army, 2006), appendix A, A-5.

24. Mao Tse-tung, *On Guerrilla Warfare* (1937; Champaign, IL: First Illinois Paperback, 2000).

25. Ironically, the ideas behind Western governments' counterinsurgency campaigns over the twentieth century were inspired by the writings of the most successful insurgent of the age.

26. John Cloake, *Templer, Tiger of Malaya: The Life of Field Marshal Sir Gerald Templer* (London: Harrap, 1985), 262.

27. Robert Thompson, *Defeating Communist Insurgency: Experiences from Malaya and Vietnam* (London: Chatto and Windus, 1966), 63–64.

28. Karl Hack, "The Malayan Emergency as Counter-insurgency Paradigm," *Journal of Strategic Studies* 32, no. 3 (2009): 383–414.

29. Kumar Ramakrishna, "'Bribing the Reds to Give Up': Rewards Policy in the Malayan Emergency," *War in History* 9, no. 3 (2012): 332–53, quote on p. 344.

30. Ibid., 350.

31. Gentile's larger point is that counterinsurgency tactics are generally not successful: i.e., the Malayan Emergency (1948–60), he claims, was not really fought with such tactics, while the Vietnam War (1955–75), Iraq war (2003–10), and Afghanistan war (2001–14) all ended

with ambiguous outcomes. This argument seems wrong to us, as it conflates strategic failure with tactical failure. Specifically, it mixes up two questions: Is it realistic to ask our military to help a foreign ally control some territory that the ally does not seem very interested in (e.g., southeastern Afghanistan)? And given that civilian officials ask the military to help a foreign ally control some territory, what are the best tactics in employing one's forces?

We return to this conflation in the conclusion, but given the relevance to Vietnam, we sketch the argument here. The evidence on the first question suggests that it is often neither realistic nor productive to try to induce weak states to use force to establish exclusive control of ungoverned spaces. Militant groups often metamorphose into more moderate parties, and sometimes they are defeated—but only by governments that are willing to invest in controlling the entirety of their territory. On this we agree with Gentile, but the source of the strategic failure in these cases is not in the tactics used to fight but in the lack of will on the part of the supported ally. (The ESOC "Proxy Wars" project provides evidence.)

For the second question, the failures with respect to country-level outcomes that Gentile so ably documents are irrelevant. What matters is which tactical approaches obtain more or less stability on the margin within ongoing conflicts. On this point, the evidence points toward counterinsurgency as defined in doctrine as being relatively efficacious—though still inherently limited by the lack of host-nation effort in many places.

The fact that the answer to the first question is negative does not imply that counterinsurgency as an approach to irregular warfare is bankrupt. It just means it has been applied in places that were better left alone, regardless of the tactics employed. For example, in *Dereliction of Duty*, H. R. McMaster demonstrates that President Lyndon Johnson and his team knew as early as 1965, when they were escalating forces in Vietnam, that the North would win in the long run. This was due to the superior political commitment of the North Vietnamese over that of our Vietnamese ally, not to the failure of counterinsurgency tactics employed. H. R. McMaster, *Dereliction of Duty: Johnson, McNamara, the Joint Chiefs of Staff and the Lies That Led to Vietnam* (New York: HarperCollins, 1998).

32. Gian P. Gentile, *Wrong Turn: America's Deadly Embrace of Counterinsurgency* (New York: The New Press, 2013), 52.

33. We use Gentile's argument to illuminate current conflicts but hesitate to accept it wholesale because (a) voluntarily shared information from civilians clearly played a contributing role in the British victory and (b) evidence that some element of public trust matters comes from many conflicts, not just Malaya. Gentile is correct in pointing out that brutal aspects of the British campaign are generally deemphasized. How critical forced population relocation was to victory in Malaya is beyond the scope of this project. It is surely not a strategy that a Western power would embrace in this century.

34. For example, the CIA and U.S. Special Forces led the Civilian Irregular Defense Group (CIDG) program.

35. Michael E. Peterson, *The Combined Action Platoons: The U.S. Marines' Other War* (New York: Praeger, 1989), 24.

36. Ibid., 123, 125.

37. Major Curtis Williamson, *The U.S. Marine Corps Combined Action Program (CAP): A Proposed Alternative Strategy for the Vietnam War* (Quantico, VA: United States Marine Corps Command and Staff College, 2002), 42.

38. Melissa Dell and Pablo Querubín, "Nation Building through Foreign Military Intervention" (NBER Working Paper 22395, 2016).

39. For a favorable but balanced account of this campaign, see William Egan Colby and James McCargar, *Lost Victory: A Firsthand Account of America's Sixteen-Year Involvement in Vietnam* (Chicago: Contemporary, 1989). For a more recent revisionist argument, see Mark Moyar, *Triumph Forsaken: The Vietnam War, 1954–1965* (Cambridge: Cambridge University Press, 2006).

40. George Veith argues that South Vietnam's defeat was the result of intersecting factors—the absence of U.S. firepower, the vast reduction of U.S. aid, and the complete abrogation of the Paris Peace Accords by the North Vietnamese—and others that devastated South Vietnamese morale and hastened collapse (*Black April: The Fall of South Vietnam, 1973–1975* [New York: Encounter, 2012]). Colby and McCargar (*Lost Victory*) argue that "massive logistical support, assistance of American advisory elements and intelligence units on the ground" were all lacking in 1975, which were present in 1972 and earlier. "This difference was the major factor producing the collapse of morale and discipline that led to the end" (363). They go on to posit, "This is not to say that the outcome certainly would have been different, but there is at least a substantial chance that it might have been" (364). For a detailed account of military failures surrounding U.S. withdrawal of troops, see James H. Willbanks, *Abandoning Vietnam: How America Left and South Vietnam Lost Its War* (Lawrence: University of Kansas Press, 2004).

    Even this stream of the argument splits: Gian Gentile contends that the change in strategy under Abrams "was one of *degree* and not of *kind*." According to his view, the successes of the U.S. military and their RVNAF allies depended on destroying the National Liberation Front (Viet Cong) infrastructure, achieved not through hearts-and-minds efforts but mostly with firepower and forced relocation. Gentile, *Wrong Turn*, 71.

41. For a survey of the policy debate surrounding Iraq and Afghanistan, see David Kilcullen, "Counterinsurgency Redux," *Survival* 48 (2006): 111–30. A review of the economic literature on mechanisms in civil wars, both asymmetric and symmetric, is in Chris Blattman and Edward Miguel, "Civil War," *Journal of Economic Literature* 48 (2010): 3–57 and in Eli Berman and Alia M. Matanock, "The Empiricists' Insurgency," *Annual Review of Political Science* 18 (2015): 443–64.

42. U.S. Army, *Field Manual 3-24*.

43. Richard Clutterbuck, *The Long, Long War: The Malayan Emergency, 1948–1960* (London: Cassell, 1966).

44. We focused on the aid component of the hearts-and-minds strategy in large part because it was more localized and was more effectively measured than the ideological and political components. That practical choice turned out to be a good one.

45. Eli Berman, Jacob N. Shapiro, and Joseph H. Felter, "Can Hearts and Minds Be Bought? The Economics of Counterinsurgency in Iraq," *Journal of Political Economy* 119, no. 4 (2011): 766–819.

46. There is an important distinction here that is often missed in press reporting. Journalist Patrick Cockburn once quoted an Afghan man who worked for a U.S. government agency as saying, "Villagers don't forgive the U.S. army for killing their sons just because it has built a road or a bridge." That kind of statement is not really relevant here because in our approach the aid need not shift the attitudes of individuals who are particularly aggrieved and thus willing to join the insurgency. Rather, aid works by shifting the beliefs of someone else who has information on what insurgents are doing regarding the value of having the government in control. Patrick Cockburn, "Billions down the Drain in Useless U.S. Afghan Aid," *Counterpunch*, 13 December 2010, http://www.counterpunch.org/2010/12/13/billions-down-the-drain-in-useless-us-afghan-aid/, accessed 16 September 2016.

47. This prediction comes with a caveat. If by "local conditions favor rebels" we mean that the insurgent advantage is in lower costs of violence, then the prediction is correct as stated. If, on the other hand, the conditions favoring rebels are local attitudes toward insurgency, then the prediction is technically ambiguous. For example, if the probability of a tip is negligible because local civilians are so predisposed to favor rebels, then the government should optimally waste no military or aid resources on that locality. For details, see Berman, Shapiro and Felter, "Can Hearts and Minds Be Bought?" 784–87.

48. CSP funded a range of small-scale economic development and community engagement activities. For an official summary, see Della McMillan, Mamadou Sidibe, Jessica Cho, and Alice Willard, "Community Stabilization Program: Final Report" (IRD Report, 2010).

49. CERP did fund a few large projects. These included $370 million to the Sons of Iraq program, the largest CERP-funded program (SIGIR, "Learning from Iraq," 100); $11.7 million to renovate the electrical distribution grid in Muhalla 312, a neighborhood in northeast Baghdad (123); $5.4 million to provide solar street lighting for the city of Fallujah (87); $4.2 million to construct the Baghdad International Airport Caravan Hotel (87); and $2.9 million for construction of a large farmer's market on a major highway in central Iraq (119).

50. Calculated using CERP's violence-reducing effect after 2007—which is greater than pre-2007, as we explain presently.

51. CSP was an exemplar for consultation with communities in Iraq. The National Solidarity Programme, which we will discuss later in the book, was the exemplar of such consultation in Afghanistan.

52. See the series of high-quality Independent Monitoring Unit (Rahman Safi Consulting) reports on CCI from 2015 including "IMU Case Study: Youth Programming in South, East, North and West Afghanistan," "IMU Case Study: The Effectiveness of Infrastructure Projects in Increasing Linkages between Local Populations and Government," "IMU Case Study: GIRoA Perspectives on OTI/CCI Programming," and "IMU Case Study: Winter Preparedness Packages," all available from RSI Consulting, http://rsiafghanistan.com.

53. Radha Iyengar, Jacob N. Shapiro, and Stephen Hegarty, "Lessons Learned from Stabilization Initiatives in Afghanistan: A Systematic Review of Existing Research" (RAND Labor and Population Work Paper WR-1191, 2017).

54. There are many well-documented examples of these dynamics in Afghanistan. For a summary of detailed case studies in five provinces—two of which, Balkh and Faryab, were secure at the time and three of which, Helmand, Paktia, and Uruzgan, were not—see Paul Fishstein and Andrew Wilder, "Winning Hearts and Minds? Examining the Relationship between Aid and Security in Afghanistan" (Finestein International Center, Tufts University, 2012). Results of other studies are summarized in Iyengar, Shapiro, and Hegarty, "Lessons Learned from Stabilization Initiatives in Afghanistan."

55. We did this in a working paper, which used a wider range of data: Eli Berman, Joseph Felter, Jacob N. Shapiro, and Erin Troland, "Modest, Secure and Informed: Successful Development in Conflict Zones" (NBER Working Paper 18674, 2013).

56. Each PRT had a military commander who led a combined civilian-military team that provided advice and coordinated development programming with military objectives. For a more recent summary, see Robert M. Perito, "Provincial Reconstruction Teams in Iraq" (USIP Special Report 185, March 2017).

57. That heterogeneity is correctly measured to the extent that the timing of PRT introduction was not too strongly influenced by trends in violence. The results on the heterogeneity of aid spending's impact depending on PRT presence are robust to controlling for pre-period trends in violence, suggesting that while this bias may be present, it is not accounting for the full effect.

58. It is possible that this increased efficiency was simply because the PRTs provided additional bodies to coordinate aid spending with raids and other tactical operations.

59. We cannot be certain the logic of conditionality is not what drives the results on project size as well, so our evidence refuting gratitude or grievance theories might rest on evidence for Proposition 2B.

60. "Ensure that noncompliance with government policies has an economic price. Likewise, show that compliance with those policies is profitable. In the broadest sense, counterinsurgency operations should reflect that 'peace pays.'" U.S. Army, *Field Manual 3-24*, 173, paras. 5–49.

61. Berman, Shapiro and Felter, "Can Hearts and Minds Be Bought?" 776.

62. An important paper by Renard Sexton of New York University, which we will describe in chapter 6, shows that in Afghanistan, too, security complemented aid. Sexton used violence data from an NGO and information on the location of American battalion-level Forward Operating Bases (FOBs) to show that CERP spending reduced violence only in districts controlled by pro-government forces. In contested areas, aid seemed to have gone beyond nullifying the effects of aid (as we saw in Iraq) to causing an increase in violence. Renard Sexton, "Aid as a Tool against Insurgency: Evidence from Contested and Controlled Territory in Afghanistan," *American Political Science Review* 110, no. 4 (2016): 731–49.

63. Our quantitatively grounded assessment is mirrored in qualitative analysis of reconstruction spending in Afghanistan and Iraq. On the efficacy of different kinds of CERP projects the Special Inspector General for Iraq Reconstruction argued, "Battalion commanders that used CERP money to execute wisely targeted, quick-turn-around projects helped the mission succeed. Those who spent it on large-scale rebuilding efforts, like the Baghdad Enterprise Zone, missed the mark" (SIGIR, "Learning from Iraq," 33). On the idea that smaller projects run by the UK Department for International Development performed better than large ones, see Jon Bennett, Jane Alexander, Douglas Saltmarshe, Rachel Phillipson, and Peter Marsden, "Country Programme Evaluation Afghanistan," *DFID Evaluation Report EV696* (May 2009): xiv, https://www.oecd.org/countries/afghanistan/47107291.pdf, accessed 31 August 2017.

64. Benjamin Crost, Joseph Felter, and Patrick B. Johnston, "Conditional Cash Transfers, Civil Conflict and Insurgent Influence: Experimental Evidence from the Philippines," *Journal of Development Economics* 119, no. 1 (2016): 171–82.

65. Ariel Fiszbein and Norbert Schady, "Conditional Cash Transfers: Reducing Present and Future Poverty" (Washington, DC: World Bank Policy Research Reports, 2009).

66. Seeta K. Prabhu, "Conditional Cash Transfer Schemes for Alleviating Human Poverty: Relevance for India" (New York: United Nations Development Programme, 2009); Stephan S. Lim, Lalit Dandona, Joseph A. Hoisington, Spencer L. James, Margaret C. Hogan, and Emmanuela Gakidou, "India's Janani Suraksha Yojana, a Conditional Cash Transfer Programme to Increase Births in Health Facilities: An Impact Evaluation," *The Lancet* 375 (2009): 2009–23.

67. Nazmul Chaudhury, Jed Friedman, and Junko Onishi, "Philippines Conditional Cash Transfer Program Impact Evaluation 2012" (World Bank Report Number 75533-PH, 2013), http://www.dswd.gov.ph/download/Research/Philippines%20Conditional%20Cash%20Transfer%20Program,%20Impact%20Evaluation%202012.pdf, accessed 10 October 2015.

68. Measuring a relatively subjective variable such as *influence* is tricky. They used four categories of rebel influence in a village, based on assessments made by Philippine military field operatives, in support of their campaign planning. Villages in the highest influence category were reported as being subjected to a permanent presence of rebels openly carrying arms and training members. Villages in the next highest category of influence were characterized by insurgents attempting to organize residents and create parallel government structures, as well as initiate propaganda and recruitment activities. The next-to-last category included villages where Philippine military operatives received intelligence or other information that the village was being targeted for communist organization activities but did not have an overt and enduring presence of rebels. Villages in the lowest category had no insurgent activity.

69. Author's interview with Department of Social Welfare and Development (DSWD) officials in Quezon City, Philippines, April 2012.

70. Julien Labonne, "The Local Electoral Impacts of Conditional Cash Transfers: Evidence from a Field Experiment," *Journal of Development Economics* 104 (2013): 73–88.

71. Jan Rasmus Böhnke and Christoph Zürcher, "Aid, Minds and Hearts: The Impact of Aid in Conflict Zones," *Conflict Management and Peace Science* 30, no. 5 (2013): 411–32.

72. Andrew Beath, Fotini Christia, and Ruben Enikolopov, "Winning Hearts and Minds through Development: Evidence from a Field Experiment in Afghanistan" (MIT Political Science Department Research Paper No. 2011–14, 2012).

73. Ibid., 2.

74. Management Systems International, Summary of the USAID/Afghanistan MISTI Project's Activities and Findings, Mimeo, 2015 (in authors' possession).

75. Daniel Egel and Peter Glick, *Peer Review of the MISTI Survey and Evaluation Methodology* (Santa Monica, CA: RAND Corporation, 2014).

76. Benjamin Crost, Joseph Felter, and Patrick Johnston, "Aid under Fire: Development Projects and Civil Conflict," *American Economic Review* 104, no. 6 (2014): 1833–56.

77. Susan Wong, *What Have Been the Impacts of World Bank Community-Driven Development Programs?* (Washington, DC: World Bank Social Development Department, 2012).

78. Andrew C. Eggers and Jens Hainmueller, "MPs for Sale? Returns to Office in Postwar British Politics," *American Political Science Review* 103, no. 4 (2009): 513–33.

79. This may seem a wide range; to understand its breadth requires some knowledge of the statistical methods. In our case, probably the most influential decision is whether to model the relationship between poverty and baseline violence as linear or quadratic. Doing the former, we arrive at an estimated 0.096 additional casualties in eligible municipalities, which corresponds to a 126 percent increase over the control mean of 0.076. Doing the latter, we arrive at an estimate of 0.141, or 185 percent over the mean. Further judgment calls include whether to assume that casualties follow a Poisson distribution or a Gaussian, and whether to include control variables to net out various other factors. Since economists and statisticians can disagree about what the "correct" choice is, we report the whole range of estimates—all large and positive. This is the robustness one wants to see in empirical work; exactly how you slice the data should not matter much.

80. One prominent example is the bombing of the National Assembly complex in Manila on 13 November 2007, which killed a congressman and five others. The Abu Sayyaf group, later affiliated with IS, claimed responsibility.

81. Ang Bayan, "PAMANA and Kalahi-CIDSS Are Counterrevolutionary and Anti-Development," Philippine Revolution Web Central, 2012, http://www.philippinerevolution.net/publica tions/angbayan/20121107/pamana-and-kalahi-cidss-are-counterrevolutionary-and-anti-de velopment, accessed 12 March 2014; Gregorio Rosal, "U.S. Military Involvement in AFP Counter-Guerrilla Operations in Bicol," Philippine Revolution Web Central, 2003, http:// www.philippinerevolution.net/statements/20030216us-military-involvement-in-afp-coun ter-guerrilla-operations-in-bicol, accessed 12 March 2014.

82. Scholars discuss such theft—and other ways insurgents extract money and resources from civilians—as *extortion* and *taxation*, so it is worth drawing a clear distinction. Both are co- ercive, but extortion suggests a target-specific rate and a threat of high levels of violence, with pernicious effects on investment and utility (for the risk-averse), respectively. Taxation suggests a fixed rate and perhaps service provision.

83. Linda Polman, *The Crisis Caravan: What's Wrong with Humanitarian Aid?* (New York: Henry Holt, 2010).

84. Ibid., 90–95.

85. Ibid., 100–103.

86. Jennifer Morrison Taw argues that the Somalia example "makes it clear that the common misperception of humanitarian assistance as apolitical and neutral is dangerously coun- terproductive and can create unintended negative consequences for donors and intended recipients alike." Jennifer Morrison Taw, "The Perils of Humanitarian Assistance in Armed Internal Conflicts: Somalia in the 1990s," *Small Wars & Insurgencies* 15, no. 2 (2004): 5–19.

87. Alex de Waal, *African Issues: Famine Crimes, Politics, and the Disaster Relief Industry in Africa* (Indianapolis: Indiana University Press, 1997), 162.

88. From an October 2014 interview with IRIN News: "They don't give anything, they just take. If someone has a truck of aid on the street, they will ask for money from them to allow

them to pass." Eva Svoboda and Louise Revers, "Aid and the Islamic State" (IRIN News/ Humanitarian Policy Group Crisis Brief, 2014).

89. Nathan Nunn and Nancy Qian, "U.S. Food Aid and Civil Conflict," *American Economic Review* 104, no. 6 (2014): 1630–66.

90. Ibid., 1635.

91. The authors also exploited the fact that certain countries received aid more frequently throughout the period because of historical ties to the United States, while others received it more sporadically. Comparing the relative differences in violence these types of countries experienced also allowed the authors to further reduce statistical noise and rule out alternative explanations.

92. Ulrike Putz, "The Problem with Aid: International Donations Not Always Welcome in Gaza," *Spiegel Online*, 4 June 2010, http://www.spiegel.de/international/world/the-problem-with -aid-international-donations-not-always-welcome-in-gaza-a-698766.html, accessed 17 October 2015.

93. Svoboda and Revers, "Aid and the Islamic State."

94. Maria Abi-Habib, "Islamic State Poaches International Aid for Syrians: Thefts Are Latest Weapon in Quest for Power," *Wall Street Journal*, 17 November 2015, http://www.wsj.com/articles/islam ic-state-poaches-international-aid-for-syrians-1416158609, accessed 2 January 2018.

95. United Nations World Food Programme, "World Food Programme Alarmed by Images Showing ISIS Distributing WFP Food in Syria," WFP News, 2 February 2015, https://www .wfp.org/news/news-release/world-food-programme-alarmed-images-showing-isis-dis tributing-wfp-food-syria, accessed 10 October 2015.

96. The *Wall Street Journal* reported, "Islamic State militants have been seizing foreign aid destined for the neediest Syrians to redistribute under the extremist group's black flag, the latest tactic in its quest for power." Abi-Habib, "Islamic State Poaches International Aid for Syrians."

97. A. Heather Coyne, presentation at panel titled "Aid, Governance and Counter-insurgency: Mindanao, Iraq, Afghanistan" (UC Institute on Global Conflict and Cooperation Conference on Terrorist Organizations, May 2007), quoted in Eli Berman, *Radical, Religious, and Violent: The New Economics of Terrorism* (Cambridge, MA: MIT Press, 2011).

98. USAID, "MISTI Stabilization Trends and Impact Evaluation Survey Analytical Report, Wave 5: Sep. 28–Nov. 3, 2014" (Arlington, VA: Management Systems International, 2015), 14.

99. Ibid., 350–51.

100. Ibid., 357. As we will see in chapter 6, Jason Lyall found complementary results—an increase in support for the Taliban—in his analysis of the Afghan Civilian Assistance Program II (ACAP II). Jason Lyall, "Civilian Casualties and the Conditional Effects of Humanitarian Aid in Wartime" (working paper, 2016).

101. A recent review of nineteen studies on the impact of aid on conflict finds that "aid in conflict zones is more likely to exacerbate violence than to dampen violence. A violence-dampening effect of aid appears to be conditional on a relatively secure environment for aid projects to be implemented. A violence-increasing effect occurs when aid is misappropriated by violent actors, or when violent actors sabotage aid projects in order to disrupt the cooperation between the local population and the government." Christoph Zürcher, "What Do We (Not) Know About Development Aid and Violence? A Systematic Review," *World Development* 97 (2017): 506–22.

102. J. Stephens and David B. Ottaway, "A Rebuilding Plan Full of Cracks," *Washington Post*, 20 November 2005.

103. See our discussion of the Host Nation Trucking scandal in chapter 5.

104. Alexander de Waal, *Famine Crimes: Politics and the Disaster Relief Industry in Africa* (Bloomington: Indiana University Press, 1997).

105. Linda Polman, *The Crisis Caravan: What's Wrong with Humanitarian Aid?* (New York: Metropolitan Books, 2010).
106. SIGIR, "Learning from Iraq," 3.
107. Ibid., 52.
108. Ibid., 42.
109. Aram Roston, "How the U.S. Funds the Taliban," *The Nation*, 11 November 2009.
110. United States House of Representatives, "Warlord, Inc.: Extortion and Corruption along the U.S. Supply Chain in Afghanistan" (Washington, DC: United States House of Representatives, 2010), 17.
111. Ibid., 1.
112. Stanley McChrystal, Commander's Initial Assessment, NATO International Security Assistance Force, U.S. Forces Afghanistan (30 August 2009), quoted in ibid., 45.
113. Table 1 in Zürcher, "What Do We (Not) Know About Development Aid and Violence" provides a nice review of findings from many of the studies cited in this chapter along with a number we do not cite.
114. David Bryer and Edmund Cairns, "For Better? For Worse? Humanitarian Aid in Conflict," *Development in Practice* 7, no. 4 (1997): 363–74.
115. Ibid., 365.

6 THE ROLE OF SUPPRESSION

1. The most thorough English-language account of these changes using interviews with Iraqis is Gary Montgomery and Timothy S. McWilliams, eds., *The Anbar Awakening*, vol. 2, *Iraqi Perspectives* (Quantico, VA: Marine Corps University Press, 2009). For an excellent academic account that synthesizes a broad range of evidence, see Marc Lynch, "Explaining the Awakening: Engagement, Publicity, and the Transformation of Iraqi Sunni Political Attitudes," *Security Studies* 20 (2011): 36–72.
2. Office of the Special Inspector General for Afghanistan Reconstruction (SIGAR), "Commander's Emergency Response Program in Laghman Province Provided Some Benefits, but Oversight Weaknesses and Sustainment Concerns Led to Questionable Outcomes and Potential Waste," Office of the Special Inspector General for Afghanistan Reconstruction, 2011, https://www.sigar.mil/pdf/audits/2011-01-27audit-11-07.pdf, accessed 20 November 2017.
3. United States Department of Defense, "Money as a Weapon System MNC-I CJ8 SOP (Multi-National Corps-Iraq CJ8 Standard Operation Procedures)," chap. 4, 2009, https://info.pub licintelligence.net/MAAWS%20Jan%2009.pdf, accessed 26 September 2015.
4. In chapter 4, we showed that CERP spending in Iraq did indeed follow insurgent violence.
5. United Nations, World Development Indicators, 2015, http://data.worldbank.org/data-cat alog/world-development-indicators, accessed 13 December 2016.
6. John F. Burns, "Afghan Dream: A Smooth Road to Anywhere," *New York Times*, 19 September 2002, http://www.nytimes.com/2002/09/19/world/threats-and-responses-develop ment-afghan-dream-a-smooth-road-to-anywhere.html, accessed 16 September 2016.
7. SIGAR, "Commander's Emergency Response Program in Laghman Province," 4.
8. Ibid., ii.
9. Ibid., 5.
10. Richard K. Morgan, a postdoctoral researcher-scholar at the Varieties of Democracy Institute, University of Gothenburg, Sweden, who did two combat tours in the U.S. Army in Afghanistan, theorizes a very different mechanism through which roadbuilding might affect the balance of power in an asymmetric conflict. He reports evidence from surveys in the Bodoland conflict areas in Assam, which has had an active separatist insurgency since the late 1980s, and the state of Bihar, which has long suffered a Maoist insurgency, that "(1) road

construction increases the probability that security forces patrol an area, and (2) that the probability of an area expressing support for the state decreases as state presence increases." It is possible, in other words, that certain kinds of aid projects matter because of their effect on the probability that one side or the other is able to apply its military forces, and not because of shifts induced in civilian attitudes. See Richard Morgan, "Road Warriors: State Power, Territorial Control, and Popular Support in Insurgencies" (working paper, 2017). Morgan's broader dissertation argues that within information-centric conflicts we should expect the deployment of security forces to have different effects depending on the preexisting views populations hold of the government and its allies.

11. SIGAR, "Commander's Emergency Response Program in Laghman Province," 5.

12. J. Stephens and David B. Ottaway, "A Rebuilding Plan Full of Cracks," *Washington Post*, 20 November 2005.

13. Patrick Fine, memo, 10 October 2004, http://www.washingtonpost.com/wp-srv/world /documents/USAIDcorrespondence.pdf, accessed 16 September 2016.

14. Azmat Khan, "Ghost Students, Ghost Teachers, Ghost Schools," *Buzzfeed News*, 9 July 2015, https://www.buzzfeed.com/azmatkhan/the-big-lie-that-helped-justify-americas-war-in -afghanistan?utm_term=.xl4MpD27G#.vtQKjP7dp, accessed 16 September 2016.

15. See our discussion of the Host Nation Trucking scandal in chapter 5.

16. Quoted in Patrick Cockburn, "Billions down the Drain in Useless US Afghan Aid," *Counterpunch*, 13 December 2010, https://www.counterpunch.org/2010/12/13/billions-down-the -drain-in-useless-us-afghan-aid/, accessed 31 August 2017.

17. Whether fried chicken and waffles are complements, substitutes, or additively separable is a debate we hesitate to wade into.

18. More precisely, g and m are *strategic* complements, as opposed to complements in (some) people's preferences for fried chicken and mashed potatoes. An exogenous increase in one will lead to increased use of the other, both ceteris paribus and in equilibrium. See Eli Berman, Jacob N. Shapiro, and Joseph H. Felter, "Can Hearts and Minds Be Bought? The Economics of Counterinsurgency in Iraq," *Journal of Political Economy* 119, no. 4 (2011): 766–819 for details.

19. But let's be careful here; the politics also changed dramatically.

20. For example, some Nazi occupation forces in (what is now) Ukraine during World War II experimented with providing services to local populations. See Ben H. Shepherd, *War in the Wild East: The German Army and Soviet Partisans* (Cambridge, MA: Harvard University Press, 2004), especially chap. 5.

21. From a technical perspective, the assumptions that imply complementarity between suppression and service provision are quite natural. The first assumption is that government has diminishing returns to suppressing violence. That is, the value of going from 151 to 150 IED attacks in Fallujah in mid-2005 for the government was less than that of going from 11 to 10. The second assumption is that the probability that government controls the territory increases in level of suppression effort, m. The third assumption is that the patrol has a better chance of finding the IED and the insurgents if the father provides the tip, i.e., that a given unit of m does more to enhance the government's probability of controlling the territory in the presence of information. Finally, we assume that civilians care at least a little about services they will get if the government controls the territory.

22. For a formal proof, see Berman, Shapiro, and Felter, "Can Hearts and Minds Be Bought?" 785.

23. This graphical analysis holds the response of government services constant. In the full analysis of the effect of a change in attitudes, the resulting change in the level of government services is also ambiguous, though violence will decrease. See Berman, Shapiro, and Felter, "Can Hearts and Minds Be Bought?" for details.

24. That point highlights the importance of directly measuring attitudes, which we will report on in chapters 8 and 9.

25. United States Energy Information Administration, "Iraq Country Overview," http://www .eia.gov/beta/international/analysis.cfm?iso=IRQ, accessed 7 July 2016.

26. Office of the Special Inspector General for Iraq Reconstruction (SIGIR), "Learning from Iraq," 2013, http://cybercemetery.unt.edu/archive/sigir/20131001083907/; http://www.sigir .mil/learningfromiraq/index.html, p. 84, accessed 9 July 2016.

27. Office of the Special Inspector General for Iraq Reconstruction (SIGIR), SIGIR PA-08-137, "Sustainment Assessment: Kirkuk to Baiji Pipeline Exclusion Zone—Phase 3, Kirkuk, Iraq," 2008, http://www.dtic.mil/dtic/tr/fulltext/u2/a509188.pdf, p. 3, accessed 7 July 2016.

28. Ibid., 4.

29. SIGIR, "Learning from Iraq," 84.

30. In the following discussion, we draw on our own experiences and on conversations with various operations officers in the U.S. military—those overseeing how troops, supplies, vehicles, etc., move from one spot to another. One such officer is Lieutenant Commander Brendan Gallagher, a U.S. Army infantry officer with 15 years' army experience, about 3.5 of which were spent on the ground in Iraq and Afghanistan. In 2007, Gallagher moved a cavalry unit around Baghdad—from one Iraqi police station to another, then to one of Saddam's old bunkers. Later in Afghanistan he served as a Brigade Executive Officer at a time when units were withdrawn from areas, and merged, in preparation for exit. Brendan Gallagher, personal interview conducted on 8 July 2016 and email to the authors, 1 August 2016.

31. Lieutenant Colonel (Ret.) Douglas Ollivant, private communication with the author, 8 September 2009.

32. This fact may seem surprising to researchers, but the need to manage such complex constraints, and to replace units incapacitated in combat, is one reason that military units are organized with seemingly redundant "core" capabilities. Moreover, it is not clear that the information exists to properly anticipate a given unit's capabilities in combat. The near complete personnel turnover in many units between deployments and the many differences in conditions between then and there versus now and here mean that any planner who wanted to place units based on how she thought they would perform would have a far harder empirical challenge than the one we take on in this book.

33. The picture of troop deployment as a game of chess may find resonance in a more recent picture of warfare as a video game—technicians using joysticks and watching on monitors as drones strike targets. However, the type of suppression we are talking about—troop presence in a given area during an asymmetric civil war—does not move so swiftly for the reasons Brendan Gallagher explained.

34. Eli Berman, Joseph Felter, Jacob N. Shapiro, and Erin Troland, "Modest, Secure and Informed: Successful Development in Conflict Zones" (NBER Working Paper 18674, 2013).

35. Carrie Lee, "Battalion Dataset Codebook" (working paper, Stanford University, 2011); Carrie Lee, "Holding Hearts and Minds: The Effect of Boots on the Ground in Iraq" (working paper, Stanford University, 2012).

36. When we crunched these numbers in a basic way we saw that there was initially no decrease in violent incidents associated with troop strength alone—in fact, the relationship was weakly positive. This is not inconsistent with the model, as those increases in troop strength could have been responding to changes in political norms, and, as we discussed earlier, when norms change in ways that would lead to more violence, troop levels could go up or down. Moreover, there is a built-in upward bias in reporting of violent incidents in areas where troops are deployed; it is often the troops themselves who do the reporting and the more of them there are, the greater the opportunities for combat incidents. The data also showed that the short-term increase in violence after troop levels increased faded after about six months. (We suspect that this was due to a learning process in which new troops were initially challenged by insurgents, who then withdrew as the troops got to know their area of operations.)

37. Renard Sexton, "Aid as a Tool against Insurgency: Evidence from Contested and Controlled Territory in Afghanistan," *American Political Science Review* 110, no. 4 (2016): 731–49.

38. Ibid.

39. We depart from Sexton's terminology. He used the presence of a military base as a proxy for government control and divided districts into ones that are "already controlled by pro-government forces" and ones that are "contested" (Sexton, "Aid as a Tool against Insurgency," 731). We are doubtful that presence of a base corresponds to control over a district; for us, military bases better indicate a measure of force, not of control, so we discuss the article in those terms. Sexton interprets his findings as evidence that the hearts-and-minds usefulness of aid is primarily in solidifying government control in areas already won; we see a large gray area worth exploring.

40. Sexton, "Aid as a Tool against Insurgency," 740.

41. Stephen Biddle, Jeffrey A. Friedman, and Jacob N. Shapiro, "Testing the Surge: Why Did Violence Decline in Iraq in 2007?" *International Security* 37, no. 1 (2012): 7–40.

42. Iraq Body Count, https://www.iraqbodycount.org/database/, accessed 7 July 2016.

43. iCasualties, http://icasualties.org/Iraq/index.aspx, accessed 7 July 2016.

44. See, e.g., *British Army Field Manual*, vol. 1, pt. 10, "Countering Insurgency," Army Code 71876, October 2009. Also, John McCain gave pride of place to the surge in the first presidential debate (26 September 2008, Debate Transcript, Commission on Presidential Debates, http://www.debates.org/index.php?page=2008-debate-transcript, accessed 5 August 2016).

45. John McCain and Joe Lieberman, "The Surge Worked," *Wall Street Journal*, 10 January 2008, http://www.wsj.com/articles/SB119992665423979631, accessed 28 May 2016.

46. Also writing in the *Wall Street Journal* in May 2008, Max Boot, a senior fellow at the Council on Foreign Relations, argued that a recent spike in casualties "could be a sign that the enemy is gaining strength. Or it could be a sign that tough combat is under way that will lead to the enemy's defeat and the creation of a more peaceful environment in the future. The latter was certainly the case with the casualty spike during the summer of 2007. (More than a hundred soldiers died each month in April, May, and June.) Those losses were widely denounced as evidence that the surge wasn't working, but in fact they were proof of the opposite" ("The Truth about Iraq's Casualty Count," *Wall Street Journal*, 8 May 2008, http://www.wsj.com/articles/SB120977505566564207, accessed 7 July 2016). Colonel Craig A. Collier wrote in 2010, "The prevailing narrative is that a holistic effort emphasizing nonlethal effects led to our tentative success. Economic development may have played a role, but our lethality was the most important factor" ("Now That We're Leaving Iraq, What Did We Learn?" *Military Review* 90, no. 5 [2010]: 88–93). And Lieutenant General Raymond T. Odierno, commander of the Multi-National Corps-Iraq, said that before the surge, U.S. forces "were incapable of 'holding' the ground we had won" and that the addition of troops "set the stage for progress in governance and economic development." Quoted in Dale Andrade, *Surging South of Baghdad: The 3d Infantry Division and Task Force Marne in Iraq, 2007–2008* (Washington, DC: United States Army Center of Military History, 2010), 389.

47. Biddle, Friedman, and Shapiro, "Testing the Surge," 23.

48. Austin Long, "The Anbar Awakening," *Survival* 50, no. 2 (2008): 67–94, quote on p. 87.

49. Daniel R. Green, "The Fallujah Awakening: A Case Study in Counter-Insurgency," *Small Wars and Insurgencies* 21, no. 4 (December 2010): 591–609.

50. Jon Lee Anderson, "Inside the Surge: The American Military Finds New Allies, but at What Cost?" *New Yorker*, 19 November 2009, 58–69.

A related argument was that any temporary reductions in violence due to the surge were at the expense of long-term stability. Steven Simon, a senior fellow at the Council on Foreign Relations, wrote:

The surge may have brought transitory successes . . . but it has done so by stoking the three forces that have traditionally threatened the stability of Middle Eastern states:

tribalism, warlordism, and sectarianism. States that have failed to control these forces have ultimately become ungovernable, and this is the fate for which the surge is preparing Iraq. A strategy intended to reduce casualties in the short term will ineluctably weaken the prospects for Iraq's cohesion over the long run.

Steven Simon, "The Price of the Surge," *Foreign Affairs*, May/June 2008, https://www .foreignaffairs.com/articles/iraq/2008-05-03/price-surge, accessed 5 July 2016. For other arguments in this vein, see Stanley Kober, "Did the Surge Work?" *Daily Caller*, 16 July 2010, http://www.cato.org/publications/commentary/did-surge-work, accessed 5 August 2016; Nir Rosen, "The Myth of the Surge," *Rolling Stone*, 6 March 2008, 46–53.

As we discuss more in the conclusion, the distinction between what it takes to win a village and what it takes to win a war is important here. The surge and associated tactical innovations very likely helped win many villages, but that was not the same as resolving Iraq's deep political tensions, as we all learned in 2014 when many of the areas brought under central government control during the surge were quickly taken by IS forces.

51. Note that the fall 2006 Anbar realignment that initiated the Awakening occurred in Colonel Sean MacFarland's area of operations (AO), where one of the occasional early experiments with population-centric counterinsurgency methods was ongoing. The surge expanded such methods across the theater and was thus instrumental in the Anbar Awakening's ability to spread beyond its origin in this AO.

52. Also contributing were indirect effects: faced with a reduced Sunni threat, Shia militias got less support from their own communities and less tolerance of their predation; U.S. troops freed up from fighting AQI were able to exact important victories against the main Shia militia, the Jaish al-Mahdi.

53. One last theory claimed that sectarian cleansing led to the drop in violence in 2007. Sunnis had been killed or run out of mixed areas, this line of reasoning went, so fighting between sects decreased. Journalist Patrick Cockburn presented evidence on this in a 2008 article. He quoted Iraqis as saying, "The killing stopped because there was nobody left to kill," then went on to attribute the reduction in Coalition casualties to the fact that "the Sunni and Shia now hate and fear each other more than they do the Americans." Patrick Cockburn, "Who Is Whose Enemy?" *London Review of Books*, 6 March 2008, http://www.lrb.co.uk /v30/n05/patrick-cockburn/who-is-whose-enemy, accessed 10 June 2016. An uneasy peace had been achieved through the sects coalescing into contiguous areas of uniform makeup with defensible borders between them.

This "cleansing thesis" requires either that combat in areas where cleansing was happening made up the bulk of the pre-2007 violence or that nonsectarian violence in other areas (e.g., against Coalition forces) was a by-product of cleansing. Neither assertion is consistent with the evidence. Violence was higher in 2005–6 in unmixed Sunni areas and it started to decline in these areas long before it did in mixed ones. And reduction of sectarian violence did not precede combat violence (attacks against U.S. troops and civilian casualties from combat); it followed it. Biddle, Friedman, and Shapiro, "Testing the Surge," 14–15.

Looking at how fighting progressed after AQI bombed the Golden Dome Mosque in Samarra in 2006 shows how the patterns of violence are inconsistent with the cleansing thesis. Shia militias did indeed remove Sunnis from mixed districts in Baghdad, and violence increased. However, they didn't stop when they had created secure, cleansed zones; they moved on to attack homogeneously Sunni neighborhoods. This initiated a pattern of battlefronts moving across *unmixed* neighborhoods, with violence concentrated at the front, *not* in mixed neighborhoods—a process that had by no means run its course by mid-2007, when violence declined.

54. Melissa Dell and Pablo Querubín, "Nation Building through Foreign Intervention: Evidence from Discontinuities in Military Strategies" (NBER Working Paper 22395, 2016).

55. A number of studies found the Hamlet Evaluation System (HES) to be crude and inaccurate. Thomas Thayer, *War without Fronts: The American Experience in Vietnam* (Boulder, CO: Westview, 1985); David W. P. Elliott, *The Vietnamese War: Revolution and Social Change in the Mekong Delta, 1930–1975* (Armonk, NY: M. E. Sharpe, 2003). Other authors consider the HES advanced for its time but have pointed out flaws in how the data were used: an excess of indiscriminate violence in rebel-held areas may have meant less use of force in contested zones where it may have been most effectively applied. Stathis N. Kalyvas and Matthew Adam Kocher, "The Dynamics of Violence in Vietnam: An Analysis of the Hamlet Evaluation System (HES)," *Journal of Peace Research* 46, no. 3 (2009): 335–55.

56. If this policy strikes you as having been, well, evil, then you are in good company. We agree. One possible explanation is that the Air Force was mistakenly deploying forces and strategy designed for a symmetric conflict in an asymmetric setting.

57. Dell and Querubín, "Nation Building through Foreign Intervention," 2.

58. Jason Lyall, "Does Indiscriminate Violence Incite Insurgent Attacks? Evidence from Chechnya," *Journal of Conflict Resolution* 53, no. 3 (2009): 331–62.

59. Ibid., 349.

60. Ibid., 331.

7 HOW CIVILIANS RESPOND TO HARM

Note to epigraph: Victor Corpus, interview with the author, Camp Aguinaldo, Quezon City, Philippines, 5 February 2009.

1. Carter Malkasian, *War Comes to Garmser: Thirty Years of Conflict on the Afghan Frontier* (New York: Oxford University Press, 2013), 168.

2. Richard Tomkins, "Anti-American Riot Rocks Afghan Town," *Human Events*, 13 January 2010, http://humanevents.com/2010/01/13/antiamerican-riot-rocks-afghan-town/, accessed 13 December 2016.

3. NATO/ISAF Tactical Directive, 6 July 2009, http://www.nato.int/isaf/docu/official_texts /Tactical_Directive_090706.pdf, accessed 18 February 2016.

4. Dexter Filkins, "Deadly Protest in Afghanistan Highlights Tensions," *New York Times*, 12 January 2010, http://www.nytimes.com/2010/01/13/world/asia/13afghan.html?_r=0, accessed 18 February 2016.

5. Malkasian, *War Comes to Garmser*, 169.

6. Ibid., 170–72.

7. Ibid., 166.

8. Carter Malkasian, email to the authors, 20 February 2016.

9. Aisha Ahmad, "Security Challenges in Afghanistan: 'Operation Enduring Freedom' and the Role of Canada," *Policy Perspectives* 4, no. 1 (2007): 1–16 (p. 4 especially); Alan K. Kronstadt and Kenneth Katzman, "Islamist Militancy in the Pakistan-Afghanistan Border Region and US Policy" (Library of Congress, Washington DC, Congressional Research Service, 2008), 10.

10. To be clear, this is true of asymmetric conflict in Western societies as well, as Richard English kindly pointed out to us. The case of the Irish conflict with the United Kingdom clearly shows that clumsy state actions can benefit non-state rebels, even when the latter are themselves being quite brutal to the population. This was true during the Irish rebellion of 1919–21, as shown in Charles Townshend, *The British Campaign in Ireland, 1919–21: The Development of Political and Military Policies* (New York: Oxford University Press, 1975), as well as during the insurgency in Northern Ireland, as Richard English demonstrates in *Armed Struggle: The History of the IRA* (New York: Oxford University Press, 2005).

11. Chris Kolenda of King's College London and coauthors present a range of compelling evidence that civilian casualties result in decreased community cooperation and intelligence sharing; see Christopher D. Kolenda, Rachel Reid, Chris Rogers, and Marte Retzuis,

"The Strategic Costs of Civilian Harm: Applying Lessons from Afghanistan to Present and Future Conflicts" (London: Open Society Foundations, 2016). As analyst Matt Waldman described to Kolenda, "People were unwilling to side with the government and Americans. So they won't inform, or warn the coalition of Taliban presence." See also Sebastian Schutte, "Violence and Civilian Loyalties: Evidence from Afghanistan," *Journal of Conflict Resolution* 61, no. 8 (2016): 1595–625.

12. Formally, as long as civilians perceive some probability that the harm is not accidental but deliberate, civilian casualties should reduce civilian beliefs about how much the side causing the harm is mindful of their welfare, and thus the value of having that side control the territory.

13. "Legal zoning, the surrender schemes, the humane handling of prisoners, and the pseudo-gang operation may all be seen as important examples of restraint in the British military policy. The Legal distinction between PAs and Special Areas gave the troops, and the population, a clear understanding of what could be done, to whom, and where. Inspired by Malaya, and carried out in close collaboration with Special Branch, the attempts at securing mass surrenders showed the army's preference for the accurate application of violence instead of overwhelming attrition." Huw Bennett, *Fighting the Mau Mau: The British Army and Counter-Insurgency in the Kenya Emergency* (Cambridge: Cambridge University Press, 2013), 158–59.

14. We acknowledge that we're going out on an intellectual limb here but one we believe can support our weight. If harm to a civilian were unrelated to protective efforts by combatants (restraint) then it shouldn't affect attitudes. We're assuming that the probability of harm declines with a combatant's effort in restraint and that the citizen understands that relationship but does not perfectly observe the effort. Thus when citizens suffer harm, they downgrade their beliefs about how much the party responsible is trying to avoid hurting the community.

15. The line between intended and unintended harm is often blurred, or looks different from one side or the other. If a commander sets rules of engagement that allow extensive use of imprecise artillery, should we consider the resulting harm to civilians an unintended consequence or a foreseeable outcome of a tactical decision? Operation Cedar Falls was a case in point. During three weeks in January 1967, over 30,000 American and South Vietnamese troops conducted a sweep of a Communist stronghold northwest of Saigon called the "Iron Triangle" attempting to establish a "Free-Fire Area" where anyone encountered could be considered a combatant: "A free-fire area (FFA) is a specific area into which any weapon system may fire without additional coordination with the establishing headquarters" (United States Army Field Manual 6-20, appendix F). Accounts differ on whether the operation was a success. Compare, for example, Lt. Gen. Bernard William Rogers, *Cedar Falls-Junction City: A Turning Point* (Washington, DC: Department of the Army, 1989), http://www.history.army.mil/books/Vietnam/90-7/cont.htm, accessed 26 May 2016 and Stanley Karnow, *Vietnam: A History* (New York: Viking, 1983). Troops in Operation Cedar Falls deported around 6,000 civilians, leveled the area's four main villages, cleared the rice paddies, and denuded the forest (Karnow, *Vietnam*, 463). While they did capture and kill hundreds of National Liberation Front operatives and uncover large caches of weapons and explosives, most leaders of the insurgency successfully hid or fled over the Cambodian border and returned within a year to use the Iron Triangle as a base for major attacks on Saigon. The villagers stayed away, though, struggling to make a new life in cities (439–40). To treat such destruction as unintended is a mistake: it discounts harm to civilians and skews the judgment of military leaders and historians as to whether a tactical decision was successful.

16. Technically, following the logic of note 12 in this chapter, the key issue for civilians is their inference about restraint—effort by combatants to prevent civilian casualties. Analytically, intended harm to civilians could be interpreted as negative effort in that context, so it is encompassed by the same model as an extreme case.

17. The entire letter can be read on the Harmony Project's website: https://www.ctc.usma.edu/v2/wp-content/uploads/2013/10/Zawahiris-Letter-to-Zarqawi-Translation.pdf.

18. Brian Fishman, "Dysfunction and Decline: Lessons Learned from inside al-Qa'ida in Iraq" (West Point, NY: Harmony Project, Combating Terrorism Center at West Point, 2009), http://www.dtic.mil/dtic/tr/fulltext/u2/a502816.pdf, accessed 29 March 2016.

19. Ibid., 6.

20. Ibid., 7.

21. *Property Loss; Personal Injury or Death: Incident to Noncombat Activities of the Armed Forces; Foreign Countries*, 10 United States Code §2734, https://www.law.cornell.edu/uscode/text/10/2734, accessed 30 March 2016.

22. United States Government Accountability Office (GAO), *The Department of Defense's Use of Solatia and Condolence Payments in Iraq and Afghanistan*, Report to Congressional Requesters, GAO-07-699, 2007, https://www.propublica.org/documents/item/627368-gao-report-on-condolence-payments-2007.html#document/p15/a98457, p. 15, accessed 30 March 2016.

23. Ibid., 46.

24. Ibid., 15, 36.

25. David S. Cloud, "Compensation Payments Rising, Especially by Marines," *New York Times*, 10 June 2006, http://www.nytimes.com/2006/06/10/world/middleeast/10payments.html?_r=1&, accessed 30 March 2016.

26. GAO, *Department of Defense's Use of Solatia and Condolence Payments*, 29.

27. *Frontline* interview, 1 August 2007, http://www.pbs.org/wgbh/pages/frontline/haditha/interviews/petraeus.html, accessed 30 March 2016.

28. How accurate? To put it in perspective, consider another experiment Jake and other co-authors ran in the United States to validate indirect survey methods and direct questions. In this case, for the sensitive topic they used a controversial anti-abortion referendum in a Mississippi state election. Voting "no" was the socially undesirable behavior: a direct question asking people if they did so led to a severe underestimation compared to actual no-votes cast—by about 21 percentage points. Employing an endorsement experiment did much better, coming within 3 percent of the true rate of "no" votes. In addition, non-response fell from 20 percent in the direct question to 6 percent in the endorsement experiment. Bryn Rosenfeld, Kosuke Imai, and Jacob Shapiro, "An Empirical Validation Study of Popular Survey Methodologies for Sensitive Questions," *American Journal of Political Science* 60, no. 3 (2016): 783–802.

29. Graeme Blair, C. Christine Fair, Neil Malhotra, and Jacob Shapiro, "Poverty and Support for Militant Politics: Evidence from Pakistan," *American Journal of Political Science* 57, no. 1 (2013): 30–48.

30. Controls included subjects' province of residence; their gender, marital status, age, and access to the Internet; whether they possessed a cell phone, the ability to read, write, and do math; and their education level and sectarian affiliation (Sunni or Shia).

31. Jason Lyall, Graeme Blair, and Kosuke Imai, "Explaining Support for Combatants during Wartime: A Survey Experiment in Afghanistan," *American Political Science Review* 107, no. 4 (2013): 679–705.

32. For a review, see Miles Hewstone, Mark Rubin, and Hazel Willis, "Intergroup Bias," *Annual Review of Psychology* 53, no. 1 (2002): 575–604.

33. Formally the authors draw on item response theory, a technology most commonly used to turn answers on multiple choice tests like the SAT, where questions vary in difficulty, into an overall score.

34. For an explanation of standard deviations, see note 31 in chapter 4.

35. To be sure, the offers were quite different. As the authors write, "To be approached by ISAF signifies that an individual or family received a one-time *solatia* payment, typically around $2,500, that absolved ISAF of criminal liability for civilian casualties or property damage.

By contrast, to be approached by the Taliban signifies that the aggrieved party received a funeral oration by the Taliban extolling the virtues of the fallen individual(s) as well as modest monthly payments or basic staples such as kerosene or foodstuffs." Lyall, Blair, and Imai, "Explaining Support for Combatants during Wartime," 687.

36. Ibid., 693.
37. Ibid., 687.
38. Kolenda et al., "The Strategic Costs of Civilian Harm," 9.
39. Kimberley Wade, Maryanne Garry, J. Don Read, and D. Stephen Lindsay, "A Picture Is Worth a Thousand Lies: Using False Photographs to Create False Childhood Memories," *Psychonomic Bulletin & Review* 9, no. 3 (2002): 597–603; S. Porter, J. C. Yuille, and D. R. Lehman, "The Nature of Real, Implanted, and Fabricated Memories for Emotional Childhood Events: Implications for the Recovered Memory Debate," *Law and Human Behavior* 23, no. 5 (1999): 517–37.
40. Eleanor Singer, Martin Frankel, and Marc Glassman, "The Effect of Interviewer Characteristics and Expectations on Response," *Public Opinion* 47, no. 1 (1983): 68–83.
41. Herbert Weingartner, W. Adefris, J. E. Eich, et al., "Encoding-Imagery Specificity in Alcohol State-Dependent Learning," *Journal of Experimental Psychology-Human Learning and Memory* 2, no. 1 (1976): 83–87.
42. Penelope Lewis and Hugo Critchley, "Mood-Dependent Memory," *Trends in Cognitive Sciences* 7, no. 10 (2003): 431–33.
43. Peter Frost, Bridgette Casey, Kaydee Griffin, Luis Raymundo, Christopher Farrell, and Ryan Carrigan, "The Influence of Confirmation Bias on Memory and Source Monitoring," *Journal of General Psychology* 142, no. 4 (2015): 238–52.
44. Luke Condra and Jacob N. Shapiro, "Who Takes the Blame? The Strategic Effects of Collateral Damage," *American Journal of Political Science* 56, no. 1 (2012): 167–87.
45. In our analysis of the surge, described in chapter 5, Jake and coauthors also used IBC data to corroborate other sources and to look at whether the locals' shift to providing information during the Awakening reduced the rate of Coalition-caused harm.
46. This was in 2007–8, before Google Earth made it possible to instantly match locations from press reports to high-resolution satellite imagery and map data. We had to order, scan, and geo-reference tourist maps of Baghdad to properly locate events.
47. Jake and Luke looked at the data by week for each of Iraq's 104 districts from February 2004 through February 2009, linking IBC data on 19,961 incidents (59,245 civilian deaths) with 193,264 SIGACT reports, which include data on violent incidents, such as IED explosions, direct fire, and "escalation of force" events (where an increasing perception of a threat ends in violence).
48. Recall also that the findings in Lyall, "Civilian Casualties and the Conditional Effects of Humanitarian Aid in Wartime," depended on natural randomization based on the trajectory of shrapnel and bullets.
49. Urban/rural was classified using as a cutoff the median district where 48.5 percent of the population lives in urban areas, according to data from the World Food Programme.
50. On the reasons why suicide attacks tend to be more resistant to compromise during the preparation phase, see Eli Berman and David D. Laitin, "Religion, Terrorism and Public Goods: Testing the Club Model," *Journal of Public Economics* 92, no. 10 (2008): 1942–67. The basic argument is that because suicide attacks can succeed against high-value targets government forces will pay a great deal for information that can stymie them. In equilibrium the only groups that will use such tactics are those that are very effective at preventing their members from sharing information with government intelligence agencies.
51. Efraim Benmelech, Claude Berrebi, and Esteban F. Klor, "Counter-Suicide-Terrorism: Evidence from House Demolitions," *Journal of Politics* 77, no. 1 (2015): 27–43.

52. Their data on punitive demolitions cover September 2000 to December 2005, while their data on clearing-operations demolitions cover all of 2004 and 2005.

53. Dror Moreh, *The Gatekeepers* (New York: Skyhorse Publishing, 2015). A documentary film with the same title appeared in 2012. The result is also consistent with targeted demolitions having a deterrent effect where punitive ones have only an anger-producing effect.

54. Andrew Shaver and Jacob N. Shapiro, "The Effect of Civilian Casualties on Wartime Informing: Evidence from the Iraq War" (Households in Conflict Network Working Paper #210, 2016). The paper was later published in the *Journal of Conflict Resolution* under the same title.

55. It speaks to the relationship ESOC affiliate Andrew Shaver has cultivated with the military to note that U.S. Central Command could have evoked an exemption not to release secret data from a recent engagement. Instead, they voluntarily invested in the laborious process of declassification and release.

56. A median is the halfway point in a distribution: half the observations are larger and half smaller.

57. As with the other results from Iraq and Afghanistan, whether you interpret these findings as causal depends on whether you believe that the spikes in civilian casualties from week to week result from bad luck on either or both sides (remember the random element of civilian cars caught in an IED explosion) and are thus conditionally independent of the next week's trend in informing. They could be linked: Coalition forces might become more active in an area for some other reason, pressing for tips; casualties could therefore increase because they are more active; and tips also increase because some of these activities work. We claim that the controls Jake and Andrew put in place rule this possibility out, but the skeptical reader should examine the paper and its appendix directly.

58. Luke N. Condra, Joseph H. Felter, Radha K. Iyengar, and Jacob N. Shapiro, "The Effect of Civilian Casualties in Afghanistan and Iraq" (NBER Working Paper 16152, 2010).

59. CCTC data included perpetrator (ISAF, insurgents, other, or unknown), type of weapons used by ISAF and insurgents, nationality of any ISAF units involved, and the number of killed and wounded in three categories: men, women, and children. Data were culled of any casualties involving people with ambiguous combatant status under the Law of Armed Conflict, including Afghan government personnel, interpreters, security guards, and contractors. We cross-checked the data against media reports for completeness.

60. Jason Lyall, "Civilian Casualties and the Conditional Effects of Humanitarian Aid in Wartime" (working paper, Yale University, 2016).

61. All residents of treatment villages received the village-level food deliveries and other aid, so this is the difference between those who get an additional individual benefit and those who share only in the collective benefit.

62. Lyall, "Civilian Casualties and the Conditional Effects of Humanitarian Aid in Wartime," tables 5 and 6.

63. Ibid., tables 3 and 4. Table 4 reports that ACAP II payments did reduce subsequent Taliban attacks following Taliban-initiated civilian casualties but only when Kabul, the capital, is included in the sample. Since attacks in Kabul originate outside of the city and are carried out without local civilian support—terrorism rather than insurgency—while ACAP payments occur in the city, the role of civilian attitudes is likely irrelevant as a test of any of these models as explanatory.

64. Austin Wright, Luke Condra, Jacob N. Shapiro, and Andrew Shaver, "Civilian Abuse and Wartime Informing" (working paper, Princeton University, 2017).

65. A geographic unit fixed-effect (e.g., village, district, or province fixed-effect) is a series of variables that account for the average level of the outcome across time in each geographic unit. A time fixed-effect is a series of variables that capture the average level of the outcomes across space in each time period.

66. Jason Lyall, "Does Indiscriminate Violence Incite Insurgent Attacks? Evidence from Chechnya," *Journal of Conflict Resolution* 53, no. 3 (2009): 331–62.

67. Melissa Dell and Pablo Querubín, "Nation Building through Foreign Intervention: Evidence from Discontinuities in Military Strategies" (NBER Working Paper 22395, 2016).

68. Though, as he notes, "the small number of observations available here can provide only an initial test of the relationship between severity of indiscriminate violence and observed insurgent responses."

69. Antonio Giustozzi, "The Afghanistan Papers, No. 5: The Taliban beyond the Pashtuns" (Ontario: Centre for International Governance Innovations, 2010).

70. One paper reports that if a Pashtun man is dishonored, he must avenge that dishonor "or he will lose face and social status to the point of becoming an outcast." Thomas H. Johnson and M. Chris Mason, "No Sign until the Burst of Fire," *International Security* 32 (2008): 63. A 2010 news report stated, "To a great extent . . . the Taliban remain motivated by revenge. The massacre in 2001 of hundreds, perhaps thousands, of Taliban detainees at the hands of an Uzbek warlord in northern Afghanistan still motivates Taliban to fight. 'That massacre was the base or foundation for all the fighting that is now going on,' [Vahid] Mojdeh [former Taliban foreign ministry official] said. The senior ISAF general agreed the massacre was 'absolutely' a recruiting tool for the Taliban. 'Those kinds of things thicken the hatred and cause more people to join.'" Roy Gutman, "We've Met the Enemy in Afghanistan, and He's Changed," *McClatchy Newspapers*, 14 March 2010, http://www.mcclatchydc.com/2010/03/14/90083/weve-met-the-enemy-in-afghanistan.html, accessed 10 February 2016.

71. U.S. soldiers in Afghanistan were aware of this cultural tradition and some thought concerns with avoiding creating long-term feuds should influence how they operated. David W. Kummer, comp., *U.S. Marines in Afghanistan, 2001–2009: Anthology and Annotated Bibliography* (Quantico, VA: History Division, United States Marine Corps, 2014), 246–47.

72. For a thorough discussion in the Afghan context, explaining why survey-based measures of who caused harm in Afghanistan attribute a much higher share of civilian casualties to ISAF than did either ISAF or United Nations Assistance Mission in Afghanistan reporting, see Jason Lyall, Graeme Blair, and Kosuke Imai, "Explaining Support for Combatants during Wartime," *American Political Science Review* 107, no. 4 (2013): 679–705, especially 688 and 694.

73. See, e.g., Open Society Foundations, "The Trust Deficit: The Impact of Local Perceptions on Policy in Afghanistan" (Regional Policy Initiative on Afghanistan and Pakistan, Policy Brief No. 2, 2010).

74. See, among many others, Geoffrey Evans and Robert Andersen, "The Political Conditioning of Economic Perceptions," *Journal of Politics* 68, no. 1 (2006): 194–207; Brian J. Gaines, James H. Kukinski, Paul J. Quirk, Buddy Peyton, and Jay Verkuilen, "Same Facts, Different Interpretations: Partisan Motivation and Opinion on Iraq," *Journal of Politics* 69, no. 4 (2007): 957–94; and Toby Bolsen, James N. Druckman, and Fay Lomax Cook, "The Influence of Partisan Motivated Reasoning on Public Opinion," *Political Behavior* 36, no. 2 (2014): 235–62.

75. Authors' calculations based on numbers from the Syrian Network for Human Rights: http://sn4hr.org, accessed 31 August 2017.

76. Sebastian Abbot, "A Medal for 'Courageous Restraint'? NATO Seeks to Avoid Killing Afghan Noncombatants," Associated Press, 4 May 2010.

77. Michael Hastings, *The Operators: The Wild and Terrifying Inside Story of America's War in Afghanistan* (New York: Plume, 2012), 262–65.

78. Amitai Etzioni, "Rules of Engagement and Abusive Citizens," *Prism* 4 (2014): 87–102.

79. Jason Lemieux, "No, Really: Is the US Military Cut Out for Courageous Restraint?" *Small Wars Journal* (2010), http://smallwarsjournal.com/jrnl/art/no-really-is-the-us-military-cut

-out-for-courageous-restraint, accessed 31 August 2017. See also Corporal Scott R. Mitchell, "Observations of a Strategic Corporal," *Military Review* (July–August 2012): 58–64; and Celeste Ward Gventer, "Counterinsurgency and Its Critics," *Journal of Strategic Studies* 37, no. 4 (2014): 637–63.

80. Thomas Harding, " 'Courageous Restraint' Putting Troops' Lives at Risk," *Daily Telegraph*, 6 July 2010, www.telegraph.co.uk/news/worldnews/asia/afghanistan/7874950/Courageous-restraint-putting-troops-lives-at-risk.html, accessed 28 June 2016; Jason Motlagh, "Petraeus Toughens Afghan Rules of Engagement," *Time*, 6 August 2010, http://content.time.com/time/world/article/0,8599,2008863,00.html, accessed 28 June 2016.

81. H.R. 1540, Section 1087, 112th Cong., 1st Sess., http://www.gpo.gov/fdsys/pkg/BILLS-112hr1540eh/pdf/BILLS-112hr1540eh.pdf, accessed 13 December 2016. The U.S. Senate ultimately left the provision out of its amended bill, citing concerns over civilians interfering with military judgment.

82. Brent Clemmer, *Challenges for This Kind of War: Modifying Army Awards for a New Century of Conflict* (Fort Leavenworth, KS: School of Advanced Military Studies, Army Command and General Staff College, 2011).

83. Rush Limbaugh, "Medal for 'Courageous Restraint,' " *Rush Limbaugh Show*, 12 May 2010, http://www.rushlimbaugh.com/home/daily/site_051210/content/0112515.guest.html, accessed 20 April 2011. See also CNN, "Military Proposes Medal for Troops Showing Restraint," *CNN Afghanistan Crossroads*, 13 May 2010, http://afghanistan.blogs.cnn.com/2010/05/13/military-proposes-medalfor-troops-showing-restraint/, accessed 29 June 2016.

84. Christian Davenport, "Should Soldiers Get a Medal for Holding Fire?" *Washington Post*, 19 May 2010, http://voices.washingtonpost.com/impact-of-war/2010/05/a_medal_for_holding_your_fire.html, accessed 29 June 2016. See also "Now Hear This," *VFW Magazine*, August 2010, http://digitaledition.qwinc.com/display_article.php?id=441040, accessed 29 June 2016.

85. Christopher Sims, Fernando Luján, and Bing West, "Both Sides of the COIN: Defining War after Afghanistan," *Foreign Affairs* 91 (2012): 178.

86. Sergio Catignani, " 'Getting COIN' at the Tactical Level in Afghanistan: Reassessing Counter-Insurgency Adaptation in the British Army," *Journal of Strategic Studies* 35, no. 4 (2012): 513–39.

87. Lemieux, "No, Really: Is the US Military Cut Out for Courageous Restraint?"

88. To be sure, "tying the hands" of soldiers and Marines confronting the enemy on the battlefield was never the intent of General McChrystal as Commander of International Security Assistance Force (COMISAF). Reflecting on this in his memoir he argued, "I wrote [the Tactical Directive] not to prescribe tactical decisions for sergeants and junior officers closest to the fight, but to help them understand the underlying logic of the approach I was asking them to employ." Stanley McChrystal, *My Share of the Task: A Memoir* (New York: Penguin, 2013), 312.

89. NATO-OTAN, "Honoring Courageous Restraint," 2010, press release, http://www.rs.nato.int/article/caat-anaysis-news/honoring-courageous-restraint.html, accessed 29 June 2016.

90. See Joseph H. Felter and Jacob N. Shapiro, "Limiting Civilian Casualties as Part of a Winning Strategy: The Case of Courageous Restraint," *Daedalus* 146, no. 1 (January 2017): 44–58.

8 ECONOMIC CONDITIONS AND INSURGENT VIOLENCE

1. Quoted from the 2006 statement of work, Office of the Special Inspector General for Iraq Reconstruction (SIGIR), "USAID Spent Almost $400 Million on an Afghan Stabilization Project Despite Uncertain Results, but Has Taken Steps to Better Assess Similar Efforts," 2012, https://www.sigar.mil/pdf/audits/2012-04-25audit-12-08.pdf, p. 2, accessed 23 September 2015.

2. USAID Afghanistan, "Fact Sheet Local Governance and Community Development (LGCD)," 2011, https://www.usaid.gov/sites/default/files/documents/1871/Fact%20sheet%20 LGCD%20FINAL%20June%202011.pdf, accessed 23 September 2015.

3. USAID Afghanistan lacks a single definition of "stability"; an ESOC review of 89 different lessons learned studies on stabilization (broadly defined) found over 200 indicators used to measure the concept. In our experience it has been taken to mean "under government control at low levels of violence." Radha Iyengar, Jacob N. Shapiro, and Stephen Hegarty, "Lessons Learned from Stabilization Initiatives in Afghanistan: A Systematic Review of Existing Research" (RAND Corporation Working Paper WR-1191, 2017).

4. Andrew Shaver and Austin Wright generously shared FOIA'd data from the ISAF CIDNE database and provided research assistance with the LGCD data. For the original use of the data, see Shaver and Wright, "Are Modern Insurgencies Predictable? Evidence from Afghanistan and Iraq" (working paper, Princeton University, November 2015).

5. SIGAR, "USAID Spent Almost $400 Million on an Afghan Stabilization Project," 24. In 2009 the employment goal was 10,250 and the number employed was 17,723. The training goal was also exceeded by 7,000.

6. Recalling the discussion of causal identification in chapter 2, estimating a causal effect on violence requires randomized LGCD treatment or some other evaluation design that allows us to eliminate the effects of confounds (omitted variables) to generate counterfactual comparisons.

7. USAID's final review stated, "After more than 250 interviews with various stakeholders, beneficiaries, implementers and [Provincial Reconstruction Team] offices as well as conducting more than 50 project site visits, the evaluation team reached the conclusion that the program has *not* met its overarching goal of extending the legitimacy of the Afghan government nor has it brought government closer to the people or fostered stability." U.S. Agency for International Development (USAID) Afghanistan, "Local Governance and Community Development Program (LGCD) Evaluation" (2009), 3.

8. "Our analysis of Defense Intelligence Agency data showed that each of the eight provinces with the most LGCD activity experienced increases in the level of violence between 2006 and 2010, ranging from almost two to twenty times. In these eight provinces, enemy-initiated attacks increased by 50 percent between 2006 and 2010, a higher increase than throughout the country for the same period." SIGAR, "USAID Spent Almost $400 Million on an Afghan Stabilization Project," 11.

9. Stoking growth in the near term and leading to violence in the longer run is also one interpretation of what happened with the Helmand River Valley Project that we will discuss in chapter 10. A major irrigation program in the 1950s brought short-term prosperity but hurt agricultural productivity in the long run, attracting migrants who ended up in conflict with the locals in the 1990s and 2000s. Rajiv Chandrasekaran, *Little America: The War within the War for Afghanistan* (London: Bloomsbury Publishing, 2012).

10. George W. Bush, "National Strategy for Victory in Iraq" (Washington, DC: The White House, 2005), quoted in Andrew Shaver, "Employment Status and Support for Wartime Violence: Evidence from the Iraq War" (ESOC Working Paper #1, 2016).

11. Barack Obama, "Remarks by the President at the Summit on Countering Violent Extremism," 19 February 2015, quoted in Shaver, "Employment Status and Support for Wartime Violence." These ideas surface in statements by government ministries, such as the CIA: "Underlying conditions such as poverty, corruption, religious conflict and ethnic strife create opportunities for terrorists to exploit. . . . Terrorists use these conditions to justify their actions and expand their support." U.S. Central Intelligence Agency, "National Strategy for Combatting Terrorism," 2003, https://www.cia.gov/news-information/cia-the-war-on-ter rorism/Counter_Terrorism_Strategy.pdf, accessed 23 September 2015. A policy statement by the UK Department for International Development (DFID) posits that "poverty and lack

of access to basic services contribute to perceptions of injustice that can motivate people to violence." UK Department for International Development, "Fighting Poverty to Build a Safer World," 2005, http://webarchive.nationalarchives.gov.uk/+/; http://www.dfid.gov.uk /pubs/files/securityforall.pdf, accessed 23 September 2015.

12. For recent reviews that cover the impact of development spending in asymmetric and symmetric conflicts, respectively, see Eli Berman and Aila Matanock, "The Empiricists' Insurgency," *Annual Review of Political Science* 18 (2015): 443–64; and for an older but extremely thorough review of research on economic conditions and civil war, see Chris Blattman and Edward Miguel, "Civil War," *Journal of Economic Literature* 48, no. 1 (2010): 3–57.

13. Fearon proposed some alternative explanations. In poor countries, labor is cheaper and prices are lower, so insurgents get more "bang for their buck." Meanwhile, there are features of rich countries that make it difficult for insurgencies to take root. Their natural and social landscapes make it harder for insurgents to conduct their business—rich countries are more urbanized, making it harder for rebels to hide, while poor ones are more village oriented, making it easier for rebels to issue threats via social networks. The national armies in rich countries have more resources to root rebels out. And individuals and businesses in rich countries are harder to extort because they are more mobile and hold less of their capital in cash or easily stolen assets. He built a rebel-versus-government model. The way he sees it, the most important factor that will allow rebels to continue their insurgency is secrecy. As rebel groups grow and create more links between members, they will start to see diminishing returns (the bigger they are, the easier they are to see), and this explains why so many of the civil wars in his time span are "small, stable, and stalemated," with insurgent groups embedding in a rural periphery. There are quite a few hurdles for rebel groups to clear in order to exert real influence over policy, either by becoming a participatory political party or by overthrowing the government—and attempting to surmount any of those hurdles involves exposing themselves to capture. From the government's perspective, there is a point with such a simmering insurgency at which their efforts won't produce enough captures to make it worthwhile. So rebels and government get stuck in an enduring war—one that the landscape lends itself to. James Fearon, "Economic Development, Insurgency, and Civil War," in *Institutions and Economic Performance*, ed. Elhanan Helpman (Cambridge, MA: Harvard University Press, 2008), 2. For more recent work on the relationship between terrain and conflict, see Andrew Shaver, David B. Carter, and Tsering Wangyal Shawa, "Terrain Ruggedness and Land Cover: Improved Data for Most Research Designs," *Conflict Management and Peace Science* (first published online, 1 November 2016), https://doi.org /10.1177/0738894216659843.

14. Ted Robert Gurr, *Why Men Rebel* (Princeton: Princeton University Press, 1970), 37.

15. Ibid., 24.

16. Indeed, James C. Scott's classic ethnography *The Moral Economy of the Peasant: Rebellion and Subsistence in Southeast Asia* (New Haven: Yale University Press, 1976) argues that peasants (i.e., poor agricultural workers) rebel only when economic conditions push them into choosing between starvation and rebellion. They know rebellion rarely works, so it is preferable to starvation but not to remaining poor and aggrieved.

17. This references joint work by Esteban Klor, Jake Shapiro, and Andrew Shaver using sixty months of public opinion surveys from Baghdad in 2004–10.

18. Jason Lyall, Graeme Blair, and Kosuke Imai, "Explaining Support for Combatants during Wartime: A Survey Experiment in Afghanistan," *American Political Science Review* 107, no. 4 (2013): 679–705.

19. This would complicate the task of economic development somewhat, since even if people's material well-being improves, they may still feel *relatively* poor and perhaps report that on surveys, a traditional measure of poverty. Furthermore, an indirect relationship would have implications for the policymaker seeking to reduce violence: if perceptions influence

attitudes, then policy interventions informing people about how militants introduce violence and economic hardship into communities may be especially effective in undermining support for those militants.

20. C. Christine Fair, Rebecca Littman, Neil Malhotra, and Jacob N. Shapiro, "Relative Poverty, Perceived Violence, and Support for Militant Politics: Evidence from Pakistan," *Political Science Research and Methods*, 16 February 2016, https://doi.org/10.1017/psrm.2016.6, accessed 2 January 2018.

21. And again, they achieved a high overall response rate—over 70 percent—with the reasons for nonresponse evenly divided between refusal to answer and not being home.

22. Shaver, "Employment Status and Support for Wartime Violence." The survey was conducted by an independent firm, under U.S. Army contract.

23. M. W. Linn, R. Sandifer, and S. Stein, "Effects of Unemployment on Mental and Physical Health," *American Journal of Public Health* 75, no. 5 (1985): 502–6.

24. That approach assumes that insurgents can't tax the increase in income to increase their own labor demand—Fearon's objection, which we will return to.

25. Christopher A. Lawrence, *America's Modern Wars: Understanding Iraq, Afghanistan and Vietnam* (Havertown, PA: Casemate Publishers, 2015), 119.

26. Ibid., 120.

27. Ibid., 118.

28. Nick B. Williams, "Drive Carried to Barrios: Philippine Insurgents Now Targeting Cities," *Los Angeles Times*, 5 September 1985, http://articles.latimes.com/1985-09-05/news/mn-24900_1_new-people-s-army, accessed 23 September 2015.

29. James Bargent, "The FARC 2002–Present: Decapitation and Rebirth," *In Sight Crime: Organized Crime in the Americas*, 26 May 2014, http://www.insightcrime.org/investigations/farc-2002-present-decapitation-rebirth, accessed 23 September 2015.

30. Robert W. Schaefer, *The Insurgency in Chechnya and the North Caucus: From Gazavat to Jihad* (Santa Barbara, CA: Praeger Publishers, 2010), 243.

31. South Asia Terrorist Portal, 2011, as reported in Oliver Vanden Eynde, "Targets of Violence: Evidence from India's Naxalite Conflict," *Economic Journal*, 26 June 2017, http://onlinelibrary.wiley.com/doi/10.1111/ecoj.12438/abstract, accessed 2 January 2018.

32. David Rohde, "Rising Violence in Afghanistan: Foreign Fighters of Harsher Bent Bolster Taliban," *Spiegel Online*, 30 October 2007, http://www.spiegel.de/international/rising-violence-in-afghanistan-foreign-fighters-of-harsher-bent-bolster-taliban-a-514352.html, accessed 23 September 2015.

33. There is a clear line of descent from the AQI of 2004–6 to the Islamic State of Iraq (ISI) of 2006–13 to the Islamic State. After being routed from most of Iraq during the surge, AQI withdrew into a limited terrorist campaign in northern Iraq. Meanwhile, the United States was winnowing its military presence in Iraq in preparation for a full withdrawal in December 2011. War broke out in Syria and divided much of the population and the armed groups, which formed along sectarian lines. Leaders in ISI quietly sent fighters into Syria in 2011 to fight covertly under the alias of Jabhat al-Nusrah. Differences of opinion over strategy, tactics, and goals led the group to a split with the Jabhat al-Nusrah leadership, and in April 2013 ISI began fighting directly under its own banner in Syria and changed its name to the Islamic State in Iraq and al-Sham (ISIS, also known as the Islamic State of Iraq and Syria, or the Islamic State of Iraq and the Levant, ISIL). Following extensive antigovernment protests in Iraq's Anbar governorate, from January 2013 to December 2013, which were met by an aggressive Iraqi government response, ISIL expanded in Iraq in force with the support of some local political organizations—including many of the same tribal organizations that had fought against it in 2006—and quickly overwhelmed Iraqi army outposts in Fallujah and other cities. In June 2014, following the group's conquest of Mosul, it renamed itself the Islamic State and proclaimed a caliphate with Abu Bakr al-Baghdadi as the caliph of

all Muslims. For a useful overview with a focus on ideology, see Cole Bunzel, *From Paper State to Caliphate: The Ideology of the Islamic State* (Washington, DC: Brookings Institution, 2015). For a good general history of the group that is more focused on senior leaders, see Joby Warrick, *Black Flags: The Rise of ISIS* (New York: Doubleday, 2015).

34. Benjamin W. Bahney, Radha K. Iyengar, Patrick B. Johnston, Danielle F. Jung, Jacob N. Shapiro, and Howard J. Shatz, "Insurgent Compensation: Evidence from Iraq," *American Economic Review: Papers & Proceedings* 103, no. 3 (2013): 518–22; Patrick Johnston, Jacob N. Shapiro, Howard J. Shatz, Benjamin Bahney, Danielle F. Jung, Patrick K. Ryan, and Jonathan Wallace, *Foundations of the Islamic State: Management, Money, and Terror in Iraq* (Arlington, VA: RAND Corporation, 2016).

35. Craig Davis, "Reinserting Labor into the Iraqi Ministry of Labor and Social Affairs," *Monthly Labor Review* 128, no. 6 (2005): 53–61.

36. Benjamin W. Bahney, Howard J. Shatz, Carroll Ganier, Renny McPherson, and Barbara Sude, *An Economic Analysis of the Financial Records of al-Qa'ida in Iraq* (Santa Monica, CA: RAND Corporation, 2010).

37. Johnston et al., *Foundations of the Islamic State*.

38. Ibid., 93.

39. Ibid., 85.

40. Philip Verwimp, "An Economic Profile of Peasant Perpetrators of Genocide: Micro-level Evidence from Rwanda," *Journal of Development Economics* 77, no. 2 (2005): 297–323; Macartan Humphreys and Jeremy M. Weinstein, "Who Fights? The Determinants of Participation in Civil War," *American Journal of Political Science* 52, no. 2 (2008): 436–55.

41. Klaus Deininger, "Causes and Consequences of Civil Strife: Micro-Level Evidence from Uganda," *Oxford Economic Papers* 55, no. 4 (2003): 579–606.

42. Oeindrila Dube and Juan F. Vargas, "Commodity Price Shocks and Civil Conflict: Evidence from Colombia," *Review of Economic Studies* 80, no. 4 (2013): 1384–421; Daniel F. Hidalgo, Suresh Naidu, Simeon Nichter, and Neal Richardson, "Occupational Choices: Economic Determinants of Land Invasions," *Review of Economics and Statistics* 92, no. 3 (2010): 505–23; Edward Miguel, Shanker Satyanath, and Ernest Sergenti, "Economic Shocks and Civil Conflict: An Instrumental Variables Approach," *Journal of Political Economy* 112, no. 4 (2004): 725–53.

43. For a full articulation of the idea that an insurgency might be constrained either by information-sharing or by manpower, see Christoph Mikulaschek and Jacob N. Shapiro, "Lessons from America's Post-9/11 Wars," *Journal of Conflict Resolution*, 13 October 2016, http://journals.sagepub.com/doi/abs/10.1177/0022002716669808, accessed 2 January 2018.

44. A note on measurement: the concept of *unemployment* distinguishes between individuals without jobs who seek work and those who do not seek work, the latter referred to as "out of the labor force." Those terms are sensible in a developed economy that pays benefits to unemployed workers. In an economy without unemployment insurance and with an easy flow from working in agriculture to not working at all, a simpler classification of labor is into the employed and the nonemployed, which is what this research does.

45. Eli Berman, Michael Callen, Joseph H. Felter, and Jacob N. Shapiro, "Do Working Men Rebel? Insurgency and Unemployment in Afghanistan, Iraq, and the Philippines," *Journal of Conflict Resolution* 55, no. 4 (2011): 496–528.

46. Ibid., 510.

47. Estimate based on linear regression of U.S. casualties due to hostile action per governorate quarter on number of combat incidents, a governorate fixed-effect, and a quarter fixed-effect. Replication code and data available on the authors' websites (http://press.princeton.edu /titles/11241.html).

48. On Peterson's techniques, see Greg Jaffe, "In Iraq, an Officer's Answer to Violence: Build a Wall," *Wall Street Journal*, 5 April 2007, http://www.wsj.com/articles/SB117570845554759869,

accessed 25 September 2015; Wesley Morgan, "Task Force Warhorse: Classical Counter-insurgency on Haifa Street," *Long War Journal*, 9 August 2007, http://www.longwarjournal.org/archives/2007/08/task_force_warhorse.php, accessed 25 September 2015.

49. Alexei Abrahams, "Hard Traveling: Distributional Impact of Travel Costs on Urban Unemployment" (working paper, Princeton University, 2017).

50. Vanden Eynde, "Targets of Violence."

51. Kumar Ramakrishna, "'Bribing the Reds to Give Up': Rewards Policy in the Malayan Emergency," *War in History* 9, no. 3 (2012): 332–63.

52. Ibid., 340.

53. Ibid., 347.

54. Ibid., 333.

55. If we widen the scope beyond conflicts—where information and violence are the currencies—to other development contexts, we come across similarly discomfiting questions. It may seem wrong to pay a mother to vaccinate her child—she *should* want to do that anyway—but conditional cash transfer programs do just that, with wide success and approbation. From a utilitarian perspective, ethical questions would take a back seat: if the mother can be incentivized to produce a desirable outcome, then a utilitarian would argue that it is in the best interest of society to do so. It is certainly in the best interest of the child.

56. United States Department of Defense, "Summary of Major Changes to DOD 7000.14–R, Volume 12, Chapter 17 'DoD Rewards Program,'" 2008, http://comptroller.defense.gov/Portals/45/documents/fmr/archive/12arch/12_17_Aug08.pdf, p. 17-3, accessed 26 September 2015.

57. U.S. Department of Defense, "Money as a Weapon System MNC-I CJ8 SOP (Multi-National Corps-Iraq CJ8 Standard Operation Procedures)," 2009, https://info.publicintelligence.net/MAAWS%20Jan%2009.pdf, accessed 26 September 2015.

58. Ibid., D-6.

59. Ibid., D-5–D-8.

60. Ibid., D-12. In addition to detailed reporting requirements for large rewards, accountability mechanisms were put in place for micro and small rewards: the RAO appointed a person of contact to administer rewards who could not be the same as the person in charge of payouts, and the monthly balance sheet had to add up or further funds would be withheld. "It is imperative," the document said, "that there is some level of analysis of reward payouts to the capture/kill ratio." Ibid., D-14.

61. Ibid., D-2.

62. Office of the Secretary of Defense, "Operation Enduring Freedom Operation and Maintenance, Defense-Wide Budget Activity 04: Administrative and Service-Wide Activities," 2014, http://comptroller.defense.gov/Portals/45/documents/defbudget/fy2015/budget_justification/pdfs/amendment/01_Operation_and_Maintenance/OSD_OUSDC_OCO_Volume_I_Book.pdf, p. OSD-85, accessed 26 September 2015.

63. Vanden Eynde, "Targets of Violence," 1–2.

64. http://www.satp.org.

65. Stathis N. Kalyvas, *The Logic of Violence in Civil War* (Cambridge: Cambridge University Press, 2006).

66. This is the same type of instrumental variables approach as Jake and coauthors' work on civilian casualties and informing in Afghanistan that we discussed in chapter 7.

67. Vanden Eynde, "Targets of Violence," 1–2.

68. Thiemo Fetzer, "Social Insurance and Conflict: Evidence from India" (EOPP Working Paper No. 53, 2014). One innovative aspect of this research is the use of natural language processing to code incident reports in order to extract perpetrator and victim types.

69. Eli Berman, Jacob N. Shapiro, and Joseph H. Felter, "Can Hearts and Minds Be Bought? The Economics of Counterinsurgency in Iraq," *Journal of Political Economy* 119, no. 4 (2011): 766–819, appendix A, p. 813.

70. Gaurav Khanna and Laura Zimmermann, "Guns and Butter? Fighting Violence with the Promise of Development," *Journal of Development Economics* 124, no. 1 (2017): 120–41.

71. Aditya Dasgupta, Kishore Gawande, and Devesh Kapur, "(When) Do Anti-Poverty Programs Reduce Violence? India's Rural Employment Guarantee and Maoist Conflict," 22 April 2016, available at SSRN: https://ssrn.com/abstract=2495803 or http://dx.doi.org/10.2139 /ssrn.2495803.

72. Dube and Vargas, "Commodity Price Shocks and Civil Conflict."

73. Ibid., 1387.

74. "To the Edge and Back Again," *The Economist*, 31 August 2013, http://www.economist.com /news/americas/21584384-hiccup-serves-confirm-government-and-farc-are-making-pro gress-edge-and, accessed 23 September 2015.

75. Jeremy McDermot, "Colombia Cracks Down on Oil Theft," BBC News, 15 February 2005, quoted in Dube and Vargas, "Commodity Price Shocks and Civil Conflict," 1389.

76. Dube and Vargas, "Commodity Price Shocks and Civil Conflict," 1385.

77. Given that Afghanistan also has farmers who can shift from legal crops to raising poppy to produce opium, which is easily taxed by the Taliban, an alternative use of LGCD funds has been to import more Afghan melons.

78. Eli Berman, Joseph Felter, Ethan Kapstein, and Erin Troland, "Predation, Taxation, Investment, and Violence: Evidence from the Philippines" (NBER Working Paper 19266, 2013).

79. Investment might induce either an increase or a decrease in rebel violence; violence raises the rate at which rebels can extort but may reduce the effective incidence of their extortion by antagonizing civilians who in turn deliver territorial control to government. Increased economic activity only increases violence if the rate effect dominates the incidence effect in an information-centric model.

80. In developing countries, even those without insurgencies, data on private investment are usually hard to come by. However, the Philippines requires permits for any new construction project as well as any renovation of an existing structure, including in areas where rebels are entrenched. The government keeps records of the industrial permits, which are available at the province level for the entire country. The value of building permits can serve as a proxy for private investment.

81. Austin Wright, "Economic Shocks and Rebel Tactics: Evidence from Colombia" (Households in Conflict Network Working Paper No. 232, 2015).

82. Ibid., 7.

83. SIGAR, "USAID Spent Almost $400 Million on an Afghan Stabilization Project," 7.

9 WHAT WORKS? LEVERAGING THE INFORMATION MECHANISM

1. Integrated Regional Information Networks, "Anbar Province Plagued by Violence," IRIN News, 15 January 2007, http://www.irinnews.org/report/64374/iraq-anbar-province -plagued-violence, accessed 9 August 2016.

2. Colin Supko, interview by the author, 25 July 2016.

3. The specific tower described was located on Camp Habbaniyah (IVO 33–22'-39.89'N, 43–35'-14.97'E).

4. Ryan Shann, email to the authors, 17 August 2012.

5. Andrew Montalvo, email to the authors, 21 July 2016.

6. For a cellular tower to provide coverage, signals from phones to the tower must be relayed back to a switch, which then connects them to the tower serving the person they are talking

with. In most developed countries that switching happens via fiber optic cables, but in Iraq in 2007 it had to happen via microwave transmission from tower to tower. Reestablishing the microwave backhaul link through Camp Habbaniyah enabled towers farther out in Anbar to connect to Iraqna's switches and therefore to offer service.

7. Joseph H. Felter, "Sources of Military Effectiveness in Counterinsurgency: Evidence from the Philippines," in *The Sword's Other Edge: Tradeoffs in the Pursuit of Military Effectiveness*, ed. Daniel Reiter (New York: Cambridge University Press, 2017).

8. Jason Lyall, "Are Coethnics More Effective Counterinsurgents? Evidence from the Second Chechen War," *American Political Science Review* 104, no. 1 (2010): 1–20.

9. A technical issue with this design is that the number of individuals abused during a sweep is likely a function of what force is conducting it; it is a post-treatment variable in program evaluation terms. By matching on it Lyall (ibid.) effectively estimates the differential between sweeps by Chechen and Russian units that does not run through different patterns of abuse. Since we expect that Chechens would be less abusive of civilians than Russians in this context, and since abuse would likely trigger more violence, the article might underestimate the counterinsurgency benefits of having local forces conduct sweeps.

10. Operatives from the Intelligence Service, Armed Forces of the Philippines (ISAFP), and Intelligence Service Group (ISG), for example, deployed Military Intelligence Groups (MIGs) and Military Intelligence Companies (MICOs) across all regional commands and division areas of operations.

11. Joseph H. Felter, "Taking Guns to a Knife Fight: A Case for Empirical Study of Counterinsurgency" (PhD diss., Stanford University, 2005), ESOC Philippines Data Set.

12. One concern with this research agenda is that people punish incumbents for things that are entirely out of their control. See, e.g., Christopher H. Achen and Larry M. Bartels, "Blind Retrospection: Electoral Responses to Drought, Flu, and Shark Attacks" (working paper, Princeton University, 2004). While highly influential, much this work has been shown to be problematic for a range of technical reasons. See, e.g., Anthony Fowler and Andrew B. Hall, "Do Shark Attacks Influence Presidential Elections? Reassessing a Prominent Finding on Voter Competence," *Journal of Politics* (forthcoming). Our own work suggests that voters in developing countries behave much more like rational, forward-thinking actors (such as the father considering sharing tips, depicted in chapter 3) than like irrational, emotionally driven individuals. See Asad Liaqat, Michael Callen, Ali Cheema, Adnan Khan, Farooq Naseer, and Jacob N. Shapiro, "Candidate Connections vs. Party Performance: Evidence on Vote Choice in a Low Information Environment" (working paper, 2017).

13. Shawn Cole, Andrew Healy, and Eric Werker, "Do Voters Demand Responsive Governments? Evidence from Indian Disaster Relief," *Journal of Development Economics* 97, no. 2 (2012): 167–81.

14. Egor Lazarev, Anton Sobolev, Irina V. Soboleva, and Boris Sokolov, "Trial by Fire: A Natural Disaster's Impact on Support for Authorities in Rural Russia," *World Politics* 66, no. 4 (2014): 641–68.

15. Ibid., 660–61.

16. Ibid., 664.

17. Jorge Gallego, "Natural Disasters and Clientelism: The Case of Floods and Landslides in Colombia" (Universidad del Rosario Working Paper 178, 2015).

18. Just as increased food aid gave local officials more currency to buy votes, victims, having just endured a financial shock, became more inclined to sell them. Gallego ruled out the demonstration effect, which had been important in Russia, as Colombian officials in municipalities that were flagged for having delays in relief projects were not punished. A number of studies have shown that disasters increase voter turnout in elections, which can influence results, but Gallego ruled out this effect as well, since victimization did not predict higher voter turnout.

19. Tahir Andrabi and Jishnu Das, "In Aid We Trust: Hearts and Minds and the Pakistan Earthquake of 2005," *Review of Economics and Statistics* 99, no. 3 (2017): 371–86.

20. These numbers paint a grim picture of trust among Pakistani citizens, but they are consistent with trust levels in developing countries as measured by the World Values Survey, which has been applied in one hundred countries in six waves since 1981.

21. Andrabi and Das, "In Aid We Trust," 379.

22. Ibid., 382.

23. Ibid., 385.

24. Andrew Beath, Fotini Christia, and Ruben Enikolopov, "Winning Hearts and Minds through Development: Evidence from a Field Experiment in Afghanistan" (MIT Political Science Department Research Paper No. 2011–14, 2012).

25. Ibid., 16.

26. Ibid., 17.

27. NSP projects were unusual in being modest and informed. Researchers conducting 574 interviews across Afghanistan in 2011 found that citizens generally reported a negative impression of development projects, citing poor planning and execution and lack of understanding of community needs, with the NSP standing as a notable exception. Paul Fishstein and Andrew Wilder, "Winning Hearts and Minds? Examining the Relationship between Aid and Security in Afghanistan" (Medford, MA: Feinstein International Center, Tufts University, 2011).

28. C. Christine Fair, Rebecca Littman, Neil Malhotra, and Jacob N. Shapiro, "Relative Poverty, Perceived Violence, and Support for Militant Politics: Evidence from Pakistan," *Political Science Research and Methods*, 16 February 2016, https://www.cambridge.org/core/journals/political-science-research-and-methods/article/relative-poverty-perceived-violence-and-support-for-militant-politics-evidence-from-pakistan/3AEAF20C324355E612F10AF59BC1DC38, accessed 17 December 2017.

29. Simone Dietrich, Minhaj Mahmud, and Matthew S. Winters, "Foreign Aid, Foreign Policy, and Domestic Government Legitimacy: Experimental Evidence from Bangladesh" (AidData Working Paper 16, 2015).

30. Kate Baldwin and Matthew S. Winters, "Can International Aid Change the Politics of Service Delivery?" (paper presented at annual meeting of American Political Science Association, Philadelphia, 2 September 2016).

31. USAID Office of Inspector General, "Audit of USAID/Afghanistan's Afghanistan Stabilization Initiative for the Southern Region" (Audit Report No. F-306-12-001-P, 2011), 9.

32. Cesi Cruz and Christina J. Schneider, "Foreign Aid and Undeserved Credit Claiming," *American Journal of Political Science* 61, no. 2 (2017): 396–408.

33. Raymond P. Guiteras and Ahmed Mushfiq Mobarak, "Does Development Aid Undermine Political Accountability? Leader and Constituent Responses to a Large-Scale Intervention" (NBER Working Paper 21434, 2015).

34. The conclusion that information can shift attitudes is also supported by *qualitative* research by the professional military community. A 2012 RAND study evaluated the effectiveness of information operations (IO) during the first decade of ISAF's involvement in Afghanistan. Specifically, it took priority messages (such as "The war on terror justifies U.S. intervention" and "Support from local Afghans is needed to eliminate IEDs") that ISAF had disbursed using a range of methods from leaflets to posters to publically screened videos, and used opinion polls and interviews with U.S. military personnel to assess how effective they had been. Findings were mixed, with the greatest successes reported to result from face-to-face communications with citizens and from ISAF staff attending meetings of Afghan community leaders. Recommendations included testing messages with local focus groups. Arturo Munoz, "U.S. Military Information Operations in Afghanistan: Effectiveness of Psychological Operations 2001–2010" (Santa Monica, CA: RAND Corporation, 2012). Similarly, a workshop on IO across U.S. military engagements held by the U.S. Army War College and the

Advanced Network Research Group, University of Cambridge, reported on the importance of information campaigns and how to carry them out effectively. A top recommendation was to produce a clear, consistent message to attract and retain civilian support. Deirdre Collings and Rafal Rohozinski, "Shifting Fire: Information Effects in Counterinsurgency and Stability Operations" (Center for Strategic Leadership U.S. Army War College and the Advanced Network Research Group, University of Cambridge, 2013). The report said, "Kinetic action to counter insurgents can create negative informational effects with the wider population, and thereby lead to strategic losses" (3). Those reports do not pass the causal identification test: the findings of opinion polls, for example, did not control for possible confounding variables, such as response bias. However, it is important and reassuring that military thinkers and practitioners drawing on qualitative evidence come to the same conclusion.

35. "Abdullah Abdullah Pulls out of Afghan Presidential Election Run-off," *Telegraph*, 1 November 2009, http://www.telegraph.co.uk/news/worldnews/asia/afghanistan/6478225/Abdullah-Abdullah-pulls-out-of-Afghan-presidential-election-run-off.html, accessed 14 July 2016.

36. "COMISAF Initial Assessment (Unclassified)—Searchable Document," *Washington Post*, 21 September 2009, http://www.washingtonpost.com/wp-dyn/content/article/2009/09/21/AR2009092100110.html, accessed 3 October 2016.

37. Michael Callen and James D. Long, "Institutional Corruption and Election Fraud: Evidence from a Field Experiment in Afghanistan," *American Economic Review* 105, no. 1 (2015): 354–81.

38. Ibid., 355.

39. Ibid., 379.

40. There is reason for caution as the effect of such policies when scaled up is unclear. If the risks of being caught committing voter fraud increase uniformly everywhere, then in an environment with limited enforcement capacity the risk to election officials from engaging in fraud at any one polling station might be very small.

41. Eli Berman, Michael Callen, Clark Gibson, and James D. Long, "Election Fairness and Government Legitimacy in Afghanistan" (NBER Working Paper No. 19949, 2014).

42. Mike, Eli, and their coauthors also theorized that if respondents viewed the election improvements as the results of actions external to government (i.e., caused by researchers performing a study), then that would undermine the shift in attitudes. Sure enough, when they separated out the effect on respondents who were aware of the intervention (about 11 percent—by self-report) the effects on attitudes were weaker on two of the four measures. Note, however, that while the study provided causal identification in its *main* findings of increased legitimacy, these *secondary* findings—that respondents crediting the improvement to nongovernmental actors were less likely to become more trustful of government—cannot be considered causal. Someone who reports being aware of the intervention might also be more critical of the government for other reasons.

43. Michael Callen, Clark C. Gibson, Danielle F. Jung, and James D. Long, "Improving Electoral Integrity with Information and Communications Technology," *Journal of Experimental Political Science* 3, no. 1 (2016): 4–17.

44. Martina Björkman and Jakob Svensson, "Power to the People: Evidence from a Randomized Aid Experiment on Community-Based Monitoring in Uganda," *Quarterly Journal of Economics* 124, no. 2 (2009): 735–69; Esther Duflo, Pascaline Dupas, and Michael Kremer, "School Governance, Teacher Incentives, and Pupil-Teacher Ratios: Experimental Evidence from Kenyan Primary Schools," *Journal of Public Economics* 123 (2015): 92–110; Benjamin Olken, "Monitoring Corruption: Evidence from a Field Experiment in Indonesia," *Journal of Political Economy* 115, no. 2 (2007): 200–249; Michael Callen, Saad Gulzar, Ali Hasanain, Yasir Khan, and Arman Rezaee, "Personalities and Public Sector Performance: Evidence from a Health Experiment in Pakistan" (NBER Working Paper 21180, 2015).

45. Eli Berman, Michael Callen, Luke N. Condra, Mitch Downey, Tarek Ghanik, and Mohammad Isaqzadeh, "Community Monitors vs. Leakage: Experimental Evidence from Afghanistan" (working paper, UCSD, 2017).

10   THE ENDURING IMPORTANCE OF UNDERSTANDING ASYMMETRIC CONFLICT

1. This account is primarily drawn from Henry I. Shaw Jr., "The United States Marines in Northern China, 1945–1949" (Washington, DC: Historical Branch, G-3 Division, Headquarters, U.S. Marine Corps, 1962).

2. Benis M. Frank and Henry I. Shaw Jr., *Victory and Occupation: History of U.S. Marine Corps Operations in World War II*, vol. 5 (Washington, DC: United States Marine Corps, 1968), 533, quoted in Michael Parkyn, "Operation Beleaguer: The Marine III Amphibious Corps in North China, 1945–49," *Marine Corps Gazette* 85, no. 7 (2001): 32–37, https:// www.mca-marines.org/gazette/2001/07/operation-beleaguer-marine-iii-amphibious -corps-north-china-1945-49, accessed 14 January 2017.

3. Frank and Shaw, *Victory and Occupation*, 547.

4. Parkyn, "Operation Beleaguer."

5. Australian Government Department of Foreign Affairs and Trade (AGDFAT), "Development Assistance in Timor-Leste," http://dfat.gov.au/geo/timor-leste/development-assistance /Pages/development-assistance-in-timor-leste.aspx, accessed 22 November 2016.

6. The most recent Human Development Index placed Timor-Leste at position 133 out of 188 countries, while Indonesia came in at 110. United Nations Development Programme, "Human Development Report 2015: Work for Human Development," http://hdr.undp.org /en/2015-report, accessed 21 November 2016. Nutrition remains a major concern: over half of the country's children are stunted. AGDFAT, "Development Assistance in Timor-Leste."

7. Paul D. Williams, "Paying for AMISOM: Are Politics and Bureaucracy Undermining the AU's Largest Peace Operation?" IPI Global Observatory, 11 January 2017, https://theglobalobser vatory.org/2017/01/amisom-african-union-peacekeeping-financing/, accessed 2 February 2017; European Union External Action, "European Union Training Mission—Somalia," 2016, https://eeas.europa.eu/csdp-missions-operations/eutm-somalia_en, accessed 14 January 2017.

8. Kenneth Waltz, *Theory of International Politics* (New York: Addison Wesley, 1979); Hans Morgenthau, *Politics among Nations* (New York: A. A. Knopf, 1948); John Mearsheimer, *The Tragedy of Great Power Politics* (New York: W. W. Norton, 2001).

9. World Bank Group, *World Development Report 2011: Conflict, Security, and Development* (Washington, DC: World Bank, 2011), 2. In his foreword (p. xi), Robert B. Zoellick, president of World Bank Group, reminded readers that the World Bank is just a nickname for the IBRD—the "R" standing for "reconstruction"—which had been founded in the wake of World War II.

10. Author analysis of UCDP and OECD data accessed through World Bank. UCDP data accessed 10 June 2017, http://ucdp.uu.se; World Bank data accessed 10 June 2017, http://databank .worldbank.org/data/reports.aspx?source=world-development-indicators. OECD data on ODA also available at oecd.org/dac/stats/idsonline.

11. World Bank, "Fragility, Conflict, and Violence," http://www.worldbank.org/en/topic/fra gilityconflictviolence, accessed 30 November 2016; Organisation for Economic Cooperation and Development (OECD), "States of Fragility 2016: Understanding Violence," 2016, http:// www.oecd.org/dac/states-of-fragility-2016-9789264267213-en.htm, accessed 3 February 2016.

12. Since markets can barely operate in those settings, market building might be precisely the wrong thing to spend money on, for example.

13. Some aid agencies are already supporting such policy. USAID, for example, operates very differently in various regions of Pakistan, often in ways that are quite sensitive to how it

can help local governments earn goodwill and thereby reduce conflict in a given village or valley.

14. The petition can be found at http://www.dailymail.co.uk/news/article-3510811/Stop-for eign-aid-madness-12bn-taxes-splurged-hand-outs-terrorists-killers-care-UK-s-spending -Foreign-Aid-sign-petition-now.html, accessed 6 June 2017.

15. In that time, the *Boston Globe*, *Newsday*, the *Philadelphia Inquirer*, and some Tribune Co. papers completely shut down all foreign offices, while the "big four"—the *New York Times*, *Wall Street Journal*, *Los Angeles Times*, and *Washington Post*—downsized their foreign offices. Of major U.S. news organizations, only NPR and Bloomberg expanded overseas. Jodi Enda, "Retreating from the World," *American Journalism Review* 22 (December 2010).

16. Justin D. Martin, "Loneliness at the Foreign 'Bureau,'" *Columbia Journalism Review* 23 (April 2012), http://www.cjr.org/behind_the_news/loneliness_at_the_foreign_bureau.php, accessed 3 November 2016.

17. American Society of News Editors 2016 Census, http://asne.org/content.asp?contentid =415, accessed 3 November 2016.

18. Jeffrey Gottfried and Elisa Shearer, "News Use across Social Media Platforms, 2016," Pew Research Center (2016), http://www.journalism.org/2016/05/26/news-use-across-social -media-platforms-2016/, accessed 3 November 2016.

19. David Samuels, "The Aspiring Novelist Who Became Obama's Foreign-Policy Guru," *New York Times Magazine*, 5 May 2016, http://www.nytimes.com/2016/05/08/magazine/the-as piring-novelist-who-became-obamas-foreign-policy-guru.html?_r=0, accessed 3 November 2016.

20. For a good early summary of Russian techniques, see Andrew Weisburd, Clint Watts, and J. M. Berger, "Trolling for Trump: How Russia Is Trying to Destroy Our Democracy," *War on the Rocks*, 6 November 2016, https://warontherocks.com/2016/11/trolling-for-trump -how-russia-is-trying-to-destroy-our-democracy/, accessed 29 August 2017.

21. For an outstanding analysis of Chinese government use of social media, see Gary King, Jennifer Pan, and Molly Roberts, "How the Chinese Government Fabricates Social Media Posts for Strategic Distraction, Not Engaged Argument," *American Political Science Review* 111, no. 3 (2017): 484–501.

22. Operation Enduring Freedom, the official U.S. government name for the war in Afghanistan, lasted from October 2001 through December 2014. It was followed by Operation Resolute Support and Operation Freedom Sentinel, the mission under which combat operations were taking place in August 2017 as we drafted this concluding chapter.

23. David E. Sanger, "A Test for the Meaning of Victory in Afghanistan," *New York Times*, 13 February 2010.

24. Oliver Poole, "Iraqis in Former Rebel Stronghold Now Cheer American Soldiers," *Telegraph*, 19 December 2005, http://www.telegraph.co.uk/news/worldnews/middleeast /iraq/1505872/Iraqis-in-former-rebel-stronghold-now-cheer-American-soldiers.html, accessed 4 September 2017.

25. In December 2017, as this book was going to press, Iraqi prime minister Haider al-Abadi declared that Iraq's security forces recaptured the last of the remaining territory held by IS and that Iraq was "fully liberated" from the "ISIS terrorist gangs" that had occupied parts of the restive country for over three years. "Iraq Announces Defeat of ISIS," *Financial Times*, https://www.ft.com/content/d6636416-dcf3-11e7-a8a4-0a1e63a52f9c, accessed 2 January 2018.

26. On the quality of governance for Sunni citizens in Anbar after the U.S. withdrawal in 2011 and how it enabled the return of IS in late 2013, see, e.g., Anand Gobal, "The Hell after ISIS," *The Atlantic*, May 2016, https://www.theatlantic.com/magazine/archive/2016/05/the-hell -after-isis/476391/, accessed 31 August 2017.

27. See, e.g., "A Spectre Haunting India," *Economist*, 17 August 2006.

28. We thank Abbey Steele and Juan Vargas for tremendously helpful guidance on the history of the 2017 Colombian peace deal.

29. Basta Ya!, "Civiles Muertos En Acciones Bélicas 1988–2012," *Bases De Datos—¡Basta Ya! Colombia: Memorias De Guerra y Dignidad*, http://www.centrodememoriahistorica.gov .co/micrositios/informeGeneral/basesDatos.html, accessed 20 January 2017.

30. Consultoria para los Derechos Humanos y el Desplazamiento (CODHES), https://data .humdata.org/dataset/municipal-statistics-of-forced-displacement.

31. Internal Displacement Monitoring Centre (IDMC)-Norwegian Refugee Council, "Internal Displacement: A Global Overview of Trends and Developments in 2005," *IDMC*, http://www.internal-displacement.org/assets/publications/2006/2006-global-over view2005-global-en.pdf, accessed 20 January 2017. Tragically, as of this writing the number of internally displaced people in Syria exceeds 7.6 million, by credible estimates. IDMC-Norwegian Refugee Council, "Global Overview 2015: People Internally Displaced by Violence," http://www.internal-displacement.org/assets/library/Media/201505-Global-Over view-2015/20150506-global-overview-2015-en.pdf, accessed 21 January 2017.

32. Andrés Castañeda and Juan Vargas identify the following as critical events and use a financial event study to confirm that markets thought so as well:

1. On 01/02/2004 FARC's leader, aka "Simon Trinidad," was captured in Ecuador, the highest-ranked guerrilla apprehended up to that point. He was responsible for famous FARC attacks such as the murder of former minister Consuelo Araujo.

2. On 01/04/2005 FARC's leader and spokesman, aka "Rodrigo Granda," was captured in Venezuela without acquiescence of the local government, arguably with the help of Colombian paramilitaries.

3. On 03/01/2008 the Colombian government forces killed FARC's deputy chief commander, aka Raul Reyes, by bombarding his camp, located near the Colombian border but on Ecuadorian territory. Ecuador accused Colombia of a violation of its sovereignty.

4. On 07/02/2008 former presidential candidate and iconic politician Ingrid Betancourt, kidnapped by FARC during the 2002 presidential campaign, was liberated by the Colombian forces in Operation Checkmate.

5. On 09/22/2010 the Colombian army killed FARC's military chief, aka "Mono Jojoy," one of the most sanguinary guerrillas in the history of the armed conflict.

6. On 11/04/2011 the Colombian military bombed the camp of FARC's commander in chief, Alfonso Cano.

See Andrés Castañeda and Juan F. Vargas, "Hitos Del Conflicto y Riesgo Pais" (University of Rosario Economics Department Working Paper No. 151, 2014).

33. For details, see Stephen Biddle, Julia Macdonald, and Ryan Baker, "Small Footprint, Small Payoff: The Military Effectiveness of Security Force Assistance," *Journal of Strategic Studies*, 12 April 2017, http://www.tandfonline.com/doi/abs/10.1080/01402390.2017.1307745, accessed 12 December 2017. Other ESOC scholars on that project include Gerard Padró i Miquel of LSE, Pierre Yared of Columbia, Esteban Klor of the Hebrew University, and others mentioned elsewhere in this volume.

34. A principal is any party that engages another, the agent, to act on their behalf and in their interest. Principals delegate to agents for a number of reasons, either because they need more labor to get a task done or because the agents have specialized knowledge or skills that let them do a task more efficiently than the principals themselves. Interesting issues arise in principal-agent relationships when principals cannot observe exactly what their agents are doing. Employers and managers are often viewed as principals who do not fully observe the actions of their employees—agents who might have their own agenda—but these models have been extended to a number of different contexts, e.g., legislature as principal and

executive branch as agent, and citizen as principal who pays taxes and government as agent who provides services. Both Eli and Jake have used principal-agent theory to understand terrorist organizations, Eli in *Radical, Religious, and Violent: The New Economics of Terrorism* (Cambridge, MA: MIT Press, 2009), and Jake in *The Terrorist's Dilemma: Managing Violent Covert Organizations* (Princeton: Princeton University Press, 2013).

35. Eli Berman and David Lake, eds., *Proxy Wars: Suppressing Violence through Local Agents* (Ithaca: Cornell University Press, forthcoming).

36. Estimate of Human Rights Watch, as reported in "Horror of Mosul Where Sinkhole Became Mass Grave for 4,000 of Isil's Victims," *Telegraph*, http://www.telegraph.co.uk/news/2017/02/25/horror-mosul-sinkhole-became-biggest-mass-grave-iraq/, accessed 4 September 2017.

37. For an explanation of those methodological distinctions, see Berman and Lake, *Proxy Wars*.

38. "Obituary: Anwar al-Awlaki," *BBC News Online*, 30 September 2011, http://www.bbc.com/news/world-middle-east-11658920, accessed 4 September 2017.

39. Patrick B. Johnston and Anoop K. Sarbahi, "The Impact of U.S. Drone Strikes on Terrorism in Pakistan," *International Studies Quarterly* 60, no. 1 (2016): 203–19.

40. Shapiro, *The Terrorist's Dilemma*.

41. For evidence on the impact of drone strikes on political attitudes outside the region being targeted, see Daniel Silverman, "Perceptions and Misperceptions in War: Civilian Beliefs about Violence and Their Consequences in Pakistan, Iraq, and Beyond" (PhD diss., Ohio State University, 2017), 89–93.

42. ESOC is not the only organization taking this approach. The AidData project out of the College of William and Mary has taken tremendous steps to build microlevel data on aid spending in countries around the world, forging relationships across the foreign aid and development communities. It too funds young scholars, creates data resources, and offers networking opportunities, thereby driving down the costs and risks of doing high-quality microlevel empirical work on foreign aid.

43. On the idea that local factors played a key role in determining how much violence was produced locally, in a particular area within the context of a larger conflict, see Peter Hart, "The Geography of Revolution in Ireland: 1917–1923," *Past and Present* 155 (May 1997): 142–76. Hart collects incident-level data on violence during the Irish revolution and seeks to explain why IRA activity varied so much at the county and district levels. On the value of the discriminate use of force by government forces and on the centrality of local factors in driving grievances and participation, see Huw Bennett, *Fighting the Mau Mau: The British Army and Counter-Insurgency in the Kenya Emergency* (Cambridge: Cambridge University Press, 2013), 158–59. The idea that a series of small-scale conflicts can lead to a larger national-level political narrative that limits the scope for conflict resolution—the converse of our point that solving local conflicts can create opportunities for political deals—appears in Rashmi Singh, *Hamas and Suicide Terrorism: Multi-Causal and Multi-Method Approaches* (London: Routledge, 2011). On the importance of local factors, as opposed to ideology or feudal norms, in motivating participation, see Sam Popkin's classic *The Rational Peasant: The Political Economy of Rural Society in Vietnam* (Berkeley: University of California Press, 1979), Joesba Zulaika's magisterial anthropological study *Basque Violence: Metaphor and Sacrament* (Reno: University of Nevada Press, 1988), and Richard Reid's excellent *Warfare in African History* (Cambridge: Cambridge University Press, 2012). For perspectives on why local factors dominate decision making in conflict settings from other disciplinary perspectives, see Charles Tripp, *A History of Iraq* (Cambridge: Cambridge University Press, 2000) and Thomas J. Barfield, *Afghanistan: A Cultural and Political History* (Princeton: Princeton University Press, 2010).

44. We thank one of our anonymous reviewers for this excellent formulation of the issue. We have borrowed terminology from that review liberally here.

45. The most widely cited work in this literature is James D. Fearon and David D. Laitin, "Ethnicity, Insurgency, and Civil War," *American Political Science Review* 97, no. 1 (2003): 75–90. The authors argued that civil wars tended to start where the opportunity to do so was good (because of rough terrain and weak state capacity) and not because of specific grievances or opportunities to secure resources (which they argued were pervasive across places that had civil wars and those that did not).

46. For a great nontechnical summary of the state of research on civil war termination, see Barbara F. Walter, "The Four Things We Know about How Civil Wars End (and What This Tells Us about Syria)," *Political Violence at a Glance*, 18 October 2013, http://political violenceataglance.org/2013/10/18/the-four-things-we-know-about-how-civil-wars-end -and-what-this-tells-us-about-syria/, accessed 30 August 2017. Sadly Walter's predictions about Syria based on the literature have so far proven correct.

47. Berman and Lake, *Proxy Wars*.

48. Christoph Mikulaschek, Saurabh Pant, and Beza Tesfaye, "Winning Hearts and Minds in Civil Wars: Governance and Support for Violence in Iraq" (SSRN Working Paper, 2016), https://papers.ssrn.com/sol3/papers.cfm?abstract_id=2702219, accessed 12 October 2017.

49. Carter Malkasian, *War Comes to Garmser: Thirty Years of Conflict on the Afghan Frontier* (New York: Oxford University Press, 2013), Kindle Edition, p. 4.

50. Ibid.

51. Ibid., 110. In his book *Little America: The War within the War for Afghanistan* (London: Bloomsbury Publishing, 2012), Rajiv Chandrasekaran also tells the story of the Helmand River Project but attributes a greater role to the progressive king Mohammed Zahir Shah, who invested the profits his country had made through trade during World War II into infrastructure projects with the help of Western allies. Chandrasekaran similarly attributes some of the region's enduring instability to the displacement of peoples. Another scheme sometimes credited with inefficiency and counterproductive effects is Gezira Scheme in Sudan, also a British colonial project and which similarly created a network of canals (the largest centrally managed system in the world, for its time) diverting the waters of the Nile to create the country's agricultural hub. The project took most of the first half of the twentieth century to complete, and according to a 1986 UN report, it disrupted the pastoral nomadism of the area (whereby people practiced agriculture only part of the year), drew the nation's resources to one district to the detriment of others, and upset the ecological equilibrium of the area. H.R.J. Davies, *Rural Development in White Nile Province, Sudan* (Tokyo: United Nations University Press, 1986). While the evidence on its inefficiency is widespread, views on its net impact on agricultural productivity are mixed.

52. James Manor, *Aid That Works: Successful Development in Fragile States* (Washington, DC: World Bank, 2007).

53. For a remarkable analysis of the challenges of using data to make tactical, operational, and strategic assessments during asymmetric conflicts, see Ben Connable, *Embracing the Fog of War: Assessment and Metrics in Counterinsurgency* (Santa Monica, CA: RAND Corporation, 2012).

54. Because of the asymmetric analytical advantage the United States and its allies enjoy, sharing almost certainly provides more benefits than cost. Jake and long-time coauthor David Siegel have analyzed the conditions under which information-sharing is net positive for security using a game-theoretic model in Jacob N. Shapiro and David A. Siegel, "Is This Paper Dangerous? Balancing Secrecy and Openness in Counterterrorism," *Security Studies* 19, no. 1 (2010): 66–98.

INDEX

Note: Page numbers in *italic* type indicate figures or tables.